COUNTRY MUSIC

COUNTRY MUSIC

THE COMPLETE VISUAL HISTORY

Edited by Paul Kingsbury and Alanna Nash

LONDON, NEW YORK, MUNICH,
MELBOURNE, DELHI

Managing Editor Debra Wolter
Managing Art Editor Karen Self
Art Director Bryn Walls
Publisher Jonathan Metcalf
DTP John Goldsmid
Production Controller Rita Sinha

Produced for Dorling Kindersley by
Palazzo Editions Limited
15 Gay Street
Bath, BA1 2PH

US Executive Editor Jay Orr
US Picture Editor F. Lynne Bachleda
Managing Editor Sonya Newland
Editor Marion Dent
Indexer Michael Dent
Picture Researcher Emily Hedges
Designer Terry Jeavons
Art Director David Costa
Managing Director Colin Webb

First published in 2006 by
Dorling Kindersley Limited
80 Strand, London WC2R 0RL

A Penguin Company

2 4 6 8 10 9 7 5 3 1

A CIP catalogue record for this book is
available from the British Library.

ISBN-13: 978-1-40530-969-1
ISBN-10: 1-4053-0969-5

Colour reproduction by Colourscan, Singapore
Printed and bound by Toppan, China

See our complete catalogue at
www.dk.com

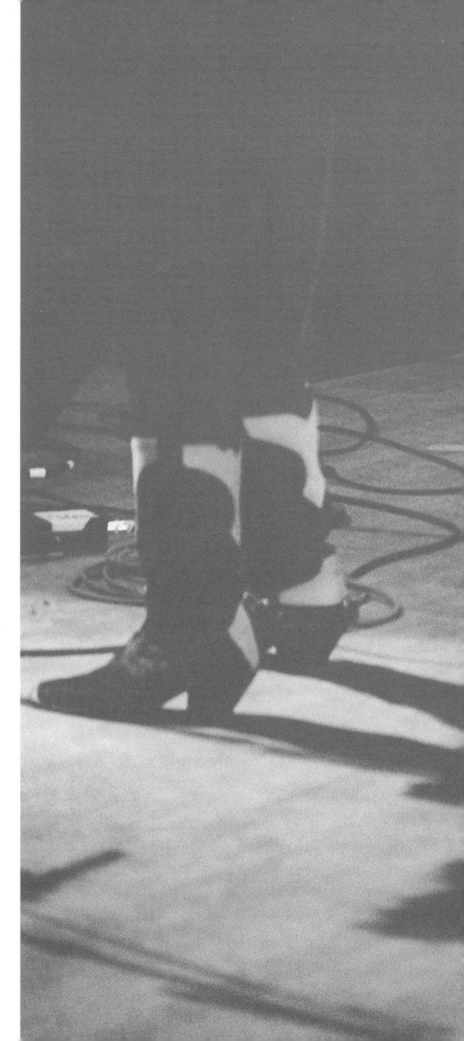

CONTENTS

Foreword by Willie Nelson

I've loved country music for a long time. It was all around me when I was growing up in Abbott, Texas. The oldest country music recordings I remember hearing were by fiddle players like Gid Tanner and the Skillet Lickers and Fiddlin' John Carson. I heard country music from Gene Autry, but I also heard it from Bing Crosby, and Bob Wills put it all together for me. He came out of our old Philco radio set with his Texas Playboys, and I fell in love with the sound. The radio taught me I was born to country music.

Both sides of my family were talented musicians. My Nelson grandparents, Mom and Dad Nelson, were descended from English and Irish immigrants who brought their traditions as storytellers, singers, dancers, and fiddlers to this country. They filled our house with music and music books. Daddy Nelson, my grandfather, would sing to me—"Polly Wolly Doodle All the Day," "She'll Be Comin' Round the Mountain," or "Where Have You Gone Billy Boy"—while I sat in his lap, barely out of diapers. My sister Bobbie played the piano and could read music. Before I got a guitar, I would sit on the bench beside her while she practiced. She would tell me what chord she was hitting and what key she was in. When I got a guitar, a Stella out of the Sears catalog, I would find the chords and play along with her. We were performing from an early age. We sang a lot of gospel songs when we went to church, Sunday school, and prayer meeting.

So I grew up loving country music. It was everywhere then, and it's everywhere now. It comes from the soul of America, but it has gone around the world. Today, people can hear country music on a computer or on an iPod; the Grand Ole Opry is going strong, carried by satellite radio and the Internet, and still booming out at night on 50,000 watts of radio power; country music has gone to the moon; you can hear country music in ads for pickups, sodas, and snacks. But the beautiful thing is, Texas is still full of dancehalls, and some people still play music on their front porches and in their living rooms on a Saturday night.

This book from the Country Music Hall of Fame and Museum will tell you a lot about the history of country music. It has a lot of great photos from the music's past, right on up to today, so that you can see what country music has looked like over the years. There's also a lot of good information here from people who've studied the history of country music and know what they're talking about. Read this book, and you'll learn about the Skillet Lickers and Gene Autry and Bob Wills.

I hope this book makes you want to go out and hear live country music, too. When country artists open their hearts to an audience, they're sharing their deepest feelings. Music is a motivator. It will make you leap up and move. It will make you dance. It will make you do jumping jacks. Country music gets people to feeling good. You don't want to miss that—especially when it's live and in person. Then you can come home again and read about it here.

Prologue: Unbroken Circle

Country music has changed a great deal since it became a commercial art form in the 1920s. In less than 100 years, it has evolved from acoustic folk music performed communally by amateurs, to amped-up productions written by full-time professional songwriters and performed by practiced entertainers for audiences unknown to them.

And yet in many ways country music hasn't really changed at all. It's still a music about real people and real lives. It's still unashamedly sentimental. It's still corny sometimes; bad puns are encouraged and savored—unlike rock music where today's musicians seem incapable of singing anything that might diminish their aura of cool superiority. In contrast, country as a musical form—and as a culture—doesn't concern itself with being hip or chic or superior; it's focused instead on communicating common experiences, on storytelling.

More than most musical forms, country music has tended to break down the barriers between performer and audience. Loretta Lynn and George Jones may dress in rhinestone finery, but fans know that Loretta and George are at heart still just plain folks. In earlier years fans felt the same way about Hank Williams and Kitty Wells. The same holds true for recent stars like Garth Brooks, Kenny Chesney, and Reba McEntire.

The following reminiscences are intended to offer an intimate point of entry into this history. Reading these stories, one can almost imagine them as conversations over the garden fence with a neighbor. And yet they're more than that, because through these performers' recollections about their formative musical experiences, we see where country music comes from and how the voice schooled on the front-porch can become the hit single on the radio.

The illustrations in this Prologue are courtesy of Jim Sherraden at Hatch Show Print, the venerable Nashville poster print shop that has long designed posters for country music stars. Using Hatch lettering and graphics, Sherraden also illustrated the opening panels of each chapter, as well as the book's cover. Hatch art was the perfect complement to this book, and not just because Hatch has been owned by the Country Music Hall of Fame and Museum since 1992. For in an era of digital images, Hatch Show Print keeps alive the painstaking tradition of handmade commercial artwork and letterpress printing—just as, in this age of hypertext and virtual reality, country music keeps us in touch with our age-old heritage of plainspoken musical storytelling about the things that matter most in life.

DOC WATSON

Born in Deep Gap, North Carolina, 1923

FROM THE time I was just a little fella I began to notice music. It was everybody from the Skillet Lickers and the original Carter Family to Mississippi John Hurt. There was a little pile of 78s we had—there might have been one or two by Furry Lewis, maybe two sides. As time come along, there was Jimmie Rodgers. Of course, he had to be in there. All kinds of people came up through the years, and I listened to all of them. Radio helped play a big part. I was influenced by the whole, full scope of the Grand Ole Opry on Saturday nights. I learned ballads from

Mama. I listened to music, whoever and whatever they played, even some of the old Dixieland jazz on a few old 78 records. I listened to any and everything I could get hold of where the flattop guitar was featured.

I found my way. After all, music is found. If you fool around with a guitar, you're gonna find out where the notes are, find out how to tune the thing. You do that by sound. Music is really sound. That's what it is. You don't have to see to learn it.

BUCK OWENS

Born in Sherman, Texas, 1929

I'VE BEEN around music all my life. My mother played the piano–terrific Christian-type music. Everywhere we lived, my mother would play the piano in church. My dad played a French harp and was a good singer, although the only time he did that was when we were going down the road somewhere.

For years and years in Texas and Arizona we listened to the Grand Ole Opry every Saturday night. When I was about three or four years old, we had a radio on top of this shelf, and it played music in the morning. It was a Dallas station, and W. Lee O'Daniel & the Light Crust Doughboys were famous [on it] in those days.

My ambition to play music came really strong and really fast. As a small kid, I was working in the

fields. It was hot and it was miserable. Once I'd been in a honky-tonk, I found that as bad as the honky-tonk might have been, it was cool in the summer and warm in the winter. I played from the time I was 15 or 16, when I started hanging around the honky-tonks. That's where the music was. I went there to listen and to try to learn, to hear what those people were doing.

LORETTA LYNN

Born in Butcher Holler, Kentucky, 1935

I WAS 27 when I started singing for a living. My four little kids were all in school. I never did think I could sing, and the only song Doo ever heard me sing was "White Christmas." He would sneak in and hear me sing while I was rocking the babies to sleep. So one day he come in and said, "I'm gonna put you on the road and let you sing for two years. We'll buy us a new home and that'll be it, and we'll be a family again." Well, two years from the time I started singing, I didn't hardly have enough money to buy a hamburger on the road, let alone a house.

When I wrote my songs, I just wrote about the things I knew—the sad times and good times. Growing up in Butcher Holler, Christmas was our only holiday. You didn't hear the Christmas songs, even though the family was pretty musical. I was 11 when Daddy got his job in the mines, and that was the greatest Christmas we ever had. Mommy usually made me a doll out of patched-up socks, but that year, I got a plastic doll. It wasn't big—it was like about eight or nine inches tall—but that was the greatest thing I ever seen. That was a great life, even though I've been to bed hungry, and I wouldn't trade it for nothing I've done since I've been married. I think that's what's made me what I am today.

CHARLEY PRIDE

Born in Sledge, Mississippi, 1938

MY HOMETOWN of Sledge, Mississippi, is the same as when I left there 40 years ago. It's about 300 or 400 population. It's just one street. You had one grocery store and one general store. It's just a small town sitting on Highway 3 that runs just out of Memphis.

A lot of people didn't have radios back when I was growing up. But we were fortunate enough to be able to have a Philco radio; it was battery operated, and my dad ran the knobs on it because he didn't want the battery run down. We would all gather around the radio just during the evenings. Most of the day, of course, we worked in the fields. Because by the time we got through chopping cotton, getting the hogs fed and the chickens bedded down, and picked up the chips for the wood to make fires the next morning, it was dark.

I remember listening to the Grand Ole Opry and shows like *Gangbusters* on Sunday, *Inner Sanctum* mystery, these kind of things. But the Opry was the music part that I remember listening to the most on Saturday nights. The stars then were Ernest Tubb, Roy Acuff, the Fruit Jar Drinkers, and George D. Hay (the Solemn Old Judge), and Uncle Dave Macon and David Cobb, the show's announcer.

A lot of people have said to me over the years, "Charley, why country music? With a voice like yours you could have sung anything you wanted to." Well, I always emulated the music I heard. I believe the basics of American music consist of three basic ingredients—country, gospel, and the blues. And they all have had an influence on one another, and they have borrowed from one another. That's what I grew up listening to, and they influenced me.

TAMMY WYNETTE

Born in Itawamba County, Mississippi, 1942

MY DAD was a musician. He had a band that sounded like bluegrass. They tried to copy and sound an awful lot like the old-fashioned Delmore Brothers. He died when I was nine months old. Mother said that before he died he was sitting at the piano with me on his knees and said, "Give her music lessons. I want her to play this thing when I'm gone." And she did, but the music teacher told Mother and me, "You're wasting my time and your time, Mrs. Lee. She's not listening to what I tell her. She has me to play it, and she goes on and plays what she hears." And that's what I did. So he told her I might as well quit.

My father and his mother, I guess, were my biggest inspiration. She played organ, and she taught the old [sacred] harp singings, where you teach the notes and not the words. My grandma taught the fa-so-la singings, which is where they teach you to sing [demonstrates] "Do-fa-mi-re"—you sing all the notes and never the words. I didn't want to learn it. I just wanted to play what I heard. But she was my biggest booster. She wanted me to go and do everything I could when it came to music. Later, she would always tell me, "You go back to Nashville. You sound better than them girls on the radio now. I know you can do as good as they can." So I did it, and she was a big, big help to me. She'd keep my kids for me when I'd come to Nashville [to audition].

VINCE GILL

Born in Norman, Oklahoma, 1957

MY VERY first memories are of music, of my grandmother playing "How Great Thou Art" on the piano, and my dad singing. My mom could play two songs on the harmonica—and then she was out of breath and couldn't play anymore. And I remember as a small boy, going to a hoedown with my father in Piedmont, Oklahoma, and listening to a skinny cowboy named Herman Stover play "Listen to the Mockingbird" on his violin. Later, I got to look into the f-holes. I said, "Where are the birds, Daddy? I know they're in there. I heard 'em."

My [older] brother played "Six Pack to Go" and "Long, Tall Texan" on the guitar, and we sang those together. When I got a little older, he was always there to chord for me while I practiced.

I wasn't the kind of kid who stood in front of the mirror with a hairbrush and pretended to be Elvis. I was the guy who had a guitar and buried his face in it and tried to learn what Chet Atkins and all of those guys played. I just wanted to be a musician. I didn't want to be a singing star. I played guitar for years

before I ever got up the nerve to sing. And then as I started to discover all this music, I'd buy these records and read the jackets [to see] who played on this, who played on that. If I had a dream, it was to be one of those guys that could really play and made records.

I think a lot of the pain you hear in my music is my love of bluegrass. I just love how real and honest those songs are. I always loved sad things. My favorite song is "Old Shep." It doesn't get any sadder than shooting your own dog.

PATTY LOVELESS
Born in Pikeville, Kentucky, 1957

MY EARLIEST memories are of a house in Belcher Holler, Kentucky, not all that far from where Loretta Lynn grew up in Butcher Holler. It was hollerin' distance, you might say. I used to sit up in the kitchen with Mother all the time and sing, and sing to the Grand Ole Opry while she was mopping the floor on Saturday night. There were seven kids, and a lot of my family sang, and Mother enjoyed singing. She'd invite people over for me to sing, but I was too shy to sing around my cousins and aunts and uncles.

The first time I ever saw anybody outside of my family perform was Lester Flatt and Earl Scruggs. It was at the Pollyanna Drive-In Theater in Pikeville, Kentucky. My dad loved Flatt & Scruggs, and he wanted me to see them perform on top of the concession stand during the movies' intermission. It was really the neatest thing. I thought, "This is great!" I was five years old.

All my grandfathers and great-grandfathers worked in the mines. But when I was ten, we moved to Louisville so my father—who went into the coal mines at eighteen and had black lung disease—could seek medical treatment. A lot of my older brothers were living in Louisville, but the move was still really

traumatic for me. It was almost like New York to me now. At school, it took the kids awhile to understand me, and at the time I thought they were kind of cruel.

What happened was, I learned to make friends through my music. That's the reason I'm always trying to look for the right songs to communicate with people now. I communicate better through the language of music.

RANDY TRAVIS
Born in Marshville, North Carolina, 1959

MY EARLIEST memories of country music were hearing my mom and dad playing records and the radio in the car or at home. My mom and dad both were great lovers of country music. My dad was, you could even say, a fanatic about country music. So it was really all I knew probably until I was in my teenage years.

I did hear other kinds of music. I heard blues, some rock, whatever the kids in school were listening to at that time. But when I put something on my record player or in my tape player, or when I turned on the radio for myself, it was country music. I listened to everything on country radio.

Country music can touch, say, a 12-year-old kid and his dad at the same time. A lot of things I heard lyrically in country music were things I could relate to—and things obviously my mom and dad could relate to—because country music is storytelling, basically.

What I do now as a singer and songwriter and what I have always done is basically the same thing.

From [the time I was] eight years old, it hasn't changed. The kind of music I like to sing now still is music that Merle Haggard would have recorded if he had found the song. So would George Jones. So would Hank, Waylon, Willie. I don't care to hear anything else. I don't care to sing anything else.

TURKEY IN THE STRAW

THE ROOTS OF COMMERCIAL COUNTRY MUSIC

BILL C. MALONE

WHEN AMERICA'S SETTLERS ARRIVED IN THE NEW WORLD, THEY BROUGHT THEIR FOLK MUSIC WITH THEM. BUT BY THE EARLY 1900s, THIS HAD CHANGED IN REMARKABLE WAYS THAT NO ONE COULD HAVE ANTICIPATED. MANY MUSICAL STYLES COALESCED TO PRODUCE WHAT WE KNOW TODAY AS "COUNTRY."

1877–1919 TIMELINE

1877 Thomas Edison invents and tests the first phonograph, which plays tinfoil cylinders. Emile Berliner invents the flat-disc phonograph.

1892 Union Gospel Tabernacle is built in downtown Nashville, Tennessee; renamed the Ryman Auditorium, this eventually becomes the longtime home of the Grand Ole Opry.

1898 Spanish-American War takes place.

1900 The mandolin becomes all the rage throughout urban America, with mandolin orchestras flourishing.

1901 President William McKinley is assassinated and is succeeded in office by Theodore Roosevelt. Queen Victoria dies.

1903 The Wright Brothers fly the first manned, motor-powered airplane. The wreck of the *Fast Mail No. 97* railroad train occurs near Danville, Virginia, which inspires "The Wreck of the Old 97" ballad and many early country-music recordings.

1904 The first double-sided records are issued.

1905 Albert Einstein publishes his special theory of relativity.

1908 N. Howard "Jack" Thorp compiles and publishes *Songs of the Cowboys*, introducing the public to genuine cowboy folk songs.

continues opposite

Country music did not exist prior to the 1920s—that is, there was no cohesive, commercially marketed product in American popular entertainment that bore that name, nor any body of music that consistently projected a rural flavor or sound. Country music is a commercial art form that coalesced only after rural American music met the technologies of radio and records, beginning in the 1920s. True, in the late 19th and early 20th centuries, minstrel and vaudeville entertainers, such as Cal Stewart, who performed under the name "Uncle Josh," had frequently played the comedic role of country bumpkins, or "rubes," and venerable skits like "The Arkansas Traveler" often graced the stage and appeared on cylinder and disc recordings.

At the same time, New York's Tin Pan Alley tunesmiths—conscious that the nation's growing cities contained a multitude of people fresh off the farm, or others who longed for a rural past that they had never experienced—also frequently published songs that commemorated rustic values, the old home place, and other rural scenes. There were also periodic examples of fiddle and banjo renditions of folk tunes on commercial recordings prior to 1920, but no one ever assumed that these performances were anything more than occasional dabblings in the rural genre by popular or vaudeville entertainers.

On the other hand, songs and dances—performed by rural and small-town people for their own entertainment or for largely noncommercial purposes—flourished all over North America prior to country music's emergence on radio and records in the 1920s. While vital enclaves of ethnic entertainment—such as that fashioned by French-speaking musicians in Canada and southwest Louisiana and by Spanish-speaking entertainers in southern Texas—certainly existed, most American rural music was largely a product of styles brought from the British Isles. Nowhere, however, did those styles endure as untouched replicas of the music originally brought to these shores by British immigrants. Even in the semi-isolated Appalachian Mountains, music by the end of the 19th century had been touched and modified by modernity and by the styles and songs contributed by other ethnic and racial groups that came to the United States.

TECHNOLOGY'S ROLE
It took the spark of radio and records to create the commercial amalgam known today as country music. This early microphone is from the Nashville station WSM.

Stories in song

Rural music everywhere in America shared certain characteristics. For example, ballads were a common component of the repertoire of every ethnic group across the nation, and folklorists have extensively collected traditional British songs in New England and other regions outside the Appalachians. Ballads from the British Isles represent some of the earliest and most substantial building blocks of country music. Although today the term "ballad" is commonly understood to mean "a romantic love song," the word also has a more technical meaning. For folklorists, who study the traditional customs of people, a ballad is a long, impersonal, narrative song that tells a story, usually with concise but dramatic clarity.

These ballads came to America in the consciousness of many immigrants and in the repertoires of professional entertainers. Ballad texts were often preserved in writing, in newspapers or magazines, and sometimes in handwritten form in personal "ballet books." However, most were preserved and disseminated orally, from generation to generation—a process that typically and unconsciously altered texts and transformed melodies.

Academic folklorists have generally categorized Anglo-American ballads in two ways—as Child or Broadside ballads. The Child ballads were those that were referenced in the massive, multivolume collection compiled by Harvard scholar

Francis James Child—*The English and Scottish Popular Ballads* (volumes published between 1882 and 1898). These 305 ballads and their variants, which were gathered from old manuscripts and books, were valued by Child and his disciples not so much as music but more as the vestiges of ancient poetry. However, when the English collector Cecil Sharp came to the southern Appalachians in 1916, he found an extensive body of songs from the Child canon still being sung by the people who lived there.

The Broadside ballads, on the other hand, were not as highly regarded by scholars as those collected by Child. Since they had been printed cheaply on large black-letter sheets or posters, called "broadsides," and peddled on English street corners and in taverns, or posted on walls, they were considered to be little more than doggerel that had been aimed

FRONT PORCH MUSIC *A farmer at home with his music, near Natchitoches, Louisiana, 1940.*

1910 Folklorist John Lomax publishes *Cowboy Songs and Other Frontier Ballads.*

1911 Irving Berlin composes "Alexander's Ragtime Band."

1912 The *Titanic* sinks off the coast of Newfoundland on its maiden voyage.

1914 The Panama Canal is completed. Cecil B. DeMille directs the first feature-length film, *The Squaw Man.* World War I begins in Europe. "Carry Me Back to Old Virginny," recorded by Alma Gluck, is Victor Records' first Red Seal disc to sell more than one million copies.

1915 Bob Wills (age ten) first plays the fiddle in public, filling in at a dance for his father, who fails to show.

1916 Vernon Dalhart begins recording light opera for Edison. Albert Einstein publishes the general theory of relativity.

1917 Cecil Sharp's *English Folk Songs from the Southern Appalachians* collects the musical notation and lyrics for hundreds of southern traditional songs. The Original Dixieland Jass Band makes the first authentic jazz recordings, for Victor Records. The USA enters World War I.

1918 World War I ends.

1919 Lloyd Loar fashions his finely crafted F5 mandolin for the Gibson Company.

at the semiliterate masses. For subject matter, these ballad-makers often quickly exploited any newsworthy event, such as a shipwreck or hanging, that caught the public's fancy, and circulated thousands of copies of such newly made songs married to popular melodies.

Neither the American folk nor their British ancestors had made distinctions concerning ballads; they simply embraced any song that told a good story. As a consequence, both Child and Broadside ballads made the transit to America as part of the cherished possessions of immigrants.

Variants or fragments of such Child ballads as "Barbara Allen," "The Wife of Usher's Well," and "Black Jack Davy" endured in the repertoires of American singers alongside such Broadside stalwarts as "Mary of the Wild Moor," "The Wexford Girl," and "The Butcher's Boy." Many of them eventually wound up on hillbilly records—which, in effect, functioned as modern broadsides—alongside such newly made American creations as "The Death of Floyd Collins" and "The Hills of Roane County."

Among musical instruments available in rural America, the fiddle was king—popular with every ethnic and racial group, and dancing was a universal passion, both North and South. Everywhere in America, folk music was a community resource that provided a bonding sense of identity, an outlet for physical and emotional release, and a means for individual creativity. Anyone who ventured into a community or house dance as far afield as Georgia, Maine, Wisconsin, or California, would have found similar scenes of conviviality and merriment, and probably even a stash of similar and familiar fiddle tunes that may or may not have borne the same names.

The southern sound

When commercial country music emerged in the early 1920s—bearing a variety of labels such as "Old Familiar Music" and "Hillbilly"—it had a decidedly southern sound and complexion. Although music that appeared on the early recordings and radio shows—especially on radio barn dances, such as those heard in Chicago and Nashville, where nostalgia and down-home informality prevailed—carried the flavor of rural music listened to throughout the USA, the country musicians themselves were overwhelmingly southern. The great majority of men and women who made the music came from that broad arc of territory extending southwest from Virginia to Texas. When the early recording scouts ventured out to find potential talent, they did not go to Maine, Wisconsin, Nebraska, or California, but to Virginia, Georgia, Texas, and other southern states instead.

The romance of the South and the presumed exoticism of its people—popularized by generations of songwriters

BROADSIDE BALLAD
Essential wellsprings for what became country music were broadside ballads—that is, songs printed on large poster sheets for common consumption. Broadside ballads, such as "Mary of the Wild Moor," originated in the British Isles and found their way to America. "Mary" has been recorded by numerous country singers, including the Blue Sky Boys, Dolly Parton, and Johnny Cash.

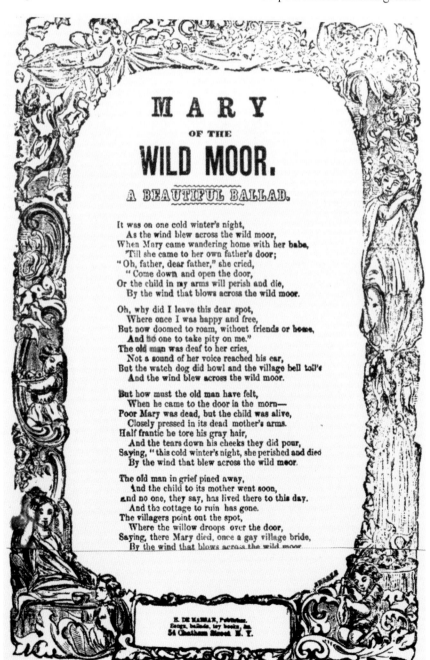

AFRICAN INFLUENCE *The music of black Americans has been a key component of country music. The banjo originated in Africa and was originally associated with slave music.*

like Stephen Foster and local-color novelists and short-story writers, and accentuated by the Lost Cause mythology that followed the Civil War—generated an interest in the region that has really never flagged. Most importantly, by the early 1920s, the South was perceived as a land of music. However, people could not be blamed for thinking that southern music was essentially black music, a perception fed first in the 1830s by blackface minstrels—white men who blackened their faces with burnt cork and performed music and dances purportedly borrowed from African-Americans—and then in the late 19th century by the recurring "discoveries" of such black musical forms as spirituals, ragtime, "coon" songs, the blues, and jazz. When OKch Records' talent scout Ralph Peer traveled to Atlanta in 1923—the visit that led to the recording of Fiddlin' John Carson and the release of the first documented hillbilly hit record—he actually was looking for black music.

Although rural music bore some similarities all over the USA, that of the South was distinctly different from other rural expressions in certain crucial ways. The men and women who made the first recordings came from an ethnically and racially diverse culture, one that was strongly flavored by evangelical Protestant Christianity, and one that had been undergoing dramatic economic and social transformation since the Civil War. Blacks and whites had met and mingled since the early Colonial era, absorbing much from each other across a racial barrier that held firm socially but remained porous culturally. In many ways, poor blacks and poor whites shared a folk culture with a common body of songs, dances, and instruments that moved freely across racial lines.

Musical miscegenation

Black fiddlers were ubiquitous in the 19th-century South and, in fact, were described much more often than white musicians in the newspapers, travel accounts, and other literature at the time. Slaves frequently attended religious revivals in the antebellum (pre-Civil War) era, and while they were typically segregated from white worshipers, their singing was recognized and admired nevertheless.

During the years following the Civil War, rural whites had ample opportunities to experience the musical skills of their black neighbors. White musicians did not simply learn from blacks to sing more expressively, with full, open-throated emotion; they were inspired also to take up new instruments, such as the banjo, and to experiment with unorthodox chord progressions, blue notes, slide-guitar techniques, and unusual rhythms. Folklorist Norm Cohen argues that southern white string-band music was more interesting than that heard in the North, because white southerners had embraced and incorporated rhythms and styles learned from black musicians.

THE SOURCES OF COUNTRY MUSIC *(Overleaf) The many strands of music that intertwined to create country music— gospel singing, country fiddling, African-American banjo, and more—are depicted in* The Sources of Country Music *(1975), the last painting by American master Thomas Hart Benton. Today the painting is displayed at the Country Music Hall of Fame and Museum.*

Poor whites also certainly knew the blues—that is, they knew poverty, pain, and social exclusion during the bleak economic years of the late 19th century. They also knew the blues—after all, they heard it everywhere in the South—on street corners, in barrooms and brothels, in medicine shows and tent shows, minstrel performances and black theaters, and, of course, on phonograph recordings.

While southern rural musicians exhibited a fondness for the spontaneity and freedom of black music, and for the

and the bottle, they should not forget that God would mete out the ultimate reward or punishment. Religion left southerners with an enormous repertoire of songs, various styles of singing them, and a powerful measure of guilt that prompted a cautionary view of life and may even have reinforced the tight-throated style of singing that often prevailed in the backwoods. The paradoxes and contradictions inherent in these opposing poles of sensuousness/libertinism and religious restraint helped

RURAL RHYTHMS *Music-making and dancing were deeply ingrained in American working-class culture, as depicted in* The Jolly Flat Boat Men *(ca. 1847), painted by George Caleb Bingham.*

hedonism that white people believed typical of black culture at that time, they also labored under restraints and inhibitions, which came from the indoctrination of Calvinist-style, religious faith. At least from the early 1800s, when huge outdoor revivals, or "camp meetings," began in Kentucky and spread throughout the South, evangelists conducted major campaigns for the souls of southerners. In a very real sense, the preachers and devout lay people promoting the religious revivals did so to "tame" southern men—to curb their passions, to divert their hedonism into an enthusiasm for God, and to civilize them. So men were reminded that in their passion for the fiddle, the dance,

to give southern music an emotional and psychic edge that generations of listeners have found compelling.

Influence of the wider world

The men and women who made the first country recordings and radio broadcasts were not innocent rustics who knew nothing of the world. Some of them had ventured off to fight for America in 1898 (the Spanish-American War) and 1917 (World War I), and their forebears had

FOREIGN FIELDS *Early in the 20th century, young men from America's rural communities joined by the thousands to fight America's foreign wars. As a result, new ideas—and music—spread. Here are two US soldiers of the Spanish-American War with an instrument soon to gain popularity: the guitar.*

> # "ANYONE WHO WANTS TO BE A SONGWRITER SHOULD LISTEN TO AS MUCH FOLK MUSIC AS THEY CAN, STUDY THE FORM AND STRUCTURE OF THE STUFF THAT HAS BEEN AROUND FOR 100 YEARS."

BOB DYLAN

fought in the Civil War. In each case, when they returned to their home communities, they brought part of the outside world with them. More importantly, that world had been intruding upon them and their society since the guns fell silent at Appomattox, marking the end of the Civil War in 1865.

The industrial juggernaut that made possible the defeat of the Confederate armies had solidified its supremacy by pushing its railroads into every corner of the South, including the once-isolated Appalachians. Largely through this penetration, old industries like textile manufacturing and lumbering expanded rapidly, and new ones like coal mining, meat packing, and oil production grew dramatically. Industrialization provided jobs that either supplemented or replaced farm work, and it encouraged a measure of material consumption that had never been possible before.

Out on the farms, where loneliness, declining commodity prices, and an encroaching system of tenant farming challenged the older dream of security,

rural folk became increasingly aware of the products of modernism. Peddlers and traveling salesmen brought samples of the city's wares, and mail-order catalogs offered easy material consumption. Sheet music, instruments, and phonograph records became increasingly available. Movie houses were emerging in many towns well before World War I, and vaudeville theaters opened in the larger cities, making available the latest songs and musical fashions.

Actually, new songs had been seeping into the rural South long before the Civil War, creeping into the repertoires of singers alongside the old ballads and folk songs that the original settlers had brought. To the despair of many of the region's political leaders, who longed to make the South self-sufficient in every way, Dixie was a colonial society that imported much of its fashions and material goods. The South had no popular culture that it could call its own, and even during the Civil War, when regional nationalism reached a feverish peak, the Confederacy borrowed its most popular songs, such as

FLICKERING IMAGES *The arrival of movie houses in many American towns in the early years of the twentieth century introduced country folk to new ideas and fashions. This movie-house photo dates from 1903.*

"Lorena," "Listen to the Mocking Bird," and "Dixie" itself, from northern sources. Traveling shows had been the principal dispensers of various forms of music in the South since at least the 18th century. Dramatic troupes, traveling down the rivers as far south as New Orleans and Mobile, invariably included musical skits and specialty dances as fillers between acts. Virtually all itinerant forms of entertainment, whether equestrian, puppet, circus, medicine, or burlesque, featured music as integral features or backdrops for their presentations. If the tune played or sung was good, it could easily insinuate itself into the consciousness of the audience.

Minstrel music

Blackface minstrel shows unquestionably provided the most popular and influential traveling entertainment of the 19th century. From the 1830s, white song-and-dance men, masquerading in blackface, and performing music and dances that allegedly came from African-American sources, toured throughout North America and Europe. Most of the minstrels seem to have been northern-born entertainers who had performed in circuses or other traveling shows, which took them to the South, where they encountered the music of slaves and free blacks. However, white southerners did make crucial contributions to the minstrel genre. For example, Joel Walker Sweeney, the famous banjo player from Appomattox, Virginia, toured the upper South with a wagon show in the 1830s, and then took his talents to the British Isles. During the antebellum period, minstrel shows traveled frequently through a broad expanse of southern territory, mostly to the larger towns and cities, but also far back into the hills via riverboats, which journeyed up the tributaries of the Ohio River.

During the Civil War, Confederate soldiers sometimes found diversion playing fiddles and banjos, and took new tunes and styles home when they returned to civilian life. Surviving banjo instruction books from the mid-19th century, such as those compiled by Thomas Briggs, Philip Rice, and Frank Converse, describe methods (probably learned from African-American musicians)

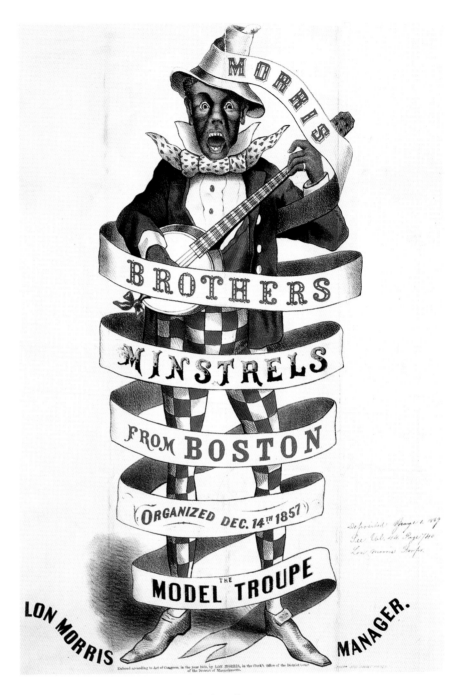

that are analogous to the "frailing" and "clawhammer" styles, which emerged in old-time country music. The minstrels' banjo and fiddle music accompanied solo dances, such as the pigeon wing, buck-and-wing, and double shuffle, which also eventually found favor in rural homes and in early country-music stage shows.

In the days before the songwriting industry became concentrated in New York City, in the theater district called Tin Pan Alley, the minstrel shows were the principal purveyors of pop music in the USA. Like Stephen Foster, many

DARK BEGINNINGS *Country songs were influenced by blackface minstrelsy, the most popular traveling entertainment of the 19th century. In minstrelsy, white performers "blacked up" with burnt cork, imitated black music, and caricatured black behavior.*

VAUDEVILLE THEATER *Beginning with the end of the Civil War, vaudeville theater—staged musical variety shows—became one of America's favorite entertainments. Though vaudeville began in New York, it eventually encompassed theater circuits across the nation. Through vaudeville, many popular songs entered early country music.*

CLASSIC COUNTRY RECORDING

UNCLE DAVE MACON
"Bile Them Cabbage Down"

Oh, bile them cabbage down, bile them cabbage down, The last word I heard old Mistress say, Bile them cabbage down.
TRADITIONAL, RECORDED JULY 11, 1924

Uncle Dave Macon's **"Bile Them Cabbage Down"** was the very first recording of what would become known as a classic country-music "shout tune"—the kind that an entire vaudeville show's cast would sing together at the end of a performance. Between Uncle Dave's boisterous singing, loud banjo playing, and foot stomping, the engineers had to keep on their toes—he made it difficult to maintain a balanced sound level with the giant acoustical horn used to capture sound in the days before microphones.

The song itself seems to be cobbled together from a series of floating folk stanzas from black and white sources alike; such recomposition was common with many Macon songs, and subsequent recordings held fast to his method. During the 1920s, "Bile Them Cabbage Down" was often recorded by fiddle bands like the Skillet Lickers, Earl Johnson & His Dixie Entertainers, and Crockett's Mountaineers. In 1937, fiddler Clayton McMichen even recorded a swing version.

CHARLES K. WOLFE

---

aspiring composers strived for genteel acceptance in the salons and fashionable parlors of the nation, but nevertheless wrote often for the earthier minstrel business, where widespread exposure and commercial viability seemed more possible. Nonsense or dance tunes, such as "Camptown Races," "Jordan Am a Hard Road to Travel," "Old Dan Tucker," "Turkey in the Straw," and "Dixie," appeared prominently in minstrel performances, yet the minstrel entertainers also understood that American audiences loved sentimental music, too. Consequently, minstrel men often sang nostalgic songs of home, or love songs such as "Lorena," "Sweet Kitty Wells," or "Listen to the Mocking Bird," or songs about faithful or heartbroken slaves such as "Yellow Rose of Texas," "Old Folks at Home," and "My Pretty Quadroon."

Except for a few names like Daniel Decatur Emmett and James K. Bland (the composer of "Carry Me Back to Old Virginny"), most of the writers who supplied songs to the minstrel shows have been forgotten. However, one writer

RURAL DANCE *(opposite) By the time of "Uncle Josh's Huskin Dance," a song from 1898, New York music publishers had begun to see that there was a market for rural music.*

whose songs have endured to the present day and who seems to have had the most direct link to country music was Will S. Hays, a journalist and businessman from Louisville, Kentucky. Hays wrote a regular column on the life and lore of the Ohio and Mississippi rivers for the *Louisville Courier-Journal* and spent much of his life as a riverboat pilot. He was also a prolific poet and songwriter whose songs appeared mainly in the mid-19th century. When he died in 1907, Hays may not have been fully aware that his songs had circulated far and wide in rural and small-town America, and certainly could not have known that some of them—such as "We Parted by the River Side," "Nobody's Darling on Earth," "Molly Darling," "I'll Remember You, Love, in My Prayers," and "You've Been a Friend to Me"—would win renewed and enduring life in commercial country and bluegrass music. His most famous song, "Little Old Log Cabin in the Lane," was present at country

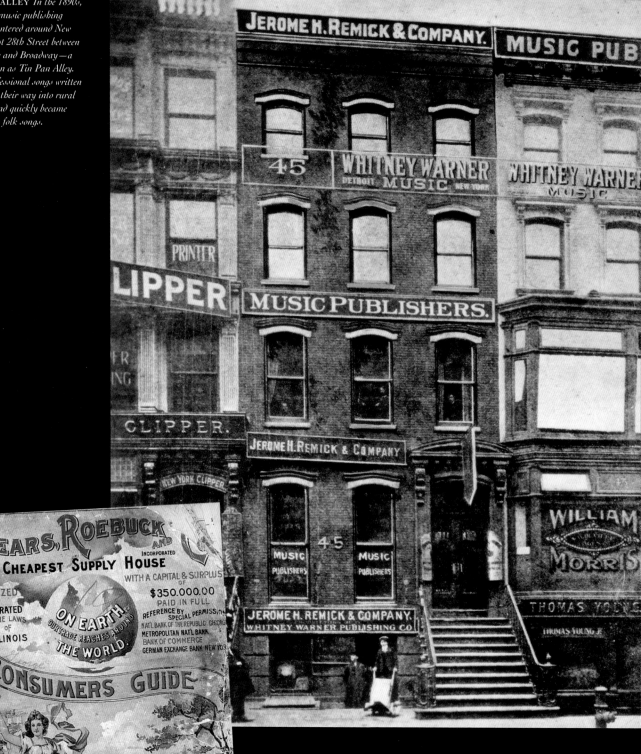

TIN PAN ALLEY *In the 1890s, America's music publishing industry centered around New York's West 28th Street between 5th Avenue and Broadway—a place known as Tin Pan Alley. Many professional songs written here found their way into rural America and quickly became accepted as folk songs.*

SEARS CATALOG *Mail-order department stores such as Sears Roebuck and Montgomery Ward helped spread Tin Pan Alley sheet music as well as guitars and harmonicas into the hinterlands across America.*

music's earliest commercial glimmerings; it was one side of Fiddlin' John Carson's seminal recording of 1923.

After the Civil War, when vaudeville and other varieties of entertainment began to mount serious challenges to the minstrel form, the blackface troupes continued to tour throughout the South. Increasingly, their casts included southern-born entertainers, with the most notable acts being real African-Americans, such as the Georgia Minstrels, who, ironically, preserved the fashion of corking their faces. Minstrelsy's contributions to southern music were enduring. Blackface costuming and dialect figured prominently in country entertainment as late as World War II, when a popular duo named Jamup & Honey toured with Grand Ole Opry casts. Minstrel-derived humor remained a basic ingredient of country comedy at least into the 1980s, when *Hee Haw* remained a staple of syndicated television. Minstrel fiddle and banjo players were early and vital role models for southern musicians, such as Uncle Dave Macon, and were probably the first "string bands" that would-be rural entertainers ever saw.

The rise of Tin Pan Alley

Although minstrelsy was the principal disseminator of entertainment in 19th-century America and continued to demonstrate great appeal well into the 20th century, it was eventually supplanted by its more urbane descendant—vaudeville theater. New York served as headquarters for the most famous vaudeville theaters and chains, but the expanding railroad network of the late 19th century permitted entertainers to move freely throughout the nation. Vaudeville's ascendancy accompanied the emergence of Tin Pan Alley as the center of popular music publishing in the USA. Publishers such as Charles K. Harris, M. Witmark & Sons, and Shapiro & Bernstein opened up businesses on West 28th Street, between 5th and Broadway, and began capitalizing on the burgeoning vogue for pianos and sheet music that accompanied the urban revolution of the late 19th and early 20th centuries. Songs written there, on the cheap, tinny pianos that probably inspired the name Tin Pan Alley, were

aimed originally at big-city music purchasers. However, they became increasingly available to rural southerners, often through the performances of vaudeville entertainers who came south, but also through the colorfully illustrated sheet music advertised in Sears Roebuck and Montgomery Ward catalogs or offered in southern department stores.

Hard-boiled New York writers, who were capable of converting any theme or emotion into a saleable song, realized that Americans were torn between tradition and innovation, and that the insatiable Victorian hunger for sentimental songs about mother, home, and the old village green continued to linger in middle-class, urban households. They also realized that touring vaudeville entertainers, or other performers who learned from them, would take these songs far into the nation's hinterlands. Consequently, a large body of sentimental, nostalgic Tin Pan Alley songs eventually lost their original identities and became "country" songs through repeated performance and oral transmission. Although often dramatically altered in form and melody, they appeared in great profusion on early hillbilly recordings, over radio broadcasts, in songbooks, and at personal appearances. Some of these writers are remembered for only one or two songs. Among these are Hattie Nevada, who wrote "Letter Edged in Black," and Will Thompson, who wrote "Softly and Tenderly" and "Gathering Shells from the Seashore." Others, however, should figure prominently in any account of the personalities who compiled the country-music canon. These should include Gussie Davis, who wrote "Maple on the Hill," "The Baggage Coach Ahead," "The Fatal Wedding," and other sentimental parlor songs, and Charles K. Harris, the writer of "After the Ball," "Hello Central, Give Me Heaven," and "Break the News to Mother." Long before any folklorist or record talent scout ventured into the southern hinterlands, rural singers were already embracing such songs and according them the same kind of affection and respect given to the British ballads of old.

Musical influences

Many types of songs had an impact on the music that would coalesce as country music. These ranged from ancient folk songs to popular songs of the 19th and early 20th centuries.

1 *Sentimental songs such as "I Wanna Go Back" (1919) were key building blocks of what would become country music.*

2 *British folk song "Barbara Allen" became well known in America.*

3 *"Hello Central, Give Me Heaven" (1901) was a big Charles K. Harris success.*

4 *"Dixie" (1850), written by Dan Emmett, became a patriotic anthem of the South during the Civil War.*

5 *"After the Ball" (1892) by Charles K. Harris was a huge popular hit in America.*

6 *By the time of this 1913 song, blackface minstrelsy was fading in popularity.*

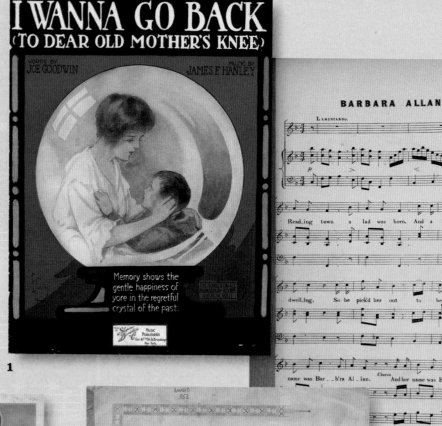

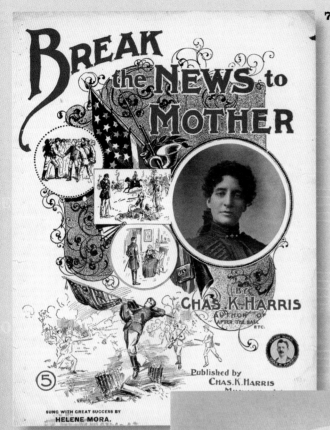

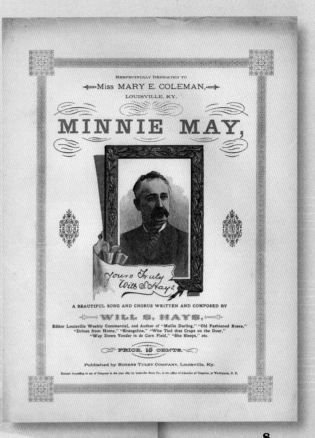

9

7 *"Break the News to Mother,"
also by Harris, was a sentimental
song originally written in 1891
about the dying words of a
fireman. In 1897, Harris rewrote
it about the death of a soldier in
the Spanish-American War.
Blind Andrew Jenkins recorded
it in 1925.*

8 *"Minnie May" was written
by Will Hays, whose "Little Log
Cabin in the Lane," "Molly
Darling," and "Jimmie Brown
the Newsboy" proved popular
with country recording artists.*

9 *"Carry Me Back to Old
Virginny" (1878) was a widely
popular minstrel song written
by James K. Bland, a black,
college-educated professional
songwriter. In 1914, Alma
Gluck's recording of it sold
a million copies.*

10 *A minstrel song by Charles H.
Fox, published by William Hall
& Son around 1858. Minstrel
shows helped popularize the banjo.*

10

PROFILES IN COUNTRY

CECIL SHARP

MOUNTAIN MUSIC *Sharp combed the Appalachians to find centuries-old British ballads still being sung.*

BORN LONDON, ENGLAND, NOVEMBER, 1859
DIED 1924
BUSINESS AFFILIATION
SCHOLAR AND RESEARCHER

The son of a slate merchant, Cecil Sharp received a degree in music from Cambridge and, by 1903, was collecting folk songs and studying folk dancing in rural England. From an American collector, he learned that many of the old English and Scottish ballads were still being sung in the southern Appalachians. By July, 1916 he had arrived in Asheville, North Carolina, to begin his preservation work.

Almost at once, Sharp found rich pockets of ballad singers in the mountains north of Asheville, and found that Appalachian singers often sang songs that had virtually died out in England. These included familiar ballads such as "Barbara Allen," "The House Carpenter," and "The Farmer's Curst Wife." They also included prototypes of the early country favorites "Three Nights Drunk," "The Knoxville Girl," and "Black Jack Davy." In the days before tape or disc recording, he notated the melody lines by hand.

Sharp roamed through North Carolina, Virginia, Tennessee, and Kentucky for three summers, gathering more than 1,600 songs. His collection, *English Folk Songs from the Southern Appalachians*, was first published in 1917. It was superseded in 1932 by a two-volume collection, which remains the best song collection from that region.

CHARLES K. WOLFE

Singings and dances

How was this vast and diverse trove of music performed? Although there were few examples of professional singing in the pre-1920s rural South, there were itinerant ballad vendors, often blind, who were heard singing their songs and hawking their printed ballads on street corners, in railroad stations, and at county fairs, hangings, and other community venues. A few of these musicians, such as Charlie Oaks and Dick Burnett, made the transition to commercial recording in the early 1920s. Otherwise, most singing was done at home and probably for private entertainment—for the family or for small, invited gatherings of neighbors or relatives.

Such occasions were sometimes called "musicales" or simply "singings." Singings and dances most often occurred in slack farming seasons, or at the end of work periods, or in homes that had achieved some degree of middle-class security and had a piano or parlor organ. Singing was not confined to age or gender, but women apparently played a central role as preservers of culture, and as guardians and dispensers of morality. Emma Bell Miles, who lived among mountain people in southeastern Tennessee in the early 1900s, described the women there as "repositories of tribal lore." They were the principal ballad singers, and the ones most likely to write a favorite song down in a "ballet book" or clip a desired song from a magazine or newspaper. Women sang often for emotional release, and, in a society where patriarchy reigned and the lot of females was generally lonely and hard, they may even have vented their frustrations or resentments in the old songs that spoke of murder, seduction, and revenge. They also sang while working at household or field chores, churning butter, cooking, shelling peas, washing clothes, sewing, or rocking their babies. Any kind of song could serve their emotional or psychological needs, but the venerable ballads and love songs (sometimes called "old lonesome songs") became particularly cherished companions. Thinking of traditional folk songs like "Barbara Allen," "The Wife of Usher's Well," and "Mary Hamilton," Emma Bell Miles noted that "it is over the loom and the knitting that old ballads are dreamily, endlessly crooned."

While an important body of British balladry and folk songs endured throughout the South, it existed side by side, and often in interaction with, religious material and popular secular pieces. Although much of the music that flowed into southern repertoires came from outside sources, southerners also made much of their own religious music. Nowhere else do we find stronger evidence of the powerful role played by evangelical religion in the historical South. In the very early 1800s, pocket-sized "songsters," containing the lyrics of songs heard at the Kentucky camp meetings, began to appear and won circulation outside the South. Distinguished by their simple, repetitive verses, familiar melodies, and use of choruses or refrains, these songs were easy to learn and won widespread popularity where songbooks were not easily available. About the same time, southern composers such as Joseph Funk and Andrew Law, in Virginia and Kentucky, began publishing "tune-books"—oblong books that printed familiar tunes used repeatedly with various religious texts. These books circulated widely in the upper South and sometimes were transported to the North, where they influenced the making of religious hymns.

The gospel sound

Throughout most of the 19th century, and well into the 20th, the songbooks that circulated in the South were printed in shape notes (also called character or patent notes). Influenced largely by *The Easy Instructor*, a publication compiled in 1801 by William Little and William Smith, itinerant singing teachers carried the method out of New England into Pennsylvania, and from there into Virginia's Shenandoah Valley, which became the seedbed for the teaching of a style that ultimately spread as far west as Texas. The earliest singing schools and their songbooks featured the method of four-note *fa-sol-la* singing (brought to the American colonies from England) and the practice of presenting the musical syllables—*fa, sol, la, mi*—as geometric shapes to indicate their position on the scale. The four-note system survives today—most notably among those singers

VAUGHAN QUARTET *Gospel music spread widely across the South in the early 20th century, as enterprising hymnal publishers such as the James D. Vaughan Company of Tennessee and the Stamps-Baxter Company in Texas sent singing quartets across the South and Southwest to teach hymns — and to sell hymnals.*

who use the book *The Sacred Harp* (1844). But the seven-note *do-re-mi* pattern, also indicated by shapes, proved to be far more popular. Promoted first in 1846, in Jesse Aikin's *Christian Minstrel*, the seven-note method was taught and circulated by the firm of J. H. Ruebush and Aldine Kieffer in Singer's Glen, Virginia, which sent its teachers and songbooks throughout the rural South. James D. Vaughan, one of Ruebush and Kieffer's many disciples, made revolutionary innovations at his publishing company in Lawrenceburg, Tennessee. He introduced traveling quartets, who served as salesmen for his methods and songbooks. In 1922, one of his many quartets recorded for a Vaughan-owned label, and, in 1923, at Whitehaven

near Memphis, Vaughan established WOAN, one of the earliest radio stations in the South, and an important medium through which his songbooks were advertised and disseminated.

To the extent that rural southerners could read music and sing harmony, they probably learned from the ten-day, shape-note schools, or from the models provided by such commercial singers as the barbershop and black gospel quartets. And they received some of their most cherished songs, such as "Keep on the Sunny Side," "Will the Circle Be Unbroken," "Life's Railway to Heaven," and "Just Over in the Glory Land," from religious sources. By the time the first hillbilly recordings appeared in the early 1920s, a large body of religious musical material was widely available in the South, including old spirituals, English hymns, camp-meeting songs, shape-note songs, and hymns from the big-city revivals led by Dwight Moody, Billy Sunday, and other evangelists.

"What singin' I did early in life was at the church. Everybody did that."
COUNTRY SINGER AND LOUISIANA STATE GOVERNOR JIMMIE DAVIS

CROWNING PRAISES *This gospel hymnal was published in 1911 by the James D. Vaughan Company of Lawrenceburg, Tennessee. Such hymnals influenced early country harmony singing.*

> ## RECORDINGS OF OLD-TIME MUSIC CAN STILL THRILL US IN THE 21ST CENTURY. THEY HAVE INSPIRED MODERN MUSICIANS SUCH AS BOB DYLAN, MARIA MULDAUR, AND TAJ MAHAL.

MIKE SEEGER

Those ancient ballads and the native pieces that emerged from the American experience, along with the religious songs and pop tunes that gradually moved into southern rural homes, constituted the vocal repertoire of early country entertainers. Although these pieces were vital components of rural music, they were not the crucial agents that shaped public performance. Community dances and fiddle contests, on the other hand, were competitive public arenas where musicians learned to play with each other, and for the entertainment of listeners and dancers who were not always easy to please.

Fiddling and frolics

The fiddle was the preeminent rural instrument in North America and was played by the broadest spectrum of people. Fiddlers had long carried the reputation of being wastrels or vagrants, people often given to drinking and debauchery, who eschewed family and responsibility in order to pursue their art. According to legend, the Devil himself was a fiddler, and his bewitching instrument was often called "the Devil's Box." While elements of truth may support the legend of irresponsibility, available evidence indicates that fiddling was a highly respectable profession in the South and was practiced by women as well as men. Its devotees ranged from the lowliest of society—slaves, farmers, and laborers—to the ranks of the most powerful and prestigious. Planters, businessmen, judges, preachers, politicians, and officeholders proudly practiced the art of fiddling, and some of them used the instrument in their quests for political power, knowing full well that their constituents valued a man who possessed such talents. In 1886, brothers Alf and Bob Taylor waged a spirited campaign against each other for the governorship of Tennessee, debating on the political stump during the day and serenading their audiences with their fiddles at night. Democrat Bob won that particular race, but Republican Alf won later elections to Congress and to the governorship, and eventually made two recordings with a group called the Old Limber Quartette.

Fiddle contests provided public exposure for talented musicians, and some fiddlers became widely known far beyond their home locales as contest participants. The earliest documented contest in North America occurred on November 30, 1736, in Hanover County, Virginia, as part of a St. Andrew's Day celebration. Long before the mid-1920s, when automobile magnate Henry Ford sponsored widespread fiddle contests,

fiddling had already gained the reputation of being an old-time art and was widely identified as a survival of Old South culture. The art was often associated with Confederate memories, and contests were frequently held at old soldiers' reunions. But, as the affairs held after 1913 in Atlanta suggested, old-time fiddle contests were also useful vehicles for New South "boosterism"—well-publicized events employed by chambers-of-commerce and other civic-minded groups to lure country people into town and to support local business establishments.

Contests were popular attractions for aspiring musicians, but fiddling's most popular venue was the local community dance, generally held in a private home, in one or two rooms stripped bare of furniture. In the 18th and 19th centuries, these community dances had been universally described as "frolics"—a term

THE GOSPEL TRUTH *Gospel music spread far and wide across the South, in part through religious revival meetings, such as this one in Hattiesburg, Mississippi, in 1912.*

GID TANNER & HIS SKILLET LICKERS
"Soldier's Joy"

TRADITIONAL, RECORDED OCTOBER 29, 1929

A clutch of hillbilly all-stars, originally assembled in 1926 by Columbia Records A&R man Frank Walker, the Skillet Lickers were one of the most popular and influential string bands of country's early days. The group combined raucous humor with fiddle-heavy treatments of minstrel songs and old tunes. Gid Tanner was nominally the group's leader, but by the time **"Soldier's Joy"** was recorded he, like banjo player Fate Norris, had moved to a support role. Instead, the focus was on singer-guitarist Riley Puckett, and on the relatively polished, innovative twin fiddles of Clayton McMichen and Lowe Stokes. Recorded on "Black Tuesday"—the date of the stock-market crash that ushered in the Great Depression—"Soldier's Joy," with its seamless shifts from unison to harmony fiddle playing and its confident vocal by Puckett, is a stellar example of the Skillet Lickers' best work. Oddly, while this was an influential version, several common lyrics were absent, with standard "floating" verses like the opening, "Chicken in the bread pan, picking out dough," being substituted in their place. Still, this rendition pulled no punches, and it was Puckett's closing allusion to the combination of morphine and alcohol that most likely gave the song its name.

JON WEISBERGER

GID
TANNER

used earlier in Britain to describe similar rustic gatherings. Although these affairs were closely identified with communal labor, as celebrations of the end of harvest, or as accompaniments for house raisings, corn huskings, quiltings, and other group projects, frolics were convened for all kinds of social celebrations, or for no reason other than the desire for fun and social companionship. Food and drink were plentiful, and group (circle, square, or line) and solo dances alike were encouraged. Although much of the dancing performed at the frolics was little more than boisterous improvisation, many of the steps and group formations, and shouted instructions—*promenade*, *allemande*, *chassez* or *sashay*, *dos-a-dos*—betrayed their formal French origins. American square dancing was an adaptation of quadrilles (French dances involving four couples arranged in a square). Old World dancers had probably learned the movements of the dances from instruction books, but southern rural dancers followed the commands of a caller. Solo or step dancing might be similarly improvised, a survival

from some forgotten ancestral ethnic past or a borrowing from minstrel or African-American sources. The term "break-down"—now used to describe an old-time fiddle piece—probably evolved from the concluding portion of a public dance, when individual dancers let go of their inhibitions and competed against each other for the favor of the crowd.

Fiddlers had an immense repertoire of traditional tunes on which to draw. Like "Soldier's Joy" and "Paddy on the Turnpike," many were of Old World vintage, part of the immense variety of tunes and dances inherited from Britain and Ireland. Many more were products of the American frontier experience as it moved westward. Some tunes commemorated historical incidents or the lives of real people, such as "Eighth of January" (about the 1815 Battle of New Orleans), "Bonaparte's Retreat," "Gray Eagle" (about an 1830s Kentucky race horse), and "Jenny Lind" (the popular

COMMUNITY FROLIC *The ever-present fiddle usually provided the music for social celebrations in rural America during the 18th and 19th centuries.*

Those Way-Back Country Sounds

Anyone who listens to CD reissues of those fabled late 19th- and early 20th-century country musicians who recorded on old 78-rpm discs will be amazed at the diversity and richness of instrumental and vocal sounds—and by the many ways people chose to make music in the days when, if you wanted to hear music, you had to make it yourself or be near someone who could. More people played then, and they all sounded different from one another, which shows how many ways there are of putting a bow to a fiddle or picking a banjo.

Folks from different places still sounded different in the 1920s and '30s. Just listen to Texas fiddler Eck Robertson's brilliant virtuoso solo recording of "Sallie Gooden," and contrast it with the droll singing and playing on "The Little Old Log Cabin in the Lane" by Georgia's own Fiddlin' John Carson. Or compare the way the Mississippi Carter Brothers & Son careen forward, helter-skelter, on "Give the Fiddler a Dram," or the high-spirited, near-manic, banjo-driven string band of Tennessee's Uncle Dave Macon on "Rabbit in a Pea Patch," to the sedate sound of Charlie Poole's North Carolina Ramblers, who had an almost Haydn-like chamber-music quality.

African-American musicians also played country fiddle, banjo, and guitar, but their music was rarely recorded.

The Mississippi Sheiks, Peg Leg Howell, and Lonnie Johnson, to name a few such acts, give us some idea of black fiddling traditions. But the commercial companies mostly recorded black groups who played the newer blues, rags, and jazz, despite the fact that there were traditional black string bands all over the South and into the near North during the 1920s and '30s.

Recordings of these old-time musicians can still thrill us in the 21st century. They have inspired modern musicians, such as Bob Dylan, Tim O'Brien, Maria Muldaur, Taj Mahal, and Ry Cooder, to incorporate traditional sounds into contemporary music. And these sounds have motivated thousands of others—both amateur and professional—to absorb that traditional feeling and to try playing it themselves. Some of us sound close to the old musicians, some don't—and some want to and some don't.

Playing traditional music that is connected to a long past and making this music for yourself is a greatly satisfying feeling. And it can be really good music to share with others as well.

MIKE SEEGER

MIKE SEEGER *As a multi-instrumental musician and historian, Mike Seeger has spent a lifetime preserving America's old-time music and fueling its steady-burning flame.*

STRING BAND *The quintessential hillbilly string-band sound took shape by the turn of the century. Typically, it would incorporate the sound of a fiddle, a guitar, and a banjo.*

> **THE FIDDLE AND BANJO REMAINED A POPULAR COMBINATION AMONG RURAL MUSICIANS, PARTICULARLY IN THE SOUTH EAST, WELL INTO THE 1920s.**

Swedish singer who performed in America in 1850), or were inspired by local scenes and places, like "Cripple Creek" and "Cumberland Gap." Some fiddle pieces were named after the dances that inspired them ("The Virginia Reel" or "Durang's Hornpipe"), but the tunes quickly became divorced from the dances, and both fiddlers and dancers soon forgot their origins.

String-band instruments

The banjo came to America as a four-string, fretless gourd instrument played by African slaves, but its shape and construction changed after it was appropriated by white entertainers, who sought a louder and more resilient sound, and after it was popularized nationally by touring blackface minstrels. Long before the S. S. Stewart Company began issuing its own brand of banjos in the 1880s, a

shorter fifth string had been added to the instrument by some unknown innovator. The five-string banjo apparently became known to white rural southerners in the antebellum period through a variety of sources, most notably through the playing of slaves and free blacks, the process by which Joel Walker Sweeney had learned the instrument in the 1830s. By the 1880s, if not earlier, black workers had also taken the banjo and their styles of playing far into Appalachian coal country and to other once-remote regions. Blackface minstrels, who presumably had learned their styles from black sources, introduced their own varieties of style among rural southerners during their wide-ranging tours in the 19th century.

The fiddle and banjo remained a popular combination among rural musicians, particularly in the Southeast, well into the

1920s. But in the early 1900s, musicians gradually began to adopt other instruments, a consequence of the greater exposure and availability made possible by urbanization, improved communications between town and country, technological progress, and mass production. It was not unheard of for a piano, accordion, or even a cello to be included in a country band, but the more common stringed instruments tended to be the norm in southern groups.

Given the directions that country music took later in the 20th century, the adoption of the guitar was the most revolutionary innovation. The guitar had been present in America since the Colonial era, but it had been identified as a polite, upper-class instrument with a light and delicate sound that rendered it unsuitable for ensemble performance. Starting early in the 20th century, itinerant black, Hawaiian, and Latino musicians demonstrated the guitar's versatility and potential, but white country musicians did not truly recognize its utility until improvements in its tone and volume were made. When the Martin and Gibson guitar manufacturers strengthened the fingerboard, making possible the substitution of metal for gut strings, the guitar became loud enough to compete with the banjo and other instruments. Mass production of the instrument lowered its cost, and mail-order catalogs made it widely available throughout the nation. These catalogs also advertised other instruments, including mandolins, French harps, autoharps, and Hawaiian steel guitars, along with instruction books on how to play them.

> **"Southerners received some of their most cherished songs, such as 'Keep on the Sunny Side' and 'Just Over in Glory Land,' from religious sources."**

OUT OF THE PARLOR *Shortly after the turn of the century, the guitar began to penetrate America's most rural enclaves, bringing music to the hearths of families like this.*

Tools of the trade

The sound of country music has been shaped primarily by stringed instruments, such as guitars, banjos, fiddles, and mandolins. Indeed the sound of strings is so pervasive that in Nashville even piano players are known as "pickers." These historic instruments, with the exception of the Willie Nelson and Jimmie Rodgers guitars, all come from the Country Music Hall of Fame and Museum.

1 *The mother of all country guitars: Maybelle Carter's 1928 Gibson L-5 archtop guitar, purchased by Maybelle's husband for $275 shortly before she used it on the epochal recording of "Wildwood Flower."*

2 *This 1928 Martin 000-45 guitar was custom-made for Jimmie Rodgers. The guitar had "Thanks" emblazoned on the back, so that he could flip the guitar at a show's end and flash the message to his audiences—an idea adopted by Ernest Tubb (pictured above).*

3 *Gene Autry endorsed this "Round Up" guitar, meant for children and sold for $9.98 through Sears catalogs.*

4 *Cowboy star Gene Autry owned this 1926 Martin 00-42 guitar, which the Gibson company customized for him in the early 1950s.*

38

5 Bluegrass patriarch Ralph Stanley began playing the banjo before he was a teen; pictured is his well-worn Gibson banjo.

6 Active from the 1920s to the 1950s, Bonnie Dodd played this National resonator guitar on tour with Tex Ritter and as a featured singer.

7 Born into a family of Texas fiddlers, Bob Wills took country music in an exciting new direction with western swing. Pictured is the ornate back of one of his fiddles.

8 One of the most famous guitars in country music is Willie Nelson's battered classical guitar, which Nelson dubbed "Trigger," after the famous horse of Roy Rogers.

9 Bill Monroe purchased this Gibson F-5 mandolin for $150 around 1945. Designed by Gibson master craftsman Lloyd Loar, this mandolin remained Monroe's primary instrument until his death in 1996.

The advent of radio

Although the evidence is impressionistic or scattered, it is apparent that country bands did exist and perform in the years prior to radio and recording. However, they probably did not identify themselves as "country" bands. They were aware of the stigma associated with southern rural life, and their only models in popular culture were the city bands that played various forms of pop music. Consequently, they may have identified themselves variously as ragtime, minstrel, or even Hawaiian bands. However, most groups were known simply as "fiddle bands," and they played wherever they could receive a hearing—at dances, neighborhood gatherings, church socials, and sometimes in medicine or tent shows.

Radio and recording gave these country bands a focus, providing a new kind of commercial exposure that brought disparate groups together—the first radio barn dance to air on American radio was broadcast by WBAP in Fort Worth in 1923, and it featured the music of an old-time fiddler, Captain M. J. Bonner, and that of Fred Wagner's Hilo Five Hawaiian Orchestra. The uncertainty that was characteristic of the 1920s, as urbanizing Americans yearned for the verities that they thought had existed in rural life, contributed to a fascination with the music that these groups made. The nostalgia that seemed so prevalent in American culture in the 1920s animated people like Henry Ford, who hoped to recreate the spirit and morality of a presumably simpler and more virtuous time.

When southern rural musicians began making the first commercial recordings and radio broadcasts in the early 1920s, it is clear that they drew upon a vast array of styles and songs—from many sources—that had been taking shape during the previous decades. And it is also

RUSTIC REVELERS *Unidentified Tennessee musicians brandish the preeminent rural instruments of the early 1900s: the fiddle and the banjo. Soon the guitar would overtake them in popularity.*

apparent that their music was molded by attitudes and stereotypes, both benign and negative, that had been present in American popular culture for just as long. Henry Ford may have hoped for a body of rural tunes and dances that would lure young people away from the sensuous African rhythms of jazz, but other people merely wanted to enjoy the seemingly wholesome or humorous feelings that had supposedly characterized the music of yesteryear. Early country musicians, and their promoters, could not escape the temptation to try to fulfill these stereotypical expectations, whether by playing the role of a lonesome cowboy, an individualistic mountaineer, or a buffoonish hillbilly. Many years passed before these roles could be relinquished, and before independent and more realistic stage images could be created. But America was apparently ready for any role that the country musician might be ready to play, and our popular musical culture has been infinitely richer because of this effort.

> **WHEN SOUTHERN RURAL MUSICIANS BEGAN MAKING THE FIRST COMMERCIAL RECORDINGS AND RADIO BROADCASTS, IT IS CLEAR THAT THEY DREW UPON A VAST ARRAY OF STYLES AND SONGS.**

SKILLET LICKERS *The Skillet Lickers boasted several talented pickers, including (at various times) fiddlers Clayton McMichen and Gid Tanner, singer-guitarist Riley Puckett (seated, right) and fiddler Bert Layne (standing, right).*

RED HOT AND RARIN' TO GO

THE COMMERCIAL BEGINNINGS, 1922–1930

CHARLES K. WOLFE

IN THE 1920s, TWO NEW TECHNOLOGIES—RADIO AND RECORDS—SUDDENLY OPENED THE DOOR FOR RURAL MUSIC TO REACH MASS AUDIENCES. LIKE WILDFIRE, HILLBILLY MUSIC CAUGHT ON WITH RADIO AUDIENCES AND RECORD BUYERS, FUELED BY ACTS LIKE THE CARTER FAMILY AND JIMMIE RODGERS.

1920–1929 TIMELINE

1920 Women vote for the first time in the USA. Prohibition of the production and sale of alcohol begins in the USA. Commercial radio broadcasting begins in the USA.

1922 Fiddlers Eck Robertson and Henry C. Gilliland make the first recordings ever by southern country musicians, inadvertently launching the country-music industry. Atlanta, Georgia, radio station WSB, a pioneer in broadcasting country music, goes on the air.

1923 Fort Worth, Texas, radio station WBAP broadcasts the first radio barn dance. Fiddlin' John Carson records "The Little Old Log Cabin in the Lane" and "The Old Hen Cackled and the Rooster's Going to Crow" in Atlanta for Ralph Peer; released on a 78-rpm single, the two sides become the first hit record in country music.

1924 "The Prisoner's Song"/"The Wreck of the Old 97," recorded by Vernon Dalhart, becomes country's first million-selling disc. First recording session for Emmett Miller, the minstrel singer who powerfully influenced Hank Williams and Bob Wills, among others. Old-time musicians Gid Tanner and Riley Puckett make their first recordings, for Columbia Records. Chicago, Illinois, radio station WLS, home of the *National Barn Dance*, begins broadcasting. Uncle Dave Macon's first recording session, for Aeolian-Vocalion Records, takes place in New York City.

continues opposite

The two men from Texas stood nervously in the outer office of the Victor Talking Machine Company on West 38th Street in New York City. One was a lean, raw-boned man of 35 dressed in a western shirt, cuff protectors, bandana, jodhpurs, and cowboy boots. His companion was much older, in his 70s, and wore an old uniform from the Confederate Army. He, too, was part of the real West—a former Indian fighter, justice of the peace, and Confederate veteran. Both carried fiddle cases. It was June 29, 1922.

They had introduced themselves to the secretary as Mr. Eck Roberton and Mr. Henry Gilliland. A friend of theirs—a lawyer who did work for Victor—had set up the appointment to discuss making Victrola records. But they hadn't been greeted with open arms, and now they were beginning to have doubts about the whole plan. Suddenly, a man in shirtsleeves rushed into the room, carrying a long piece of paper with a list of names. He turned to Robertson and barked, "Young man, get your fiddle out and start off on a tune! I can tell that quick whether I can use you or not." Startled and miffed, Robertson responded, "Mister, I've come a long way to get an audition with you. Maybe I better wait and come back some other time." But the manager insisted, and Robertson took out his instrument and started to play his signature tune, "Sallie Gooden," with its bagpipelike drones and skirling high notes. He was barely halfway through it when the manager stopped him. "By Ned, that's fine! Come back in the morning at nine o'clock, and we'll make a test record." And with no more than that, southern music entered a new era.

The following day, the two Texans returned and began recording a series of unaccompanied fiddle duets—familiar standards like "Arkansas Traveler" and "Turkey in the Straw" were among them. Far from being doubtful about or hostile to

JOHN CARSON'S FIDDLE
Country music's first hitmaker inherited this 300-year-old fiddle from his Irish great-grandfather.

the music, the Victor A&R men were excited and enthusiastic. They invited Robertson back the next day for some solo sides, including his masterpiece, "Sallie Gooden," and other Texas classics like "Done Gone" and "Ragtime Annie." They were tunes that Robertson had been hearing all his life at Texas fiddling contests. He had also been playing them since 1906, when he and his wife began performing in theaters and silent-movie houses. Eventually, he was invited to the annual reunions of Confederate veterans, and it was at such a gathering in Richmond, Virginia, that he met the man who urged him and Gilliland to go north to preserve his old tunes on records. On that day in 1922, the Victor Talking Machine Company— later to become RCA Victor—was one of the two most successful and prestigious record companies in America.

An untapped market

Victor was a big, proud, distinguished company, which could boast on its roster classical giants like Enrico Caruso and popular stars like Paul Whiteman and John McCormack. But Victor's executives knew that record sales were plummeting, mainly because of the sudden explosion of

PIONEER *Texas fiddler Eck Robertson, the first country musician to be recorded, had to make an uninvited visit to the Victor company in New York to get the opportunity.*

1925 Acoustic recording horns for phonographs are superseded by more sensitive electrical microphones developed by Bell Laboratories. The term "hillbilly" is first used to describe commercial country music of the South, during an OKeh recording session in New York City for the band soon known as "The Hill Billies." Crystal Springs Dance Hall, the birthplace of western swing, officially opens near Fort Worth.

1926 Uncle Jimmy Thompson wins a regional old-time fiddling competition in Nashville, part of Henry Ford's series of national fiddle contests. "Harmonica Wizard" DeFord Bailey debuts on the Grand Ole Opry and quickly becomes one of the program's most popular performers.

1927 The Carter Family and Jimmie Rodgers make their first records for Ralph Peer, in a vacant hat warehouse in Bristol, on the Tennessee-Virginia state line. Jimmie Rodgers records his first "Blue Yodel."

1928 The Carter Family records "Wildwood Flower" on Maybelle Carter's 19th birthday, in Camden, New Jersey. The first Nashville recording session takes place when a field-recording unit from the Victor company comes to town.

1929 Gene Autry's first recording session. America's stock market crashes, signaling the start of the Great Depression. Jimmie Rodgers begins production on his only movie, *The Singing Brakeman*, a ten-minute musical short.

"Fiddlin' John Carson, champion southern bow-man, fresh from Fannin County ... is an institution in himself."

ATLANTA JOURNAL,
SEPTEMBER 10, 1922

VICTOR HEADQUARTERS *The Victor Talking Machine Company (later RCA Victor Records) took an early lead in the hillbilly business, signing Jimmie Rodgers and the Carter Family in 1927.*

radio stations around the country beginning in 1920. All the record companies were looking for new, untapped markets, whether it was ethnic music, jazz, or blues. Fiddle music—and southern music in general—was one of these untapped markets, but nobody was sure how to break into it. On the session sheets the producer noted "First recordings—records to be listed in the black label class." This meant that even though they were violin records, they were not to be confused with the classical recordings on the label's Red Seal series, but would be released in Victor's popular black-label series. After a delay of several months, the company finally issued "Sallie Gooden" and "Arkansas Traveler" as two sides of one disc during March, 1923.

Today, Eck Robertson's recording of "Sallie Gooden" is recognized as the definitive version of that tune, and although it is a challenge for hundreds of fancy fiddlers even now, in 1923 it barely caused a ripple in the music world. In the following weeks, Victor issued four more of the Robertson solo pieces and Robertson-Gilliland duets, but they, too, failed to cause much excitement. The company then

gave up, leaving in their vaults four other recordings, which eventually were destroyed. Robertson returned to Texas, waiting for a callback that never came. He would not record again for five more years.

Fiddlin' John Carson

Around the same time Robertson was first recording, events were unfolding in Atlanta, Georgia, that would have a dramatic impact on country music. The venerable *Atlanta Journal* newspaper opened the WSB radio station in March, 1922, and invited some local fiddlers and pickers to play informally. Informally was putting it mildly. In late June, 1922, several of them gathered in the men's room of the station to drink a jug of "moonshine." Among them was a 54-year-old man named John Carson, a former factory worker from nearby Marietta, who drove his 1913 Ford all over Georgia, playing at fiddling contests, circuses, political rallies, auctions, dances, and on courthouse lawns. He was known to his cronies simply as "Fiddler." According to legend, a brash young man was pouring a drink into Carson's glass. Unaccustomed to the

Victor Talking Machine Works, Camden, N.J.

FIDDLIN' JOHN CARSON IS COMING!

Fiddlin' John Carson
AND HIS WORLD-DISTINGUISHED ORCHESTRA
OF BLUE RIDGE MOUNTAIN, GEORGIA
WILL GIVE A SERIES OF
INSTRUMENTAL AND VOCAL CONCERTS IN THE CITY AUDITORIUM

FIDDLIN' JOHN CARSON
Although his first recording session came a year after Eck Robertson's, it was Carson's record that got the country-music business started.

FIRST HIT RECORD
The A-side of the record that jump-started the country-music business. Although OKeh Records' A&R man Ralph Peer pronounced the music "pluperfect awful," Carson's record sold hand over fist.

OKeh

4890-A

Fiddling Solo
Vocal Chorus

THE LITTLE OLD LOG CABIN
IN THE LANE

FIDDLIN' JOHN CARSON

GENERAL PHONOGRAPH CORPORATION NEW YORK

PROFILES IN COUNTRY

RALPH PEER

BORN KANSAS CITY, MISSOURI,
MAY 22, 1892
DIED JANUARY 19, 1960
BUSINESS AFFILIATIONS COLUMBIA
RECORDS, OKEH RECORDS, VICTOR
RECORDS, SOUTHERN MUSIC, PEER
INTERNATIONAL CORPORATION

Ralph Peer never saw himself as
a folklorist or romantic visionary
preserving America's roots
music; he was first and foremost
a businessman, with an uncanny
ear for good music and how to
promote it. He was responsible
for recording dozens of legendary country-music acts as
well as blues, jazz, and Cajun
groups. His record production
ranged from King Oliver's
Creole Jazz Band to Louis
Armstrong, from blues singer
Mamie Smith to Fiddlin' John
Carson.

He struck a key deal with
Victor in 1926. He would
provide his services as a talent
scout, A&R man, and recording
supervisor at no charge, if he
was allowed to control copyrights of the songs that he
recorded. He began signing all
the artists he recorded in field
sessions to two contracts—one
for a recording fee, and a second that transferred copyright
of the song to himself. In
January, 1928, Peer formed
Southern Music, which
grew into one of the largest
independent publishers in
the nation. Peer was elected to
the Country Music Hall of Fame
in 1984.

CHARLES K. WOLFE

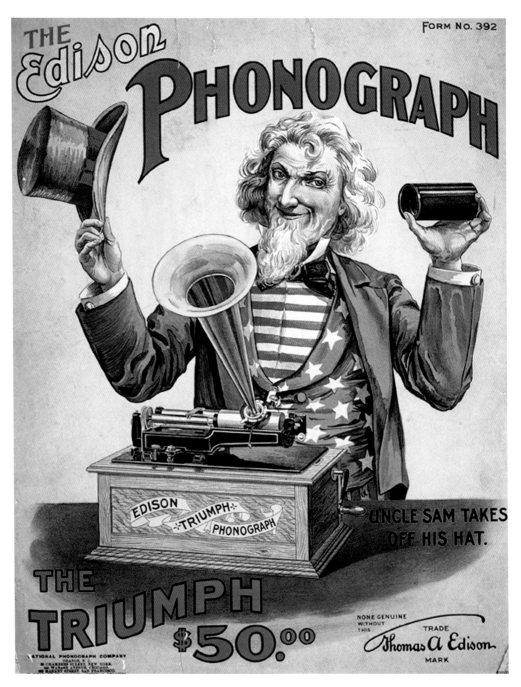

FORM No. 392

THE Edison PHONOGRAPH

EDISON ✦ TRIUMPH ✦ PHONOGRAPH

THE TRIUMPH $50.⁰⁰

NATIONAL PHONOGRAPH COMPANY

UNCLE SAM TAKES OFF HIS HAT.

NONE GENUINE WITHOUT THIS

TRADE *Thomas A Edison* MARK

EDISON'S TRIUMPH *The Edison Triumph phonograph
of 1898 could play 14 two-minute records per winding of its
spring motor. Although pricey at $50, it was not beyond most
middle-class incomes.*

thirst of Georgia mountain men, he asked
Fiddler to say "when." Carson remained
silent, and the young man kept pouring.
"Say when, now." More silence. More
pouring. Finally, Fiddler said, "I reckon
you can tell when it's runnin' over, can't
you?" Well-fortified with the moonshine,
Carson and the pickers headed for the
studio to set the airwaves alight with a
rendition of "Alabama Gals."

For the next several months, the WSB
programs were fluid and improvised, with
Carson and his pals likely to show up at
any time. That June, the newspapers were
full of stories about Georgia's "champion"
fiddler, with headlines reading, "Georgia
Fiddlers Invade the Radio World." Early
radios were crystal sets, to which one
person at a time could listen with an
earphone. The demand to hear Carson
was so great that WSB set up remote
loudspeakers in two nearby parks. It was
at this juncture that 31-year-old Ralph
Peer came to Atlanta. He was an A&R

man for the General Phonograph Company, maker of OKeh Records, and had won his spurs three years earlier when he recorded one of the first blues records, "Crazy Blues," by black singer Mamie Smith. It became a surprise best-seller, opening up the market for many more blues singers. Now Peer was in Atlanta, where he thought he would find even more blues musicians, but he didn't have much luck—a so-so jazz band, a college quartet, and a movie-theater pianist. He asked his local contact, furniture-store dealer Polk Brockman, to find a place to record, so Brockman rented the top floor of a vacant building on Nassau Street. As Peer was lining up his acts, Brockman urged him to add Fiddlin' John Carson to the list. He was so popular that Brockman guaranteed to buy the whole pressing himself.

An immediate hit

So on June 14, 1923, John Carson sat with his fiddle before one of the big recording horns still used in the acoustic record-making of the day. He began playing "The Little Old Log Cabin in the Lane," an 1871 minstrel song by Louisville riverboat man Will S. Hays. Carson's fiddling was adequate, but what set things off was his singing. He was a fine country singer, with colorful inflections, mannerisms, ornamentation, and unusual rhythm, echoes of which were still heard generations later in the songs of George Jones and Lefty Frizzell. For the record's flip side, he chose an old southern dance tune, "The Old Hen Cackled and the Rooster's Going to Crow." It contained a few scattered stanzas that Carson sang in full voice, but the performance was mostly a fiddle solo. As Peer watched the needle cut into the heavy wax master, he must have wondered if he was wasting his company's money. A midwesterner by birth, he had never heard anything resembling Carson's strange singing—"I thought it was pluperfect awful," he later recalled. But true to his word, he took the masters back to New York, had 500 copies of the Carson disc pressed, and shipped them to Brockman—with his invoice.

A few days later the records arrived in Atlanta, at the same time as an Elks club convention was beginning downtown. Brockman, eager to promote his investment,

staged a fiddling contest for the evening entertainment and invited Carson to be his special guest. He sat Fiddlin' John in a chair on stage, next to a table with a Victrola, and put on the new OKeh disc, so listeners could hear Carson's voice singing "The Little Old Log Cabin in the Lane." Immediately afterwards, Carson played and sang the same song live—the audience went wild. Brockman then repeated the process with the flip side, and again Carson played the tune in person. Finally, Brockman brought out a box of Carson's records, which he and Carson began selling over the footlights—within minutes, they sold out. Next day Brockman wired Peer in New York to send more, and a few days later, still more. Peer had considered the record a custom job, strictly for local sales, but now he released the record nationwide—and still the sales continued. Nobody today knows why Carson chose the two songs he did, but they were representative of the two key sources for early country music— traditional folk music ("The Old Hen Cackled") and old 19th-century music-hall fare ("Little Old Log Cabin").

Thus, the first artists to record what we now know as country music were both fiddlers. But whereas Robertson returned to Texas without much fanfare, Carson was asked back to the OKeh studios repeatedly in the next few years. Carson was by no means the virtuoso fiddler Robertson was, but he was a singer and a practiced entertainer. J. B., Cranfill, a Texas fiddler and admirer of Robertson's, wrote of Carson, "I have some of this fiddler's records, and there are dozens of fiddlers in Texas who can beat him eight times over, but this singing stuff with which he accompanies his fiddling sees him through." This singing—this "pluperfect awful" singing– was the thing that sold Carson and won him his place as the first successful country recording artist.

The New York record companies became curious but were unsure of the market for this kind of music. However, their doubt was answered on May 14, 1924, when a 41-year-old studio and cabaret singer, Vernon Dalhart, recorded a ballad called "The Wreck of the Southern Old 97," first for Edison and then for Victor.

HEY! HEY! COMING

Uncle Dave Macon

...test Comical Trick Banjo Player in the South; Bruns-...Vocalion Record and Radio Artist. The Only Man ...Ever Accomplished Playing Two Banjos at the Same ... Hear UNCLE DAVE Play and Sing on His Famous ...o and Songs That Everybody Enjoy . -:-   -:-   -:-

...ddlin' Sid Harkreader

...nswick Vocalion Record and Radio Artist; Violionist; ...Time Fiddling; Guitarist and Radio Star. HEAR ...Play and Sing Songs on his Violin that Has Made Him ...ous All Over the World.   -:-   -:-   -:-   -:-

UNCLE DAVE AND SID

Play One Hour of Solid Entertainment. Something New Every Minute. Song, Jokes and Music of Various Kinds. Hear Them Sing the Songs They Sang in Monte Carlo.

MONEY BACK IF NOT SATISFIED!

Will Appear *Barthelia School*

Place *June 17th Tuesday*

Time *8-15 P.m.*   Adm. *15 / 25.*

Dalhart's singing was stiff and formal, with none of the swaggering appeal of Carson and other early southern singers, but his versatility and diction made him popular with all sorts of fans. Throughout 1925 and 1926, his records consistently outsold everything else released by his companies, Victor and Columbia. He recorded "event" songs like "The Death of Floyd Collins" and "The Santa Barbara Earthquake," older ballads and sentimental songs like "Little Rosewood Casket," "Frank Dupree," and "In the Baggage Coach Ahead"—and even uptempo songs, such as "The Roving Gambler." Many of Dalhart's hit songs were well known throughout much of the 20th century, and more than a few have been collected, mistakenly, as folk songs. Dalhart's career was largely confined to the studio; he recorded under dozens of pseudonyms for dozens of labels—one of his favorites being "Al Craver." When asked why he had so many Dalhart records in his collection, a farmer from Deepwater, Missouri, replied, "Because you can hear the words to what he's singing good and clear through all that hiss."

New vocal stars

In the wake of such success, many southern singers made their way into northern studios over the next two years. Some came to seek easy money; others, such as Ernest Stoneman (from Virginia) and Uncle Dave

Macon (from Tennessee), came because they had heard earlier records by nondescript singers like Henry Whitter and George Reneau, and were convinced they could do better. Tennessee freight hauler David Harrison Macon ("Uncle Dave") had already won a reputation on the vaudeville stage, although he had not started performing professionally until he was past 50. In July, 1924, encouraged by a local record dealer, he appeared for the first time in the New York studios of the staid Aeolian-Vocalion company. In a boisterous voice, accompanied by his banjo and an occasional whoop, he strutted through a bawdy piece called "Keep My Skillet Good and Greasy," which he had learned from a black handy-man in Tennessee. Engineers scurried around to accommodate the performer's sudden changes in volume and frequent foot stomping. It was one of the first times that an old vaudeville singer, used to an age before microphones or monitors, encountered recording technology. During that session, Uncle Dave also rendered his impression of a fox chase, a remake of Carson's hit "The Little Old Log Cabin in the Lane," and a song that was the first to use the word "hillbilly"—"Hill Billie Blues." These first 78-rpm records, issued on colorful red shellac, started a career that, eventually, included some 180 sides, establishing Macon as one of the most visible country recording stars of the 1920s.

EDISON RECORD *Vernon Dalhart made his first recording of "The Wreck on the Southern Old 97" for Edison Records in May 1924. It was his first hillbilly recording. In August he re-recorded it for the Victor company. Released with "The Prisoner's Song" on the flip side, it became country music's first million-selling release.*

THE HILL BILLIES *After their first recording session, in January 1925, A&R man Ralph Peer asked the string band what they were called. Leader Al Hopkins said, "Call us anything you want. We're nothin' but a bunch of hillbillies from North Carolina and Virginia anyway." Soon after, all string-band and fiddle music became known as "hillbilly."*

> **BY 1927, ALL MAJOR RECORD COMPANIES AGREED THERE WAS A HEALTHY MARKET FOR COUNTRY MUSIC.**

RILEY PUCKETT *Blinded shortly after birth, Riley Puckett nevertheless made his living as a singer even before he made his first recordings at age 30 in 1924. One of the most popular string-band musicians of the 1920s and '30s, he went on to make more than 200 recordings.*

Another early figure who began a long recording career in 1924 was a blind guitarist and singer from Alpharetta, Georgia, named Riley Puckett. He was a generation younger than Macon—he turned 30 that year—and was eager to try his hand at the new medium. Puckett had spent his time busking on street corners and in train stations and picking up odd jobs at carnivals and medicine shows. Now he was looking for better work. He had already appeared regularly on Atlanta's WSB radio, where he won fame as country's first yodeler. A talent scout for Columbia Records, looking for an act that the label could use to counter the success that rival OKeh enjoyed with Carson, he invited Puckett and a friend, fiddler Gid Tanner, to New York. In March and then again in September, Puckett and Tanner recorded several dozen sides for Columbia, laying the groundwork for the label's country series. By mid-June, Columbia was heavily promoting their new artists in full-page ads in *The Talking Machine World*—"The fiddle and guitar craze is sweeping northward," they trumpeted. "Columbia leads with records of old-fashioned southern songs and dances."

By 1927, all major record companies agreed there was a healthy market for country music and decided the best way to get it was to send out field-recording units to set up temporary studios in cities around the South. Most of the major companies designated special numerical series devoted to this old-but-new music, but there was still no agreement on just what to call it. Each company tried its own label, resulting in a patchwork of names, none of which were "hillbilly" or "country." They included Brunswick's "Songs from Dixie"; Columbia's "Familiar Tunes Old and New" and "Old Familiar Tunes"; Gennett's Unnamed 6,000 and 300 series; OKeh's "Old Time Tunes"; Paramount's Unnamed series with catalogue numbers 3,000 plus;

Victor's "Native American Melodies" and, after 1929, "Old Familiar Tunes"; and Vocalion's "Old Southern Tunes."

Together, these series released a total of 3,577 two-sided records between 1925 and 1932—some selling as many as 300,000, others as few as 18. The leading recording site was Atlanta, but other locations included Memphis, Dallas, New Orleans, Bristol and Johnson City (both in Tennessee), Knoxville, Nashville (one lone session), Birmingham, Indianapolis, Charlotte, Winston-Salem, San Antonio, St. Louis, Ashland (in Kentucky), and Jackson (in Mississippi). Most companies had today's equivalent of an A&R man in charge of finding new talent, setting up the sessions, and deciding what to release. Columbia had Frank Walker, Vocalion had Jack Kapp, and OKeh hired Polk Brockman after Ralph Peer went to Victor. These men relied, in turn, on a network of local record dealers, promoters, and radio-station managers to recommend candidates for recording. Often blues and gospel artists were recorded at the same sessions as old-time music.

The Bristol sessions

The mother lode of these prospecting trips was mined by Ralph Peer. By early 1927, he had found dozens of delta blues singers in Memphis, and that summer he sought old-time music in Atlanta, Savannah, Charlotte, and Bristol—a small sleepy city on the Virginia-Tennessee state line. In late July, Peer, his wife, and two engineers pulled into Bristol and set up a temporary studio on the second floor of an empty building near the railroad tracks. The sessions that took place there were so successful and influential that one historian calls them "the big bang of country music."

The two-story building on Main Street had been occupied by the Taylor-Christian Hat Company; Peer hung old quilts on the walls of the second floor to serve as sound baffles. Although he had a number of artists scheduled, Peer planned to put out a "cattle call" to ask other performers to come in for auditions. To do this, he invited the local newspaper editor to one of Ernest Stoneman's sessions. The result was a front-page story in the Bristol newspaper that described the group recording "Skip to

My Lou, My Darling." The story also mentioned that Stoneman and his group were getting $200 a day for the sessions, and that he had earned some $3,000 in royalties the year before. This was the fact that most impressed the area's musicians, and soon people were making their way to Bristol from Kentucky, Virginia, West Virginia, North Carolina, and Tennessee— on foot, and by rail, horseback, or car.

In two weeks of intensive work, Peer recorded some 19 acts, including several days' worth of the popular Stoneman family who were already Victor stars. He recorded a blues harp player, a fervent Pentecostal church group from Kentucky, a couple of street singers, and a bevy of string bands; but two acts were to change the face of the music. The first was a family trio from Maces Springs, Virginia— the Carter Family. When Peer first heard the lead singer, Sara Carter, sing "Single Girl," he recalled, "I knew it was going to be wonderful." It was. For the next 14 years the Carters would define country harmony singing, and produce hit after hit.

The Carter Family

Today, they look like 19th-century royalty, peering solemnly from dozens of old album covers and yellowing publicity photos. No one cracks a smile, no one makes a gesture, A. P. Carter always standing behind or between the two women. There's no flashy jewelry, no makeup, just dark, simple, serviceable suits and conservative dresses, like a southern family going to church. It's almost as if they knew that they were setting out to change the face of American music, and that it was a serious business requiring a serious image.

The Carter Family moniker—"the First Family of Country Music"—is richly deserved. They created and circulated dozens of songs that became country, bluegrass, and gospel standards. They also developed a simple yet effective style of vocal harmony that generations of singers would use as a model. Maybelle Carter

crafted a guitar style—the "Carter scratch"—that defined the way country guitar was played, at least until the arrival of Merle Travis in the 1940s. In short, it is hard to imagine the sound of country music today without the Carter Family.

The trio hailed from Poor Valley, which runs roughly parallel to the Virginia-Tennessee state line, under the shadow of Clinch Mountain, a few miles north of Kingsport, Tennessee. A. P. and Sara Carter were husband and wife. Married in 1915, they began singing together at church and social gatherings. By 1927, they were joined by Sara's young cousin Maybelle, whose voice blended seamlessly with Sara's. On July 31, 1927, they drove to Bristol, Tennessee, and the next day made their first recordings—"Bury Me Underneath the Weeping Willow," "The Storms Are on the Ocean," "Little Log Cabin by the Sea," and "The Poor Orphan Child"—for Ralph Peer.

These sessions inaugurated a career that would encompass more than a decade and eventually include nearly 300 recordings for Victor, Decca, and other labels. The recordings included gospel

THE CARTER FAMILY *From left: Maybelle, A. P., and Sara. The Carter trio's legacy is not only one of song. Their extended family includes such prominent musicians as Johnny Cash, June Carter, and Rosanne Cash.*

Carter Family Tree

ROBERT C. CARTER married 1890 **MOLLIE ARVELLE BAYS** (8 children)

ALVIN PLEASANT (A. P.) DELANEY CARTER (1891–1960)
married 1915/divorced 1936
SARA DOUGHERTY CARTER (1898–1979)

MAYBELLE ADDINGTON CARTER (1909–1978)
married 1926
EZRA J. (ECK) CARTER (1898–1975)

GLADYS CARTER MILLARD (1919–1994)
JANETTE CARTER (1923–2006)
JOE CARTER (1927–2005)

HELEN MYRL CARTER (1927–1998)
VALERIE JUNE CARTER (1929–2003)
INA ANITA CARTER (1933–1999)

VALERIE JUNE CARTER (1929–2003)
married (1st) 1952/divorced 1956
CARL SMITH (b. 1927)

REBECCA CARLENE SMITH
[A.K.A. CARLENE CARTER] (b. 1955)
3rd marriage to pop singer/producer **NICK LOWE**

VALERIE JUNE CARTER (1929–2003)
married (2nd) 1957/divorced 1962
EDWIN (RIP) NIX

ROZANNA (ROSEY) LEE CARTER
(1958–2003)

JOHN R. (JOHNNY) CASH (1932–2003)
married (2nd)
VALERIE JUNE CARTER (1929–2003)
married (3rd)

married (1st) 1954/divorced 1967
VIVIAN LIBERTO (1934–2005)

ROSANNE CASH (b. 1955)
KATHLEEN CASH (b. 1956)
CINDY CASH (b. 1958)
TARA CASH (b. 1961)

JOHN CARTER CASH (b. 1970)

hits like "Keep on the Sunny Side" and "Can the Circle Be Unbroken," old ballads like "John Hardy" and "Black Jack Davy," topical songs like "The Cyclone at Rye Cove" and "No Depression in Heaven," and blues like "Coal Miner's Blues" and "Worried Man Blues." In 1938, the Carters traveled to Del Rio, Texas, and began broadcasting over XERA, a far-reaching Mexican border station that gave the Carters a national following.

Just as they were on the verge of fame beyond the hillbilly market, Sara and A. P. split up, and Maybelle decided to start her own band with her daughters. Sara moved to California, and A. P. returned to Poor Valley, where he opened a general store and seemed content to sit on his porch and dream of what might have been. Although the group's career ended earlier than A. P. had hoped, their music has proved to be among the most evergreen of all country performers from the 1920s and 1930s.

The day after Peer recorded the Carters, he auditioned another singing act, this one from Asheville, North Carolina, but originally from Mississippi—Jimmie Rodgers.

BRISTOL'S STANDOUTS *Jimmie Rodgers meets the Carter Family in Louisville, Kentucky, June 1931. Ironically, they didn't meet at Bristol in 1927, when they all first recorded.*

CLASSIC COUNTRY
RECORDING

THE CARTER FAMILY
"Wildwood Flower"

*Oh, I'll twine with my mingles
and waving black hair,
With the roses so red and
the lilies so fair.*

**ARRANGED BY A. P. CARTER
AND RECORDED ON MAY 10, 1928**

"Wildwood Flower" became one of the best loved of all Carter songs—one they would continue to perform throughout their career, and one that would become a country standard for generations to come. Ironically, the session sheets show that the song was done by Sara and her cousin Maybelle only, without group leader A. P. Carter. Sara sang it as a solo, and Maybelle played the famous guitar run that would later become a basic test for all aspiring country pickers. Sara later recalled about the song, "My mother sang it, and her mother sang it. It's been handed down for years and years."

In fact, the song has been traced back to an 1860 vaudeville song written by lyricist J. P. Webster and pioneer singer-songwriter Maud Irving, who published it as "I'll Twine Mid the Ringlets." It started appearing in folk-song collections as early as 1911, sometimes with the alternate title, "The Pale Amaranthus," which was, indeed, a mountain flower.

The Carters' recording was released by Victor on January 4, 1929, and went on to sell over 120,000 copies, making it one of the best-selling country records of the year. A later remake by the Carters easily sold that many again.

CHARLES K. WOLFE

COUNTRY STORE *After the Carter Family disbanded in 1943, A. P. Carter (left with guitar) retired in Poor Valley, Virginia, and opened this general store, which he ran until he died in 1960.*

RODGERS LETTER *Although Jimmie Rodgers and the Carters got along well during their June 1931 recording sessions in Louisville, and Rodgers wrote hopefully of sessions to come, there were no more joint recordings for the two most famous acts in early country music.*

To my good friends the Carter Family. I hope we have many more Recordings together as Pleasant as this one. I wish you the best of every thing dont forget your friend

Jimmie Rodgers

6-12-31

CLASSIC COUNTRY
RECORDING

JIMMIE
RODGERS
"Blue Yodel"

*T for Texas,
T for Tennessee.*
WRITTEN BY JIMMIE
RODGERS AND RECORDED
NOVEMBER 30, 1927

"Blue Yodel" was Jimmie Rodgers's first big hit and the inspiration for 12 numbered sequels. Recorded in Camden, New Jersey, at Rodgers's second session for Victor, the first "Blue Yodel" was included solely because Rodgers lacked material for the four sides needed to fill two 78-rpm records. The only song of that session attributed to Rodgers as composer, "Blue Yodel" was actually an amalgamation of traditional blues stanzas, which Rodgers had pulled together and recast into a fairly consistent narrative of betrayed love and projected revenge. No older variants have been traced, however, and those who first heard Rodgers's recording of "Blue Yodel" could not decide whether the singer was black or white.

Ralph Peer, the Victor talent scout who oversaw that session, later implied that he was responsible for naming the song—"When we recorded the first blues, I had to supply a title, and the name 'Blue Yodel' came out." But as early as 1923, Rodgers had been calling some of his compositions "blue yodels," so he clearly had a hand in naming it. In any event, as country-music historian Bill Malone has remarked, the Blue Yodels were "Rodgers's unique contribution to American folksong."

NOLAN PORTERFIELD

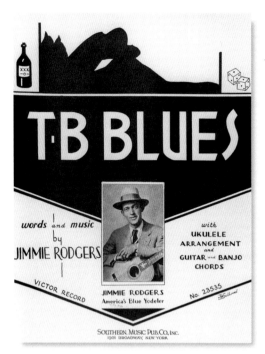

words and music by JIMMIE RODGERS

with UKULELE ARRANGEMENT and GUITAR and BANJO CHORDS

VICTOR RECORD

JIMMIE RODGERS
America's Blue Yodeler

No. 23535

SOUTHERN MUSIC PUB. CO., INC.
1501 BROADWAY, NEW YORK

If the Carters defined rural harmony, Rodgers set the standard for country solo singing. His warm, pliant, laid-back voice, his ability to slide into a falsetto yodel, his sense of blues—all these made him the biggest star of the decade. Ironically, Peer only recorded two sides of Rodgers at Bristol, but they were not truly typical—one was an old ballad, the other a lullaby. Nor did they sell especially well when they were released. They did, however, provide the singer with a calling card when he went on his own to the Victor studio in Camden, New Jersey, where Ralph Peer allowed him to record what would become Rodgers's biggest hit and career song—"Blue Yodel," otherwise known as "T for Texas." Until his premature death in 1933, Rodgers recorded hit after hit, many of them a genre he virtually invented—white blues.

Noticing the huge sales figures of the Carter and Rodgers releases, other companies kicked their programs into high gear. Columbia's Frank Walker created an all-star string band by combining Georgia musicians into the oddly named Skillet Lickers. Built around Gid Tanner, a lanky red-headed chicken farmer who played the fiddle and banjo, the band included a second fiddler—wise-cracking auto mechanic Clayton McMichen—plus the veteran vocalist Riley Puckett, who also contributed resounding bass runs on

T B BLUES When Jimmie Rodgers was diagnosed with tuberculosis in 1924, it was a virtual death sentence. And yet he persevered, even recording this jaunty blues about the malady in 1931.

the guitar, and street musician Fate Norris who played banjo. For later sessions, a third fiddler was added. The band had an eccentric, undisciplined sound, full of impromptu shouts and cackles, and the rumor spread that Columbia provided a bathtub full of Georgia "white lightning" on days when they were scheduled for sessions. At the start of one of their biggest hits, "Soldier's Joy," McMichen introduces the group by saying, "Well, folks, here we are again, the Skillet Lickers, red hot and rarin' to go. Gonna play you another little tune this morning. Want you to grab that gal and shake a foot. And Mom, don't let 'em dance on your new carpet—you make 'em roll it up."

New stars emerge

Other recording stars emerged throughout the 1920s—from Galax, Virginia, a vaudeville-tinged band called the Hill Billies; from Georgia, the team of Darby & Tarlton, who did the classic "Birmingham Jail"; from West Virginia, the innovative fiddler Clark Kessinger; and, from eastern Kentucky, the fiddler and singer Doc Roberts—one of the first old-time musicians to record with African-American artists. Gospel music was dominated by Smith's Sacred Singers from Lawrenceville, Georgia, and the McCravy Brothers from South Carolina. Riley Puckett and Hugh Cross recorded some of the first close-harmony duets, and Puckett and McMichen had a major hit with the sentimental "My Carolina Home." Record companies began issuing catalogs listing their old-time series, and creating posters and advertisements to spread the word. Many records were sold from dealers by mail, even though only three out of four of the fragile shellac 78-rpm discs ever arrived intact. By 1926, Sears Roebuck and Montgomery Ward's, the two giant mail-order houses, were listing old-time records in their catalogs, and

JIMMIE RODGERS *Country music's first superstar and most powerful musical influence, Rodgers also set the template for country-music tragedy, dying of tuberculosis at age 35.*

PROFILES IN COUNTRY

JIMMIE RODGERS

BORN NEAR MERIDIAN,
MISSISSIPPI, SEPTEMBER 8, 1897
DIED MAY 26, 1933
PLAYED GUITAR
FIRST RECORDED 1927
INFLUENCED GENE AUTRY,
ERNEST TUBB, LEFTY FRIZZELL,
AND MANY OTHERS
HITS "BLUE YODEL
(T FOR TEXAS),"
"WAITING FOR A TRAIN,"
"IN THE JAILHOUSE NOW"

Jimmie Rodgers was an American original. When he began his heady climb to stardom in the late 1920s, there was nothing quite like him—a roguish southerner with a winning grin, a liquid voice like hard rain rippling down a window pane, and some booming, unorthodox guitar licks.

Rodgers spent his early years as a desultory railroad brakeman, baggage handler, and flagman. Diagnosed with tuberculosis about 1924, he increasingly turned his attention to music. At the famous Bristol Sessions, Rodgers made his first recordings—"Soldier's Sweetheart" and "Sleep, Baby, Sleep"—on August 4, 1927. The two songs attracted modest attention when released that fall, so Ralph Peer called Rodgers for a second session. That produced Rodgers's breakthrough hit, "Blue Yodel," the first of a series of 13 "Blue Yodels."

He died in New York of a lung hemorrhage, less than 36 hours after his final recording session. At the time of his death, he left behind 110 titles, including classics such as "In the Jailhouse Now," "Treasures Untold," and "Miss the Mississippi and You."

Rodgers's influence can scarcely be overstated. Inducted in the first-ever election of the Country Music Hall of Fame, he has been an inspiration to dozens of others through the years.

NOLAN PORTERFIELD

Radio and Records—
Capturing the Hillbilly Sound

Combined, nothing had greater impact on country music than the phonograph and radio, and the influence of both began to be felt in the 1920s. It's true that records had been around for a while—Thomas Edison filed a patent in 1877—and there had been experiments with radio for almost as long. But it took time for both technologies to develop into industries, and even longer for those industries to embrace country music.

The first complete symphony (released on 40 single-sided discs) was released nearly 20 years before the first country record, and the first recordings of other types of music (like jazz and blues) preceded the earliest country discs. The first performing rights society—ASCAP (American Society of Composers, Authors, and Publishers)—was almost ten years old when the first country records appeared, and the first battle of the recording technologies had already been decided in favor of the flat disc over the cylinder. The economic reality was that the record business only began to consider the hillbilly market after radio began to usurp the phonograph as the new toy. Panicked, the phonograph manufacturers turned to those who couldn't receive radio—namely, those without electricity.

Once country-music recording began in earnest in the 1920s, it had an immediate and incalculable impact. Songs that had lain hidden in hollows for decades were suddenly available country-wide, with little copyright notices appended to them. The best musician for miles around suddenly heard others playing much better. Ballads of indeterminate length were shortened to approximately three minutes. And the experience of music, which had so often been communal, frequently became passive and even solitary.

Country music had never been a career option for anyone except a few itinerant singers, but now it was—and radio opened even wider vistas. Battery-powered receivers, together with rural electrification, brought radio to many isolated communities, and the stations knew that if they were to appeal to rural listeners, they must program rural music.

By the end of the 1920s, the hills were alive with the sound of music as never before, and young musicians could dream big. They could also learn from radio and records in a way that was unthinkable a generation earlier, and take their music to a regional, perhaps even national, audience.

COLIN ESCOTT

HOEDOWN BAND *The early Grand Ole Opry of the 1920s and '30s featured many Nashville-area string bands, including the Binkley Brothers' Dixie Clodhoppers. The quartet was the first act to record in Nashville, in 1928.*

leasing masters for release on their own labels, including Challenge, Silvertone, and Supertone.

Radio was a constant presence throughout all these events, but it had not sufficiently developed to allow musicians to make a living from playing on it. For much of the 1920s, radio stations produced their own live programming; it was not until 1927 that network radio became established with NBC (National Broadcasting Company). Initially, radio schedules were informal and improvised. Most stations, such as WSB in Atlanta (the first of the big southern outfits), were owned by local newspapers or other established businesses, and operated as a public service, and as advertising outlets for their parent companies. Although many early stations were broadcasting only between 1,000 and 5,000 watts, the uncluttered, signal-free atmosphere often permitted signals to carry for hundreds of miles. WSB would invite local fiddlers and singers to perform but not on any regular basis. The first "barn dance" program— that is, a musical variety show—was staged on January 4, 1923, on WBAP in Fort Worth. The shows were still very casual and were aired once or twice a month. However, the prototype for regular country programming began in one of the most unlikely places—Chicago, Illinois.

Hillbillies in Chicago

Although Chicago in the 1920s was known as a hotbed of jazz and home to pioneers like King Oliver and Louis Armstrong, it was also the headquarters of the giant mail-order firm of Sears Roebuck. On April 12, 1924, the company signed on the air with a powerful, new radio station—WLS—the call letters reflecting Sears's motto, "World's Largest Store." Edgar Bill, the first station manager, oversaw the initial week of programming but then began to worry. He recalled, "We had so much highbrow music for the first week that we thought it would be a good idea to get on some of the old-time music." He learned that a janitor at the building housing the studio was an old-time fiddler; a week after the station signed on, Bill put Tommy Dandurand (born in Kankakee, Illinois, the last year of the Civil War) on the air. Dandurand

was not a transplanted southerner, and his fiddle repertoire included midwestern favorites like "Haste to the Wedding" and "Pig Town Fling." After he began appearing, telegrams flooded the station. The Sears executives were at first skeptical, but then they realized that since most of their customers lived in the rural Midwest, old-time music programming would be a sound business move. Soon the show was christened *The National Barn Dance*, and a group of regulars began to show up. They included banjo-playing Chubby Parker, whose signature songs included "I'm a Stern Old Bachelor" and an old British ballad he called "Nickety Nackety Now Now Now," and Walter Peterson. The latter billed himself as "the Kentucky Wonder Bean" and accented his singing with his own accompaniment on guitar and harmonica, which he played with the aid of a rack hung around his neck (as Bob Dylan did years later).

The WLS management defined "old-time music" more broadly than the record companies did. It was not strictly southern music that WLS offered, but music of the "good old days." Favorites on the show included barbershop quartet the Maple City Four, light-opera singer Grace Wilson, and comedian Rube Tronson. But the biggest star arrived in 1926, when Kentuckian Bradley Kincaid began to sing folk and sentimental songs. In a high, soft, lilting tenor, he charmed audiences with songs like "The Fatal Wedding," "Gooseberry Pie," and the ancient ballad "Barbara Allen." Kincaid recalled that when he first introduced "Barbara Allen," the fan response was so overwhelming that he had to sing it every Saturday night for the next year. Kincaid was a master of public relations, and in the late 1920s he became one of the first country singers to issue his own souvenir songbooks and sell them by mail.

An important announcer for these early days of the *Barn Dance*—and the man largely responsible for its folksy image—was 29-year-old journalist

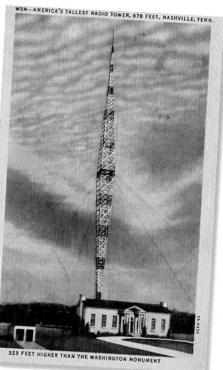

TALLEST ANTENNA *In October 1952, Nashville's WSM erected the world's tallest radio antenna—878 feet high—to broadcast a far-reaching signal and the Grand Ole Opry across much of the USA.*

THE EMERGENCE OF RADIO BARN DANCES

The dawn of commercial radio broadcasting in 1920 sparked a massive expansion of country music's popularity. By 1922, country musicians were performing on Atlanta radio station WSB. In 1923, Fort Worth's WBAP began a multi-artist, musical variety show featuring old-time music—the first of many radio barn-dance programs that took root before World War II.

By 1924, Chicago powerhouse WLS launched the *National Barn Dance*. Nashville's WSM followed in 1925 with its own Barn Dance—rechristened the Grand Ole Opry in 1927. After 1932, WSM's 50,000-watt transmitter, and network exposure via NBC (from 1939 to 1957), made the show a household name. During the Great Depression, the barn-dance format spread to the coastal metropolises of New York and Los Angeles, and numerous points in between—Wheeling, West Virginia; Cincinnati, Ohio; Charlotte, North Carolina; Knoxville, Tennessee; Fort Wayne, Indiana; and Renfro Valley, Kentucky.

To create the aura of old-fashioned rural gatherings, radio producers deliberately cultivated a homespun approach, encouraging performers to assume countrified personas and wear rustic outfits. Their studied use of nostalgia won the hearts of millions, especially listeners who lived in the countryside or in small towns. The 1920 census was the first to report that more than half of all Americans lived in communities of 2,500 or more, with many city dwellers having strong country ties.

Even in hard times, barn dances thrived because they moved merchandise for sponsors and helped radio stations earn profits. In turn, sponsors paid talent fees, helping amateur musicians turn professional. Most barn dances drew live audiences, and ticket sales further strengthened the shows' financial footing. By the late 1920s, barn-dance acts began touring, making their biggest money through gate receipts and sales of songbooks advertised on the air.

As World War II sparked prosperity's return, dozens of new radio jamborees sprang up from Philadelphia to Dallas and from St. Paul to Shreveport. By the early 1950s, these shows were flourishing in Indianapolis, Little Rock, Boston, Topeka, Oklahoma City, and countless other locations.

However, by the early 1960s, the heyday of the radio barn dance was over. Broadcasters and sponsors shifted their dollars to television, and live country-radio shows faded into history. Today, Wheeling's *Jamboree USA* and WSM's Grand Ole Opry strive to keep the barn-dance tradition alive.

JOHN W. RUMBLE

RENFRO VALLEY BARN DANCE *One of the popular radio barn dances that vied with the Grand Ole Opry for listeners on Saturday nights was broadcast from Kentucky's Renfro Valley. The poster advertised a traveling performance of the show's cast.*

OPRY BEGINNINGS *The men who started the Grand Ole Opry: announcer George D. Hay (with trademark steamboat whistle in arm) and Uncle Jimmy Thompson, ca. 1925.*

George Dewey Hay. Although he was assumed to be a southerner, Hay was born in Attica, Indiana, and grew up on the streets of Chicago. He began his journalism career at the *Memphis Commercial Appeal*, and when that newspaper started its own radio station, WMC, Hay became an announcer. He found that he had a flair for broadcast work, and, in 1924, Sears hired him to return to Chicago to be an announcer for WLS. Here he was heard by a larger national audience, and that summer he was awarded a gold cup by the magazine *Radio Digest* as America's best announcer. A year later, on October 5, 1925, Hay was invited to the grand opening of Nashville's new radio station, WSM—the brainchild of the city's major insurance company, National Life and Accident. Company executives had decided to spare no expense in creating a state-of-the-art facility. In its plush studios on the fifth floor of the new National Life building, visitors marveled at the luxurious Oriental carpets, the heavy crimson drapes, the ornate crystal chandeliers, and the fact that there were not one but two grand pianos available. At that time, National Life envisioned WSM as

something akin to what National Public Radio is today—a dignified, high-minded schedule full of classical music, poetry readings, lectures, and all sorts of public-service programs. To run the station, they wanted the best and put together an offer that would tempt Hay out of Chicago—not only would he be chief announcer, he would be station manager and allowed to develop the new programming.

A Nashville barn dance

Hay accepted the position in November, 1925 and moved to Nashville. Almost at once, he began thinking of how successful the *National Barn Dance* had been, and how much easier it might be to mount such a show in the Tennessee hills, which were full of the kinds of musicians needed for a radio barn dance. He was still pondering this on November 28, when he brought into the studio Uncle Jimmy Thompson, a 78-year-old, white-bearded fiddler from nearby Wilson County. Accompanied by his niece, Eva Thompson Jones, a studio piano player for the station, Uncle Jimmy tore into "Tennessee Waggoner" and followed it with pieces like "When You and I Were

> **"WSM had a good-natured riot on its hands. After three or four weeks of this fiddle solo business we were besieged with other fiddlers, banjo pickers, guitar players, and a lady who played an old zither."**
>
> **GEORGE D. HAY**

POSSUM HUNTERS *(Overleaf) A physician by trade, Dr. Humphrey Bate (seated with guitar) led the popular Possum Hunters string band on Saturday nights at the Opry. The group routinely kicked off Opry broadcasts with a rousing rendition of "There'll Be a Hot Time in the Old Town Tonight."*

PROFILES IN COUNTRY

DEFORD BAILEY

BORN SMITH COUNTY, TENNESSEE, DECEMBER 14, 1899
DIED JULY 2, 1982
PLAYED HARMONICA, GUITAR, BANJO
HITS "THE FOX CHASE," "PAN AMERICAN BLUES"

DeFord Bailey—"The Harmonica Wizard"—was one of the most creative and complex artists on the early Grand Ole Opry. The first African-American to become a regular on any country-music radio show, he played almost every week from 1926 to 1941. More than an accidental pioneer, he was possibly the greatest technical virtuoso the harmonica had ever seen. But his association with the Opry came to an abrupt end in 1941, when Bailey was fired under mysterious circumstances. "They turned me loose to root hog or die," he said in later years.
Fortunately, in the 1970s, a young housing officer, David Morton, won Bailey's confidence and encouraged him to do a number of public shows, including several on the Opry. Bailey was posthumously elected to the Country Music Hall of Fame in 2005.
CHARLES K. WOLFE

Young, Maggie," "Lynchburg," and "Leather Britches"—some of which he had learned during the Civil War. Telegrams and phone calls poured in—according to WSM legend, they came from every state in the Union—and Hay knew his idea for a new, more authentic barn dance was valid.

By early 1926, WSM announced that because of the increased popularity of old-time tunes, they would schedule "an hour or two" of them every Saturday night and call the show *The Barn Dance*. Soon a cast of about 20 acts became regulars. In contrast to the Chicago

BRADLEY KINCAID *At the* National Barn Dance *in Chicago, Bradley Kincaid was one of the leading stars of the 1920s with sentimental folk songs such as "Barbara Allen" and "The Fatal Wedding."*

country physician Dr. Humphrey Bate, the Possum Hunters were the cornerstone for the entire broadcast; they usually led off the Barn Dance at 8:00 p.m. with "There'll Be a Hot Time in the Old Town Tonight." The band had been active in middle Tennessee since the turn of the century and had even played on the old riverboats cruising the Cumberland. Bate himself played the harmonica and occasionally sang a few verses of "How

FRUIT JAR DRINKERS *Despite their genteel appearance, the Fruit Jar Drinkers were a fast, driving ensemble in the '20s and '30s. In one incarnation or another, the act played hoedowns at the Grand Ole Opry until the '70s.*

show, Nashville's strong suit was hard-driving fiddle bands, with colorful names (courtesy of Hay) like the Gully Jumpers, the Fruit Jar Drinkers, the Dixie Clodhoppers, and the Possum Hunters. A large string ensemble led by genial

Many Biscuits Can You Eat This Morning?" and "Ham Beats All Meat." He became a father figure to many of the younger musicians; when he died in 1936, Hay referred to him as "The Dean of the Opry."

OLD DOMINION BARN DANCE *(Opposite) Another popular Saturday-night billbilly showcase, the Old Dominion originated from Richmond, Virginia, from 1946 to 1957. Stars included Chet Atkins, Grandpa Jones, and Joe Maphis.*

PROFILES IN COUNTRY

CHARLIE POOLE

BORN RANDOLPH COUNTY, NORTH CAROLINA, MARCH 22, 1892
DIED MAY 21, 1931
HITS "DON'T LET YOUR DEAL GO DOWN BLUES," "THE GIRL I LEFT IN SUNNY TENNESSEE"

Charlie Poole & the North Carolina Ramblers were one of the most distinctive string bands to emerge during the late 1920s. Poole's unmistakable voice and banjo virtuosity anchored their sound, supported by precise parallel runs by fingerstyle guitarist Roy Harvey, while the fiddler—usually Posey Rorer—rigidly maintained the melody.

Poole's first coupling—"Don't Let Your Deal Go Down Blues" and "Can I Sleep in Your Barn Tonight Mister"—sold more than 100,000 copies in an era when sales of 20,000 records constituted a hit. When the Ramblers' second release sold more than 65,000 copies, Columbia offered Poole an exclusive contract, promising $150 per side royalties.

When the Depression leveled the record industry, Poole's professional career evaporated. None of the records he made in 1930 sold more than 2,000 copies, and the financially troubled Columbia label dropped him from its roster. Poole returned to millwork in his hometown of Spray, North Carolina, where he died following an extensive bout with the bottle. He was 39 years old.

DAVE SAMUELSON

Hay renamed the show "The Grand Ole Opry" in an impromptu ad lib one night in 1927—NBC had been carrying grand opera, and Hay said it was now time for some down-to-earth "Grand Ole Opry." In the 1920s, the show had still not found a blockbuster, breakout star like Bradley Kincaid. The best-known performer was Uncle Dave Macon, who had already established his reputation in vaudeville and on records. Popular singers included Obed "Dad" Pickard (an amazing jaw-harp player who featured songs like "Sweet Kitty Wells"),

Jack Jackson (a Lebanon, Tennessee, singer who was WSM's answer to Jimmie Rodgers), and brothers Sam and Kirk McGee (exciting instrumentalists who often worked with Uncle Dave Macon and offered duet singing on their own). Harmonica players, led by Dr. Bate and the young, black virtuoso DeFord Bailey, were in abundance. Many of these artists made records, but only Macon did so on a regular basis; to this first generation of radio regulars, low-paying recordings did not seem as important as radio fan mail.

And Opry performers received a great deal of it, for the WSM signal—one of the strongest in the nation—covered the South, as well as the Northeast, Midwest, and Southwest.

By the late 1920s, radio and records—the two main commercial outlets for country music—were heading in opposite directions. After the stock-market crash in 1929, record sales began to fall off, and soon even genuine stars like the Carter Family, Charlie Poole, and Jimmie Rodgers were selling drastically less. Royalties and recording fees

dropped dramatically, and soon even well-established radio singers were being offered a flat ten dollars a side to record. Radio, on the other hand, was starting to learn how to promote its acts, attract paying advertisers, and offer its artists a way to make a modest wage. The first country-music professionals were starting to come forth when traditional jobs in America were vanishing like the morning dew. By now they had a foothold in the new industry, and, armed with a passion for the music, they were ready for the struggle.

RECORD SLEEVES *An abundance of record labels entered the country market in the 1920s and '30s.*

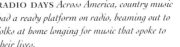

RADIO DAYS *Across America, country music had a ready platform on radio, beaming out to folks at home longing for music that spoke to their lives.*

TOP TEN

BOB PINSON'S TOP TEN 78-RPM RECORDS

Bob Pinson (1934–2003) served for nearly 30 years as the chief researcher and record collector for the Country Music Hall of Fame and Museum library, which now holds more than 200,000 recordings. He was one of the world's foremost experts on country-music history and a lifelong record collector. But more than that, he was an enthusiastic music fan, always eager to share music and facts about it. Here is a list of his Top Ten 78s, which originally appeared in the *Old-Time Herald* magazine.

1. **"San Antonio Rose"/ "The Convict and the Rose"** Bob Wills (Vocalion 04755)

2. **"Get Along Home Cindy"/ "Right or Wrong"** Bob Wills (Vocalion 03451)

3. **"Just Sitting on Top of the World"/"Loveless Love"** Milton Brown (Bluebird 5715)

4. **"Spanish Fandango"/ "New Spanish Two Step"** Bill Boyd (Bluebird 7921)

5. **"Jole Blon"/"Basile Waltz"** Harry Choates (Gold Star 1313/14)

6. **"Georgia Wildcat Breakdown"/ "Hog Trough Reel"** Clayton McMichen (Crown 3385)

7. **"Sunny Side of Life"/ "Where the Soul of Man Never Dies"** Blue Sky Boys (Bluebird 6457)

8. **"Roanoke"/"Cheyenne"** Bill Monroe (Decca 29406)

9. **"Swanee River Hodown"/ "The Memory of Your Smile"** Stanley Brothers (King 5210)

10. **"Georgia Bust Down"/ "Pickin' Off Peanuts"** Dilly & His Dill Pickles (Vocalion 5436)

I'LL LEAVE THIS W
OF TOIL AND TROU
MY HOME'S IN HEA
I'M GOING THER

NO DEPRESSION IN HEAVEN

COUNTRY MUSIC IN THE 1930s

RONNIE PUGH

DURING AMERICA'S GREAT DEPRESSION, FARMS GAVE OUT AND UNEMPLOYMENT WAS RAMPANT. THE RECORD BUSINESS SUFFERED HUGE DROP-OFFS IN SALES. YET IN THE MIDST OF ALL THIS, THE DEMAND FOR HILLBILLY MUSIC GREW, AND BRANCHED OUT INTO A DAZZLING VARIETY OF NEW SOUNDS.

continues opposite

America has endured panics and depressions many times—usually such short-lived credit crunches as those of 1837, 1873, 1893–94, and 1907—but for severity, duration, and impact, none of these economic downturns matched the worldwide Great Depression of the 1930s. There is no universal agreement as to its causes or timing, but the decade-long disaster, with only brief periods of temporary relief, extended from the stock-market crash of September–October, 1929 to the start of World War II in Europe ten years later. No part of American life was unaffected by the Depression.

A watershed realignment of the political forces in America took place, with the Democratic party gaining a Congressional hegemony that would last virtually unbroken for 60 years. Attitudes toward work, home, family, savings, investment, and the Government's role in all of this changed radically. It was the era of the Bonus Marchers, bread lines, and the Dust Bowl and its migrants, and over it all towered the figure of President Franklin D. Roosevelt with his New Deal and its alphabet soup agencies (TVA, WPA, CCC, SEC, NRA, and so many others).

Government assistance helped millions through the economic crisis, but beyond doubt millions more found solace, escape, relief, and sometimes wry commentary on the dreadful situation in the media of the day—such as newspaper comics, the talking movies, the radio, and the phonograph. Although barely a decade old as a commercial music at the depths of the Depression, country music managed not only to survive these prolonged hard times, but actually to expand, to grow, to change and adapt. In fact, during the 1930s, a number of new country-music

FRANKLIN D. ROOSEVELT
America's 32nd president, elected to four terms, offered citizens a New Deal to combat the Great Depression.

styles—cross-pollinated by far-reaching radio and records—emerged and flourished across the nation.

Paradoxically, it was during these years of business crisis that country music became a business—that is, a viable form of commercial music. By the 1930s, record talent scouts, such as Ralph Peer, Art Satherley, Don Law, Dave Kapp, and W. R. Calaway, were scouring the South and West for both established and new rural musicians. In this era, newly written songs largely displaced the folk and traditional favorites that had provided the material for the earliest country records—although these new songs were often written in the style of folk songs.

Commercializing country

Supplying the new songs was a growing class of professional songwriters, including Bob Miller, Carson Robison, Andrew Jenkins, A. P. Carter, Albert E. Brumley, Bob Nolan, Tim Spencer, and others. Songs took printed form on sheet music

HARD TIMES *Oklahoma migrant children, near Calipatria, California, 1937, during the Great Depression. Many families left their homes to seek a new life away from the Dust Bowl.*

1935 The Carter Family record the immortal "Can the Circle Be Unbroken."

1936 Miles of Great Plains farmland turn into a Dust Bowl. Ernest Tubb has his first recording session. The Monroe Brothers—Bill and Charlie—make their first recordings. Western-swing pioneer Milton Brown dies at age 32 from injuries sustained in an automobile accident. Roy Acuff makes his first recording of the classic "Wabash Cannon Ball." Carson Robison tours Great Britain.

1937 Roy Rogers becomes Republic Studios' newest singing-cowboy star. First broadcast of Kentucky's *Renfro Valley Barn Dance*. Pablo Picasso paints *Guernica*, his artistic commentary on the Spanish Civil War. *Snow White and the Seven Dwarfs*, the first full-length animated film, is released by Walt Disney Pictures.

1938 Roy Acuff, at age 34, joins the cast of the Grand Ole Opry. The Columbia Broadcasting System (CBS) acquires the ARC family of record labels and makes Columbia its flagship record label. The Carter Family begins performing on Mexican station XERA. Floyd Tillman's song "It Makes No Difference Now" becomes a major hit record for both Cliff Bruner and Jimmie Davis.

1939 Bill Monroe, at age 28, joins the cast of the Grand Ole Opry. The Grand Ole Opry is first broadcast over NBC's national radio network. Germany invades Poland, triggering World War II.

"These unhappy
times call for the
building of plans
that . . . build from
the bottom up . . .
that put their faith
once more in the
forgotten man at
the bottom of the
economic pyramid."
FRANKLIN D. ROOSEVELT

and in illustrated songbooks, which artists could sell by mail or at concerts. Not surprisingly, the earliest publishing firms that concentrated heavily on country music—Southern Music, owned by Ralph Peer in New York, and M. M. Cole, owned by Morris M. Cole in Chicago—flourished in this era. The Depression also witnessed the rise of professional booking agents and promoters in country music (Larry Sunbrock, O. W. Mayo, J. L. Frank, and Oscar Davis) and the first national radio sponsors (Alka-Seltzer, with a segment of Chicago's *National Barn Dance* in 1933, and Prince Albert Smoking Tobacco, which took on an NBC segment of Nashville's Grand Ole Opry in 1939).

The first prerecorded radio programs (known then as "electrical transcriptions") date from the 1930s; these disc recordings were cut live and circulated widely. By allowing performers to make seemingly live broadcasts hundreds of miles from their home bases, transcriptions helped many regional radio artists become nationally known. Even the earliest overseas junkets by country artists were undertaken in the 1930s—Carson Robison took his popular troupe to England in 1936, and, in 1939, movie cowboy Gene Autry played Ireland and England literally days before the outbreak of World War II.

A depressed market

However, not all elements of the country-music business were booming. Record sales plummeted during the Depression. Just 6,000,000 records (of all types of music) were sold in 1932, a small fraction of the 104,000,000 sold just five years earlier. Country sales suffered along with the rest, but even during the Roaring Twenties the only million-selling country record was Vernon Dalhart's "Wreck of the Old 97"/"The Prisoner's Song." For all his popularity, Jimmie Rodgers's "Blue Yodel" sold about half that figure, and an average country record in the 1930s sold about 10,000 copies.

After the first full year of the Depression—1930—many previously successful recording acts never recorded

PICKIN' Boys in rural Alabama, 1937. With just an inexpensive guitar or a fiddle, country folk could chase the blues away.

ART SATHERLEY

BORN BRISTOL, ENGLAND, OCTOBER 19, 1889
DIED FEBRUARY 10, 1986
BUSINESS AFFILIATIONS PARAMOUNT RECORDS, AMERICAN RECORD COMPANY/BRUNSWICK RECORDS, COLUMBIA RECORDS

As a talent scout and record producer, British-born Arthur Satherley helped shape country music as it developed in the first half of the 20th century—an accomplishment recognized by his election to the Country Music Hall of Fame in 1971.

Initially a salesman for Paramount Records (for which he recorded Blind Lemon Jefferson), Satherley gradually developed into a recording executive. He joined the American Record Company in 1929 and stayed in his post when the company was acquired by CBS and Columbia Records in 1938. It was as a talent scout and producer of records for the race and hillbilly series that he came into his own. Often with the astute assistance of his eventual successor, Don Law (another Englishman), Satherley produced a number of important blues and country artists, including Roy Acuff, Bob Wills, and Bill Monroe. In addition, his steering of Gene Autry toward a western image, and his later lobbying for Autry's initial film contract, had enormous repercussions in the American entertainment industry. Satherley retired from Columbia as a vice president in 1952. After a long, comfortable retirement, he died at age 96 in 1986.

KEVIN COFFEY

EMMETT MILLER

BORN MACON, GEORGIA,
FEBRUARY 2, 1900
DIED MARCH 29, 1962
HITS "LOVESICK BLUES,"
"I AIN'T GOT NOBODY,"
"ST. LOUIS BLUES"

Although Emmett Miller worked out of New York and never considered himself a country singer, he was a major inspiration for many early hillbilly singers, who admired his vocal embellishments and his easy way with the blues. Artists such as Bob Wills, the Callahan Brothers, Rex Griffin, Hank Williams, and Merle Haggard covered Miller songs.

He began his career as a teenager by joining a traveling blackface minstrel show, still quite popular in the late teens and 1920s. When the show played in New York, Miller's "trick yodeling" was hailed by newspaper reviews, and, in 1924, he was asked to make his first record, "Pickaninny's Paradise," backed with "Any Time" (later an Eddy Arnold hit).

Throughout the 1930s and 1940s, Miller toured the South as a solo act, playing clubs and second-class theaters. Ironically, he was playing such a club in Nashville's Printer's Alley in the late 1940s, when Hank Williams caused a sensation in the nearby Ryman Auditorium by singing Miller's version of "Lovesick Blues."

Although Miller could have laid claim to being a jazz singer, a blues singer, a pop singer, or a country singer, he saw himself as none of these. He was first and foremost a minstrel man.

CHARLES K. WOLFE

again. Among the names on that list are Jules Verne Allen, DeFord Bailey, the Georgia Yellow Hammers, Frank Hutchison, the Leake County Revelers, Eck Robertson, Carl T. Sprague, and Ernest Thompson. But with new, low-priced record labels, such as Bluebird and Decca, a second wave of wider-ranging A&R men, and demand for records for the newly popular roadside jukeboxes, there was never a year in the 1930s without the discovery and first recording of some new country act. The Delmore Brothers of Elkmont, Alabama, sold only 511 copies of their first recording ("Got the Kansas City Blues" for Columbia in 1931); but for RCA's Bluebird label just two years later their "Brown's Ferry Blues" sold an impressive 100,000. Gene Autry eventually sold a million copies with a 1931 release, "That Silver Haired Daddy of Mine," and yodeling cowgirl Patsy Montana claimed a million sales from her 1935 recording "I Want to Be a Cowboy's Sweetheart."

Reaching their audiences

Generally, low Depression-era record sales meant that even those country artists who had records made no living from them, especially since most artists were paid a flat fee for recording sessions (in the $15–$50 range), with no royalties on sales. And those who were lucky enough to gain royalties were usually paid at the rate of half a cent per record sold. At that rate, even an average seller of 10,000 copies would make only $50 in royalties. Still, records were gratifying to the ego and useful for career promotion—for example, being labeled as an "Exclusive Bluebird Recording Artist."

Typically, the full-time, professional hillbilly artist of the 1930s was a radio musician, whose stock-in-trade was the live show broadcast at farmer's hours (either early morning or noon). Comic skits and religious songs were often included in a fast-paced, carefully timed, and balanced program. The main benefit of a radio show to a musician was the chance to publicize tour dates booked at area schoolhouses, theaters, fairs, or town squares in the days or weeks just ahead. When one area was "played out" and the repeat

business declined, the radio bands pushed on to another radio station in a new area, whose listeners were as eager for new artists as those performers were for new listeners.

Those artists fortunate enough to appear weekly on a weekend barn-dance show from one of the powerful radio stations—WWVA in Wheeling, West Virginia, WLS in Chicago, Illinois, WHO in Des Moines, Iowa, WSM in Nashville, Tennessee, or Kentucky's *Renfro Valley Barn Dance*—benefited from the wide broadcast range of such stations. In addition, talent agencies at those stations booked and arranged artists' personal appearances through the week. The development of electrical transcription recordings of live radio programs, by firms such as World, Orthacoustic, Thesaurus, and Sellers, gave country artists and their music even wider exposure, as did the super-powerful radio stations built just across the border in Mexico, which—unfettered by FCC wattage limitations—boomed country music literally across the North American continent. Together, radio and recordings set higher performance

RURAL RADIO *By 1938, 69 percent of rural families had radios. Hillbilly musicians, record companies, and magazines like* Rural Radio *all aimed to reach them.*

" WOODY
(GUTHRIE)
VOWED HE WAS
GOING TO MARRY
ONE (OR TWO
OR THREE) OF THE
COON CREEK
GIRLS "

**MILLARD LAMPELL OF
THE ALMANAC SINGERS**

standards for would-be country musicians. It was no longer enough to be the best in your region when you could hear singing and playing on a 35-cent disc or from a Mexican-border radio station that was significantly better than your own. But if this discouraged some, it challenged and encouraged others. Records, especially, became a learning tool, and musical styles began to slowly merge and, in an odd way, become increasingly standardized. Through records, a relatively obscure minstrel singer like Emmett Miller could prove to be a powerful influence on performers ranging from Bob Wills to Hank Williams. Overall, the bar was set higher, but there it was for all to see and reach if they could. Backwoods regional variations of musical performance style slowly diminished, for as historian Colin Escott has noted, "The irony of the record business is that it preserved these regional musics even as it was helping to destroy them."

Records and radio undoubtedly made for increased musical homogeneity, but in fact there remained considerably more regional and stylistic diversity in the country music of the 1930s than the genre would see in years to come.

NATIONAL BARN DANCE *(Overleaf) Chicago radio station WLS was home to the* National Barn Dance. *In this cast photo are such favorites as the Girls of the Golden West (front row), Lulu Belle (2nd row, center), and Patsy Montana (back row, left).*

PROFILES IN COUNTRY

THE COON CREEK GIRLS

LILY MAY LEDFORD (FIDDLE, BANJO, VOCAL)
BORN POWELL COUNTY, KENTUCKY, MARCH 17, 1917 **DIED** JULY 14, 1985

CHARLOTTE "ROSIE" LEDFORD (GUITAR, VOCAL)
BORN POWELL COUNTY, KENTUCKY, AUGUST 16, 1915 **DIED** JULY 24, 1976

ESTHER "VIOLET" KOEHLER (MANDOLIN)
BORN WILTON, WISCONSIN, FEBRUARY 6, 1916 **DIED** OCTOBER 4, 1973

EVELYN "DAISY" LANGE (BASS, FIDDLE)
BORN ST. HENRY, OHIO, JULY 7, 1919 **DIED** FEBRUARY 10, 2002

MINNIE "BLACK-EYED SUSAN" LEDFORD (BASS)
BORN POWELL COUNTY, KENTUCKY, OCTOBER 10, 1923 **DIED** JULY 22, 1987

HITS "BANJO PICKIN' GIRL," "FLOWERS BLOOMING IN THE WILDWOOD," "SOWING ON THE MOUNTAIN"

When The Coon Creek Girls ran to the microphones for the *Renfro Valley Barn Dance*'s initial WLW radio broadcast in 1937, no one expected that any gingham-frocked string band could play old-time music with such driving abandon. Their leader, fiddler and clawhammer banjo player Lily May Ledford, hailed from northeastern Kentucky's coal-mining region. In 1937, WLS talent broker John Lair auditioned young women for an "all-girl" band to be built around Lily May and her guitar-playing sister, Rosie. Mandolinist Esther Koehler and fiddler-bassist Evelyn Lange were hired only two weeks before the show went on the air.

Aware of the group's earning potential, Lair kept The Coon Creek Girls working virtually seven days a week for the next two years. Besides the Saturday night WLW broadcast, he set up a daily show for the band over WCKY. And in June, 1939, folklorist Alan Lomax brought the band to Franklin D. Roosevelt's White House. Unfortunately, lineup changes in the 1940s slowed the group's early momentum, and The Coon Creek Girls formally disbanded in 1957. The sisters reunited for occasional folk-festival appearances during the late 1960s and early 1970s.

DAVE SAMUELSON

BROTHER DUET AND FRIEND *The Delmore Brothers—Rabon (left) and Alton—with Uncle Dave Macon at station WSM in the 1930s. Preeminent brother duet stylists, the Delmores influenced many acts not only with their harmony singing but also with their intricate playing on these Martin guitars.*

Even though a good many of the 1920s string bands were never heard on records again, the Southeast especially was home to some talented and popular string bands during the Depression years—most notably J. E. Mainer's Mountaineers, brother Wade Mainer's Sons of the Mountaineers, and Roy Hall's Blue Ridge Entertainers (all from North Carolina), and a talented band of young women from Kentucky, the Coon Creek Girls. Building on these traditional sounds, many fiddle-based southeastern bands incorporated more elements from pop and jazz. Most notable among them were the Georgia Wildcats (a Louisville, Kentucky, radio band of former Skillet Licker, Clayton McMichen), and a very popular group from Chicago, Illinois—the

Kentucky Ramblers, who became better known after westernizing their name to the Prairie Ramblers. Successors to such earlier breakdown fiddlers as Eck Robertson, Mellie Dunham, Uncle Bunt Stephens, and Uncle Jimmy Thompson were newer and better players—Fiddlin' Arthur Smith, Georgia Slim Rutland, Big Howdy Forrester, Tommy Magness, and Curly Fox.

Harmony duets

The same southeastern region that produced most of the string bands was also home to what many will recall as the hallmark style of the 1930s—the "harmony duets," often dubbed "brother duets" because of the many successful sibling pairings. Like so much of what was going on in country music during the Depression, this was a case of innovation upon a base of tradition. There had been sibling acts in country music almost from the beginning, such as the Allen Brothers and the Johnson Brothers from Tennessee. And there had been a tradition of guitar and mandolin playing close-harmony duet acts, such as the popular WLS teams McFarland & Gardner ("Twenty-One Years") and Karl & Harty ("I'm Just Here to Get My Baby out of Jail," and "Kentucky"). Combining these two traditions with stylistic touches all their own were such great 1930s duets as the Carlisle Brothers, the Callahan Brothers, the Delmore Brothers, the Dixon Brothers, the Monroe Brothers, and the Blue Sky Boys (the Bolick brothers), the Girls of the Golden West, and the DeZurik Sisters (aka the Cackle Sisters).

The music of the Depression-era duet acts varied. Some, like the Carlisles of Kentucky and the Dixons of South Carolina, favored guitar and steel-guitar instrumental pairings in the early Darby & Tarlton tradition. The Carlisles favored rowdy, blues-based song material, both together and separately—as Cliff on dobro and Bill on guitar often recorded solo as well. The Dixons stayed close to the moralistic fare that brother Howard

HOOSIER HOT SHOTS *Comic stars of Chicago's National Barn Dance in the 1930s, the Hoosier Hot Shots blended elements of vaudeville and hillbilly music in their zany novelty songs, such as "From the Indies to the Andes in his Undies" and "When There's Tears in the Eyes of a Potato."*

"Typically, the full-time, professional hillbilly artist of the 1930s was a radio musician. Comic skits and religious songs were often included in a fast-paced, carefully timed, and balanced program."

Great duet teams

The 1930s saw the rise of a number of outstanding harmony duos in country music.

1 *The hard-driving, dapper Monroe Brothers—Bill and Charlie (ca. 1936)—set high standards for brother duets with their powerful harmony singing and playing.*

2 *Hailing from North Carolina, the Callahan Brothers incorporated blues influences and duet yodeling into their harmony act.*

3 *Karl & Harty—mandolin player Karl Davis and guitarist Hartford Connecticut Taylor—exemplified the country duet tradition at Chicago's WLS in the '30s and '40s.*

4 The Carlisle Brothers (Cliff and Bill) performed together for 13 years at WNOX in Knoxville; in the late '40s they pursued separate careers.

5 The Blue Sky Boys—brothers Bill (on mandolin) and Earl Bolick—lifted country harmony singing to a high art in a career that began on radio in 1935 and continued into the '60s.

6 Blind duo Mac & Bob (Lester McFarland, on mandolin, and Robert Gardner) brought a polished, polite approach to old-time songs at Chicago's WLS in the '30s.

7 Married in 1934, the year they teamed up, Lulu Belle & Scotty Wiseman starred on the National Barn Dance for 25 years, singing novelties, folk songs, and modern love songs.

> **DESPITE THE SOCIAL AND CULTURAL BARRIERS THAT SEPARATED THE RACES, SOUTHERN MUSIC HAS ALWAYS REFLECTED THE CROSS-POLLINATION BETWEEN BLACKS AND WHITES.**

Dixon composed, such as their *Titanic* song, "Down with the Old Canoe," or the immortal "I Didn't Hear Nobody Pray"—later a hit for Roy Acuff as "Wreck on the Highway."

Other duos, such as the Callahan Brothers and the Delmore Brothers, featured two guitars to underpin the harmonized voices. Hailing from North Carolina, the Callahan Brothers specialized in high-register tandem yodeling and showed the same occasional fondness for rowdy blues that the Carlisles had. The Delmore Brothers, Alton and Rabon, played guitar and tenor guitar, respectively, and were masters of instrumental and vocal interplay, as evidenced by their work on "Brown's Ferry Blues," "I've Got the Big River Blues," and other much-requested songs, which they featured for most of the Depression years on Nashville's Grand Ole Opry. The same improvement in microphone fidelity that made possible the phenomenal success of the caressing crooning of pop legend

Bing Crosby also helped the Delmores, whose gently blended harmonies were anything but loud and strident.

The Monroe Brothers and the Blue Sky Boys played the guitar-mandolin combination of Karl & Harty and McFarland & Gardner, but there the similarities with their predecessors ended. Kentuckians Bill (on mandolin) and Charlie (on guitar) Monroe were magnificent musicians. The 60 or so recordings that they made for Bluebird Records, between 1936 and 1938, were often characterized by fast tempos and hard-driving instrumental breaks, as evidenced on "Roll in My Sweet Baby's Arms" and "My Long Journey Home." Bill always took the instrumental lead on mandolin, supported by Charlie's lightning-paced runs and fills on guitar. On the vocals, Charlie took the lead, as Bill reached for the sky with high harmony. In 1938, despite a growing fan base, incompatibility drove the Monroes apart, with Charlie launching his Kentucky Pardners and Bill the Blue Grass Boys—and, ultimately, the bluegrass music he and his band inspired.

The Blue Sky Boys—Bill (on mandolin) and Earl (on guitar) Bolick—came from a devout Holiness church family in the Piedmont section of North Carolina. In their relatively long career on Bluebird and RCA Victor (1936–1951, interrupted by both men's military service in World War II), they consistently recorded many traditional folk ballads ("Katy Dear" and "The Butcher's Boy") and gospel hymn-book songs ("The Royal Telephone" and "Whispering Hope"). Bill's mandolin took the melody on breaks and, even during the vocals, never seemed to slip into a chorded "sock" rhythm. They remained a rare example of a brother duet act still recording after World War II—their only concession to modernity was the addition of a spare and tasteful supporting fiddle and string bass.

Yodeling and blues

Even before he died in 1933, a growing number of rural artists were clearly under the spell of the ultracommercial Jimmie Rodgers. He created the "blue yodel" by combining African-American blues with his own variant of Swiss yodeling; most

UNSUNG HERO *Black musician Arnold Shultz (left) was a key influence on Bill Monroe and the fingerstyle guitar playing of Merle Travis.*

The Color of the Blues in Early Country

Despite the social and cultural barriers that separated the races through much of the 20th century, southern music has always reflected a cross-pollination between blacks and whites. Two of the earliest country performers on record—Uncle Dave Macon and Emmett Miller—drew heavily from 19th-century minstrel traditions. The most innovative and enduring musicians in country-music history —Jimmie Rodgers, Bob Wills, Bill Monroe, Merle Travis, Hank Williams, and Elvis Presley—were all deeply rooted in the blues.

Some white rural performers honed their skills by observing local black singers and bluesmen. Frank Hutchison, the West Virginia singer considered the first white country bluesman on record, learned slide-guitar techniques from a black railroad worker. Arnold Shultz, an African-American longbow fiddler and finger-style guitarist, influenced two youths from Rosine, Kentucky— Prairie Ramblers fiddler Shelby "Tex" Atchison and bluegrass patriarch Bill Monroe. Even Merle Travis's innovative, fingerpicking guitar style is directly traceable to Shultz. Similarly, Hank Williams learned guitar from an itinerant black guitarist, Rufus "Tee-Tot" Payne.

Pioneering country acts who drew heavily from the blues include Grand Ole Opry stalwart Sam McGee, Virginia banjoist Dock Boggs, the Allen Brothers from Chattanooga, Tennessee, and Darby & Tarlton, a Georgia duo whose slide guitar-driven 1927 record of "Columbus Stockade Blues" and "Birmingham Jail" reportedly sold 200,000 copies.

Indeed, many white country musicians were inspired by blues and jazz musicians. Some early 1930s bands like Clayton McMichen's Georgia Wildcats, the Prairie Ramblers, and Milton Brown's Musical Brownies largely eschewed the standard fiddle repertoire in favor of jazz and syncopated dance tunes. Bob Wills was fond of Harlem jazz and the tightly arranged swing of Detroit's Casa Loma Orchestra. His earliest recordings fused traditional Texas fiddle music with horns, reeds, and Leon McAuliffe's hot steel guitar. For Wills, the blues bug bit early. He claimed that in his teens he once rode 40 miles on horseback to see the "Empress of the Blues," Bessie Smith. Years later, he described the experience as "the greatest thing I ever heard." Indeed, many white country musicians had idols among black blues and jazz musicians. Good taste knows no color.

DAVE SAMUELSON

of his imitators and disciples, lacking his genius, tended to specialize in either blues or yodeling.

The yodelers went in one direction, some of them displaying a technical virtuosity unreached by Rodgers—like Wilf Carter, Roy Rogers, Elton Britt, the Girls of the Golden West, the Callahan Brothers, the Delmore Brothers, and Patsy Montana. The blues singers went in another direction but, like the yodelers, took their craft to greater heights (and lower depths) than Rodgers had dared, many drawing even more directly from black sources. Rodgers was content with a highly commercial, watered-down, anglicized blues that borrowed the song structure, the best lines, and the symbols he heard in the black blues all around him, or on the latest blues records. But he didn't go nearly as far with some facets of the blues—such as its sensuality and boasts of sexual prowess, and its tales of explicit drug and alcohol use—as did some of the younger, white country-blues artists, no doubt inspired in large part by Rodgers and his success. Rodgers's success no doubt also encouraged other hillbilly musicians to listen more closely to the black sources that had obviously inspired him. Indeed, during the 1930s the influence of black blues and jazz became more pronounced in country music.

Gene Autry, "Oklahoma's Yodeling Cowboy," who covered many of Rodgers's own songs on a variety of labels, ventured far into graphic sensuality with "Do Right Daddy Blues" and many others. Cliff Carlisle, the singing dobroist from Kentucky and sometime half of the Carlisle

Brothers, did the same with "Tom Cat Blues" and "Shanghai Rooster Yodel." Jimmie Davis, the future governor of Louisiana, who late in his long life sang nothing but gospel, recorded "Red Nightgown Blues," "High Behind Blues," and other risqué numbers for Victor Records, between 1929 and 1932, sometimes using black musicians for accompaniment.

Southwestern styles

In southwestern Louisiana, Cajun musicians also took advantage of the new platforms that radio and records offered. While traditional Cajun acts like Leo Soileau and Joe Falcon and his wife, Cleoma, preserved their folk-based music on records, more progressive Cajun acts like the Hackberry Ramblers string band blended traditional Cajun music with

JIMMIE DAVIS *In the 1930s, Jimmie Davis specialized in risqué blues numbers such as "Red Nightgown Blues." By the time of this 1940s songbook, however, he was better known for the huge hit "You Are My Sunshine" (1940).*

blues and country styles, adding drums and electric amplification for dance halls.

Across the Sabine River from Cajun country, southern and eastern Texas enjoyed relative prosperity during even the worst Depression years, thanks to the booming oil industry. This region was home to perhaps the most successful of country music's new styles—a fiddle-driven, danceable hybrid of hoedown fiddling, pop, jazz, and blues, which became known as "western swing." Texas-born Bob Wills was the music's cofounder and most enduring performer; his Texas Playboys became country's version of the big band, and they cranked out hit after hit in the late 1930s and 1940s. Wills and cofounder Milton Brown, leader of the Musical Brownies, both came out of W. Lee O'Daniel's seminal Fort Worth band—the Light Crust Doughboys.

CAJUN SPICE *In southwestern Louisiana, Cajun musicians created their own tasty variety of country music, which frequently included accordions, French lyrics, and elements of Cajun folk songs. Here, popular Cajun bandleader Leo Soileau (on fiddle) holds court at the Pleasure Club with his Rhythm Boys, late 1930s.*

One of the seminal figures in country music, Bob Wills helped pioneer the jazzy, dance-hall hybrid known as western swing.

Born into a long line of fiddlers, Wills grew up in west Texas hearing both frontier fiddle music and the emotive sounds of black field-workers. In 1930, he and guitarist Herman Arnspiger teamed with vocalist Milton Brown in Fort Worth, Texas, to form a trio that, in 1931, became the Light Crust Doughboys, soon the most popular string band in the Southwest. Problems with alcohol led to his dismissal in 1933, but Wills rebounded and established a base in Tulsa, Oklahoma, in 1934, with his Texas Playboys band. Following Brown's death in 1936, Wills became western swing's major figure, while the Playboys became *the* band, featuring such important figures as vocalist Tommy Duncan, steel guitarist Leon McAuliffe, guitarist Eldon Shamblin, and country music's first permanent band drummer, Smoky Dacus.

Wills's popularity rose steadily in the 1930s, and he enjoyed major successes with "Steel Guitar Rag" and the self-penned "San Antonio Rose." A 1969 stroke ended his fiddling days, but when he died in 1975, western swing was experiencing a revival, and his music is still revered by committed fans and artists.

KEVIN COFFEY

> **"He had an aura so strong it stunned people.... You had to see him in person to understand his magnetic pull."**
>
> **WILLIE NELSON ON BOB WILLS**

Eventually, each major Texas city boasted a thriving musical scene, heavy on this new, hot dance music. Houston had Cliff Bruner, Leon Selph, Moon Mullican, Ted Daffan, and Floyd Tillman. Fort Worth had the Light Crust Doughboys and the Crystal Springs Ramblers. Dallas had Bill Boyd's Cowboy Ramblers, Roy Newman, and the Shelton Brothers. San Antonio boasted Jimmie Revard, the Hofner Brothers, and the Tune Wranglers. Much of their music combined the hard drive of a breakdown fiddle with the improvisational feel of jazz music, taking a melody and playing off it on the numerous instrumental breaks. Aimed at the dance halls and jukeboxes, most of what they played (and recorded) was fast-paced. It was what dancers wanted to hear, and that suited the era's record producers just fine.

Further west in America's Depression-era landscape, Southern California was home to the motion picture—the flourishing

medium of entertainment and escapism. The terrible Depression was, paradoxically, a golden era for Hollywood movies, and a now-famous assortment of country singers today known as the "singing cowboys" gravitated to a low-budget niche in this prosperous industry—the "B-Western," or "Budget Western," akin to the record company's 35-cent budget labels.

In addition to the singing star, most of these low-budget, musical westerns featured some singing sidekick or guest bands—roles that provided invaluable national exposure for some of the more popular country or hillbilly acts of the 1930s and 1940s. The list of southern and southwestern hillbilly stars who made one or more appearances in cowboy films of this era is a long one, including Patsy Montana, Pee Wee King, the Hoosier Hot Shots, Ernest Tubb, Jimmie Davis, Red Foley, Bob Wills & His Texas Playboys, Bill Boyd, the Callahan

Brothers, the Village Boys—even Fiddlin' Arthur Smith, as a Jimmy Wakely sidekick in the 1940s.

With the exposure and respectability that the cowboy movies provided, hillbilly or country musical acts were soon dressing up as cowboys and using western names for their bands, even if they'd never been west of the Mississippi. Examples are legion, but two Alabamians suffice—Hank Penny, who named his band the Radio Cowboys (they first hit it big on Atlanta radio), and Hank Williams, who dubbed his group the Drifting Cowboys, and used as his theme "Happy Roving Cowboy," a classic Bob Nolan tune, written for the Sons of the Pioneers.

Singing movie cowboys prettied up the reality of the Old West and, in the

COWBOY BIG BAND *Bob Wills & His Texas Playboys band with Gene Autry at KCMC in Texarkana, Texas, ca. 1959. By this time Wills's band had grown to 10 members, including two trumpeters and two saxophonists.*

RY THE TRAIN

LAX Southern Pacific

process, provided escape from the often harsh reality of Depression life, if only for a few hours on Saturday afternoons at the local movie theater. At the same time, however, country musicians, drawn overwhelmingly from the white Southern working class, were well acquainted with hard times and didn't mind singing about the manifold troubles that their class, region, and nation endured. Thus, they provided some of the Depression's best contemporary accounts — a veritable chronicle of hard times.

Hard Times

The region was used to it. The South had been in an agricultural depression since the collapse of cotton prices in the early 1920s. For that reason, many of the music's finest hard-time laments actually predate the stock-market crash and the Great Depression, and deal with the farmer's plight. Among them are "Dixie Boll Weevil" (by Fiddlin' John Carson in 1924), "Down on Penny's Farm" (by the Bentley Boys in 1929), "Farm Relief Song" (recorded by Vernon Dalhart the month of the stock-market crash, in which he lost a considerable sum), Uncle Dave Macon's "Farm Relief" (also 1929), and songwriter Bob Miller's "Eleven Cent Cotton and Forty Cent Meat," from 1928.

Bob Miller, a Memphis-born pianist, composer, and bandleader, went to New York in 1928 to work for Irving Berlin Music, write his own songs, and make records. He wrote pop and light classical works, but he preferred to chronicle news events and famous persons from the common man's perspective, much as Carson Robison did. A prolific tunesmith, Miller in his heyday wrote between 50 and 200 songs a year.

NO. 1 COWBOY *Gene Autry, America's most popular singing cowboy star of the 1930s, rose to be a Top 5 box office attraction among all Hollywood stars. This movie dates from 1938.*

EXODUS *This famous photo by Dorothea Lange captures the exodus of poor folk from America's plains and farms to California in the '30s. When they moved west, they brought their music with them, and country music soon took root in California.*

"I am a mother of seven children, and utterly heart broken, in that they are hungry, have only 65¢ in money. The father is in L.A. trying to find something to do."

LETTER FROM MRS. H. L. TO PRESIDENT ROOSEVELT, 1934

Besides the tearjerkers for which he is best remembered ("Twenty-One Years," "Seven Years with the Wrong Woman," "Things That Might Have Been," "Rocking Alone in an Old Rocking Chair"), Miller wrote a great many Depression commentaries. His "Farm Relief Blues" took a wry view of politicians' promises for relief, as witnessed by its original title, taken from its refrain: "Those Campaign Lyin,' Sugar Coated Ballot-Coaxin' Low Down Farm Relief Blues." And yet at the very beginning of the Depression, his "Bank Failures" (1930) maintained that "Folks, something's gotta be done." Two years later, in "The Poor Forgotten Man" (1932), his call for political action at the ballot box was explicit: "Who's gonna vote on election day? Who's gonna finally have his say? Who's gonna cause a change— Hey! Hey! It's the poor forgotten man!"

In the 1932 update of "Eleven Cent Cotton and Forty Cent Meat" came the same call to action: "Votin' time is coming, and just watch us all; you can bet there's gonna be a change somewhere this fall." Miller played up class antagonisms in such classics as "The Rich Man and the Poor Man" (1932), in his many calls for the repeal of Prohibition ("Dry Votin' Wet Drinkers," "Page Mr. Volstead," "Five Cent Glass of Beer," and "Good Old Beer"), and "I Can't Go to the Poorhouse" (Why? No room. "All the millionaires are there.")

> **"**
> ## WHEN THE DEPRESSION HIT IN '29, MY DADDY WAS ONE OF THE FEW MEN IN CLEVELAND COUNTY, ARKANSAS, WHO COULD USUALLY FIND WORK OF SOME KIND.
> **"**
>
> **JOHNNY CASH**

Everyone is suffering

"I Can't Go to the Poorhouse" points up a theme of almost vengeful, egalitarian glee that everybody's suffering now—the stock-market crash and the subsequent Great Depression had spread the misery to all regions and classes of the nation, ultimately to the world at large. The same thread appears in a 1933 recording by W. Lee O'Daniel & His Light Crust Doughboys—"In the Fall of '29." The word "fall," of course, carries a dual meaning in the song, as verse upon verse recounts how the mighty fell in the stock-market crash—a "great big banker" is now an iceman; a stock-and-bond holder now drives a taxi; a musician is reduced to selling apples; a "Mrs. Swell" who once led "the whole four hundred" now

sells magazines door to door. Despite this, the chorus strikes a hopeful note, anticipating the "Let's all pull together now" optimism of another O'Daniel classic of the era, "My Million Dollar Smile."

In the fall of '29, in the fall of '29,
That's when we started sliding,
In the fall of '29
'Twas a fall of 50-50,
You lost yours and I lost mine,
But it made us all more human
Since the fall of '29.

The bleak four years of descent from stock-market crash to bank failures, business failures, farm foreclosures, Bonus Marchers, and full-blown Depression resounded with a variety

STREET MUSIC *In the depths of the Depression, musicians like this blind fiddler in West Memphis, Arkansas, frequently played for tips on city streets.*

of complaints from country musicians. Obscure artists cut some of the best, such as Bernard (Slim) Smith's "Breadline Blues" (1931). That same year, Happy Jack cut "I'm Only Suggesting This," which championed the repeal of Prohibition as a cure to the economic woes, and agreed with "Prohibition Is a Failure," the cry of Lowe Stokes of the Skillet Lickers.

Striking a more personal note was "Prohibition Has Done Me Wrong," written and recorded by another former Skillet Licker, Clayton McMichen, and also recorded in a lost, unreleased version by Jimmie Rodgers. Rodgers, the giant among rural recording artists, saw his sizable royalty income dwindle in these years, so much so that in 1933 he

sold his four-year-old mansion, "Blue Yodeler's Paradise," at a considerable loss. Considering it all, Carson Robison was properly skeptical to ask of the Hoover administration, "Prosperity Is Just Around Which Corner?"

As the Depression deepened in the late 1930s, and as droughts caused farms across the Great Plains and Southwest to turn to worthless dust, Woody Guthrie emerged as a voice for displaced Okies and others migrating west for a better life. In the fall of 1932, Americans voted by a huge majority to replace Herbert Hoover with Franklin D. Roosevelt, then reelected him three more times.

CLASSIC COUNTRY RECORDING

WOODY GUTHRIE
"This Land Is Your Land"

*This land is your land,
this land is my land,
from California to the New
York Island,
From the redwood forest
to the Gulf Stream water,
this land was made for you
and me.*

WRITTEN BY WOODY GUTHRIE,
FEBRUARY 23, 1940
FIRST RECORDING
DATE UNKNOWN, 1940s

"This Land Is Your Land" is far and away Woody Guthrie's best-known song. Indeed, it's one of the most widely sung songs in the USA and has even been championed as a new national anthem.

Guthrie's stated reason for writing it was that he was tired of hearing Kate Smith sing Irving Berlin's popular "God Bless America." So Guthrie voiced a different perspective, ending each verse with *"God blessed America for me."* That final line was too limiting, however, so he changed it to *"This land was made for you and me."*

Guthrie freely adapted many melodies from other songs and singers, and he was always more of a lyricist than a musical composer. "This Land Is Your Land" is no different. The melody of the song is derived from the gospel song "When the World's on Fire," which the Carter Family recorded in 1930, and which the Carters also used as the melody for "Little Darling Pal of Mine." Guthrie loved the Carter Family, and they had a great influence on his melodies in general.

The first release of a Guthrie recording of the song came in 1951, on the 10-inch Folkways Records LP *This Land Is Your Land.* The song "was really his response to Irving Berlin's false optimism," Woody's daughter, Nora Guthrie, has said. "It was so obvious that God hadn't blessed America for everybody."

GUY LOGSDON

Dusty Old Dust:
The Dust Bowl Songs
of Woody Guthrie

With such songs as "Do-Re-Mi," "I Ain't Got No Home," and "Dust Bowl Refugee," Woody Guthrie became the preeminent voice of the Dust Bowl migrants during the 1930s and 1940s. His songs dramatized the problems that afflicted a group of more than 200,000 displaced souls—victims of the twin ravages of the Depression and fierce droughts, who were forced to leave their farms on the Plains in search of a better life in California.

Guthrie himself was from Okemah, Oklahoma, some 300 miles east of the Dust Bowl region. In 1937, he joined the tide of migrants headed toward California, desperate to find work. Guthrie's goal was to be a country-radio singer, and he soon gained his own radio show in Hollywood on station KFVD.

By 1938, Guthrie became more outspoken about the country's social problems. Actor Will Geer, himself a social activist, heard Guthrie's broadcasts and went to the studio to meet the singer. They became fast friends, and soon Geer and Guthrie began traveling throughout California, spreading the word about migrant issues. During this time, Guthrie also met John Steinbeck—whose best-selling novel about the migrants, *The Grapes of Wrath*, was published early in 1939. Guthrie also became Steinbeck's music advisor for the film adaptation of the book, which featured Guthrie's song "Blowin' Down the Road."

In 1940, folk-music impresario Alan Lomax recorded a lengthy interview with him for the Library of Congress. During this interview, Guthrie sang "Dusty Old Dust," which became the well-known "So Long, It's Been Good to Know You." Afterwards, RCA Victor Records approached Lomax for help in finding an artist to record a collection of migrant songs. The result was two albums of Guthrie's *Dust Bowl Ballads*, which further cemented his reputation as the voice of the downtrodden. Guthrie ultimately became known for writing many songs outside his Dust Bowl roots— "Oklahoma Hills," "Philadelphia Lawyer," and "This Land Is Your Land"—and influenced a wide scope of performers (Bob Dylan chief among them). But his *Dust Bowl Ballads* will always occupy a special place in the cultural documents of the American experience.

GUY LOGSDON

DUST STORM *An Oklahoma family flee a dust storm in 1936. Woody Guthrie (right), a fellow Oklahoman, reported in song the plight of those displaced by drought and depression.*

"I am out to sing songs that will prove to you that this is your world and that if it has hit you pretty hard and knocked you for a dozen loops, no matter what color, what size you are, how you are built, I am out to sing the songs that make you take pride in yourself and in your work."

WOODY GUTHRIE

ROY ACUFF & HIS SMOKY MOUNTAIN BOYS

"Wabash Cannon Ball"

From the great Atlantic Ocean to the wide Pacific Shore.

WRITTEN BY WILLIAM KINDT AND RECORDED ON JANUARY 28, 1947

"Wabash Cannon Ball" is so closely identified with Roy Acuff that it's hard to believe he wasn't singing on his band's first recording of the song. In 1936, when Acuff and his Crazy Tennesseans band included it on their second session, band member Sam "Dynamite" Hatcher handled the vocal. Hatcher probably learned the song from Hugh Cross's 1929 recording. The Carter Family also recorded their own arrangement of the song in 1929, and A. P. Carter's name often appears as composer, sometimes with that of William Kindt, who had published a version in 1904.

After Acuff joined WSM's Grand Ole Opry, in 1938, he reorganized his group in early 1939, and changed its name to the Smoky Mountain Boys. Kindt's story of a train on the Wabash Railroad (based on J. A. Roff's "Great Rock Island Route!") became one of Acuff's two most-requested songs—the other being the gospel number "Great Speckled Bird."

The bandleader recorded his now-definitive 1947 rendition of "Wabash Cannon Ball" in Hollywood for Columbia Records. This time around, Beecher "Oswald" Kirby's swooping dobro and Acuff's whining train-whistle sounds ("a combination of a whistle and a field holler," as he described them) provided the signature introduction.

JOHN W. RUMBLE

Roosevelt's early New Deal programs found wide and almost unquestioned favor from country singers, ranging from W. Lee O'Daniel ("On to Victory, Mr. Roosevelt"), West Virginia balladeer Billy Cox ("NRA Blues," "Franklin D. Roosevelt's Back Again," and "The Democratic Donkey Is in His Stall Again"), Texas honky-tonk pioneer Al Dexter ("Let Me Join the CCC"), and Chattanooga's Allen Brothers ("New Deal Blues"). In Louisiana, Huey Long's "Share Our Wealth" plans found wide support, and his assassination was widely lamented in song (even predicted two years before the fact by a Bob Miller song recorded in 1935 by Hank Warner, "The Death of Huey P. Long").

The only skeptical note in country music on any of the actual or proposed social programs was sounded in "When Our Old Age Pension Check Comes to Our Door," recorded in several different versions by the Sons of the Pioneers (1935) and Roy Acuff (1939). The earlier version, credited to a "Manny Stone," actually predates the Social Security Act and satirizes Dr. Francis E. Townsend's plan to give every nonworking American over the age of sixty a monthly pension of $200, every cent of which had to be spent in the month received.

The strong strain of evangelical Protestantism in southern culture added a dose of otherworldly hope and earthly resignation to the era's bleak news in

some of its best-remembered songs—such as "I'll Fly Away" (recorded by the Chuck Wagon Gang and others) and "Meeting in the Air" (cut by the Carter Family in 1940, and much later by Roy Acuff as "Little Moses"). Best remembered of all, and not least because it became the title of an alternative country magazine, is "No Depression" (1936) by the Carter Family, with its haunting refrain:

I'm going where there's no depression
To the lovely land that's free from care
I'll leave this world of toil and trouble
My home's in heaven, I'm goin' there.

"All generalizations are false, including this one," President Dwight D. Eisenhower once said in a great epigram, which parallels the difficulty of summing up country music's Depression era. It was a time of contrasts, of a rich musical variety teeming with anomalies and seeming contradictions. It was an era of contraction and expansion; the Depression ended many promising country careers and gave birth to many others. It was a time of unapologetic escapism but also of harsh realities, squarely faced. Records, radio, and motion pictures standardized, professionalized, and even nationalized the music far beyond what its 1920s discoverers could have envisioned, and yet regional variations (as between southeastern and southwestern musical styles) persisted and in a way intensified. That country music not only survived, but actually prospered during these hard years, testifies to two of its hallmark characteristics and enduring qualities — the loyalty of its listeners and the great adaptability of its artists. The country careers that last tend to find new ways to sound timeless and to be traditional.

SEEKING SOLACE *In the depths of the Depression, everyday people like these guitar players from Maynardsville, Tennessee, found comfort in country music.*

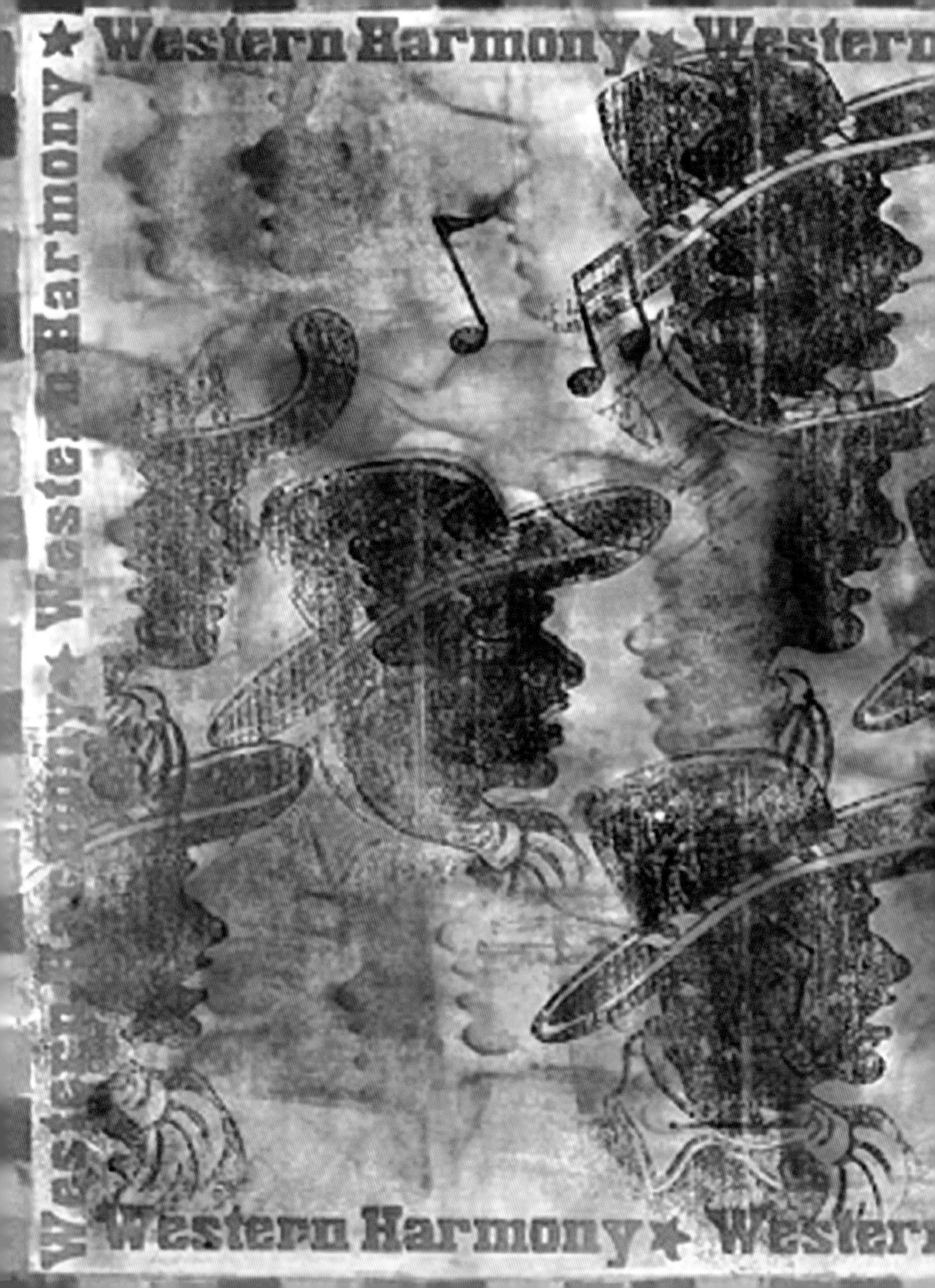
Western Harmony ★ Western
Western Harmony ★ Western Harmony ★
Western Harmony ★ Western

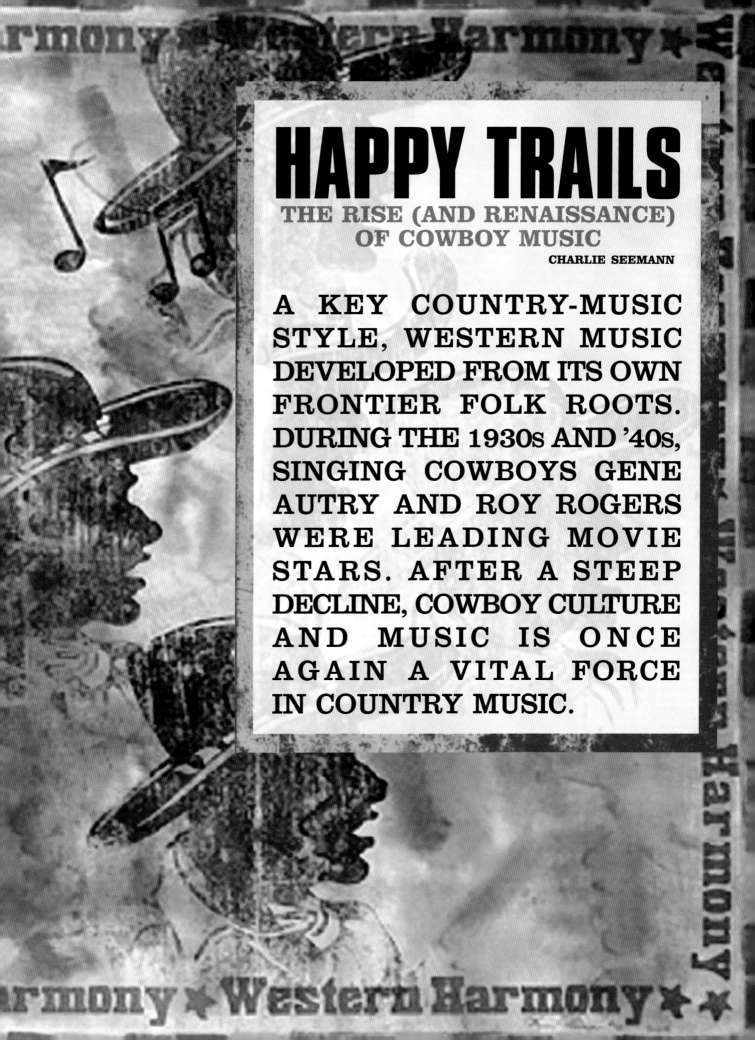

HAPPY TRAILS

THE RISE (AND RENAISSANCE) OF COWBOY MUSIC

CHARLIE SEEMANN

A KEY COUNTRY-MUSIC STYLE, WESTERN MUSIC DEVELOPED FROM ITS OWN FRONTIER FOLK ROOTS. DURING THE 1930s AND '40s, SINGING COWBOYS GENE AUTRY AND ROY ROGERS WERE LEADING MOVIE STARS. AFTER A STEEP DECLINE, COWBOY CULTURE AND MUSIC IS ONCE AGAIN A VITAL FORCE IN COUNTRY MUSIC.

SINGING COWBOY TIMELINE

1883 William F. Cody (Buffalo Bill) opens his first Wild West show.

1903 *The Great Train Robbery*, a silent western film, jump-starts the American film industry.

1908 N. Howard "Jack" Thorp publishes *Songs of the Cowboys*, the first compendium of such songs.

1910 John A. Lomax publishes *Cowboy Songs and Other Frontier Ballads*.

1917 Buffalo Bill dies.

1919 Trained concert singer Bentley Ball makes the first commercial recordings of cowboy songs.

1925 Carl T. Sprague becomes the first genuine cowboy to record a cowboy song with "When the Work's All Done This Fall" for Victor Records.

1929 Gene Autry makes his first recordings. Billie Maxwell becomes the first cowgirl singer to make a commercial record.

1934 Gene Autry appears in his first movie, *In Old Santa Fe*. The Sons of the Pioneers record "Tumbling Tumbleweeds," their first release.

1935 With Gene Autry's first starring role in a feature film, *Tumbling Tumbleweeds*, the singing cowboy era is launched. Patsy Montana's "I Want to Be a Cowboy's Sweetheart" is released and becomes a popular seller.

1937 Roy Rogers becomes Republic Studios' newest singing-cowboy star.

continues opposite 👉

The cowboy has long held a mythic status in American culture. He has ridden through the pages of literature and across movie screens, and he has had a huge impact on music. The once-lowly laborer on horseback from the trail-drive days of the late 1800s has been transformed through the years into the archetypal American icon, the embodiment of values Americans purport to hold dear—independence, hardiness, honesty, and self-reliance.

As Americans enter the 21st century they are still, amazingly, in the cowboy's thrall and still listening to his music. Cowboy songs originated as the occupational songs of working cowboys, in the same way that songs of sailors, loggers, and miners developed in those professions. People toiling in isolation and in perilous conditions, left to their own creativity for entertainment, have always crafted poems and songs. Those songs reflected the often-harsh realities of the life and work of the herders, from the dangerous work with horses and cattle, to the living

PORTABLE MUSIC
Out on lonely cattle drives, cowboys often sang unaccompanied or made music with small, easily portable instruments such as harmonicas.

conditions on the trail and in the cow camps. The cowboy repertoire also included non-occupational songs that dealt with other aspects of the western experience, such as immigration, outlaws, and Indians.

Many traditional cowboy songs were reworkings of folk and popular songs from the British Isles. For example, "The Streets of Laredo" was a cowboy version of a British and Irish broadside ballad, "The Unfortunate Rake." Likewise, "Bury Me Not on the Lone Prairie" came from the old sailor's song

HOME ON THE RANGE *A group of cowboys set up camp on the open range. It was here that the cowboy songs originated—in the wide-open spaces of the American West.*

"The Ocean Burial." Working cowboys also made up new songs out on the range, often setting the words to traditional or popular melodies. The borrowing of older melodies and the tailoring of lyrics to fit a new environment is a time-honored way of creating new works. These ranged from anonymous folk songs like "The Old Chisholm Trail," with verses added by many different people over time, to classic compositions, such as "When the Work's All Done This Fall," written by Montana cowboy poet D. J. O'Malley in 1893, and originally set to the melody of Charles K. Harris's popular Tin Pan Alley song of 1892, "After the Ball."

Working cowboys

The days of the long trail drives that gave rise to cowboy songs were over by the end of the 1800s. With the coming of the railroads after the Civil War and the invention of barbed wire in 1874, the open range gave way to ranches and fences strung with "the Devil's hatband." Cattle and cowboys no longer roamed as freely across the vast tracts of the West, and the cowboy's work changed accordingly. Instead of spending weeks and months on trail drives, he lived in bunkhouses or cow camps, and rode fences as he tended the cattle. In this different context, a rich new store of cowboy poetry and music was created.

WYOMING COWBOY, 1890s *The once-lowly laborer on horseback has become the archetypal American icon of today.*

1942 Gene Autry volunteers for the US Army Air Corps. Tex Ritter signs with Capitol Records.

1947 Roy Rogers and Dale Evans marry on New Year's Eve.

1951 *The Roy Rogers Show* debuts on the NBC television network.

1952 The movie western *High Noon*, starring Gary Cooper, is released. Tex Ritter sings the Oscar-winning theme song.

1954 *The Phantom Stallion*, which stars Rex Allen, is the last of the singing-cowboy westerns.

1959 Columbia Records releases Marty Robbins's popular *Gunfighter Ballads & Trail Songs* album, featuring the No. 1 country hit "El Paso."

1975 Willie Nelson's western-themed concept album *Red Headed Stranger* is released.

1977 Riders in the Sky form in Nashville.

1982 Riders in the Sky join the Grand Ole Opry.

1985 The first Cowboy Poetry Gathering is held in Elko, Nevada.

1986 The first WestFest, organized by Michael Martin Murphey, is held in Copper Mountain, Colorado.

1988 Western Music Association is formed.

1992 Warner Bros. Records launches the Warner Western subsidiary label.

2000 US Senate proclaims Elko, Nevada's cowboy convention the "National Cowboy Poetry Gathering."

The Show Goes On!
Buffalo Bill's Wild West

One of the most colorful figures of the Old West, William F. "Buffalo Bill" Cody revolutionized show business when he opened his first Wild West show in Nebraska in 1883. Almost immediately, Cody was hailed for his unique exposition, which featured a cast of authentic westerners—real cowboys and real Indians—in a series of dramatic reenactments based on his own Old West experiences. These now-historic shows formed the bedrock of America's romance with the West.

The original American western hero, Buffalo Bill lived a remarkable life. Born in Iowa in 1846, he was a wagon teamster at age 11, Pony Express rider at 14, and Union cavalryman at 17. He also distinguished himself as a dead-eye marksman and brave Indian scout. Sporting long hair and a goatee, Cody cut a dashing figure in his ten-gallon Stetson and rugged buckskins. His influence continues today in the dress of country singers, western performers, and Hollywood actors.

Buffalo Bill achieved national fame in 1869, when dime novelist Ned Buntline featured him in a wildly popular fictional story. Yet Buffalo Bill's real adventures needed no exaggeration. By October 23, 1869, he had crammed seven expeditions and nine Indian fights into one year and 23 days, and he had been widely proclaimed "Champion Buffalo Hunter of the Plains." Throughout his career, Cody used his fame as a platform for western causes—particularly the plight of Indians and conservation—and he never shied away from self-promotion. He enjoyed renown as a star actor between 1872 and 1883, portraying himself in Buffalo Bill melodramas.

But it is his Wild West exposition for which Cody is best remembered. A wily showman, he introduced the first "King of the Cowboys," Buck Taylor, to the Wild West cast. Then, in his cleverest move, he brought the teenaged "Annie Oakley" (Phoebe Ann Moses) to the spotlight as the world's most famous sharpshooter, and she soon became his star attraction. Cody also hired warriors who were once enemies, even Chief Sitting Bull, to help preserve and celebrate American Indian culture.

The show's popularity exploded when it reached Chicago, New York, and London. By 1900, Buffalo Bill was arguably the most recognizable man in the world. His great success ultimately inspired hundreds of imitation Wild West shows, which led to the development of professional rodeo.

On his deathbed, in 1917, Cody's dying words were reportedly, "Let my show go on." And so it has!

MICHAEL MARTIN MURPHEY

BUFFALO BILL *William Frederick Cody, former Pony Express rider and Union Army officer, fanned the flames of America's ardor for cowboys with his traveling Wild West shows.*

TRICK SHOT *Left: Sharpshooter Annie Oakley was one of the star attractions of Buffalo Bill's shows. Right: Buffalo Bill and Sioux Chief Sitting Bull pose for a formal portrait in 1885; the chief was a featured performer in the Wild West shows.*

MAC'S HAYWIRE ORCHESTRY

HAYWIRE MAC *Harry "Haywire Mac" McClintock (far right) sang cowboy songs on radio as early as 1925 and on recordings starting in 1928. His best-known song was the 1928 hobo anthem "Big Rock Candy Mountains."*

Since it was difficult for cowboys to carry instruments on trail drives, most singing was done unaccompanied, although smaller pocket instruments like harmonicas and Jew's harps (jaw harps) were common, and fiddles could be carried in a bedroll. Living in the bunkhouse provided a time and place for the guitar, mandolin, and banjo, and some of the finest and most enduring of traditional cowboy songs come from this ranch period—California cowboy Curley Fletcher created "The Strawberry Roan," and Arizona's Gail Gardner penned "The Sierry Petes (Tying Knots in the Devil's Tail)."

Cowboy songs owe much of their popularity and durability to the collectors and folklorists who published them. The first such printed collection

was *Songs of the Cowboys*, a small booklet privately published in 1908 by New Mexico cowboy N. Howard "Jack" Thorp. Two years later, in 1910, folklorist John A. Lomax published *Cowboy Songs and Other Frontier Ballads*. These and subsequent cowboy song collections made the words to songs widely available, not only to cowboys but also to other singers and musicians who added them to their repertoires.

New technologies

The 1920s saw the advent of three new technologies that would further transform and disseminate cowboy songs and music. These were, not coincidentally, the same technologies that expanded hillbilly music—the radio, the phonograph, and the motion picture. A number of real cowboys brought their music

HOHNER HARMONICAS *German harmonica maker Matthias Hohner introduced mass-produced harmonicas to the USA in 1862. Legend has it that famous sheriff Wyatt Earp and outlaws Billy the Kid and Frank James were harmonica players. This 19th-century advertisement shows Hohner himself selling harmonicas to buyers from around the world.*

John Lomax—Corralling the Cowboy Songs

Although John Lomax's *Cowboy Songs and Other Frontier Ballads* (1910) is considered a landmark work in America's cultural history, it was only by happenstance that Lomax set out to collect the material that gave the book its title.

At Harvard in 1907, for his master's degree in English, Lomax (1867–1948) enrolled in Barrett Wendell's "Literary History of America" course. Students came from around the country; Wendell asked each one to concentrate on the literature of his particular region. Lomax first suggested Negro music, a longstanding interest he would later pursue in depth, but Wendell, the Boston Brahmin, dismissed that as paltry and insignificant. Casting about for a second choice, Lomax came up with "songs of the cowboys," to which Wendell responded enthusiastically.

Later, there would be stories about Lomax roaming the Southwest by horseback with a primitive cylinder recorder strapped to the saddle, collecting songs from cowpunchers on cattle drives or gathered around chuck-wagon campfires. In fact, most of the contents of *Cowboy Songs* came to him through the mail or from lyrics printed in newspapers and magazines that circulated in rural regions. He did make one trip through Texas, New Mexico, and Arizona, but traveled mostly by rail. Moreover, he cribbed 19 songs from N. Howard "Jack" Thorp's little booklet, *Songs of the Cowboys*, published by the author in 1908, yet claimed those songs were "never before in print."

Lomax seems to have held a rather loose and romantic notion of what constituted "cowboy folk songs." As folklorist James McNutt has remarked, the material in *Cowboy Songs* was "neither so western nor so cowboy as [Lomax] asserted," but rather "the synthetic products of folk, popular, and elite composers." "Home on the Range," for example, was later discovered to have been printed in a Kansas newspaper in 1873, "composed" by a doctor and amateur poet from Ohio.

All of that notwithstanding, *Cowboy Songs and Other Frontier Ballads* has had a wide and enduring influence on American culture. Nearing its century mark, it remains in print today, after six editions and countless reprintings. Without it, such national treasures as "Jesse James," "Little Joe the Wrangler," "The Old Chisholm Trail," "Git Along Little Dogies," and, of course, "Home on the Range," would have disappeared into the ether.

NOLAN PORTERFIELD

SONGS OF THE CATTLE TRAIL AND COW CAMP

JOHN A. LOMAX

COWBOY SONGBOOK
John Lomax's groundbreaking collection Cowboy Songs and Other Frontier Ballads *(1910) proved to be such a success that he followed it with this 1919 sequel,* Songs of the Cattle Trail and Cow Camp, *which was reprinted in two subsequent editions.*

TURNING POINT *Ken Maynard may have been the featured star of* In Old Santa Fe *(1934), but Hollywood newcomer Gene Autry stole the picture with his melodious songs and easygoing charm.*

from the bunkhouse to the radio, and radio cowboy singers proliferated across the country. Harry "Haywire Mac" McClintock was singing cowboy and hobo songs on radio station KFRC in San Francisco as early as 1925. Jules Verne Allen, a Texas cowboy, performed on stations WFAA in Dallas and KFI and KNX in Los Angeles around the same time that the Arizona Wranglers were broadcasting on KTAR in Phoenix. John I. White, who was a not a real cowpoke but was one of the first to adopt the persona and repertoire, became well known as "The Lonesome Cowboy" on New York stations WEAF and WOR, beginning in 1926.

Taking this cue, recording companies sensed a niche market, as they had with hillbilly music, and quickly moved to record cowboy songs and music. Concert singer Bentley Ball made the first commercial phonograph record of a

TEXAN COWBOY *Carl T. Sprague grew up on a Texas ranch and had been a working cowboy when he recorded "When the Work's All Done This Fall," in 1925. It became a hit as well as the first western song recorded by a genuine cowboy.*

Ken Maynard - 6

cowboy song in 1919, when he recorded "Jesse James" and "The Dying Cowboy." Vernon Dalhart and Charles Nabell both took a stab at recording cowboy songs in 1924. However, it was a 30-year-old, ranch-born Texan, Carl T. Sprague, who really got the recording of cowboy music rolling with his 1925 classic, "When the Work's All Done This Fall." According to some accounts, the record sold as many as 900,000 copies.

A number of authentic cowboys quickly followed in Sprague's footsteps, including Oklahoma rancher Otto Gray, and the Cartwright Brothers from Texas. Pseudo-cowboys also jumped on the bandwagon, and through their affectation of cowboy attire and the popularization of western music they further developed an increasingly romantic image of the iconic cowboy. Most notable among these performers was Jimmie Rodgers. Although best known as "The Singing Brakeman" for his years of railroad work prior to his recording career, Rodgers adopted a cowboy persona when he moved to Texas. The tubercular singer was photographed in cowboy garb and recorded western-themed songs, such as "When the Cactus is in Bloom," "Cowhand's Last Ride," and "Yodeling Cowboy."

Big stars in movies

The third new entertainment medium, the motion picture, was also quick to trot up the cowboy trail—*In Old Arizona*, an early sound movie released in January 1929, included music. In October 1929, cowboy actor, stuntman, and singer Ken Maynard was featured in the film *The Wagon Master*, and he went on to become the first "singing cowboy" movie

star in a career that would continue until 1945. Being first, however, did not make him preeminent. Maynard was soon eclipsed by Gene Autry, who parlayed his success as a star of radio and records into a movie career as the nation's most popular saddle-riding singer.

The Texas-born Autry had begun his recording career in 1929. Primarily emulating his idol, Jimmie Rodgers, he enjoyed regional acclaim as a star of WLS's *National Barn Dance* radio show in Chicago. In 1934, he was picked to play a walk-on singing role in Maynard's film *In Old Santa Fe*. Autry stole the picture with his easygoing charm and earned good reviews for his singing—as well

YODELING COWBOY *Before western attire was fashionable in country music, Jimmie Rodgers tried out the look. The cowpoke image went well with the handful of cowboy songs he recorded.*

GUNSLINGER *Actor Ken Maynard became the first singing cowboy in Hollywood movies in 1929. But he was quickly eclipsed by Gene Autry.*

PROFILES IN COUNTRY

NAT LEVINE

BORN NEW YORK CITY, JULY 26, 1900
DIED AUGUST 6, 1989
BUSINESS AFFILIATIONS MASCOT PICTURES, REPUBLIC PICTURES, MGM STUDIOS

Mascot Pictures chief Nat Levine played a key role in launching Gene Autry as the biggest singing cowboy in history, but that was just part of his influential career.

Levine formed the innovative Mascot Pictures in 1926. His 1927 serial *Heroes of the Wild* was the first to have a "trio" hero, consisting of the cowboy, his gifted horse, and his dog. In 1932, he signed newcomer John Wayne. Mascot's *The Devil Horse* (1932) used Rossini's "William Tell Overture" as background music for its equine footage (a brainstorm later co-opted by *The Lone Ranger* on radio and then TV). Levine also transformed wonder dog Rin Tin Tin into a star of the talkies.

After seeing cowboy singer Ken Maynard in 1933's *The Strawberry Roan*, Levine decided to make musical westerns. Autry, then a Chicago radio star, badgered him for months, begging for a movie job. Levine initially thought the singer not virile enough. Still, Levine took a chance. In 1935, Autry starred in *Tumbling Tumbleweeds*, his first full-length feature, which made him a national star. After merging Mascot with Republic Pictures in 1935, Levine was placed in charge of production. He was bought out for $2 million in 1937.

ROBERT K. OERMANN

GENE AUTRY

BORN NEAR TIOGA, TEXAS,
SEPTEMBER 29, 1907
DIED OCTOBER 2, 1998
PLAYED GUITAR
FIRST RECORDED 1929
INFLUENCES JIMMIE RODGERS
HITS "THAT SILVER HAIRED DADDY
OF MINE," "BACK IN THE SADDLE
AGAIN," "SOUTH OF THE BORDER"

Gene Autry's popularity in the
1930s helped turn hillbilly music
into a national sensation, while
his mellifluous blend of country,
western, and pop redefined the
Saturday-afternoon western.

Orvon Grover Autry was born
the son of an itinerant horse trader
and sometime bootlegger. He
started singing at age five in his
grandfather's Baptist church.

In 1928, Autry began a stint
as "Oklahoma's Yodeling
Cowboy" at Tulsa radio station
KVOO, and went to Manhattan
in 1929 to cut his first sides. His
breakthrough came with the
plaintive ballad, "That Silver
Haired Daddy of Mine," which
he cowrote and recorded for the
American Record Corporation.

In 1931, Autry moved to
Chicago to star on the WLS
National Barn Dance. There, he
honed his western image and
focused on cowboy songs and
in 1934 moved to film. Beginning
with *Tumbling Tumbleweeds*
(1935), his work became the
prototype for the musical western,
while the songs featured in his
pictures became hits. Over four
decades, Autry recorded some
600 sides, half of which he was
credited with writing. Many have
become western standards.

HOLLY GEORGE-WARREN

"I wanted to be like Gene
Autry. I wanted to ride
off into the sunset."

MARTY ROBBINS

MARQUEE STAR *In the 1930s and 1940s, Gene Autry was a sure-fire box-office attraction. No wonder his name dwarfed the title of* Gold Mine in the Sky *(1938).*

as the attention of the executives at Republic Pictures. In 1935, he won the starring role in *Tumbling Tumbleweeds.* The film became a box-office hit and launched an acting career that would see him star in nearly 100 movies. He also went on to enjoy a long and successful recording career and to become a fixture on the emerging new medium of television in the 1950s.

Autry's success spawned a whole herd of aspiring singing cowboys. The first was Dick Foran, who enjoyed limited success at Warner Brothers Studios. He was followed by Ray Whitley, Smith Ballew, Bob Baker, Jack Randall, and Herb Jeffries (an African-American singer nicknamed "The Bronze Buckaroo"). Yet Autry's most serious competition as America's No. 1 Cowboy came from two other newcomers—Tex Ritter and Roy Rogers.

RIDING HIGH *Gene Autry astride his horse Champion. Almost singlehandedly Autry launched the singing-cowboy phenomenon in Hollywood movies. In addition, he had numerous hit records, including "South of the Border" and "Rudolph, the Red-Nosed Reindeer."*

CLASSIC COUNTRY RECORDING

GENE AUTRY
"Back in the Saddle Again"

I'm back in the saddle again, Out where a friend is a friend.
WRITTEN BY GENE AUTRY AND RAY WHITLEY AND RECORDED APRIL 18, 1939

The rousing western anthem **"Back in the Saddle Again"** became Gene Autry's theme song in 1939—the kick-off to his live performances and, from 1940 to 1956, his CBS radio show, *Melody Ranch Time.* "It kinda became part of me," Autry said in 1987.

The catchy tune was credited to Autry and Ray Whitley, a songwriter, singer, and B-western actor. The song's origins date to a 5 a.m. telephone call Whitley received from RKO Studios in 1938. The producers needed a number for an upcoming picture. Whitley reported the news to his sleepy wife, adding, "Well, I'm back in the saddle again!" "You've got a good song title right there!" she replied. Whitley quickly jotted down the first verse, and first performed the song in the 1938 film *Border G-Man.*

Autry, already a star, heard Whitley's recording and asked him to collaborate on a new version. He recorded the song on April 18, 1939, and issued it on OKeh Records that September. The release was timed to coincide with Autry's new film, *Rovin' Tumbleweeds,* which featured the number. Two years later, another Autry movie, *Back in the Saddle* (1941), was named for the song, as was Autry's 1978 memoir, published by Doubleday.
HOLLY GEORGE-WARREN

Cowboy Costumes

How did the costume of the cowboy—that hardworking drover of the plains or his gussied-up, rodeo-riding counterpart—come to epitomize the look of the country singer? Early on, rural entertainers typically wore their Sunday best. During the 1930s, though, with the huge popularity of the singing-cowboy movie, many country artists adopted a more dashing western style.

Chicago's *National Barn Dance*, on radio station WLS, was the first nationally prominent hillbilly venue to encourage its stars to don western garb. Before he started there in 1931, Gene Autry rarely dressed like a buckaroo. But station announcer Ann Williams pushed Autry to look the part, and the cowboy style became his signature, inspiring countless other WLS performers, including Patsy Montana & the Prairie Ramblers.

The style traveled to Nashville's Grand Ole Opry primarily through Pee Wee King, who along with his Golden West Cowboys, wore western shirts and matching pants, Stetsons, and cowboy boots. Although Zeke Clements had been the first to wear a cowboy outfit on the Opry stage, in 1930, the look didn't catch on with Opry performers until after King's arrival in 1937. Even then, it was not particularly welcomed by Opry MC George D. Hay. But the western look was already becoming fashionable from Nova Scotia—where Hank Snow adopted it early on—to California, where the style became widespread by the 1940s.

With the demand for eye-catching western outfits increasing, several custom tailors began wooing country stars as clients—the Philadelphia-based Ben the Rodeo Tailor, a favorite of Autry's; Nathan Turk, in Van

1 *Nudie designed this suit for Webb Pierce to commemorate his 1955 No. 1 hit "In the Jailhouse Now."*

2 *Nudie's label: a mark of quality, hillbilly status, and glamor.*

3 *Trisha Yearwood's boots emblazoned with her initials were inspired by a pair of boots owned by Hank Williams (see p. 154).*

4 *Although Patsy Cline's purple cowgirl dress looks like a Nudie creation, it was actually made by Patsy's mother, who designed many of her outfits.*

5 *This outfit belonged to Little Jimmy Dickens, the first Grand Ole Opry star to wear Nudie's rhinestone creations.*

6 *In a nod to tradition, Jason Ringenberg of Jason & the Scorchers wore this fringed cowboy shirt on the cover of the group's groundbreaking 1983 EP Fervor.*

7 *Classic-looking white boots owned by Dwight Yoakam.*

3

4

NUDIE'S CLIENTS *Nudie Cohn (center) with his customers: singers Tex Williams, Gene Autry, Roy Rogers, and Rex Allen.*

Nuys, California, whose regulars included Ernest Tubb and Rose Maddox and the Maddox Brothers, and North Hollywood tailor Nudie Cohn, more responsible than anyone else for country entertainers' over-the-top cowboy clothes. In 1950, Little Jimmy Dickens was the first Nashville-based artist to wear an embroidered Nudie suit onstage at the Opry. The next year, Lefty Frizzell became the first country singer to don a rhinestone-studded garment designed by Nudie. Other major Nudie clients included Hank Williams, Hank Snow, Webb Pierce, Ray Price, Faron Young, and Porter Wagoner. One of Nudie's staff, Manuel Cuevas, branched out on his own in the 1970s, becoming the bridge to the next generation of flashy western wearers.

HOLLY GEORGE-WARREN

HIGH STYLE *Webb Pierce, dressed in full Nudie regalia, beside his 1962 Pontiac Bonneville, spectacularly customized by Nudie.*

5

6

7

PROFILES IN COUNTRY

TEX RITTER

BORN PANOLA COUNTY, TEXAS,
JANUARY 12, 1905
DIED JANUARY 2, 1974
PLAYED GUITAR
FIRST RECORDED 1932
INFLUENCES JOHN LOMAX,
J. FRANK DOBIE
HITS "JINGLE JANGLE JINGLE,"
"I DREAMED OF A HILLBILLY
HEAVEN," "HIGH NOON"

Tex Ritter was the third most influential singing cowboy of the movies after Gene Autry and Roy Rogers, but he was arguably the most distinctive cowboy recording artist, with a thorough knowledge of frontier folklore that made his records sound authentically western.

The youngest of six children, Maurice Woodward Ritter got his early musical education through shape-note singing schools. While attending the University of Texas, he came under the influence of voice teacher and composer Oscar Fox, who kindled Ritter's interest in cowboy songs. After appearing on Houston radio, Ritter landed roles in New York stage productions and started his recording career. His 1933 ARC recording of "Rye Whiskey" became a regular component of his repertoire.

In 1936, Ritter gained his first starring role in a musical western with *Song of the Gringo*. Although his pictures were made for "Poverty Row" B studios Monogram and Grand National, he remained among the Top 10 western box-office stars.

Ritter signed with newly created Capitol Records in 1942, and went on to score 26 chart hits through four decades. In 1965, he moved to Nashville, where he joined the Grand Ole Opry, and exerted a key influence in the Country Music Association.

GUY LOGSDON

POSTER BOY *Tex Ritter made his movie debut in Grand National's* Song of the Gringo *in 1936. He went on to star in more than 50 westerns.*

> **HE WAS PRETTY MUCH IMITATED. A LOT OF THE COUNTRY ARTISTS, WHILE HE WAS LIVING AND AFTER HE DIED, TOOK GREAT JOY IN IMITATING HIS DISTINCTIVE TEAR IN HIS VOICE.**
>
> **ACTOR JOHN RITTER, SON OF TEX RITTER**

Tex Ritter became interested in cowboy songs while studying pre-law at the University of Texas, where he was influenced by folklore professors John Lomax and J. Frank Dobie. Ritter soon abandoned his pursuit of a law career and traveled to New York, where he got a job as a singing actor in the stage musical *Green Grow the Lilacs*. He also began a recording career with the American Record Corporation (ARC) in 1932. Four years later, Ritter got his first starring movie role in *Song of the Gringo* for Grand National Pictures. Although he went on to star in more than 50 westerns, he was unable to compete effectively at the box office with Autry—the studios he worked for, Grand National and Monogram, were both small and poorly financed.

Ritter made a greater impression on the public as a recording artist, singing in a rich, knotty baritone redolent of trail drives and campfires. After brief

TEX RITTER *The folksy cowboy star made a smooth transition from movies to hit records in the '40s just as his acting career was declining. In 1942, he became the first country act signed by Capitol Records, lauching a lifelong association with the label.*

KING OF THE COWBOYS *Roy Rogers,
who landed his first starring role in a western because Gene Autry was involved in a
contract dispute, assumed the role of "King
of the Cowboys" when Autry joined the
Army Air Corps in 1942.*

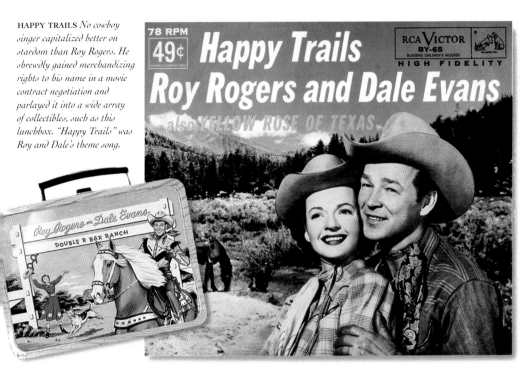

HAPPY TRAILS *No cowboy singer capitalized better on stardom than Roy Rogers. He shrewdly gained merchandizing rights to his name in a movie contract negotiation and parlayed it into a wide array of collectibles, such as this lunchbox. "Happy Trails" was Roy and Dale's theme song.*

stints with ARC and Decca Records, he was one of the first artists to sign with Capitol Records, in 1942. There, he recorded a string of popular country and western hits, including "Jingle Jangle Jingle," "Jealous Heart," "I Dreamed of a Hillbilly Heaven," and "High Noon," the Oscar-winning theme to the 1952 Gary Cooper western.

Roy Rogers—King Cowboy

Roy Rogers was a founding member of the influential Sons of the Pioneers. The Ohio-born singer subsequently left the group to take Gene Autry's place at Republic Pictures, first when Autry was boycotting the studio during contract negotiations, and later when Autry served in the Army Air Corps during World War II. Rogers quickly rose to the top ranks of western stars, becoming known as the "King of the Cowboys." During his long career he was a movie star, recording artist, and television star. Along with Autry and Ritter, Rogers did much to create the popular—if not altogether historically accurate—persona of the silver screen's singing cowboy.

This motion-picture phenomenon continued until 1954, when Rex Allen made *The Phantom Stallion*, generally regarded as the last singing-cowboy film. Unlike many other media cowboys, Allen was steeped in the western

experience. Born in Willcox, Arizona, he grew up on a ranch and competed in rodeos before becoming a professional musician. He first appeared on the *National Barn Dance* in 1945.

The image of the cowboy moved toward romantic fantasy as it was appropriated by the larger popular culture; at the same time, cowboy music and songs underwent significant changes. While cowboy songs traditionally had been sung unaccompanied or with simple guitar accompaniment, many audiences were used to more sophisticated musical arrangements from professional performers. Cowboy singers and musicians were competing in new media arenas with other contemporary musical forms, ranging from jazz and big-band swing to blues and hillbilly. As cowboy music moved from the trail to radio, records, and movies, influences from other forms of popular music were absorbed into the genre. By the 1930s, cowboy singers routinely performed with bands, utilizing guitars, fiddles, accordions, basses, and even horns on occasion, and musicians incorporated elements of pop music in their playing.

SONS OF THE PIONEERS *(Overleaf) Roy Rogers in a movie scene from the 1940s with his former band, the Sons of the Pioneers. From left: Hugh Farr, Bob Nolan, Roy Rogers, Karl Farr, Tim Spencer, Lloyd Perryman, Pat Brady.*

CLASSIC COUNTRY
RECORDING

THE SONS OF THE PIONEERS
"Tumbling Tumbleweeds"

See them tumbling down, pledging their love to the ground. Lonely but free I'll be found, drifting along with the tumbling tumbleweeds.

WRITTEN BY BOB NOLAN AND RECORDED AUGUST 8, 1934

Although its poetic, picturesque lyrics suggest a folk song of long standing, the western classic "Tumbling Tumbleweeds" was the creation of singer-songwriter Bob Nolan.

A founding member of the Sons of the Pioneers, Nolan began singing the song with the Sons during their hour-long radio broadcasts for Los Angeles station KFWB, starting around 1934. Originally, Nolan had written the song as "Tumbling Leaves," but when the radio audience kept asking for the number about "tumblin' weeds," Nolan realized the audience was on to something, and changed the tune slightly to accommodate the extra syllables. It was the second song cut at the group's first Decca recording session in 1934, and the group nailed it on the first take.

In 1935, it served as the title song for the first full-length cowboy movie starring Gene Autry, which kicked off the musical western trend. "Tumbling Tumbleweeds" was soon covered by such pop acts as Bing Crosby. The group recorded the song several times, and their 1948 version was a No. 11 country hit—yet another acknowledgment of the song's enduring power to evoke the beauty of the west.

GUY LOGSDON

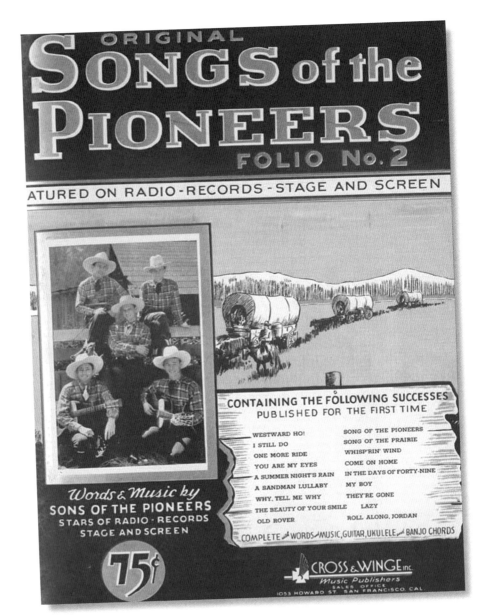

During the heyday of westerns from the 1930s to the 1950s, Hollywood attracted scores of actors, stuntmen, musicians, and songwriters, and a thriving western musical scene developed in southern California. Among the active cowboy groups were the Beverly Hill Billies and Jimmy LeFevre & His Saddle Pals. But the most influential group to come out of this scene was the Sons of the Pioneers, co-founded by Roy Rogers. The Pioneers featured a blend of close trio and (later) quartet harmony singing, backed with hot guitar and fiddle accompaniment that was noticeably influenced by the jazz records of guitarist Django Reinhardt and violinist Stephane Grappelli.

Two of the group's members, Bob Nolan and Tim Spencer, were among

SONGS OF THE PIONEERS *Starting in the early '30s, the Sons of the Pioneers revolutionized western music through their stirring trio and quartet harmonies. This songbook dates from 1939.*

western music's most gifted songwriters, penning such classics as "Cool Water" and "Tumbling Tumbleweeds" for the group, and helping to create a musical form more properly called "western" than "cowboy." Along with Tin Pan Alley songwriters Billy Hill, Fred Rose, and Nat Vincent and Fred Howard ("The Happy Chappies"), Nolan and Spencer established a new tradition of cowboy songs that, unlike the more realistic traditional songs, painted a highly romanticized picture of an idyllic West. The Sons of the Pioneers themselves appeared in a number of motion pictures singing behind Roy Rogers and others. The strong influence of the Pioneers continues today in the vocal harmony work of Riders in the Sky and the Sons of the San Joaquin.

A second major development in the evolution of western music took place in Texas and Oklahoma. There, Bob Wills and Milton Brown began shaping what eventually became known as western swing with their group the Light Crust Doughboys. Incorporating elements of old-time Texas fiddling, blues, jazz, and big-band swing, they forged what was then known as "hot string-band music"—a highly danceable style that took Texas and the rest of the Southwest by storm. Brown eventually left the Doughboys to form his own band, the

Musical Brownies, while Wills formed the Texas Playboys. The Playboys' style and big band-like instrumentation—which often included drums, electrified guitars, lap steel, piano, and horns, along with a heavily bowed fiddle—had a huge influence in both western and mainstream country music.

Like most of the prominent singing cowboy stars, Wills was based in the Los Angeles area in the 1940s. Wills and his Texas Playboys also starred in 13 Hollywood musical westerns, beginning in 1940 with *Take Me Back to Oklahoma* starring Tex Ritter.

BEVERLY HILL BILLIES *A popular act on L.A.'s radio station KMPC during the 1930s, the Beverly Hill Billies not only released several records but also appeared in several western movies with Ray Whitley, Gene Autry, and Tex Ritter.*

"When I watched Roy and Dale ride, shoot, and sing, for me it was always the music. They took me to another place, and I stayed there long after the film was over."

JOHNNY WESTERN

PROFILES IN COUNTRY
PATSY MONTANA

PATSY MONTANA *(center) Outside WLS studios with two friends, 1940.*

BORN (RUBY BLEVINS) JESSEVILLE, ARKANSAS, OCTOBER 30, 1908
DIED MAY 3, 1996
PLAYED GUITAR AND FIDDLE
FIRST RECORDED 1932
INFLUENCES JIMMIE RODGERS, STUART HAMBLEN
KEY HIT "I WANT TO BE A COWBOY'S SWEETHEART"

With her 1935 recording of "I Want to Be a Cowboy's Sweetheart," Patsy Montana became known as America's No. 1 cowgirl and was an early model for women in country music.

Her professional career began around 1930 in California, where she had gone to live with relatives. Stuart Hamblen, then a popular California country-music impresario, helped usher her into a trio called the Montana Cowgirls, and christened her Patsy Montana.

During a brief stint with a new group, The Prairie Ramblers, at WOR in New York, Montana recorded "I Want to Be a Cowboy's Sweetheart." When Montana and the band returned to Chicago, their music became more western in style, and the Prairie Ramblers with Patsy Montana became one of the most popular acts on the famous *National Barn Dance.*

During the later years of her career, Montana toured extensively in the USA and Europe, and continued to perform until shortly before her death in 1996.

WAYNE W. DANIEL

SISTERLY HARMONY *Known as the Girls of the Golden West, sisters Dollie and Millie Good specialized in trick yodeling and duet versions of western songs on the WLS National Barn Dance and other radio programs.*

Although working cowboys prior to the 20th century were nearly always men, women became involved in commercial western music early on. The first cowgirl to record was Billie Maxwell, an Arizonan who made six solo sides for Victor in July 1929, including "The Cowboy's Wife" and "The Arizona Girl I Left behind Me." At one of the sessions, she also recorded several other songs as part of her father's cowboy string band, the White Mountain Orchestra. Other early cowgirl singers included Kitty Lee, who performed with husband Powder River Jack Lee; Buerl Sisney, who billed herself as "The Lonesome Cowgirl"; and Louise Massey of the Massey family, who starred at the *National Barn Dance* and on records as the lead singer of Louise Massey & the Westerners.

Patsy Montana
It was a young woman from rural Hope, Arkansas—Patsy Montana—who became the first singing cowgirl star. Born Ruby Blevins, she began her singing career in Los Angeles, performing as part of a trio called the Montana Cowgirls and becoming acquainted with Stuart Hamblen and others active in the local western music scene. In 1933, she earned a slot at WLS in Chicago, where she hooked up with the Kentucky Ramblers, one of the hottest string bands of the era. The group changed its name to the Prairie Ramblers to match Patsy's cowgirl image and began recording for Victor. In 1935, the Ramblers backed Montana on the classic "I Want to Be a Cowboy's Sweetheart," which became a runaway best-seller. Patsy Montana's success paved the way for a number of cowgirl singers, including Rosalie Allen, Texas Ruby, Jenny Lou Carson, and the Girls of the Golden

West. Montana's influence is still heard today in the singing of contemporary artists, such as Suzy Bogguss, Liz Masterson, and Eli Barsi.

Years of decline
As the popularity of the singing cowboy films faded, national interest in cowboy and western music also waned. Most cowboy artists drifted into mainstream country music and, despite the ongoing currency of the term "country and western," after 1960 only a negligible trace of western influence remained in the genre. The onslaught of rock & roll also shifted popular music's center of gravity. A few performers, including the Wagonmasters, the Flying W Wranglers, and Singin' Sam Agins, continued in the western vein, but they performed mostly at dude ranches and western theme parks. A handful of traditional performers found a place in the folk-music revival of the late 1950s and early

COWBOY'S SWEETHEART *Patsy Montana became the first singing cowgirl star with her best-selling recording of "I Want to Be a Cowboy's Sweetheart" in 1935. She went on to have a long career, performing into her eighties.*

CLASSIC COUNTRY
RECORDING

PATSY MONTANA
"I Want to Be a Cowboy's Sweetheart"

I wanna be a cowboy's sweetheart, I wanna learn to rope and to ride...,
WRITTEN BY PATSY MONTANA AND RECORDED ON AUGUST 16, 1935

Leave it to a tough-minded cowgirl to record one of the biggest country records of the 1930s. Arkansas native Patsy Montana had seen her share of cow ponies—thanks to some Oklahoma relatives and several stints singing western songs in California—though she'd never ridden herd. But it was true love, along with a suggestion from Gene Autry's manager, that inspired the song.

After arriving at Chicago's WLS in 1933, Montana adopted Stuart Hamblen's "Texas Plains" as her theme song, converting it to "Montana Plains." It was popular with audiences as she toured with an outfit of WLS performers, road-managed by Paul Rose, with whom Patsy became smitten.

One day, Autry's manager, J. L. Frank, handed Montana a scrap of paper on which he'd scribbled "cowboy's sweetheart," saying he thought the idea could become a song. Soon after, Paul Rose rushed back to Tennessee to comfort his sick grandmother. One night, feeling lonely for her beau (and future husband), Montana came across Frank's note and started writing.

Backed by the Prairie Ramblers, the 26-year-old recorded the song, marked by her exuberant yodeling, for the American Record Corporation in New York. The song quickly became a runaway hit, and remained a surefire showstopper.

HOLLY GEORGE-WARREN

I WANT TO BE A COWBOY'S SWEETHEART
by PATSY MONTANA

And That's How The Riders Were Born

YOUNG RIDERS *Too Slim, Ranger Doug, and Woody Paul in the group's early days.*

Nineteen seventy-seven was not an optimal time to start a cowboy band. Western music was dead, relegated to nostalgia when thought of at all. What group of young men in their right minds would build a career on the sound and style of 40 years ago?

To us, the draw was the music itself. We found the songs of Roy Rogers and Gene Autry refreshing, the music of the Sons of the Pioneers inspirational. Their songs got hold of us and would not let us go. We knew that this band had to work in the present day as well as pay homage to the past, so we built in quips, skits, characterizations, political references, and tongue-in-cheek humor, hoping we didn't end up a dry exercise in history or a sophomoric spoof. It's a fine line we've walked from the start.

The start. It went like this. I, Douglas Green, editor at the Country Music Foundation and semiprofessional musician, had been singing cowboy songs in bands for several years. I became infatuated with the Sons of the Pioneers after seeing them live in Tulsa in 1974, and wanted to put together a harmony group. Then folk singer Patty Hall canceled an appearance at a Nashville dive due to the flu, and asked me to cover.

I called Fred LaBour and Willie Collins to join me. "Can I play the upright bass?" asked LaBour, a recent convert from the electric. "You have to play the upright bass!" I replied. "But I don't have a hat," he responded. "I'll loan you a hat!" I said.

The show went well; the eight drunks enjoyed our sketchily rehearsed set. At evening's end we split the $25 three ways, tearing the final dollar bill in thirds to celebrate. That was November 11, 1977.

Amazingly, more dates came in. Fred (Too Slim by then) and I (rechristened Ranger Doug) gave up our day jobs. Willie (Windy Bill) dropped out. Woody Chrisman (Woody Paul) joined us on fiddle, and Tommy Goldsmith sat in on guitar for awhile. We settled down as a trio for a dozen years before Joey Miskulin (Joey the Cowpolka King) made us a quartet.

Along the way, we've been blessed with two Grammy Awards, movie appearances (notably *Toy Story 2*), and more than 5,000 personal appearances. It's been a great ride.

DOUGLAS B. GREEN

1960s, among them Glenn Ohrlin, a buckaroo, rodeo rider, and rancher based in Arkansas, and Harry Jackson, who recorded an LP of cowboy songs for Folkways Records.

In the late 1970s the first signs of a cowboy and western resurgence began to appear. Willie Nelson released his western-themed album *Red Headed Stranger* in 1975 and was soon joined by Waylon Jennings, Tompall Glaser, and others in the short-lived but influential Outlaw movement. In 1977, the cowboy group Riders in the Sky formed in Nashville. The group combined close harmony singing with hot instrumental accompaniment in the style of the Sons of the Pioneers and added a clean, but clever brand of off-the-wall humor. Led by "Ranger Doug" Green, they quickly gained a cult following that led to numerous albums, a popular public radio show, a Saturday morning children's show for CBS-TV, and a 1982 membership in the Grand Ole Opry. The 1970s also saw the emergence of bronc rider Chris LeDoux, who began recording rodeo-themed songs on his own Lucky Man label. After Garth Brooks mentioned him in his 1989 song "Much Too Young (To Feel This Damn Old)," LeDoux was signed to Capitol records and had a few of his compositions covered by Brooks and other mainstream country artists.

COWBOY'S RETURN *Willie Nelson's western-themed* Red Headed Stranger *album of 1975 helped signal a revival of interest in cowboys and cowboy music.*

Other offshoots of cowboy culture, including the oral tradition of cowboy poetry, caught on during the 1980s. In 1985, a group of western folklorists led by Jim Griffith and Hal Cannon organized the first Cowboy Poetry Gathering, held in Elko, Nevada. Although it focused primarily on the traditional poetry of working cowboys, it featured a strong musical component as well. State folklorists in the West did extensive fieldwork to locate and identify traditional cowboy poets and musicians, and then brought them to Elko. The Gathering was intended to be a one-time event, but the response from the ranching community and the general public was so overwhelming that it became an annual festival, and in 2004 celebrated its 20th anniversary. In addition to reacquainting old-timers with traditional poetry and music, the event inspired younger generations to write and perform material drawn from the contemporary western and ranching experience. In 2000, the United States Senate proclaimed the annual Elko festival the National Cowboy Poetry Gathering, largely in response to its role as a model for nearly 300 similar events throughout the West. Taken together, such developments have been widely termed a "cowboy renaissance."

National revival

The rekindled interest in western writing and music inspired by the National Cowboy Poetry Gathering and its progeny has bolstered the careers of a number of contemporary performers. Traditional cowboy singers such as Glenn Ohrlin, the late Buck Ramsey, Duane Dickinson, and Don Hedgepeth have earned a special place in the hearts of cowboy music audiences. Ohrlin and Ramsey both received National Heritage Fellowships from the National Endowment for the

Arts, the nation's highest award given to traditional artists. Canadian singer Ian Tyson, formerly of the 1960s folk duo Ian & Sylvia, has become something of a western icon for his literate and powerful songs about life in the West. Red Steagall, who enjoyed success as a singer and songwriter in country music and western swing, has also become an accomplished cowboy poet. And since the mid-1980s, Texas-born singer-songwriter Michael Martin Murphey has stepped away from a career in pop and mainstream country music to become a strong force in the rejuvenation of the western genre; in 1986, he organized the first WestFest in Copper Mountain, Colorado, and continues the event in various locales today.

As the cowboy and western music revival picked up steam, a supporting infrastructure began to emerge. The proliferation of cowboy music and

ELKO FESTIVAL *In 2004, the annual Cowboy Poetry Gathering in Elko, Nevada, celebrated its 20th anniversary. This two-CD set was released to mark the occasion.*

GLENN OHRLIN *Former rodeo bronco rider Glenn Ohrlin did his part to keep authentic cowboy songs alive during the lean years of the '60s and '70s, and went on to become a mainstay of the cowboy festival circuit.*

RED STEAGALL *Originally a mainstream country singer with several chart hits in the '70s, Steagall moved easily and comfortably into cowboy music in the 1980s. Today, in addition to being a popular cowboy singer, he's also renowned as a cowboy poet.*

poetry events created a circuit that provided artists with venues and performing opportunities throughout the year. In 1988, the Western Music Association, patterned loosely after the Country Music Association and the International Bluegrass Music Association, was formed to promote western music. In 1992, at the urging of Michael Martin Murphey, Warner Bros. Records launched its subsidiary Warner Western label, with a roster that included Red Steagall, the Sons of the San Joaquin, and cowboy poet Waddie Mitchell. One of the most important artists to record for Warner Western was Don Edwards. After performing for some 40 years, Edwards saw his career take off through his Warner Western recordings and his appearances at the National Cowboy Poetry Gathering in Elko. Edwards also enjoyed a prominent supporting role as Smokey, Robert

Redford's singing sidekick, in Redford's 1997 film *The Horse Whisperer*. He continues to be one of the most popular interpreters of old-time cowboy music.

Warner Bros. eliminated the Warner Western label in the late 1990s, but the torch was picked up by Colorado-based Western Jubilee Records, now the recording home of Waddie Mitchell, the Sons of the San Joaquin, Don Edwards, Wylie Gustafson, and Rich O'Brien. Many other western artists have created their own record labels, and the level of activity continues to increase. Among the numerous western performers active today are Joni Harms, Stephanie Davis, Chuck Milner, Mike Beck, Gary McMahan, the Gillette Brothers, Andy Wilkinson, R. W. Hampton, Gail Steiger, Sourdough Slim (Rick Crowder), Lorraine Rawls, the Quebe Sisters, Stan Howe, New West, and Jesse Ballantyne.

It is somewhat surprising that what some might have seen as an anachronistic form of folk song not only persists, but continues to inspire new music in the tradition. In the 1960s, no one could have predicted that cowboy and western music would enjoy its recent resurgence, taking its rightful place as a cherished regional subgenre on the American musical scene, along with Cajun music, blues, old-time string-band music, and bluegrass. But after some 25 years of popular revival, there is no sign that interest in the genre is flagging. In fact, it continues to increase, with new events, festivals, and performers coming along all the time. Most importantly, the music continues to reflect not only the past but also the contemporary experiences of the men and women of the West who work to make a living on the treasured land today.

TOP TEN

FAVORITE COWBOY RECORDS OF RANGER DOUG OF RIDERS IN THE SKY

What a tough assignment! There is so much great western music, there are so many eras, so many decades, so many wonderful voices and recordings. How do you stop? Where do you fit in "Song of the Sierras" by Jimmy Wakely, "Hannah Lee" by Johnny Western, "The Red Headed Stranger" and "Cattle Call" by Eddy Arnold, "Riders in the Sky" by Vaughn Monroe? Where do you put Marty Robbins, the Riders of the Purple Sage, Patsy Montana, Eddie Dean? Ten is just too few to cover the spectrum of that beautiful western music I love. It would be easier to do a Top 50, but here goes. These are the recordings I don't think I could live without.
—RANGER DOUG

1 **"Blue Shadows on the Trail"**
Roy Rogers & The Sons of the Pioneers *(RCA, 1948)*

2 **"Call of the Rolling Plains"**
Andy Parker & the Plainsmen (Capitol radio transcription, ca. 1950)

3 **"Tumbling Tumbleweeds"**
The Sons of the Pioneers (RCA, 1946)

4 **"Outlaws"**
The Sons of the Pioneers (RCA, 1952)

5 **"Too Lee Rollum (I'm an Arizona Cowboy)"**
Rex Allen (Mercury, 1950)

6 **"South of the Border (Down Mexico Way)"**
Gene Autry (Vocalion, 1939)

7 **"Blue Prairie"**
The Sons of the Pioneers (RCA, 1946)

8 **"Give Me a Pinto Pal"**
Elton Britt (RCA, 1954)

9 **"Rye Whiskey"**
Tex Ritter (Capitol, 1948)

10 **"The Everlasting Hills of Oklahoma"**
The Sons of the Pioneers (RCA, 1952)

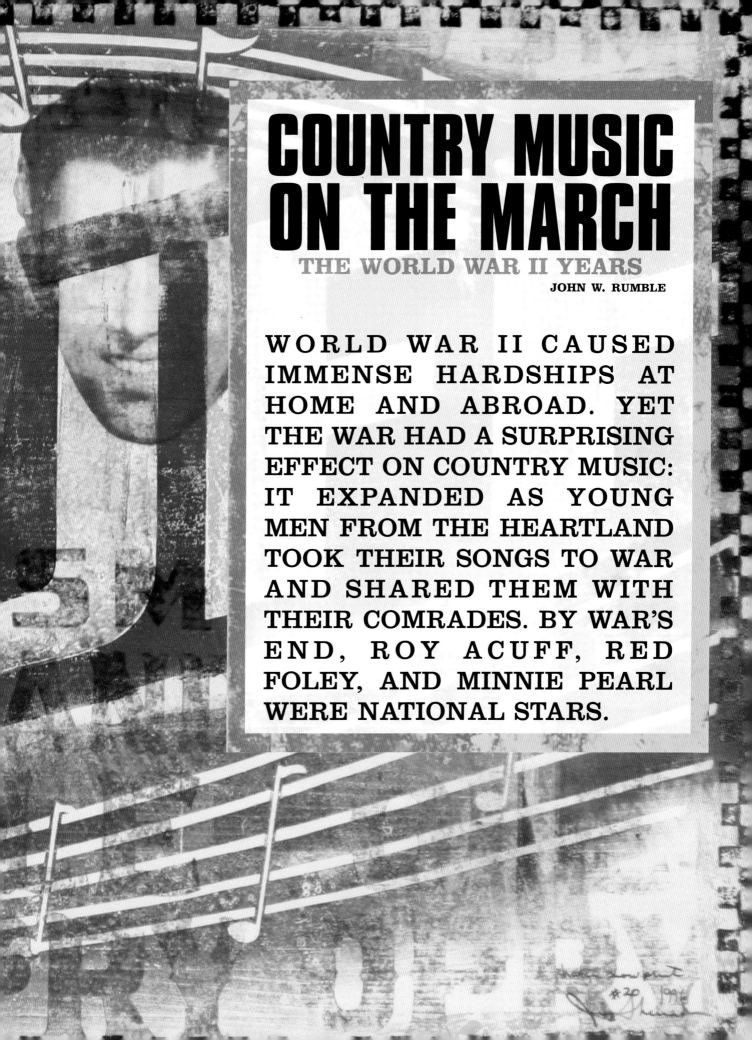

COUNTRY MUSIC ON THE MARCH

THE WORLD WAR II YEARS

JOHN W. RUMBLE

WORLD WAR II CAUSED IMMENSE HARDSHIPS AT HOME AND ABROAD. YET THE WAR HAD A SURPRISING EFFECT ON COUNTRY MUSIC: IT EXPANDED AS YOUNG MEN FROM THE HEARTLAND TOOK THEIR SONGS TO WAR AND SHARED THEM WITH THEIR COMRADES. BY WAR'S END, ROY ACUFF, RED FOLEY, AND MINNIE PEARL WERE NATIONAL STARS.

1940–1945 TIMELINE

1940 Germany invades France, the Low Countries, Denmark, and Norway. Jukeboxes number 300,000 across the USA. Jimmie Davis first records "You Are My Sunshine" for Decca Records. Sarah Ophelia Colley (better known as Minnie Pearl) makes her Grand Ole Opry debut. Franklin Roosevelt is reelected to his third term as US president. BMI (Broadcast Music Incorporated) begins licensing songs for airplay. Bob Wills records "San Antonio Rose" for the first time with lyrics; it's released as "New San Antonio Rose," soon to become a massive hit and a classic. The feature film *Grand Ole Opry*, starring Roy Acuff and Uncle Dave Macon, is released. Eddy Arnold joins Pee Wee King's Golden West Cowboys as lead singer.

1941 The day after the Japanese attack on Pearl Harbor on December 7, the USA enters World War II. Ernest Tubb records his first hit, "Walking the Floor over You," for Decca Records. Songwriter Cindy Walker lands her first hit—on the pop charts—with Bing Crosby's recording of "Lone Star Trail."

1942 Elton Britt's recording "There's a Star Spangled Banner Waving Somewhere" receives country music's first gold record, awarded by RCA Victor. The Venice Pier opens, becoming the top western dance spot in Los Angeles. Capitol Records is founded in Los Angeles. The national musicians'

continues opposite

In 1945, as Japanese soldiers charged an Allied position on Okinawa, they shouted what they considered the ultimate insult for any US soldier: "To hell with Roosevelt! To hell with Babe Ruth! To hell with Roy Acuff!" In a single epithet the enemy targeted America's most popular president, its most revered sports hero, and arguably the era's leading singer of country music. Acuff was being cursed, all right, but he was certainly in good company. In a sense, it was the highest praise he ever received.

In many ways, this Japanese battle cry spoke volumes about changes that World War II brought to country music, changes that propelled Acuff to the front ranks of the genre's rapidly maturing star system. What's more, these changes made possible his leadership in building Nashville's music industry, whose emergence symbolized a broad decentralization then evolving in the interlocking worlds of music publishing, recording, and broadcasting. Economic prosperity, increasing urbanization, and the sharing of sounds and styles by Americans in military service all boosted country music's national popularity and financial strength to new levels, while American forces stationed abroad laid groundwork for its postwar international growth. Moreover, the nation's patriotic mood raised country's status as a folk-rooted expression of American culture, whose core values of home, family, and religion Acuff projected as powerfully as any entertainer of the day. Looking back, the war years

WWII BADGES *Patriotic fervor ran high in the USA during the war.*

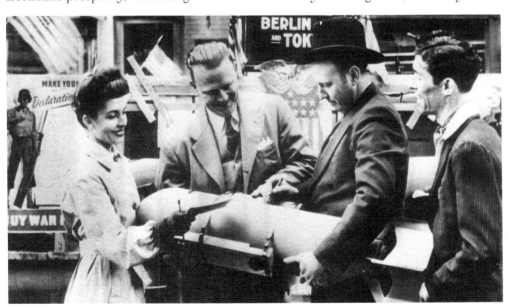

GIFT FOR THE AXIS *In a World War II publicity photo, country entertainers the Duke of Paducah, Bill Monroe, and Roy Acuff sign a bomb meant for the enemy.*

DAILY NEWS

2¢   2¢

JAPS BOMB HAWAII
DECLARE WAR ON U.S. AND BRITAIN

Stories on pages 2 and 3.

PEARL HARBOR *On December 7, 1941, Japanese carrier-launched aircraft unleashed a surprise attack on the naval base at Pearl Harbor, Hawaii, crippling the US Pacific fleet and killing some 2,500 men. The next day, America joined World War II against Japan and Germany.*

union goes on strike. For nearly two years, no new records can be made with American musicians. Roy Acuff and Fred Rose establish Acuff-Rose Publications, the first Nashville music publisher to focus on country music.

1943 The Grand Ole Opry moves to the Ryman Auditorium for a 30-year residency. Ernest Tubb joins the Grand Ole Opry cast. Soon to be a leading independent record label in country and R&B, King Records begins issuing its first records. Eddy Arnold leaves Pee Wee King's band and goes solo.

1944 D-Day—The Allies invade Normandy and begin to push the German occupiers back to Germany. President Franklin D. Roosevelt is reelected for an unprecedented fourth term. Eddy Arnold makes his first record. Jimmie Davis begins his first term as governor of Louisiana. *Billboard* begins its first "Hillbilly" record charts. The feature film *National Barn Dance*, starring Lulu Belle & Scotty and the Hoosier Hot Shots, is released. Hill & Range Songs, soon to be a major music publisher in country music, is founded in New York.

1945 President Roosevelt dies and is succeeded by Vice President Harry Truman. Winston Churchill is unseated as British prime minister. The USA drops atom bombs on Hiroshima and Nagasaki, and World War II comes to a close. Roy Acuff bests Frank Sinatra in a popularity poll of US servicemen stationed in Germany.

CLASSIC COUNTRY
RECORDING

ELTON BRITT
"There's a Star Spangled Banner Waving Somewhere"

There's a star spangled banner waving somewhere. In that heaven there should be a place for me.
WRITTEN BY SHELBY DARNELL (BOB MILLER) AND PAUL ROBERTS; RECORDED ON MARCH 19, 1942

Of the many country songs about World War II, this hit perfectly caught the initial patriotic fervor of America's entry into the war. The song's first-person narrator is a handicapped lad from the hills, eager to defend American freedoms against "the mad dictators, leaders of corruption." If death be the cost, so much the better. That would be his ticket to a flag-draped American corner of heaven, where already one new hero named in the song—Colin Kelly (who crashed his damaged plane into a Japanese ship)—has taken a place in America's pantheon alongside "Lincoln, Custer, Washington, and Perry."

This was the hit that Arkansas yodeler Elton Britt had sought throughout a whole decade of recording. Popular on jukeboxes across the country, its longevity was no doubt stretched by the musicians' union strike, which banned new recordings after August 1, 1942. It inspired pop cover versions and sheet-music sales of more than 750,000 copies. RCA Victor gratefully awarded Britt a gold record after the recording's sales passed a million. Britt eventually donated this to the Country Music Hall of Fame and Museum.

RONNIE PUGH

PATRIOTIC COWBOY *In 1942, at the height of his career, Gene Autry volunteered for the Army Air Corps. He flew transport missions in the Far East and North Africa.*

not only witnessed Acuff's emergence as a star rivaling contemporary pop idols, but also marked country music's transformation from embarrassing poor relation to American success story.

Although most Americans hoped their nation would avoid the war Adolf Hitler started by invading Poland in September 1939, many came to realize that the USA could not abandon the British, who stood alone against the dictator after France fell in June 1940. Nor could America afford to let Germany or Japan control world trade, upon which the US economy depended. Led by President Franklin D.

SEWING THE STARS AND STRIPES
With able-bodied men joining the armed forces, many American women went to work in factories to help the war effort. Here a woman sews a flag for the army, 1942.

Roosevelt, Americans began preparing for war and, as they did, the economic expansion triggered by military production pulled the nation out of the Great Depression. By December 1941, when the Japanese attack on Pearl Harbor made the USA an official combatant, factories were humming again, employment was rising, and consumers had more money to buy records and show tickets, play jukeboxes, and settle bar tabs at honky-tonks, dancehalls, and clubs. As a result, the music industry bounced back from hard times with a vengeance.

Country radio's popularity

One consequence was the growth of country radio, fueled by sponsors whose products listeners could now afford more easily. Radio stations expanded existing shows and launched new ones. By 1944, nearly 600 country programs could be heard on outlets ranging from local

100-watters to 50,000-watt giants, such as Nashville's WSM, whose signal reached cities, towns, and farmhouses from the Rockies to the Eastern Seaboard. These shows allowed hundreds of country singers to pursue full- or part-time careers by selling songbooks and advertising show dates.

Country's radio barn dances continued to flourish. WLS's *National Barn Dance*, the key to Chicago's early prominence as a country-music center, had suffered in the late 1930s when Cincinnati's WLW, gaining temporary federal permission to broadcast at 500,000 watts—ten times the usual maximum of 50,000—had lured Red Foley, Lulu Belle & Scotty Wiseman, and other top *Barn Dance* stars to the *Boone County Jamboree* (renamed the *Midwestern Hayride* by 1945). In the early 1940s, though, many of these acts returned to the *National Barn Dance*, and some also appeared in their own network shows.

"Oh, radio was big then. Real big. It just got everything going."
COUNTRY BANDLEADER BILL WOODS

TENNESSEE SATURDAY NIGHT
This 1940s advertisement features several of the Grand Ole Opry's more popular acts of the time, such as Bill Monroe & His Blue Grass Boys, old-timer Dave Macon, and blackface comics Jamup & Honey.

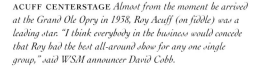

RED FOLEY

BORN BLUE LICK, KENTUCKY,
JUNE 17, 1910
DIED SEPTEMBER 19, 1968
PLAYED GUITAR
FIRST RECORDED 1933
INFLUENCES JOHN LAIR, BING CROSBY
HITS "OLD SHEP," "CHATTANOOGIE
SHOE SHINE BOY," "(THERE'LL BE)
PEACE IN THE VALLEY (FOR ME)"

One of the most versatile country
singers of his era, Clyde Julian
"Red" Foley could swing, croon,
and even turn in a credible
rockabilly recording. Over time,
he graduated from rustic string-
band musician to a suave and
urbane crooner who resembled
Bing Crosby, both in his singing
and in his relaxed, comedic style.
By 1946, when Foley was
recruited from WLS to replace
the popular Roy Acuff as host of
the Grand Ole Opry's coveted
NBC radio network segment,
the 36-year-old singer was a
seasoned stage veteran. He
remained in that role until 1953.

From his new base, Foley
and Ernest Tubb (a frequent
duet partner) built Decca
Records in Nashville; a foundation
stone was "Chattanoogie Shoe
Shine Boy," a No. 1 on the pop
charts in 1950. Afterwards,
the genial host parlayed his
enhanced profile into television
success elsewhere. From 1955
to 1960, he hosted ABC-TV's
Jubilee television programs
from Springfield, Missouri, and
in the early 1960s plied his acting
talents in Hollywood as part of
the ABC-TV cast of *Mr. Smith
Goes to Washington.*
MICHAEL STREISSGUTH

ACUFF CENTERSTAGE *Almost from the moment he arrived
at the Grand Ole Opry in 1938, Roy Acuff (on fiddle) was a
leading star. "I think everybody in the business would concede
that Roy had the best all-around show for any one single
group," said WSM announcer David Cobb.*

On country's thriving West Coast scene,
Gene Autry headlined the *Melody Ranch*
radio show from CBS's Los Angeles
studios, while KNX in Los Angeles
showcased Tex Ritter, Jimmy Wakely,
Foy Willing, Johnny Bond, and other
California-based stars on the CBS Pacific
Network's *Hollywood Barn Dance*. Country
performers could also be heard on
KMPC in Los Angeles, KYA in San
Francisco, and numerous other stations.
"Oh, radio was big then," bandleader Bill
Woods told historian Gerald Haslam.
"Real big. It just got everything going."

Hollywood beckons

Hollywood filmmakers had recruited
country radio talent ever since Gene Autry
made the groundbreaking transition from
hillbilly radio star to cowboy movie idol
in the mid-1930s. With the war's country
music groundswell, movie moguls looked
to western-swing bandleader Bob Wills,
Roy Acuff, Ernest Tubb, and others to
fill lead and supporting roles. Hollywood
also spotlighted radio barn dances. The
film *Grand Ole Opry* (Republic, 1940)
featured vaudeville greats the Weaver
Brothers & Elviry—among the first to
create hillbilly characters—and costarred
Uncle Dave Macon, Roy Acuff & His
Smoky Mountain Boys, and Opry founder
George D. Hay. *National Barn Dance*
(Paramount, 1944) starred Lulu Belle &
Scotty, the Hoosier Hot Shots, and other
Barn Dance favorites.

By World War II, the Opry had
shouldered its way to the top of the country
radio world, owing much to the efforts of
a triumvirate of young, energetic, behind-
the-scenes businessmen—Harry Stone,
who had replaced George D. Hay as
WSM manager in 1932; Stone's brother
David, who served as staff announcer
and ran the Opry's booking department
(until 1940); and program director Jack
Stapp (who arrived in 1939). In 1939,
WSM convinced the R. J. Reynolds
Tobacco Company to sponsor a half-hour
NBC radio segment known as the *Prince
Albert Show*, after Prince Albert Smoking

Tobacco. Coverage quickly grew from
26 stations to 35, and by late 1943 the
program could be heard on a coast-to-
coast, 129-station web.

Roy Acuff arrives

WSM's 50,000-watt, clear-channel signal
had helped make Acuff a national figure
after he joined the Opry in February
1938, and NBC's *Prince Albert Show*

FRONT PAGE NEWS *By the time Billboard* magazine featured Roy Acuff *in its April 1, 1944, issue, the singer had branched out to star in several Hollywood B-movies and had cofounded the Acuff-Rose music-publishing firm.*

increased his influence as an unvarnished country vocal stylist. "I was one of the first fellows who reared back and hit a microphone with a real strong voice," he later recalled. "That got me my job." Harmony vocal groups, such as the Vagabonds and the Delmore Brothers, among others, had already begun the Grand Ole Opry's transition from a program of largely anonymous and amateur string bands to a new paradigm of star lead vocalists, and Acuff gave the process a big shove. Early on, Jimmie Rodgers and other national country stars had proved that fans liked vocal solos as much as they did instrumentals. Acuff and his band offered listeners a combination of both. Fusing the homespun quality of the folk musician with elements borrowed from his sister's

The Grand Ole Opry's Prince Albert Show

By the late 1930s, more than a decade into its long life, the Grand Ole Opry was already a national radio phenomenon, thanks to WSM's 50,000-watt transmitter and clear channel of 650 AM in Nashville. Early Opry stars got fan mail from every state in the union, but no program in that golden age of radio could claim national coverage and prestige without being on a network. The Opry achieved that on October 14, 1939, with its premiere on NBC radio.

WSM had become the South's first NBC affiliate just months after the radio network's debut in late 1926, and the station had cultivated good relations with the New York-based network, feeding it one-off shows and short series during the 1930s. Then, in 1939, several key WSM executives helped their station's signature show break through. WSM manager Harry Stone sold a segment to sponsor Prince Albert, the roll-your-own tobacco made by the R. J. Reynolds company. Later that year, newly hired program director Jack Stapp used his New York network connections to get three WSM shows on NBC, including the Prince Albert segment of the Opry.

Initially a half-hour program late on Saturday, the PA Opry brought the sounds and ambience of Nashville's War Memorial Auditorium to a limited number of NBC stations. The show moved to the Ryman Auditorium and the full NBC network in 1943.

CONTROLLED CHAOS *A typical* Prince Albert Show *at the Opry in the 1950s: square dancers at left, Minnie Pearl at centerstage, announcer Grant Turner on the right, and between them singer Carl Smith and Chet Atkins (seated).*

Opry founder George D. Hay initially hosted it, and Roy Acuff emerged as the brightest star on the nation's top hillbilly show. Others who benefited from the national exposure included Red Foley and comedians Rod Brasfield and Minnie Pearl, who frequently teamed up.

The high-profile *Prince Albert Show* helped the Opry get coverage in *Time* and the *New York Times*, and it boosted its stars to new levels of fame and bankability. Listeners heard the show evolve through World War II, the birth of bluegrass, the rise and fall of Hank Williams, the flowering of honky-tonk, and the wilderness years, when many fans jilted country for rock & roll. The show survived until the very end of variety network radio. Although the *Prince Albert Show* remained on WSM until at least 1960, NBC stopped carrying it in December 1957. Because of the rock & roll onslaught, that had already been a tough year for the Opry, WSM, and country music in general. But, of course, country would rebound, and the Grand Ole Opry would endure.

CRAIG HAVIGHURST

PEE WEE KING *Along with Roy Acuff, Bill Monroe, and Ernest Tubb, King helped modernize and popularize the Grand Ole Opry in the 1940s. Joining in 1937, he brought a mellow, pop-western sound and a dapper western look to the show.*

classical training as well as contemporary pop and country styles, Acuff delivered his songs, in the words of *Collier's* magazine, "with a passion evangelist Billy Sunday might have envied. His spiritual conviction is so deep that his own eyes sometimes fill with tears as he sings."

Above all, Acuff was a consummate entertainer. "I think everybody in the business would concede that Roy had the best all-around show for any one single group," said WSM announcer David Cobb, who often introduced the bandleader on radio and emceed a number of Opry tours. Indeed, there seemed to be something for everyone, much of it laced with humor. Acuff's backup musicians, who dressed in rube (rustic) costumes that effectively contrasted with their leader's sportcoat-and-slacks outfits, were past masters of slapstick comedy. When he wasn't acting as straight man, Acuff himself amused stage audiences during radio commercials by balancing his fiddle and bow on the bridge of his nose or on his chin. In short, Acuff epitomized qualities that had made country acts successful from the outset and enhanced their wartime appeal—exciting musicianship, unpretentious self-expression, direct connection with

audiences, an underlying honesty that observers then called "sincerity" or "heart," and sheer salesmanship. All the emerging top stars of the era—such as Ernest Tubb, Bob Wills, Tex Ritter, and Eddy Arnold—were masters of these basic hillbilly skills.

The Opry in ascendance

With WSM's 50,000-watt signal strength and the NBC radio network exposure, the Opry gained a clear edge over its rivals in recruiting new stars. These stars in turn could attract audiences, improve ratings, and increase advertising income—all building a stronger station and a stronger Grand Ole Opry. WSM radio's young executives began recruiting heavily to build the radio show into the best it could be. In the late 1930s, the Stone brothers enlisted Pee Wee King and Bill Monroe. In 1943, Harry Stone added danceable western swing to the mix, hiring Paul Howard & His Arkansas Cotton Pickers. Also that year, gravel-voiced Texas honky-tonk singer Ernest Tubb, then churning out signature hits such as "I'm Walking the Floor over You," joined the cast. Both Howard and Tubb featured electric lead guitars—still a new technological development in music. Even smooth-singing Eddy Arnold featured an electric steel guitar in his band. Other talented newcomers, such as comedians Minnie Pearl, the Duke of Paducah, and Rod Brasfield, further diversified the program's lineup. This star system wasn't unique to WSM, of course—Hollywood had pioneered it for the movies, and star systems were soon prevalent at radio stations across the nation. But the Opry gathered the cream of the crop, and by the time the Allies defeated the Axis powers, Acuff, Tubb, Arnold, and their Opry companions had elevated the Grand Ole Opry to the top rank of country radio shows—and had established the hegemony of a star system that continues in country music to this day.

Much of the Opry's success turned on advertising. WSM worked hand-in-glove with its parent firm, the National Life and Accident Insurance Company; R. J. Reynolds; and the New York-based William Esty Agency—which sold airtime to sponsors nationwide—in publicizing

PROFILES IN COUNTRY

ERNEST TUBB

BORN CRISP, TEXAS, FEBRUARY 9, 1914
DIED SEPTEMBER 6, 1984
PLAYED GUITAR
INFLUENCE JIMMIE RODGERS
HITS "WALKING THE FLOOR OVER YOU," "WALTZ ACROSS TEXAS," "THANKS A LOT"

A key pioneer of honky-tonk music was Ernest Tubb. Initially a Jimmie Rodgers imitator, Tubb was forced to write his own songs and find a new musical style following a botched tonsillectomy. Tubb thereafter pioneered a honky-tonk style with a key innovation—an electrified lead guitar. Beginning with his 1941 classic "Walking the Floor over You," Tubb produced regular hits. His voice—a warm Texas baritone—was immediately recognizable.

He joined the Grand Ole Opry in 1943 and soon built around him his Texas Troubadours band, making Nashville his permanent radio and recording base after 1946. Tubb's hits began to slow in the mid-1950s. But even then he adapted well by building his band into a first-rate dance band and playing the club circuit. Thereafter, he was one of country's legendary "road warriors." In 1965, Tubb was elected to the Country Music Hall of Fame.

RONNIE PUGH

ERNEST TUBB RECORD SHOP (THEN) *In 1947, Ernest Tubb opened his first record shop and mail-order operation at 720 Commerce Street in downtown Nashville; a year later the shop became the site of his much-beloved post-Opry broadcast, The Midnite Jamboree. In 1951, Tubb's shop moved to its present location on Broadway in downtown Nashville.*

ERNEST TUBB RECORD SHOP (NOW) *Though he passed away in 1984, the shop that Tubb built is still in business at 417 Broadway in Nashville, as well as three other locations in Tennessee and Texas. The store still has a thriving mail-order business as well, run via its website.*

"The surprise attack that brought America into the conflict inspired immediate reactions in song."

the show. As network headliner, Acuff became the center of this high-powered machine, and stories about the Grand Ole Opry appeared in *Newsweek*, *Time*, and other national magazines, giving him primary coverage. Featuring Acuff on the cover of its April 1, 1944, issue, *Billboard* proclaimed, "Roy's mountain melodies may be corn, but the payoff is long and green."

Breakfast cereal and animal feed manufacturer Ralston Purina began sponsoring an Opry segment in 1943 over selected NBC stations, with Eddy Arnold soon becoming the host. In 1945, Purina added two daytime shows recorded, respectively, by Arnold and Ernest Tubb for broadcast on Mutual, and the two stars joined forces for *Opry House Matinee*, each doing a live, half-hour Mutual broadcast from Nashville's Princess Theater.

Country goes overseas

Meanwhile, the War Department's Armed Forces Radio Service (AFRS) helped spread country's popularity overseas. In 1942, AFRS began airing country music, and programming soon included the *Prince Albert Show* and a portion of the *National Barn Dance*. Like pop entertainers, country artists recorded hundreds of V-Discs, produced by the military for shipment to American forces worldwide. Acuff and other country singers did their own mailings to the military as well.

Fightin' Words—Country's World War II Songs

America's involvement in World War II inspired a torrent of hillbilly musical commentary. The surprise attack that brought America into the conflict not only quickly rallied popular support for the war but also inspired immediate reactions in song, such as Denver Darling's "Cowards over Pearl Harbor" (recorded by Roy Acuff) and Carson Robison's "Remember Pearl Harbor." Robison soon became country music's main World War II balladeer, and his war-themed songs eventually included such colloquial cries as "We're Gonna Have to Slap the Dirty Little Jap (And Uncle Sam's the Guy Who Can Do It)" and "Get Your Gun and Come Along (We're Fixin' to Kill a Skunk)."

Most war songs predictably dealt with the pain of lovers parting or the loss of a loved one in battle. Examples of the former are legion and include Patsy Montana's "I'll Be True While You're Gone" (1942). But questions about lovers' fidelity increased as the war lengthened, as suggested by Tex Ritter's "Have I Stayed Away Too Long?" (1943), Ernest Tubb's "It's Been So Long, Darling"(1945), and Gene Autry's anguished receipt of a Dear John letter, "At Mail Call Today" (1945). Fallen heroes were the theme of Ritter's "Gold Star in Her Window," Tubb's poignant "Soldier's Last Letter" (1944), and Eddy Arnold's "Did You See My Daddy Over There?"

Probably the most popular of all country's wartime songs was Elton Britt's "There's a Star Spangled Banner Waving Somewhere" (1942), in which a patriotic but crippled mountain boy longs to fight for his country. It played on radio's *Lucky Strike Hit Parade*, sold more than a million singles and 750,000 copies in sheet-music form, and even inspired pop cover versions.

Bob Wills memorialized sacrifices at key battlefields in the Pacific with his 1945 hits "Stars and Stripes on Iwo Jima" and "White Cross on Okinawa," and victory was eagerly anticipated in Zeke Clements's "Smoke on the Water" (1944).

Yet there were surprisingly few celebrations in song when the long-awaited end actually came. Most postwar songs that looked back on the hostilities were rather morbid ("The Cross on the Hill" or "Searching for a Soldier's Grave"). Happier memories did prevail in two of 1946's biggest hits— "Rainbow at Midnight" and "Filipino Baby"—and in the biggest hit of 1948, T. Texas Tyler's "Deck of Cards."
RONNIE PUGH

COUNTRY COMFORTS *Country music accompanied US servicemen almost everywhere they were posted—via jukeboxes, the Armed Forces Radio Service, and V-Discs—records that were recorded especially for the soldiers and often contained messages from the artists.*

"I used to have parties ever' once in awhile at my house, and I usually invited Minnie, because Minnie was the type of person that I knew could get along with everybody."

ROY ACUFF

MINNIE PEARL *The most successful and beloved comedienne in country-music history, Minnie Pearl was the creation of actress Sarah Ophelia Colley. One of her trademarks was her straw hat with a $1.98 price tag (below). She joined the Grand Ole Opry in November 1940 and remained a fixture on the show until 1991.*

PROFILES IN COUNTRY

MINNIE PEARL

BORN (SARAH COLLEY) CENTERVILLE, TENNESSEE, OCTOBER 25, 1912
DIED MARCH 4, 1996
INFLUENCE CLASSICAL DRAMA

For 50 years, Minnie Pearl held the Grand Ole Opry stage as the queen of country comedy, a flowered straw hat with a price tag serving as her crown. From the night she made her Opry debut in 1940, she personified the Opry's exuberant spirit and was as responsible for the show's enduring popularity as any of its famous musicians.

Pearl, née Sarah Ophelia Colley, attended Nashville's Ward-Belmont School and grew up in Centerville, Tennessee, the daughter of a prosperous lumber man who'd lost his business in the '29 crash. After college, she organized amateur productions of drama and musical comedy, and gleaned the inspiration for the character of Minnie Pearl, the country girl in the Mary Janes with an eye toward "ketchin' fellers," from an elderly woman in Brenlee Mountain, Alabama, in 1936.

Though she normally worked solo, recounting the gossip of the fictional town of Grinder's Switch, Pearl performed double comedy with Rod Brasfield for ten years (1948–58). She also made some half dozen albums, and was a prize fixture of TV's *Hee Haw.*

Sarah Cannon envied her character. "She's been quite a role model and inspiration to me," she said. "I'd like to be more like her."

ALANNA NASH

JIVIN' IN THE STUDIO *Country singer Red Foley in the Decca recording studio with pop harmony trio the Andrews Sisters, known for the popular 1941 hit "Boogie Woogie Bugle Boy."*

GUITAR MAN *GI John De Grote from Illinois wouldn't part with his Martin guitar. He brought it to Utah beach in Normandy on D-Day, and it accompanied him through Europe with General Patton's Third Army—even into the fierce Battle of the Bulge. Both survived and returned safely home.*

WRITING HOME *A servicewoman writes a letter to her soldier sweetheart in a typical image of wartime morale-boosting.*

Military service fostered the interaction of Americans from various social backgrounds, regions, and musical tastes. For many servicemen and servicewomen, barracks life brought their first exposure to country music, and whether stationed at home or abroad, thousands of soldiers found solace in country's vivid songs. Acuff proved especially popular, as did Bob Wills. After the Allied occupation of Germany, Acuff beat pop heartthrob Frank Sinatra by 600 votes in a poll conducted by the Armed Forces Network's *Munich Morning Report*, prompting AFN to create a

special country show, *Hillbilly Jamboree*, for American forces in Europe. And it wasn't just military personnel who tuned in to hear country music. In October 1945, Acuff's "The Great Speckled Bird" topped a poll of Italian audiences conducted by an "American Expeditionary Station," edging out recordings by Sinatra and rising pop star Dinah Shore. Some Europeans evidently bought Wills's music before the Allies arrived, as historian Charles Townsend discovered. "While tossin' some Jerries out of a house," two American soldiers wrote Wills from Germany, "we ran on to some old records and among them we were surprised to find one of your records — 'Rose of San Antonio'."

Many country-music performers served in the war. From teenage future stars to established superstars, they represented every facet of the business. Some were drafted; some volunteered; some lied about their age to get in (Freddie Hart) or made public performances of their inductions (George Gobel and Gene Autry). Not everyone was accepted (Jim Reeves was turned down because of a heart condition); not everyone stayed (Merle Travis and Bob Wills were discharged early). Others supported the war effort at home — Earl Scruggs worked in a North Carolina factory producing parachutes and Roy Horton toiled as a machinist in a New York City defense plant. They were Navy cooks (Billy Byrd), Army Air Corps teletype operators (Gordon Stoker of the Jordanaires), ground-pounding infantry men (Hawkshaw Hawkins), flight instructors (Gobel) — and even a Director of Special Events, Department of Psychological Warfare in the European Theater of Operations (Jack Stapp). Of course, there were inevitable deaths and imprisonments — Hardrock Gunter was a POW at Stalag IX-A, and Red Smiley nearly died from injuries sustained in Sicily. Overall, country's performers acquitted themselves well.

A music-publishing pioneer

Few country acts of World War II were as popular as Wills, Acuff, Ritter, or Tubb, and fewer still were as quick as Acuff in seizing the business opportunities fame afforded. Like many country artists, the singer began his career as a green country boy, but what he lacked in higher education he made up for in common sense. As his radio stardom grew, New York publishers offered him as much as $2,000 for some of his songs, thereby alerting him to their value. Around 1941, Acuff and his wife, Mildred, began to publish a series of songbooks, marketing them heavily over WSM. Although selling songbooks was nothing new in

country music, Acuff was among the first to set up his own publishing firm. By mid-1942, he had accumulated $25,000 to capitalize Acuff-Rose Publications, which he cofounded with singer-songwriter Fred Rose ("Deed I Do"), recently returned from a four-year Hollywood stint tailoring hits for Gene Autry. As Nashville's first country-music publishing house, the company soon attracted professional songwriters to town and helped lay the commercial and artistic foundations of Music City.

With Rose's reputation and songwriting skills, Acuff's strategic position on the Opry, and a country-music boom under way, the new company

ACUFF SONGBOOKS *Shortly after joining the Opry, Roy Acuff began advertising his own mail-order songbooks on the air. He once estimated he sold 10,000 a week. Their popularity ultimately led him to cofound Acuff-Rose Publications, Nashville's first country-music publishing firm, in 1942.*

SOLDIER BOY *Gordon Stoker, later a member of the famous Jordanaires harmony group, served in World War II as an Army Air Corps teletype operator.*

PROFILES IN COUNTRY

J. L. FRANK

BORN LIMESTONE COUNTY,
ALABAMA, APRIL 15, 1900
DIED MAY 4, 1952
BUSINESS AFFILIATION
INDEPENDENT SHOW PROMOTER
AND TALENT MANAGER

Joseph Lee Frank was a
behind-the-scenes force
who built careers and
moved country shows from
schoolhouses to concert halls.

Settling in Louisville,
Frank promoted Gene
Autry for a time before
managing his son-in-law,
Pee Wee King. With Frank's
backing, King formed the
Golden West Cowboys
band, headed for Knoxville,
and welded his band into a
tight professional unit. "Mr.
Frank taught us how to come
onstage," King explained,
"how to gesture to the
crowd with my hat, and to
never leave the stage with
our backs to the audience."

In 1937, Frank helped
King gain Opry member-
ship; in 1938 he rechris-
tened Roy Acuff's Crazy
Tennesseans as the more
dignified Smoky Mountain
Boys. He also played a key
role in landing Ernest Tubb
a spot on the Opry. By the
early 1940s, Frank was
booking Acuff, King, Tubb,
Minnie Pearl, and other
country acts on tour,
boosting them up from
small-town theaters to city
auditoriums. His death at
52 was a major loss to
country music.

JOHN W. RUMBLE

seemed destined for success. A
revolution in performance-rights licensing
also smoothed the road for Acuff-Rose
and other new country-music publishers.
Under copyright law, songwriters and
publishers were entitled to compensation
for the performance of their songs in
restaurants, in clubs, and on radio
(and later, on television). But prior to
1940, the only practical way a publisher
or writer could collect performance
royalties was through the American
Society of Composers, Authors, and
Publishers (ASCAP), which deliberately
kept its ranks small to maximize
earnings for its members. Also, in
distributing royalties, ASCAP considered
only music performed live on prime-time
network radio shows—most of which
originated in New York or Hollywood
and featured mainstream pop tunes.
Country and other roots-based styles
were virtually shut out until the formation
of Broadcast Music, Inc. (BMI) in
1940. Because BMI let anyone affiliate,
paid for both recorded and live
broadcasts, and compensated for songs
broadcast on network and non-network
shows throughout the USA, new

CAMEL CARAVAN *From mid-1941 into 1942, a group of
performers from station WSM entertained troops at US military
bases in a tour sponsored by Camel Cigarettes. Among the
group pictured: Eddy Arnold, Pee Wee King, and Minnie Pearl.*

commercial vistas opened up for
writers and publishers outside the
pop-music establishment.

By 1941, Acuff had begun licensing
his copyrights through BMI, and when
he teamed with Rose, BMI advanced
their company $2,500 against future
performance royalties. Likewise, BMI
advances provided seed money for new
publishing ventures in many cities,
democratizing the music industry and
encouraging its expansion in Nashville,
Atlanta, Cincinnati, and other music
centers. Acuff-Rose was a new kid on the
block, but by war's end it held its own with
Ralph Peer's powerful Southern Music,
Peer's newly organized Peer International
Corporation, Sylvester Cross's Los
Angeles-based American Music, and Jean
and Julian Aberbach's bicoastal Hill &
Range Songs, as an aggressive player in
the country-music market.

In the long run, Acuff-Rose would
become Roy Acuff's primary source of
wealth. During the 1940s, though, most

of his estimated $200,000 yearly income came from road shows, whose success was yet another sign of country's growing commercial muscle and national appeal. Thousands of rural folks, seeking the higher-paying manufacturing jobs involved in the war effort, left the farm for cities of the South and Southwest. Workers from these regions also streamed into urban centers, such as Baltimore, St. Louis, Detroit, Chicago, and Los Angeles. These migrants brought their love for country music with them and wanted to see their radio favorites in person. Country entertainers were happy to oblige.

Through their booking departments, WSM and other stations began to schedule country stars on live performances that grossed as much as $12,000 a day, often collaborating with the likes of show promoters, such as Nashville's J. L. Frank, Chicago-based Oscar Davis, and Memphis performer-promoter "Happy" Hal Burns. Country acts still worked the "kerosene circuit" of schoolhouses, high school gyms, and small-town theaters, but many singers also began playing big-city auditoriums and dance pavilions.

Country on the road

Billboard, which debuted its weekly "American Folk Records" column in 1942, hailed the phenomenon as a "King Korn Klondike," and reported such spectacular crowds as the 13,000 who flocked to the Cincinnati Music Hall on February 7, 1943, to see two Opry package shows headlined by Acuff and Tubb. Hitting small communities and cities alike, two *Renfro Valley Barn Dance* tent shows raked in some $5,000 weekly, and by mid-1945 the Opry was fielding three tent shows and 12 other units that collectively worked 25 states. Country troupes also played music parks in Maryland, Delaware, New York, Pennsylvania, and the Midwest.

EDDY ARNOLD *After apprenticing as a singer for Pee Wee King, Eddy Arnold (left) set out on his own in 1945. The smooth singer became country music's biggest hitmaker of the 1940s, a superstar whose hits frequently crossed over to the pop charts through the 1960s.*

Perhaps no state offered more work for country musicians than California, where newcomers from Texas, Oklahoma, and the Southeast joined farm laborers who left the state's Central Valley for busy coastal shipyards and industrial plants, many of which operated around the clock. Beginning in 1942, Bert "Foreman" Phillips leased the Venice Pier Ballroom, Compton's Town Hall Ballroom, and similar facilities for dances and shows in the Los Angeles area. Artists including Ray Whitley, Spade Cooley, and Hank Penny fronted house bands who worked all-night dances for crowds of 5,000 or more, and as many as 11,300 customers paid to see big names, such as Acuff or Wills, at special performances. Around San Francisco, Maple

CAMEL CARAVAN BACKSTAGE
Pee Wee King (with accordion) and Eddy Arnold (with guitar) backstage before a Camel Caravan servicemen's show.

Hall and Redmond Hall soon widened a circuit that sustained both local and out-of-state acts.

Wild for western swing

While these and other venues offered plenty of work for bands playing honky-tonk and straight country, western swing held sway among California country fans. A hybrid of American folk fiddling and big band jazz, this forward-looking style contrasted sharply with country's relatively conservative string-band and duet-harmony traditions. Its best-known practitioner was master showman Bob Wills. After returning from the army in 1944, Wills left his Oklahoma stronghold to settle in Los Angeles, where he assembled a large strings-and-horns orchestra and barnstormed the West Coast and the nation at large. Both Wills's and Spade

BOB WILLS SHOW *One of the most popular groups on the West Coast in the 1940s was Bob Wills & His Texas Playboys. Bandleader Wills sports the white hat and cigar.*

Cooley's groups rivaled pop swing bands in popularity, as Carolina Cotton (who sang with Cooley in those years) explained to Gerald Haslam, "We used to finish a dance with Spade ... and then they'd take us out to what they called a Swing-Shift dance out at the beach. We alternated country with pop—with Glen Gray, Stan Kenton.... It took a rugged constitution."

Military bases offered additional work for musical performers in all genres. The R. J. Reynolds Tobacco Company organized several "Camel Caravan" goodwill tours to entertain troops across the USA and Central America. One WSM unit consisted of Pee Wee King's Golden West Cowboys, pop singer Kay Carlisle, and the Camelettes—perky young women who used slingshots to lob free packs of Camel cigarettes into eager crowds. The War Department worked with United Service Organizations (USO) to hire dozens of country entertainers, including a *National Barn Dance* "Camp Show" that staged a daily performance for 139 days in 1942. Country singers, like those in other fields, also sold War Bonds, planted Victory Gardens, and autographed bombs to pound the enemy.

The Mussolini of music

Although Americans were spared fighting on their home soil, World War II forced other hardships on the populace. To aid the war effort, the War Production Board instituted a system for rationing essential goods, ranging from gasoline and tires to tomato ketchup and the shellac used in 78-rpm records. Incredibly, in the midst of these privations, the American Federation of Musicians—the national musicians' union—chose to strike, refusing to perform on records.

The instigator of the strike was the union's dictatorial president, James Caesar Petrillo, a former roughneck saloon owner aptly nicknamed "the Mussolini of Music." In June 1942, at the AFM's national convention, he announced that the union's contract with record companies would terminate on August 1, 1942, and all 140,000 AFM members would cease making recordings

until a new agreement could be reached. The reason for the recording ban, Petrillo claimed, was that records played on jukeboxes and radio were putting musicians out of work.

Immediately, record companies rushed to record as many masters as possible—of all kinds of music—before the deadline. Columbia A&R man Art Satherley may have suspected a strike was imminent because he had some of his artists stockpile recordings beginning in February 1942. "He wrote me to count on [doing] 24 sides—six recording sessions," recalled bandleader Ted Daffan of a marathon February session booking. Similarly, Roy Acuff and Bob Wills cut 18 songs apiece in three-day sessions just before the ban. During the next two years, most record companies carefully doled out their hoarded titles, although they released far fewer discs than usual.

In September 1943, Decca Records became the first label to come to terms with Petrillo. The label agreed not only to increase the musicians' hourly rates but also to pay an ongoing percentage of record proceeds (ranging from 0.25 cents to 5 cents per record) into a Performance Trust Fund for unemployed musicians. Capitol Records followed suit a month later. After waiting in vain for the federal government to intervene, the two biggest major labels—RCA Victor and Columbia—finally came to terms on November 11, 1944.

Most country musicians survived the recording ban just fine, since the bulk of their earnings came from road shows and, to a lesser extent, radio appearances. Some even prospered from the strike and the diminished competition in the marketplace. Al Dexter, for example, made a jaunty recording of his composition "Pistol Packin' Mama" for Satherley before the strike. Released by

SPEEDING TO VICTORY *During the war, everything was considered part of the war effort, including rationing essential goods and watching the speed limit to conserve much-needed gasoline.*

VICTORY SPEED 35 MILES

Charting Country's Rise

Surest of the many indications of country music's growing popularity during the World War II years was the appearance of the music's first weekly record charts in *Billboard* magazine's January 8, 1944 issue. Titled "Most Played Juke Box Folk Records," the first country-record charts had anywhere from two to eight slots (soon it was 15).

Early on, charts became the main ground on which the battle for country music's respectability was fought, as artists and their record companies lobbied *Billboard* over the name of the music as much as for chart entries. When it became clear "Folk" wouldn't work (it was so broad that popular R&B artists such as Louis Jordan appeared on the chart under that category), others were tried. "Hillbilly" was used for less than two months in the fall of 1947, then the title returned to "Folk." The first tentative use of "Country & Western" as a heading (appearing in parentheses, after the longstanding "Folk" title) came in mid-1949, then shortened to "C&W" in June 1956. "Country" first stood alone as the chart's genre title in November 1962.

Charts also tell us much about country's market changes through the years. The jukebox was the main market (and hence the only chart) for the records at the beginning. *Billboard* published its country jukebox charts until 1957; it then added a separate "Best-selling Retail Folk Records" chart (a gauge of the reviving postwar home market for record retail) on May 15, 1948; then began a third country chart, "Country & Western Records Most Played By Folk Disc Jockeys," on December 10, 1949—recognition that radio airplay was crucial to sales.

Record charts quickly became the statistical gauge of relative artist performance and popularity—the musical equivalent to sports statistics. Recording artists could even win "Triple Crown Awards" from *Billboard* when a given record topped all three charts (jukebox, sales, disc jockeys). Because of far too much overlap, the three charts were finally merged into one 30-slot "Hot C&W Sides" chart in October 1958. Goaded by competitors' charts (such as *Cash Box* magazine's) and recognizing the industry's growth, *Billboard* expanded the number of chart positions to 50 in 1964, 75 in 1966, and 100 in 1973. Today's country chart lists 60 titles.

RONNIE PUGH

FIRST RECORD CHART *The very first country-record chart published in* Billboard *was this one from the January 8, 1944 issue. Note the popularity of Al Dexter's "Pistol Packin' Mama"—with three versions pushing it to the top.*

OST PLAYED JUKE BOX FOLK RECORDS

(Hillbillies, Spirituals, Cowboy Songs, Etc.)

Special reports received from The Billboard representatives last week show the Folk rds listed below are currently the most popular Folk records on automatic phonographs out the nation. These reports stem from all the country's leading operating centers and averaged together.

SITION st This k. Wk.			
1. Pistol Packin' Mama	Bing Crosby-Andrews Sisters	Decca	
	Al Dexter	Okeh	
	Don Baxter	Musicraft	
2. No Letter Today	Ted Daffan	Okeh	
3. New San Antonio Rose	Bob Wills	Okeh	
4. They Took the Stars Out of Heaven	Floyd Tillman	Decca	
5. Rosalita	Al Dexter	Okeh	
6. Try Me One More Time	Ernest Tubbs	Decca	

Columbia in early 1943, it sold 1.6 million copies, according to the *Saturday Evening Post*, by the year's end. Indeed Dexter's song proved so popular that Decca's first release after coming to terms with Petrillo was a pop cover of "Pistol Packin' Mama" by top crooner Bing Crosby.

REMEMBER ME *In an iconic image from 1941, a GI and his sweetheart dance to the strains of a Wurlitzer jukebox. Around 500,000 jukeboxes were in use in America by 1941, and many were stocked with country records.*

Strong jukebox sales

Throughout the war and throughout the AFM strike, a healthy jukebox industry provided a ready market for country discs. As record makers found shellac substitutes, restrictions eased, and the AFM settled with the labels, country-record sales improved, joining the industry's ascent from approximately 60 million units sold in 1939 to some 275 million in 1946. Even during the strike, the demand for recordings of any kind led many jukebox operators to add country discs to their machines, as *Billboard* reported in 1944, "in locations that never before have listened to the plaint of the [cow] puncher or the moan of the mountain man." To jukebox owners' delight, country records often kept grabbing nickels well after pop records had faded.

Ted Daffan had been spinning songwriting gold for a good three years when he told a luckless bandmember during a road-trip card game that he was "born to lose." Years later, Daffan said, "I knew I had a song the moment I said it."

Daffan (1912–96) excelled at songwriting, and he followed his first hit, "Truck Driver's Blues" (1939), which sold more than 100,000 copies, with "Worried Mind" and "I'm a Fool to Care" in 1940. Just before disbanding his group, The Texans, in February 1942 due to the war, Daffan cut **"Born to Lose,"** with fiddler Leonard Seago handling the vocals. Its release was delayed, and sales were initially hindered by wartime rationing of shellac. Nevertheless, it became a phenomenal hit in 1943 and on into 1944.

Daffan's bandleading career was essentially over by the early 1950s, and his songwriting prowess seemed to dry up after he kicked a drinking habit. Still, he remained musically active. Occasional revivals of his hit songs culminated with Ray Charles's inclusion of "Born to Lose" as the centerpiece of his monumental *Modern Sounds in Country & Western Music* album in 1962, which ensured not only Daffan's financial future but also the song's status as a modern standard.

KEVIN COFFEY

Placed strategically in working-class bars near military bases or defense plants, the machines could be gold mines. "A jukebox loaded with hillbillies or westerns," *Billboard* noted, "is as good as money in the bank."

The AFM strike didn't intimidate pop singer-songwriter Johnny Mercer, music-store owner Glenn Wallichs, and songwriter-movie executive George "Buddy" DeSylva, who organized Capitol Records in 1942. The Los Angles-based venture was off and running in the country market with Tex Ritter's "Jingle Jangle Jingle." Ritter followed with six hits that made *Billboard*'s newly established country jukebox chart during 1944–45, and labelmates Jack Guthrie and Wesley Tuttle also enjoyed chart-making records during these years. Together with pop hit makers, such as Freddie Slack, Capitol quickly gained major-

1941 HITS Ralph Peer's Southern Music published this songbook featuring the company's top writers of the year, including Ted Daffan and Al Dexter.

TED DAFFAN

WINDOW SHOPPING *The uncertainty of wartime adrenalizes romance. Not surprisingly, country fans had their share of popular love songs during World War II, including such favorites as "Remember Me," "Be Honest with Me," and "You Are My Sunshine."*

label status and would become a mainstay of West Coast country after the war. The strike likewise didn't stop Cincinnati's Syd Nathan, who in 1943 signed his first artists to King Records, country's leading independent label of the postwar decade.

Of loves won and lost

Despite regional and cultural differences, country singers increasingly made love their primary subject. Although Jack Guthrie used a cowboy metaphor in "I'm Brandin' My Darlin' with My Heart," and Autry celebrated wide-open spaces in "Don't Fence Me In," country artists generally downplayed western themes, perhaps because the dreamy lyrics of many pop-western songs no longer spoke to Americans facing hardship on the home front and in foreign lands. Eddy Arnold did make "Cattle Call" his radio theme, but tellingly he relied on love songs such as "Each Minute Seems a Million Years" to build his reputation as a country-pop balladeer. And though Bob Wills's hit recording of "Cherokee Maiden" (written by newcomer Cindy Walker) may have seemed on its face a western song, it was actually a song of love for the singer's "sweet little Cherokee maiden."

While country performers kept using plenty of emotionally upbeat numbers on radio and onstage, the vast majority of country's World War II jukebox hits dealt not with romantic fulfillment, but with love gone wrong, as distilled in Al Dexter's "Triflin' Gal," Tex Ritter's "You Two-Timed Me One Time Too Often," and Ted Daffan's devastating "Born to Lose." Tapping country's folk-rooted tradition of realism, songs like these addressed life

PROMISING STARS *Eddy Arnold (top) saw his solo career take off at the end of World War II beginning with his first chart hit, "Each Minute Seems a Million Years" in 1945. Jack Guthrie, Woody's cousin, notched a No. 1 hit in 1945 with "Oklahoma Hills" and seemed destined for a long career, only to be felled by tuberculosis at age 32 in 1948.*

frankly and openly, and often reflected painful wartime realities of drinking, infidelity, and divorce.

Country music has always mirrored social change, and artists have typically given their fans many ways to cope with it. Like western swing, honky-tonk music was born in the Southwest in the 1930s and gained momentum during World War II. Whether blaring from jukeboxes or onstage PA systems, its heavy beat, incisive electric lead guitars, and crying electric steel guitars filled the smoky taverns, dancehalls, and roadhouses that mushroomed in World War II's America. Packed with soldiers and blue-collar workers looking to blow off steam, dance, or drown their sorrows, these venues pulsed with

rowdy hits, such as Daffan's "Headin' Down the Wrong Highway," Tubb's cheating song "You Nearly Lose Your Mind," Jerry Irby's "Driving Nails in My Coffin," and other similar songs recorded by southwestern singers.

Innovation pleased the writers, artists, and record executives who profited from it, but some country fans preferred familiar sounds they considered more down-to-earth. "To me," PFC (Private first class) David Young wrote to the Opry's Poe Sisters in 1945, "it seems that the Grand Ole Opera [sic] is slipping from its one-time level of good, old fashioned, truely [sic] mountain folk songs, and will soon be only a jumbled mass of lovelorn ballads sung by some cowboys with warped voices, ranging only on the subjects of 'come back home' and 'quit running around on me' ... But thank the Lord, the old standards ... are apparently trying to be held up by you girls, Roy Acuff, and Rachel and Oswald," (the latter a duet team within Acuff's band).

Enduring traditions

Millions of Americans did find reassurance in old-time fiddle tunes, story songs, and laments about home, family, trains, death, and religion—all standard country-music subjects. Acuff, Lulu Belle & Scotty, the Blue Sky Boys, and dozens of other radio acts gave their audiences a wealth of such down-home material. For instance, a partial list of Acuff's early 1940s repertoire includes the train song "Fire Ball Mail," the murder ballad "The Precious Jewel," religious numbers such as "Wait for the Light to Shine," the moralistic "Wreck on the Highway"— in which "whiskey and blood ran together"—a slew of romantic heart songs, and the tearjerker "Don't Make Me Go to Bed and I'll Be Good."

Whether helping "to gather the American family around the fireside" with string-band music and sentimental tunes, soothing jangled nerves with country-pop love songs, setting dancers in motion with western-swing numbers, or stirring honky-tonk crowds with boisterous barroom anthems, country performers met the needs of their wartime fans, old and new. And together with these fans, they made the most of the dynamic transformations that World War II brought to American life. More than ever, country had a truly national following, with national stars, national economic clout, and a new measure of respect. As early as February 1943, *Billboard* predicted that "when the war is over and normalcy returns it will be the field to watch." When the war finally did end in September 1945, country music was poised for a period of expansion the likes of which it had never seen.

POSTWAR EMISSARIES *The pride of the Grand Ole Opry—Red Foley, Little Jimmy Dickens, Minnie Pearl, Hank Williams—flew overseas to entertain American occupational forces in Germany and Austria for two weeks in November 1949.*

TOP TEN

DEEP CATALOG RECORDS —WSM DJ EDDIE STUBBS

It's very hard to say what are THE rarest or least heard country records. These are some of my personal favorites, all of which I have showcased frequently on radio since 1983. Because each recording is special in its own way, I have listed them chronologically.
—Eddie Stubbs

1. **"Just Me and My Fiddle"** Benny Martin, Hillous Butrum & the Tennessee Partners (Pioneer, 1946)

2. **"I Saw the Light"** Clyde Grubb & His Tennessee Valley Boys (RCA Victor, 1947)

3. **"She's My Curley Headed Baby"** Rachel & Oswald (Decca, 1949)

4. **"A World That's Real"** Cowboy Copas (Dot, 1958)

5. **"Nobody's Business"** The Stanley Brothers & the Clinch Mountain Boys (Blue Ridge, 1959)

6. **"Where Will This End"** Buzz Busby & the Bayou Boys (Starday, 1959)

7. **"Shakin' the Blues"** Donny Young (Decca, 1960) *Donny Young is better known as Johnny Paycheck*

8. **"Same Old Town"** Skeets McDonald (Columbia, 1961)

9. **"A Death in the Family"** Little Jimmy Dickens (Decca, 1969)

10. **"There Won't Be Any Tree This Christmas"** Kitty Wells & Johnnie Wright (Decca, 1969)

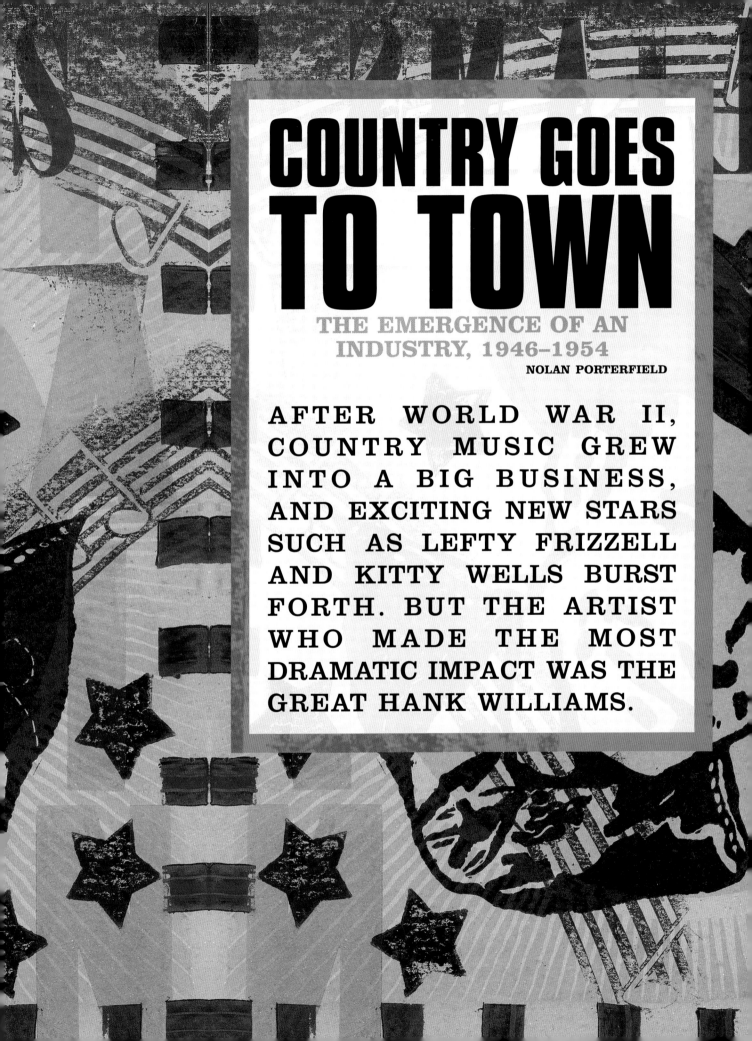

COUNTRY GOES TO TOWN

THE EMERGENCE OF AN INDUSTRY, 1946–1954

NOLAN PORTERFIELD

AFTER WORLD WAR II, COUNTRY MUSIC GREW INTO A BIG BUSINESS, AND EXCITING NEW STARS SUCH AS LEFTY FRIZZELL AND KITTY WELLS BURST FORTH. BUT THE ARTIST WHO MADE THE MOST DRAMATIC IMPACT WAS THE GREAT HANK WILLIAMS.

1946–1954 TIMELINE

1946 First General Assembly of the United Nations. Regular commercial recording begins in Nashville, Tennessee, with the establishment of the Castle Studios in the downtown Tulane Hotel. Red Foley becomes the host of the Opry's NBC network segment, *The Prince Albert Show*. Hank Williams meets and begins working with Fred Rose; by the end of the year Williams is making his first records. Merle Travis records "Nine Pound Hammer," "Dark As a Dungeon," and "Sixteen Tons."

1947 Jackie Robinson becomes major league baseball's first African-American player. Ernest Tubb hosts the first Grand Ole Opry program at Carnegie Hall in New York.

1948 Columbia Records introduces the 33 ⅓-rpm LP. Second musicians' union recording strike begins January 1 and continues to December 14. Eddy Arnold leaves the Grand Ole Opry to head his own CBS radio show. The *Louisiana Hayride* barn dance premieres. Hank Williams joins the *Louisiana Hayride* cast; Lefty Frizzell auditions and is rejected. "Tennessee Waltz" appears in the country charts for the first time, in versions recorded by Cowboy Copas, Roy Acuff, and Pee Wee King, cowriter of the song.

1949 William Faulkner wins the Nobel Prize for literature. Communist forces led by Mao Zedong take control of mainland China. *Billboard* magazine retitles its "Hillbilly" music chart "Country and

continues opposite

I n the immediate aftermath of World War II, most Americans were too busy getting their lives back to normal to notice that subtle but significant things were happening to popular entertainment. In Hollywood, the star system was developing cracks, and the Supreme Court would shortly order the powerful studios to sell off their theater chains, ending their long-time monopoly on production and distribution. By December 1946, most of the big bands had been dissolved; a few of them would regroup and struggle on, but the Swing Era was essentially over, and the day of the featured vocalist was dawning, along with something called "rhythm & blues."

Similar alterations were in store for what had been known as hillbilly music. For one thing, it was about to become "country and western." For another, its operations were increasingly centered in Nashville, Tennessee, where such entities as Castle Recording Studio and Acuff-Rose Publications laid the foundation of an infrastructure that included booking agents, promoters, artists service bureaus, and related enterprises, in addition to recording and publishing. The emergence of Broadcast Music, Inc. (BMI) as a major force in music licensing, beginning in 1940, was opening new doors—and distributing previously undreamed-of songwriting royalties—to country songwriters and publishers, who had never received much respect or support from old-line ASCAP (American Society of Composers, Authors, and Publishers).

In small towns across the country, 250-watt radio stations were sprouting like Johnson grass, programming live local string bands and country music on record. Acts that had routinely played schoolhouses and VFW halls were now being booked into state fairs, municipal auditoriums, and major movie theaters.

HANK'S BOOTS *These custom-made boots belonged to the stylish Hank Williams, whose flair for cowboy fashion complemented his memorable songs.*

In 1947, Carnegie Hall opened its doors to a troupe from the Grand Ole Opry, led by Ernest Tubb. A year earlier, Red Foley was signed to headline the Opry's network segment, replacing Roy Acuff and auguring a shift away from the raw string-band sound of earlier days, to the smoother, more polished vocals of solo stars, such as Foley and Eddy Arnold.

Then there was Hank Williams, who was neither as old-timey as Acuff's Smoky Mountain Boys, nor as slick and easy as the country crooners. He made his first records (for Sterling) in December 1946—coincidentally or not, just as the big bands were dying. Less than eight months later, he hit the charts with his first MGM release, "Move It on Over."

The soul of a poet

If some mad scientist and his assistants—Dr. Frankenstein, say, abetted by Captain Ryman and Judge Hay—had conspired to take the components and stitch together an archetypal country singer,

NOT HARMONIOUS *Audrey and Hank Williams mixed like oil and water, yet she inspired many of his greatest songs. (From left) Sammy Pruett, Audrey and Hank Williams, Jerry Rivers, 1951.*

Western." RCA Records introduces the 45-rpm single. Hank Williams makes his debut at the Grand Ole Opry, singing his hit "Lovesick Blues."

1950 United Nations forces counter communist North Korea's invasion of South Korea as the Korean War begins. Lefty Frizzell is signed to Columbia Records. Hank Snow joins the Grand Ole Opry and earns his first No. 1 hit with "I'm Moving On." Red Foley's recording of "Chattanoogie Shoe Shine Boy" tops both the country and pop charts.

1951 Lefty Frizzell places four songs simultaneously in the country Top 10. Lefty Frizzell and Hank Williams tour together for one week. Patti Page's recording of "Tennessee Waltz" is a No. 2 country hit, tops the pop charts, and sells more than a million copies.

1952 "The Wild Side of Life," recorded by Hank Thompson, and "It Wasn't God Who Made Honky Tonk Angels," the answer song recorded by Kitty Wells, both top the country charts.

1953 Hank Williams is found dead on New Year's Day. The Korean War ends and armistice is signed. Elizabeth II is crowned Queen of Great Britain and Northern Ireland.

1954 Ernest Hemingway wins the Nobel Prize for literature. A first: stations begin airing country music full time—KDAV in Lubbock, Texas, and KXLA in Pasadena, California. George Jones, at age 22, makes his first records. Elvis Presley makes his only appearance on the Grand Ole Opry.

Why Nashville?

By the end of World War II, a number of cities held the promise of becoming enduring country-music centers and, possibly, the genre's principal hub.

So why did Nashville become country's capital and primary recording center? The Grand Ole Opry had much to do with it. Its parent station, WSM, was a 50,000-watt, clear-channel giant that virtually blanketed the nation, while the *Prince Albert Show*, the Grand Ole Opry's half-hour NBC segment (1939–57), topped every other barn dance in longevity and geographic coverage. This powerful radio penetration—combined with Nashville's central location and the assistance of aggressive show promoters, such as J. L. Frank, Hubert Long, and Jim Denny— enabled Opry artists to tour more widely than most country performers. Emphasizing these advantages, WSM executives deliberately recruited star singers (such as Red Foley, lured from WLS's *National Barn Dance* in 1946), drawing many from rival shows.

By the late 1940s, arguably the best singers and musicians in country music were in Nashville. As a result, recording executives began coming to town regularly after 1947 to record Opry talent, using the Castle Studios (1946–54), the Bradley studios (established in 1952 and bought by Columbia in 1962), RCA's studios (1957–77), and other facilities that soon sprang up. Adding to the growing infrastructure was a dependable cadre of skilled session musicians and recording engineers; an exceptionally flexible musician's union chapter that accepted musicians who did not read music and allowed song demos to be recorded at reduced union rates; and a small but aggressive group of local music publishers (beginning with Acuff-Rose in 1942), whose writers could tailor songs for specific artists.

Not surprisingly, then, by 1963 most major record labels had established offices in Nashville. To be sure, Nashville did not become the sole source of country music. Other music scenes—such as Bakersfield, California, in the glory days of Buck Owens and Merle Haggard—have blossomed from time to time, and Texas continues to be a major breeding ground for country artists. But by the early 1960s Nashville's position at the heart of country music was secure.

JOHN W. RUMBLE

NASHVILLE, 1950S *A typical crowd, lined up for the Grand Ole Opry at the Ryman Auditorium in Nashville, Tennessee.*

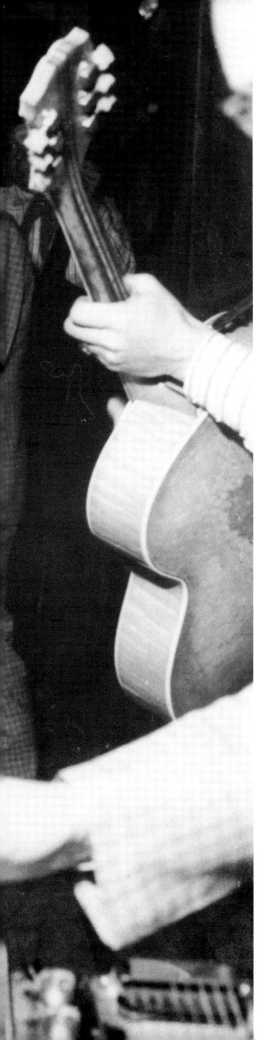

they would have come up with Hank Williams: the twig-thin, bone-and-gristle frame dressed in a faux-cowboy outfit, the starved, country-boy face, with its beady eyes and thin-lipped slash of a mouth, a face that even at 25 was already ravaged and tragic. But all that was merely external; what Hank Williams had inside was the soul of a poet and a voice inflected with all the sorrows and joys known to blue-collar Everyman—honky-tonk romances, camp-meeting revivals, lost highways, cotton fields, lonesome railroad whistles. In his own way, he was a primal cultural force, risen from the American consciousness that produced poet Walt Whitman, painter Thomas Hart Benton, and folksinger Woody Guthrie.

Recording activity was suspended throughout most of 1948 by yet another strike imposed by the American Federation of Musicians, but Williams and his mentor, Fred Rose, were ready the instant the recording ban was lifted. "Mansion on the Hill," recorded the previous year, was released in December 1948, and that same month Williams recorded "Lovesick Blues"—over the objections of Rose and most of the session musicians. (Rose complained, "That's the worst damn thing I ever heard.") By May 1949, "Lovesick Blues" was No. 1 on *Billboard*'s "Folk Records" chart (renamed "Country & Western" the following month); the record remained at the top for 16 weeks and still lingered on the list six months later. Some radio stations programmed it over and over for weeks on end.

Williams had been appearing on KWKH's *Louisiana Hayride* with only limited success. Largely on the strength of "Lovesick Blues," Fred Rose set up a regular spot for him on the Grand Ole Opry beginning in June 1949. (Stories of multiple encores at his first appearance appear to have been a myth; Opry

PROFILES IN COUNTRY

HANK WILLIAMS

BORN MOUNT OLIVE, ALABAMA, SEPTEMBER 17, 1923
DIED JANUARY 1, 1953
PLAYED GUITAR
FIRST RECORDED 1946
INFLUENCES ROY ACUFF, ERNEST TUBB
HITS "LOVESICK BLUES," "COLD, COLD HEART," "YOUR CHEATING HEART"

Hank Williams' songs were little sonograms of life itself—his own and, judging by the ongoing sales, many other lives. He wrote in plain English and set his words to simple, almost folk-based melodies, but above all he sang as if his life hinged upon every word. Even his song demos, designed to be heard by no more than a few people, were delivered with blinding intensity.

Hank had been a sickly child with a chronic back condition. Unsuited to other careers, such as logging or farming, he turned to music—and soon to alcohol. A teenage sensation on local radio, he scored his first hit, "Move It on Over," in 1947. Two years later, "Lovesick Blues" (a song he did not write) earned him an invitation to the Grand Ole Opry. In August 1952, the Opry dismissed him for drunkenness and missing shows. Four months later, Hank Williams was dead at 29.

Williams' recording career spanned just six years, and during that time he recorded 66 songs under his own name, an astonishing 37 of which were hits. More than once, in a single afternoon he cut three songs that became standards. No one will ever do that again.

COLIN ESCOTT

FRED ROSE

BORN EVANSVILLE, INDIANA,
AUGUST 24, 1898
DIED DECEMBER 1, 1954
HITS "BE HONEST WITH ME,"
"TAKE THESE CHAINS
FROM MY HEART,"
"BLUE EYES CRYING IN THE RAIN"

Fred Rose was one of country music's most influential songwriters and behind-the-scenes song doctors, as well as a publisher, talent scout, and record producer.

After an early career as a pop-music songwriter, Rose moved to Nashville and station WSM in 1933, where he became acquainted with country and western styles. From 1938 to 1942, Rose lived mostly in Hollywood writing hits for Gene Autry, Roy Rogers, and other movie cowboys.

In 1942, Rose returned to Nashville and began working at WSM, where he soon struck up a friendship with Roy Acuff, penning "Blue Eyes Crying in the Rain" for Acuff. That year, the two joined forces to form the influential Acuff-Rose music-publishing house; meanwhile, Rose kept writing, crafting hits for Bob Wills ("Roly Poly"), Eddy Arnold ("Texarkana Baby"), and Hank Williams ("Take These Chains from My Heart"). Rose also ghostwrote classics, including the Tex Ritter hit "Jealous Heart" and the Red Foley crossover smash "Chattanoogie Shoe Shine Boy." With Rose's guidance and occasional song editing, Hank Williams and other country writers learned the fine points of songwriting—and excelled. Rose was elected to the Country Music Hall of Fame in 1961, the honor's first year of existence.

JOHN W. RUMBLE

segments were rigidly structured and left no time for deviations from the script.) Despite problems with alcohol, missed show dates, and an erratic personal life, Williams climbed steadily toward national fame, and his songs were among the first in country music to cross over into the pop market. Ironically, Williams's breakthrough record was not his own composition. "Lovesick Blues" had been written and copyrighted in 1922, with words by Irving Mills (of Russian-Jewish parentage), and music by Cliff Friend, a vaudeville piano player and prolific pop composer. Once Williams joined the Opry, however, he made the decision to stick to his own songs, and after 1950 wrote virtually all of his hits, including such eventual classics as "I Can't Help It (If I'm Still in Love with You)," "Hey, Good Lookin'," and "Your Cheatin' Heart."

Williams's most serious competition appeared on the scene in September 1950, when Columbia released Lefty Frizzell's recording of "If You've Got the Money (I've Got the Time)," backed with "I Love You a Thousand Ways."

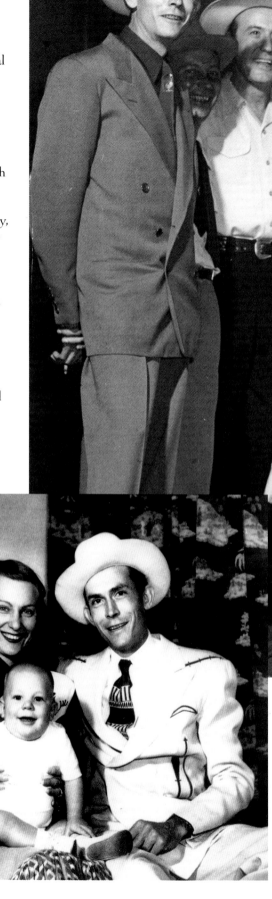

HANK AT HOME *Hank's life with his wife Audrey was never happy and peaceful for long. Here the couple poses with Lycrecia, her daughter from a previous marriage, and their son, Hank Williams Jr.*

HANK AND FRIENDS *Hank Williams with his peers from the Opry—Milton Estes (literally in Hank's shadow), Red Foley, Minnie Pearl,* Variety *magazine editor George Rosen, Wally Fowler (crouching), WSM general manager Harry Stone, Eddy Arnold, Roy Acuff, Rod Brasfield, and Lew Childre, 1950.*

Like Hank Williams, Lefty was a master of the simple, eloquent lyric line, whether tragic or lighthearted. His "If You've Got the Money (I've Got the Time)" is a jaunty classic in the mold of Hank's "Honky Tonkin'," and he wrote at least

a dozen country weepers that stand beside "Cold, Cold Heart" and "I'm So Lonesome I Could Cry." (Sadly and surprisingly, Lefty, the poet of heartbreak, wrote love letters to his wife that were only semiliterate; worse, they were mortally dull.)

At one point in 1951, four Lefty Frizzell records charted simultaneously in the *Billboard* country Top Ten. For a week that spring, Frizzell toured through the South with Hank Williams—who was

"He was just pure soul, is what it amounted to."
WAYLON JENNINGS ON HANK WILLIAMS

HANK'S LAST RIDE

KENTUCKY

TENNESSEE

ALABAMA

Birmingham

Montgomery

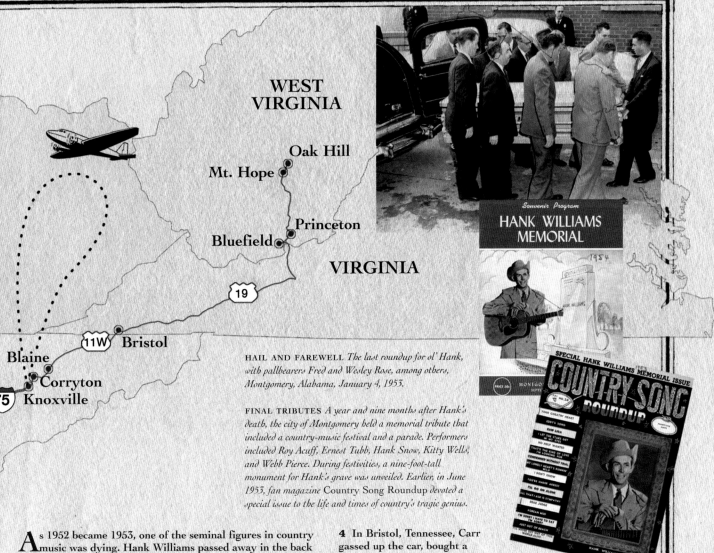

WEST VIRGINIA

Oak Hill

Mt. Hope

Princeton

Bluefield

VIRGINIA

19

11W   Bristol

Blaine

Corryton

75   Knoxville

HAIL AND FAREWELL *The last roundup for ol' Hank, with pallbearers Fred and Wesley Rose, among others, Montgomery, Alabama, January 4, 1953.*

FINAL TRIBUTES *A year and nine months after Hank's death, the city of Montgomery held a memorial tribute that included a country-music festival and a parade. Performers included Roy Acuff, Ernest Tubb, Hank Snow, Kitty Wells, and Webb Pierce. During festivities, a nine-foot-tall monument for Hank's grave was unveiled. Earlier, in June 1953, fan magazine* Country Song Roundup *devoted a special issue to the life and times of country's tragic genius.*

Souvenir Program
HANK WILLIAMS MEMORIAL

COUNTRY SONG ROUNDUP
SPECIAL HANK WILLIAMS MEMORIAL ISSUE

As 1952 became 1953, one of the seminal figures in country music was dying. Hank Williams passed away in the back seat of a powder-blue Cadillac, somewhere between Knoxville, Tennessee, and Oak Hill, West Virginia. He was supposed to play a January 1 show in Canton, Ohio, but he never made it.

1 Williams's trip began December 30 in Montgomery, Alabama, where he took a shot of morphine to ease his chronic back pain and began riding northeast with driver Charles Carr — a college student home on winter vacation — at the wheel of Williams's 1952 Cadillac. Williams took chloral hydrate, a sleep-inducing drug, with him as well. The two men stopped in Birmingham, Alabama, that night, then rode to Knoxville, Tennessee, the next morning.

2 Williams boarded a 3:30 p.m. plane for Charleston, West Virginia, where he was scheduled to play New Year's Eve, but the plane returned to Knoxville because of fog. Carr and Williams checked into the Andrew Johnson Hotel in Knoxville, where Williams drank alcohol and reportedly received two more shots of morphine and a shot of vitamin B-12. Williams was carried to the Cadillac by 11 p.m.

3 Between Corryton and Blaine, Tennessee, the Cadillac was pulled over by officer Swan H. Kitts, who remarked that the passenger looked "dead." Assured Williams was only sleeping, Kitts let Carr pay a speeding fine and drive on.

4 In Bristol, Tennessee, Carr gassed up the car, bought a sandwich, and said he spoke with Williams.

5 In Bluefield, West Virginia, Carr stopped and picked up a relief driver, Donald Surface. Carr is not sure what happened to that relief driver — he may have disembarked in Princeton, West Virginia, or he may have continued on the journey. Some reports have Williams stopping at the Bluefield Sanitarium for one more morphine shot, but Carr denies this.

6 Somewhere between Mt. Hope, West Virginia, and Oak Hill, West Virginia, in the early morning hours of January 1, Carr noticed Williams's blanket had slid from his frame. He found the singer's hand was cold and stiff.

7 Williams was pronounced dead at Oak Hill General Hospital. His Cadillac was kept in a bay at the Pure Oil station in Oak Hill. Falstaff beer bottles were found in the back floorboard. An autopsy was performed in a mortuary across from the hospital, and the official cause of death was heart failure.

PETER COOPER

LEFTY FRIZZELL

BORN CORSICANA, TEXAS,
MARCH 31, 1928
DIED JULY 19, 1975
PLAYED GUITAR
FIRST RECORDED 1950
INFLUENCES JIMMIE RODGERS,
FLOYD TILLMAN, TED DAFFAN
HITS "IF YOU'VE GOT THE MONEY
(I'VE GOT THE TIME)," "ALWAYS
LATE," "LONG BLACK VEIL"

Lefty Frizzell's songs bared his
sentimental, sensitive soul, and his
distinctive, melismatic
singing style immortalized them.

Frizzell approached Dallas
recording-studio owner Jim Beck
in 1950 about making records.
The young singer's voice left
Beck unimpressed, but one of his
original songs, "If You've Got the
Money (I've Got the Time),"
caught his ear. Beck recorded a
demo and took it to Columbia
Records A&R man Don Law, who
immediately liked both song and
singer. In the early 1950s, Frizzell
began a four-year run of Top Ten
singles. However, at the same
time, he embraced the barroom
lifestyle and became infamous
for heavy drinking
and carousing.

In 1975, at age 47,
he suffered a fatal
cerebral hemorrhage.
Elements of his famous
vocal phrasing endure in
the vocal styles of Willie
Nelson, George Jones,
Merle Haggard, John
Anderson, Randy
Travis, and Alan
Jackson.
RICH KIENZLE

less than impressed with Lefty's vocal
habit of bending his vowels and sliding
through syllables, so different from
Hank's full-tilt, bluesy style. Nonetheless,
in July, Lefty was asked to join the cast of
the Grand Ole Opry, then the pinnacle of
country fame.

Golden age of country

While it would later seem that country
music in the early 1950s was dominated
by Hank and Lefty, they were, in fact,
just two of numerous country acts that
captured national attention and created
what many feel was the Golden Age of
country music. Eddy Arnold—not yet
"country-politan," still "The Tennessee
Plowboy"—was outselling both Hank
and Lefty. Hank Snow rocketed to the
top with "I'm Moving On" in 1950
(44 weeks on the charts). Ernest Tubb
was in his prime and touring to packed
houses. Bob Wills and Spade Cooley had
created a national following
for what was increasingly
known as "western swing."
And jukeboxes were filled
with records by Webb Pierce,
Kitty Wells, Jim Reeves,
Goldie Hill, Tennessee Ernie
Ford, Carl Smith, Slim Whitman,
and many others.

As country music matured
and adapted to changing times
in the late 1940s and early 1950s,
a bedrock of tradition was
maintained by a number of stars
who had been around since the
1930s—notably Ernest Tubb and
Bob Wills. Meanwhile, innovative
newcomers, such as Eddy
Arnold, Pee Wee King,
and Merle Travis, had
begun their rise during
the war years. At the
same time, young
traditionalists like the
Louvin Brothers with
their duet sound,
kept alive and
re-energized earlier
sounds and styles.

LEFTY'S AXE *This Gibson
SJ-200 was custom-built for
Lefty Frizzell.*

LEFTY WITH DON LAW *Young Lefty Frizzell with his
producer, Don Law, in Jim Beck's Dallas recording studio,
early '50s. Frizzell's distinctive, drawling vocal style
established him as one of the decade's leading artists.*

Arnold, destined to play a key role in the
evolution of the "Nashville Sound" in the
late 1950s, got his first break in 1940,
when he was hired as featured vocalist
by Pee Wee King, whose Golden West
Cowboys were then appearing on the
Grand Ole Opry. In 1943, Arnold struck
out on his own, securing a solo spot on
the Opry and performing various
musical roles on Nashville's WSM.
But opportunities to record eluded him,
caused in part by the 1942–44 musicians'
union strike. Once the recording ban
was lifted, Arnold went into Studio B at
WSM, on December 4, 1944, and
recorded four songs for RCA Victor,
including "Cattle Call" (only a minor
success at the time, but a No. 1 hit when
rerecorded ten years later). Significantly,
this was the first recording session held by
a major label in Nashville since the 1920s.
It would be the first of thousands to come.

Beginning with "That's How Much I
Love You" in 1946, Arnold ruled the
charts in the late 1940s with such No. 1
hits as "I'll Hold You in My Heart (Till
I Can Hold You in My Arms)" (1947),
"Anytime," "Just a Little Lovin' (Will
Go a Long Way)" (1948), and "Don't
Rob Another Man's Castle" (1949). A
decade later, Arnold altered his style and
image, moving steadily into pop territory.
His smoother, more polished delivery
and uptown presentation paid off with
another string of No. 1 hits.

Innovative newcomers

Pee Wee King, without Eddy Arnold,
scored a solid hit in 1951 with "Slow
Poke" and coauthored the blockbuster
"Tennessee Waltz"—no small achievement
for a former vaudeville accordion player,
born Julius Frank Anthony Kuczynski
in Milwaukee, Wisconsin, far from the
Southland that supposedly generated
country music. In addition, King and his
Golden West Cowboys helped introduce
drums to the ever-conservative Grand
Ole Opry stage, and became pioneers
in the new medium of television,
appearing as early as 1948 on WAVE
in Louisville, Kentucky.

" LEFTY'S MAGNETISM WAS OVERWHELMING AND HIS VOICE WAS BETTER THAN HIS RECORDS.

MERLE HAGGARD

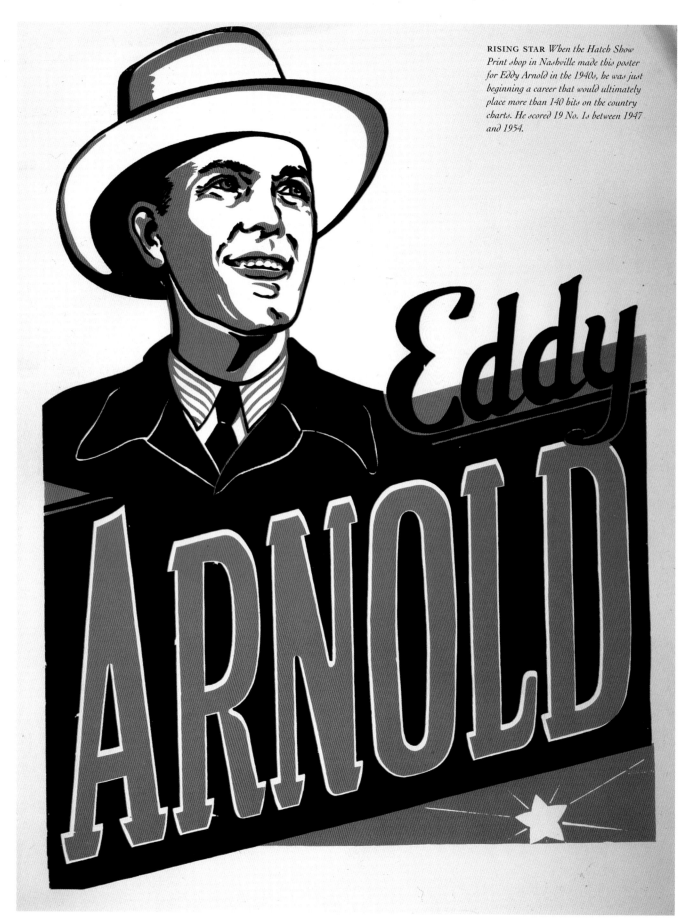

RISING STAR *When the Hatch Show Print shop in Nashville made this poster for Eddy Arnold in the 1940s, he was just beginning a career that would ultimately place more than 140 hits on the country charts. He scored 19 No. 1s between 1947 and 1954.*

Another artist who figured prominently in the country-music boom of the late 1940s was Red Foley, a multitalented vocalist who, along with Eddy Arnold and Tennessee Ernie Ford, personified the trend away from hard-edged mountain music toward a more polished, uptown style. Foley scored commercial successes with both secular and gospel tunes, ranging from "Tennessee Saturday Night" and "Sugarfoot Rag," to "Peace in the Valley" and "Just a Closer Walk with Thee." In 1950, his "Chattanoogie Shoeshine Boy" was a crossover hit, reaching No. 1 on both the country and pop charts.

Slim Whitman, a crooner-yodeler cut from different cloth, specialized in sentimental love songs and old stage ballads, such as "Love Song of the Waterfall," "Danny Boy," and "Indian Love Call." Like Foley, he suffered a decline in the late 1950s, but found a warm reception in Europe, especially England. That propelled him back onto the US charts in the 1960s, and his 1979 telemarketed LP, *All My Best*, reportedly sold four million copies.

Born in music-rich Muhlenberg County, Kentucky, in 1917, Merle Travis developed an innovative thumbpicking guitar style that quickly established him as a session musician for radio and recording on the West Coast, beginning with Tex Ritter's "Jealous Heart" in September 1944. Travis soon emerged as a singer in his

CLOSE HARMONY *The Louvin Brothers—Ira (left) and Charlie—were country music's premier harmony duo of the 1950s and early 1960s.*

PROFILES IN COUNTRY

THE LOUVIN BROTHERS

IRA LOUVIN
BORN SECTION, ALABAMA,
APRIL 21, 1924
DIED JUNE 20, 1965
PLAYED MANDOLIN, GUITAR, VOCALS

CHARLIE LOUVIN
BORN SECTION, ALABAMA,
JULY 7, 1927
PLAYED GUITAR, VOCALS

INFLUENCES THE DELMORE BROTHERS, ROY ACUFF, SACRED HARP SINGERS

HITS "WHEN I STOP DREAMING," "I DON'T BELIEVE YOU'VE MET MY BABY," "YOU'RE RUNNING WILD"

The Louvin Brothers brought the brother-duet style of the 1930s into the age of modern country music. When they signed with Capitol Records in 1952, producer Ken Nelson saw them strictly as a gospel act. However, the brothers realized they needed secular hits to make the big time. They finally persuaded Capitol to release a love song they pinned their hopes on, "When I Stop Dreaming." The record became a Top Ten single, followed by the chart-topping "I Don't Believe You've Met My Baby." They never totally dropped gospel material from their repertoire, but they began exploring a wide variety of love songs and novelty songs, and experimented with rock & roll.

In 1963, after more than 20 years, they split up to try separate careers. Ira issued one solo LP before his death in a highway crash, but Charlie began a solo career that saw him place more hits on the charts than the Louvins had ever enjoyed together. The Louvin Brothers were elected to the Country Music Hall of Fame in 2001.

CHARLES K. WOLFE

FRINGE BENEFITS *Singer-bandleader Hank Thompson wore this striking red-and-silver leather jacket in the mid-'50s, by which time he had scored more than 25 hits on the country charts.*

own right, and his songwriting skills produced such hits as "Divorce Me C.O.D." in 1946 and "So Round, So Firm, So Fully Packed" a year later. "Smoke! Smoke! Smoke! (That Cigarette)," co-written by Travis and Cliffie Stone, was a hit for Tex Williams that same year and became Capitol's first million-selling record. Travis's career was rejuvenated for a time in the mid-1950s by Tennessee Ernie's recording of "Sixteen Tons," and he was active and winning awards (a 1981 Grammy nomination for his *Travis Pickin'* LP) almost until the time of his death in 1983. An inspiration for Chet Atkins, Jerry Reed, and Billy Grammer, among others, his legacy lives on among dozens of lesser-known thumbpickers who continue to swell the ranks of Nashville sesson musicians.

Honky-Tonkin'

The style that came to be known as honky-tonk was flourishing by 1950. Its foremost exponent was Ernest Tubb, who had earlier set the pattern with "Walking the Floor Over You" (1941) and "Driving Nails in My Coffin" (1946). Others who followed in the tradition included Hank Thompson, Carl Smith, Floyd Tillman, Hank Snow, Ray Price, and even Little Jimmy Dickens, whose novelty tunes ("Take an Old Cold Tater and Wait" and "I'm Little but I'm Loud") were also popular among those who fed nickels into honky-tonk jukeboxes. Probably best known for his 1952 hit "Wild Side of Life," Hank Thompson

HANK AND THE BOYS *With the help of his crack band, the Brazos Valley Boys, Hank Thompson (right) blended honky-tonk themes and lyrics with western-swing rhythms to produce such hits as "Green Light" and "Rub-a-Dub-Dub."*

had also scored considerable success in the late 1940s with a sound that blended honky-tonk themes and lyrics with western-swing rhythms and flash ("Whoa Sailor" and "Green Light"). He became one of country's most enduring stars and was still performing 50 years later. Carl Smith may have sung in the new, smoother style, but instrumentally his No. 1 hits, such as "Let Old Mother Nature Have Her Way" and "Are You Teasing Me" (both in 1952), were solidly cast in the classic honky-tonk mold.

Lyrical themes were developing a harder, less sentimental edge during the honky-tonk era. Songs about marital infidelity and drinking came to the fore. It was during this era that Floyd Tillman's "Slippin' Around" (1949) became the quintessential cheatin' song, followed closely by Webb Pierce's "Back Street Affair" (1952). Radio programmers apparently weren't much bothered by adultery in country songs, but when Pierce recorded "There Stands the Glass" the following year many stations banned it on the grounds that it might encourage the consumption of alcohol. Nevertheless, it became a No. 1 country hit—as did a dozen other songs that Pierce recorded—marking him the premier honky-tonker of the 1950s, with more No. 1 hits than any of his contemporaries.

Canada's Snow

Hank Snow followed a long and difficult route from his native Canada before finally landing a spot on the Grand Ole Opry in 1950. His tenuous hold there was strengthened by his first No. 1 hit, "I'm Moving On," that same year, quickly followed by two more—"Golden Rocket" and "Rhumba Boogie." Snow stood firmly in the honky-tonk tradition that took root with Jimmie Rodgers and found its fullest expression in the work of Ernest Tubb, but his repertoire through the years— folk songs, jazz, blues, mambos, and recitations—transcended genre, and his masterful, flatpicking guitar style made him one of the most versatile country stars of his era. Still, he remained a traditionalist at the core and was a major force in "keepin' it country" during the rock & roll years of the 1960s and 1970s.

Jamup & Honey—Horse of a Different Color

Blackface comedy, although it declined in popularity after the 19th century, continued to be a component of country shows well into the World War II years. Although thoroughly out of favor today, in the early 1930s, when most white Americans were still struggling with how to relate to a people freed only 65 years before, such race-based humor was widely accepted, even sought out by mainstream white America.

In Nashville, WSM's Grand Ole Opry was home to a long-running and popular minstrel-comedy duo, Jamup & Honey, who had a major impact on Opry touring in the 1940s. They began as the team of Lasses & Honey, which came to Nashville around 1932, with Lee Roy "Lasses" White's minstrel troupe, of which Lee Davis "Honey" Wilds was a member. Lasses & Honey were initially booked for six weeks of guest appearances on the Grand Ole Opry. Someone, perhaps station manager Harry Stone, had been looking for an accomplished act with a minstrel and vaudeville background, and White and Wilds, both from Texas, filled the bill. It was their job to do comedy sketches between the waves of talented hillbilly singers.

For Honey Wilds, that six-week engagement turned into 21 years, during which time he became an Opry cast member. In 1936, Lasses White left the act— and blackface comedy in general—to become the sidekick to numerous handsome cowboys in B-movie westerns. Wilds continued the act as Jamup & Honey, with an assortment of partners, and even created a highly popular daily WSM soap opera with the act at its center. Around 1940, Wilds pioneered the traveling tent shows—mini-Oprys, in effect—that took Opry stars to rural audiences across the hinterlands of the South and Southwest. The tent shows proved so lucrative that Roy Acuff and Bill Monroe quickly followed suit. Like Jamup & Honey, they toured the tent-show circuit during the week and raced back to Nashville on Saturdays for the Opry's evening broadcasts.

Honey Wilds stuck it out until the bitter end. But by the early 1950s, blackface comedy was no longer tolerated by the majority of America. Unwilling or unable to change with the times, Wilds gave up performing. After 40 years as an entertainer, he effectively retired in 1956.

DAVID WILDS

ANOTHER TIME *Blackface comedians Jamup & Honey with fellow Grand Ole Opry stars Minnie Pearl, Eddy Arnold, and Uncle Dave Macon, 1940s.*

Best of the West

In the 1940s and early 1950s, there was still a strong western element in country music, concurrent with the peak popularity of singing-cowboy movies. Gene Autry recorded songs with such titles as "Cowboy Blues," "Tweedle-o-Twill," "Gallivantin' Galveston Gal," and "Can't Shake the Sands of Texas from My Shoes," as well as the you-done-me-wrong-little-darlin' standards associated with mainstream country. Tex Ritter appeared on the charts many times in those years, beginning with "I'm Wasting My Tears on You" and "Jealous Heart" in 1944, and culminating in the unlikely pop crossover hit "I Dreamed of a Hillbilly Heaven" in 1961. Other recording stars with cowboy film credits included Jimmy Wakely and Johnny Bond (a regular on Gene Autry's long-running *Melody Ranch* radio show). During the war, western night clubs had thrived in California, and in 1951 KFI radio in the Los Angeles suburb of Compton began airing *Town Hall Party*, which was soon picked up by KTTV television and attracted a huge following. At its peak, the show had a cast of 32, including Merle Travis, Joe & Rose Lee Maphis, Wesley Tuttle, Cliffie Stone, and Skeets McDonald. Tex Ritter hosted when he was in town, and the show was scripted by Johnny Bond. Guest stars included Eddie Dean, Lefty Frizzell, Gene Autry, Johnny Cash, and the Maddox Brothers & Rose—a rich mixture of authentic country and western music, however defined. (Today, anyone who calls it "Country & Western" is immediately marked as an outsider—there is no "Country & Western Music Hall of Fame," no "Journal of Country & Western Music," and no "Country & Western Music" chart.)

Western swing was also thriving on the West Coast by the 1950s. In 1947, Bob Wills had established his Wills Point ballroom near Sacramento but continued to tour nationally, playing to packed houses. Spade Cooley, who called his band an "orchestra" and popularized the term

TRAFFIC STOP *Grand Ole Opry comedian the Duke of Paducah (left) and singer Ernest Tubb bring traffic to a halt with a street concert in downtown Nashville, 1940s.*

The Vienna Connection: Hill & Range Songs

Hill & Range Songs was one of the most influential country-music publishing houses in history. It was established in New York in late 1944 by Viennese immigrant Joachim "Jean" Aberbach (1910–1992) and his brother Julian Aberbach (1909–2004), who recognized country music as both a lucrative business opportunity and a music genre deserving of wider exposure.

In the mid-1940s, few country songwriters received song royalties. Hill & Range remedied this by acquiring song catalogs, educating songwriters about royalties and copyrights, and setting up ongoing royalty accounts. Spade Cooley, Sons of the Pioneers members Tim Spencer and Bob Nolan, and Bill Monroe all collected their first-ever song royalties through Hill & Range.

Cash-poor but full of ambition, the Aberbachs also attracted top songwriter-performers by offering writers half the publishing revenues in addition to their author royalties. Such top stars as Bob Wills, Ernest Tubb, Hank Snow, Red Foley, and Marty Robbins proudly incorporated their own publishing companies in partnership with the Aberbachs. The brothers' success was reflected in the record charts: Hill & Range outpaced chief rival Acuff-Rose by anywhere from 23 percent to 75 percent in the number of Top Ten country hits produced between 1945 and 1954—except in 1953, when the publishers tied.

In late 1955 the Aberbachs gambled on a young, little-known singer named Elvis Presley. Working with Presley's manager, Colonel Tom Parker, who had previously steered Eddy Arnold to the Aberbachs' fold, Hill & Range created partnership companies with Presley and became the sole publisher for almost all the music he recorded throughout his career. Although Elvis was the top earner for Hill & Range, the company's pop success came from many sources. Between 1954 and 1966, Hill & Range contributed at least 208 songs to the *Billboard* Top 40 pop charts, half of which made the Top Ten and almost a quarter of which made No. 1.

Ultimately, Hill & Range grew to become a multimillion-dollar international publishing conglomerate with 121 domestic firms and 129 international subsidiaries in 16 countries. In 1975, retaining a 25 percent interest, the brothers sold all of their publishing, except their Hank Williams and Elvis Presley catalogs, to Chappell Music, a division of Dutch corporation PolyGram. For 30 years, the Aberbachs were key catalysts in advancing country music not only as a popular music form but also as a profitable music industry.

BARBARA BISZICK-LOCKWOOD

SIGN HERE, SON *Elvis Presley with his manager, Colonel Tom Parker, 1956. The Colonel was instrumental in making Hill & Range the primary music-publishing firm for Elvis.*

PROFILES IN COUNTRY

WEBB PIERCE

BORN WEST MONROE, LOUISIANA, AUGUST 8, 1921
DIED FEBRUARY 24, 1991
PLAYED GUITAR
FIRST RECORDED CA. 1950
INFLUENCES JIMMIE RODGERS, GENE AUTRY, BOB WILLS
HITS "BACK STREET AFFAIR," "THERE STANDS THE GLASS," "I AIN'T NEVER"

Country's most successful 1950s hitmaker after Hank Williams was Webb Pierce. Raised by his widowed mother, Pierce moved to Shreveport in his twenties. There he performed at KWKH, whose *Louisiana Hayride* boasted a huge regional following. Pierce wasn't afraid of controversy, and in 1952 cut Billy Wallace's anthem of infidelity, "Back Street Affair." The next year Pierce followed that smash with another, "There Stands the Glass."

Pierce moved to Nashville and WSM's Grand Ole Opry around the time Hank Williams died; with Hank gone, Webb was soon the field's biggest star. The No. 1 hits just kept coming—"Slowly," "Even Tho," "More and More," and "In the Jailhouse Now." While at WSM, Pierce joined Opry manager Jim Denny in launching Cedarwood Music. Pierce left the Opry after WSM fired Denny in 1956 and worked for a while on ABC-TV's *Ozark Jubilee* country showcase. Cedarwood Music kept Pierce in hit songs—"Tupelo County Jail" and "I Ain't Never"—well into the 1960s. A decade after his death, he was elected to the Country Music Hall of Fame in 2001.

RONNIE PUGH

MUNICIPAL AUD.
SAN ANTONIO, TEXAS
MON. SEPT. 16 1954
GRAND OLE OPRY

HANK SNOW
AND THE RAINBOW RANCH BOYS

"I've loved Hank Snow
for a long, long time.
Ever since 'Brand on
My Heart' was his first
big hit in Texas."

WILLIE NELSON

HANK SNOW ON TOUR *(Top left and right) Hank Snow with music executive Hubert Long during a mobbed autograph session after a concert. In the Hatch Show Print poster, Snow appears with his beloved horse Shawnee; Snow and the horse performed tricks at outdoor shows early in Snow's career.*

"western swing," was fresh from wartime success at the Venice Pier Ballroom when he recorded his first hit record, "Shame on You," in 1944. As the popularity of western swing soared in the late 1940s, Cooley joined KTLA-TV's *Hoffman Hayride*, one of the first televised country music shows. Other radio barn dances sprang up around the country after the war, most notably the *Big D Jamboree* on KRLD in Dallas in 1947, and a year later the *Louisiana Hayride*, broadcasting on KWKH in Shreveport. Eventually known as "The Cradle of the Stars," the *Louisiana Hayride*, to the chagrin of its management, ultimately served as a sort of minor-league farm club from which many stars rose to greater fame on the Grand Ole Opry. Among those who got their start on the *Hayride* were Hank Williams, Slim Whitman, Webb Pierce, Faron Young, Jim Reeves, and, eventually, Elvis Presley and Johnny Cash. In 1948, WLW's *Midwestern Hayride* in Cincinnati, Ohio, was among the first to go on television. Performers on many of these programs toured as road-show units, playing, among other venues, the growing number of "music parks" in resort areas stretching from the Northeast through the Midwest and ultimately, with the establishment of Roy Acuff's Dunbar Cave Resort in Tennessee in 1948, into the South.

The *National Barn Dance* on WLS in Chicago could lay claim to being the first major, sustained radio barn dance, beginning in 1924 and running for nearly 40 years. At one time or another, its cast included such luminaries as Gene Autry, Red Foley, Bradley Kincaid, Lulu Belle & Scotty, Patsy Montana, and the Hoosier Hot Shots. By the mid-1940s, however, its popularity was waning, and in 1946 Alka-Seltzer, which had sponsored the show since 1933, withdrew.

HANK SNOW ON STAGE *Snow had a long road to the Opry. Born in Nova Scotia, Canada, he recorded for 15 years before he gained his Opry membership in 1950. He cemented it that very year with the massive hit "I'm Moving On."*

By this time, the Grand Ole Opry had become the 800-pound gorilla of the radio barn dance shows. With its half-hour segment aired by NBC radio, it was the nation's most popular country program, and by 1948 live audiences had grown so large that the Opry instituted a Friday-night show to accommodate the overflow. Yet the Opry was also showing signs of hardening of the arteries. Its conservative management let Elvis Presley slip away after only one appearance in October 1954; they also failed to reckon with the Opry's lack of television exposure and the consequences of rock & roll. It was an ominous portent of a long, slow decline.

Girl singers

Women had long figured on the Opry and in country music, from Moonshine Kate (Rosa Lee Carson) in the 1920s to Patsy Montana in the 1930s. But until the end of World War II, they were largely relegated to secondary roles, often as the distaff member of a duo (Lulu Belle & Scotty, Texas Ruby & Curly Fox, Wilma Lee & Stoney Cooper), or as the girl singer in an otherwise male band (Laura Lee McBride with Bob Wills's Texas Playboys and Rose Maddox with her brothers). In 1947, Louise Massey scored a hit with "My Adobe Hacienda," but the billing still read, "Louise Massey & the Westerners" (male members of her family), and her career soon faded.

Earlier, Molly O'Day had helped pave the way for girl singers in country music. Born Lois LaVerne Williamson in southeastern Kentucky in 1923, she served an apprenticeship on radio stations and road tours in half a dozen states. By 1945, she arrived at radio station WNOX in Knoxville, Tennessee, where she and her husband, guitarist Lynn Davis, became stars of the *Midday Merry-Go-Round*. Her old-timey rendition of "Tramp on the Street" caught the attention of Fred Rose, who signed her to the Acuff-Rose stable of writers and helped her get a recording contract with Columbia. As a result of her Acuff-Rose connection, she became the first major artist to

CLASSIC COUNTRY RECORDING

HANK THOMPSON
"The Wild Side of Life"
KITTY WELLS
"It Wasn't God Who Made Honky Tonk Angels"

"WILD SIDE OF LIFE" WRITTEN BY
ARLIE A. CARTER AND WILLIAM
WARREN
NO. 1 COUNTRY, MAY 10, 1952
"HONKY TONK ANGELS" WRITTEN
BY J. D. MILLER
NO. 1 COUNTRY, AUGUST 23, 1952

*I didn't know God made
honky-tonk angels. I might have
known you'd never make a wife.*
("The Wild Side of Life")

*It wasn't God who made
honky-tonk angels. As you
said in the words of your song.*
("It Wasn't God Who Made
Honky Tonk Angels")

Seldom is an answer song as
popular as the original. "Honky
Tonk Angels" is the notable
exception. The song that
inspired Kitty Wells's famous
answer was "The Wild Side
of Life," recorded by Hank
Thompson for Capitol Records in
1952 and a hit for 30 weeks.

J. D. Miller, a songwriter and
promoter, heard the hit and
wrote a tart answer song from
the woman's point of view. He
sent it to Decca, who passed it
along to Johnnie Wright and his
wife, Kitty, then preparing for
her first Decca Records session.
At first, she was hesitant. "If you
want me to record it," she told
her husband, "we'll do it. At least
we'll get a session fee out of it."

The song proved to be worth
a lot more than the $125 standard
artist's session fee of the time. It
broke into the country charts in
July 1952. By August it had sold
half a million copies, and it
knocked Thompson's
"Wild Side of Life"
out of the No. 1 slot.
Not only was it
Wells's first hit,
but also the first
No. 1 hit ever for
a woman on the
country charts.
CHARLES K. WOLFE

THREE HANKS *Hank Thompson, Hank Snow, and Hank Williams, ca. 1951. Snow and Williams were two of the Grand Ole Opry's biggest stars of the early '50s; Thompson maintained his home base in Oklahoma City for most of the decade.*

record Hank Williams's songs and was later instrumental in the fledgling careers of Carl Smith and Mac Wiseman. To the traditional musical styles of her native Kentucky mountains, she brought an instinctive talent for the bad-whiskey-and-broken-hearts strains that infused country music in the 1940s, forging what Mary Bufwack and Robert Oermann have called "a sort of barroom-bluegrass sound." But in 1952, just when she was poised at the brink of national success, she left show business to join her husband's evangelical ministry.

For a brief time, Charline Arthur made waves and showed the guys a thing or two, when she emerged as the first female rockabilly artist in the early 1950s. Yet, although she attracted much attention and sold a lot of records after signing with RCA in 1953, she never had a certifiable hit. Arthur played the Grand Ole Opry and the *Louisiana Hayride* and toured widely with Lefty Frizzell, Ray Price, Webb Pierce, and other male stars of the day, but

again, they got top billing. "Most of the time I was the only female singer among the men," she said. "That's just how lopsided the music business was in favor of men in those days." Feisty and dynamic in performance, she was also tempestuous offstage, proving strong-willed and determined to go her own way. For ruffled male booking agents and record executives, that way was the highway—RCA dropped her in 1956, bookings dwindled, and her time at the top was quickly over. The day when female artists could be treated as equals and garner star billing had not yet come to country music.

Kitty Wells's breakthrough

That began to change with the rise of Kitty Wells. The undisputed Queen of Country Music in the 1950s, Wells was propelled to fame by her 1952 recording of "It Wasn't God Who Made Honky Tonk Angels," an answer record to Hank

The Cradle of the Stars—
The Louisiana Hayride

Based in Shreveport, the *Louisiana Hayride* was a frustrating study in what might have been. A radio barn dance, the *Hayride* gave the all-important first break to Hank Williams, Elvis Presley, Jim Reeves, Johnny Horton, the Browns, Kitty Wells, Webb Pierce, Faron Young, Slim Whitman, Johnny Cash, David Houston, the Wilburn Brothers, and a cast of backing musicians that included Floyd Cramer, James Burton, and Jerry Kennedy. If only a few had stayed, Shreveport might have taken a run at Nashville's country preeminence, which was newly established and vulnerable. As it was, the *Hayride* simply became a Grand Ole Opry farm club or, as it called itself after everyone had left, the Cradle of the Stars.

The *Hayride*, like the Opry, went out over a 50,000-watt, clear-channel station, KWKH. On clear nights, it could be heard in an area west of the Mississippi and east of the Rockies. Local media magnate John Ewing handed the station to his son-in-law, Henry Clay, who launched the *Hayride* on April 3, 1948, with help from commercial manager Dean Upson and program director Horace Logan. Hank Williams was hired in August, and became the show's first big star. Williams, who was little known outside Alabama when he was signed,

YOUNG JIM REEVES Like many other ambitious stars in the 1950s, Jim Reeves started out on the Hayride *(in 1952) but soon moved on to the more prestigious Grand Ole Opry.*

used the show as a springboard to success, and Clay even took him back after the Opry had beckoned him away and later fired him. The Opry also lured Webb Pierce and Faron Young, leaving Slim Whitman as the headliner.

In 1954, Horace Logan signed a then virtually unknown Elvis Presley to a long-term contract, and the show became the original "alt-country" jubilee, attracting capacity crowds to Shreveport's Municipal Auditorium every Saturday night. Elvis's manager, Colonel Tom Parker, bought Elvis off the show in March 1956, and his disappearance left a hole that the *Hayride* couldn't fill. Elvis and the rockabillies had alienated the *Hayride*'s original audience, and no one could replace him.

As the era of the radio barn dances drew to a close, the *Hayride* limped on with Johnny Horton and Slim Whitman still among the headliners. CBS radio, which networked the show sporadically from 1953, dropped it in 1958, and Henry Clay discontinued it in 1960. Attempts to revive the *Louisiana Hayride* have not met with much success, but in its heyday it gave the Opry competition and fans some great music.

COLIN ESCOTT

KITTY WELLS *A wife and mother in her 30s when she emerged as a star, Kitty Wells was the first woman to have a No. 1 on the country chart. She became an enduring favorite with such classics as "Release Me" and "Making Believe."*

Thompson's "Wild Side of Life." One of the few country stars actually born in Nashville, she came from a musical family with roots that ran deep in traditional culture. (Her real name was Muriel Deason, and she took her stage name from the title of an old 19th-century song.)

An unlikely candidate for honky-tonk stardom, Wells was a demure 32-year-old wife and mother of three when her break came, but much like Molly O'Day, she combined a sharp, lilting gospel voice with the plaintive and intense style that distinguished the cheatin' songs and beer-hall ballads of the time. Wells never had another hit comparable to her breakthrough record, but all of her subsequent releases sold well, with 35 singles in the Top Ten and 81 charted singles. She became one of country's most enduring stars, with a raft of honky-tonk standards through the years — "Release Me," "Making Believe," "I Can't Stop Loving You," and others. Many of her songs — starting with "Honky Tonk Angels" — were considered controversial at the time, but the combination of her steady, old-fashioned demeanor and impeccable family life ultimately overcame all objections. (Years before, Jimmie Rodgers had said, "If they like you when you're nice, they'll forgive you when you're naughty.")

In essence, it was Kitty Wells who convinced country-music executives that female singers were marketable, and her legacy includes introducing realistic women's themes to the genre and making possible the careers and feminist songs of such later stars as Loretta Lynn ("Don't Come Home a'Drinkin'" and "The Pill") and Tanya Tucker ("Would You Lay with Me"). Ranked by the industry as country music's top female vocalist every year from 1952

ROSE MADDOX OUTFIT *Rose Maddox and her brothers were known for their colorful stage costumes. Rose served as lead singer for the family band from 1937 to 1959, and then went on to a successful solo career. This dress designed by Nathan Turk dates from the late 1940s.*

GOLDIE HILL *She was the first woman in country music to capitalize on the breakthrough of Kitty Wells. Her big break came in 1952, when she made a trip to Nashville with Webb Pierce's band and auditioned successfully for Decca Records. The result: the No. 1 hit "I Let the Stars Get in My Eyes."*

Electric innovations

Country players had embraced electric guitars by the 1940s, and their ranks soon included some of the most influential and inventive guitarists anywhere, including Chet Atkins, Merle Travis, and Joe Maphis. With the exception of No. 2 and No. 7 here, all of these instruments reside at the Country Music Hall of Fame and Museum.

1 *This Gibson Super 400 hollow-body electric was custom-built for Merle Travis in 1951, and it remained his main instrument for over 30 years. His "Travis picking" fingerstyle influenced many, including Chet Atkins.*

2 *Invented by country-rock musicians Clarence White and Gene Parsons, the "B-bender" mechanism allows a guitarist to simulate a pedal-steel effect on the B string by pulling against the guitar strap.*

3 *Guitar maker John D'Angelico custom-built this D'Angelico for Chet Atkins around 1950.*

4 *In the late '50s, hot pickers Shot Jackson and Buddy Emmons started their own line of pedal-steel guitars under the Sho-Bud name. Here's one of their four-pedal, single-neck models.*

5 *This 1954 Mosrite double-neck electric belonged to Joe Maphis, recording artist and in-demand studio picker for numerous West Coast sessions.*

6 *Electric guitar pioneer Les Paul built this Frankenstein experiment in 1941. He dubbed it "The Log," and it was an early milestone in solid-body electric guitar design.*

7 *If there's a quintessential electric guitar in country, it's the Fender Telecaster, which has changed little since its introduction around 1950.*

8 *Ira Louvin of the Louvin Brothers built this unusual guitar himself in 1964. He called it his "Hi-G" guitar because of its high-register tuning.*

to 1965, Wells was elected to the Country Music Hall of Fame in 1976. At the time, she was only the third woman to be honored as a solo act.

Just as Kitty Wells scored her first hit with an answer song, Goldie Hill broke through in 1953 with "I Let the Stars Get in My Eyes," a response to Slim Willett's "Don't Let the Stars Get in Your Eyes" (widely covered by others and a No. 1 hit on the pop charts for Perry Como). Hill made a brief career of answer songs and recorded a popular duet with Justin Tubb ("Lookin' Back to See," in 1954). She was named Best Female Artist in 1953 by *Country Song Roundup*, but essentially left the business after she married honky-tonker Carl Smith in 1957.

Rose Maddox was another immensely popular female singer of the time (although, even as the featured vocalist for the Maddox Brothers & Rose, she was still taking second billing behind the male contingent). Rose was every bit as spunky and outspoken as Charline Arthur, but the sense that she was merely Little Sister among a batch of big brothers gave her a certain protection that Arthur didn't enjoy. The Maddox Brothers & Rose first caught national attention in 1949 with "Philadelphia Lawyer," penned by Woody Guthrie, and their 1950 recording of "Sally, Let Your Bangs Hang Down" was both controversial and widely popular, kept off the charts only because

it was considered too risqué for radio. (The song was a reprise of a 1936 recording by Billy Cox that ruffled no feathers at the time and slipped into obscurity.) Dressed in gaudy western outfits by Nathan Turk and billed as "The Most Colorful Hillbilly Band in America," the Maddox Brothers & Rose combined elements of old-time music, honky-tonk, rube comedy, and western swing. With occasional strains of gospel and rockabilly thrown in, they became one of the most flamboyant and progressive acts of that era. Rose continued to pursue a solo career after the band broke up in 1956, but although she scored several chart hits (including duets with a young Buck Owens), she never regained her former prominence, although her influence on younger performers was widespread.

New technologies and styles

Country music in the postwar era was also affected by major changes and innovations in music publishing, marketing, and technology. Many of these developments were represented in just one example—the long-playing 33 ⅓ rpm record. Introduced in 1948, it was mastered on recording tape rather than the old wax discs and could hold 14 or more tracks with a playing time of approximately 40 minutes. Furthermore, it came in a stiff jacket that had space for all kinds of promotional commentary on the musicians, composers, and discography, as well as cover graphics that in time became an art form in itself.

ABOUT FACE *Record companies were reluctant to issue albums by country's female artists until Kitty Wells proved women could sell. Pictured here are Kitty Wells's* Country Hit Parade *(1956), Rose Maddox's* The One Rose *(1960), and Goldie Hill's self-titled LP (1960).*

Pedal to the Metal—The Mystical Sound of the Pedal Steel Guitar

Buddy Emmons, the most innovative pedal steel-guitar player who ever bent a string, once described his chosen instrument as "fascinating and intimidating." How true. Fascinating, because for 50 years its shivering, crying sound has had the power to utterly etch a record as "country." Intimidating, because it may be the most complicated instrument in common use. Hands, feet, and knees each act independently on a contraption with two or three necks of ten or more strings, attached to several foot pedals and knee levers. It requires attention and artistry far out of proportion to its usual role as a backing instrument.

Pedal steel became Nashville's clarion call in 1954, when Bud Isaacs invoked the yearning of Webb Pierce's "Slowly" with a few well-chosen, quavering notes. Isaacs's novel pedal let him slur some notes while holding others steady. In the wake of that influential No. 1 country hit, a whole generation of fellow steel players began retro-fitting their instruments—some with coat hangers and automobile gas pedals—all in a feverish quest to reproduce the emotional new sound.

Little Jimmy Dickens, who had brought Isaacs to Nashville, also featured pedal player Walter Haynes and later Emmons, a technical hotshot who pushed the instrument to new heights. Jimmy Day joined Ray Price in 1956 and helped make "Crazy Arms" a signature honky-tonk record. Pierce later hired Sonny Burnette to cultivate (some say mimic) the sound pioneered by Isaacs, producing memorable records such as "More and More" and "I Don't Care."

It took a few years for the technology and technique to coalesce into a golden age of steel in the 1960s. Ralph Mooney's stabbing, gut-grabbing sound defined Bakersfield country with Merle Haggard and Buck Owens, while in Nashville Hal Rugg backed Loretta Lynn for years with a directness and authority that matched her own. Lloyd Green brightened up Warner Mack's "The Bridge Washed Out," Johnny Paycheck's "Lovin' Machine," and scores of other hits. Curly Chalker, a lap steel player of the 1940s, pushed pedal steel into jazz terrain in the 1960s, while Pete Drake emerged as Nashville's hit-making, go-to-session pedal player, famous for his "talking" steel sound, as well as for appearances on records by Bob Dylan, George Harrison, and other rockers.

Steel has come and gone on country radio with the tides of traditionalism, but a steel guitar hall of fame and regular conventions help keep the fires burning for this mystical instrument and its many ardent fans.

CRAIG HAVIGHURST

STEELIN' THE SPOTLIGHT *Little Jimmy Dickens (center) knew the value of a good pedal-steel player. He hired 18-year-old Buddy Emmons (left) in 1955 and brought him to Nashville. Emmons went on to become one of pedal steel's leading innovators.*

> **UPON MEETING ELVIS—AND HERE'S THE HISTORICAL FACT—ELVIS SAID TO ME, 'YOU LIKE MR. BILL MONROE?' I SAID, 'I LOVE MR. BILL MONROE.' ELVIS SAID, 'MAN, I DO TOO.'**
>
> **CARL PERKINS**

NEW ARRIVALS *In late 1945, Bill Monroe's music made a great leap forward with the addition of Lester Flatt and Earl Scruggs to his band. (From left) Birch Monroe, Chubby Wise, Bill Monroe, Lester Flatt, Earl Scruggs.*

The extended playing time of the LP also made possible so-called "concept albums" (Hank Snow was one of the first to explore the potential of this form).

Perhaps the most significant development in country music of the time was the emergence of what came to be known as "bluegrass." The form reached an apotheosis of sorts in the period 1946–1948, as defined by the ground-breaking musicianship of Bill Monroe & His Blue Grass Boys, notably the rapid-fire, three-finger banjo style of Earl Scruggs, the cast-iron rhythm guitar chords of Lester Flatt, and the virtuoso mandolin chops of Bill Monroe.

By the mid-1950s, two of country's towering icons had fallen—Hank Williams was dead and Lefty Frizzell had slipped into decline. But country-record sales were booming, and, according to *Billboard*, hillbilly music was played on some 1,400 radio stations. In 1954, at least two stations programmed it full time (the first was either KXLA in Pasadena,

BREAKING LOOSE *Elvis Presley at the* Louisiana Hayride, *ca. 1954. As the '50s reached the halfway point, the shocking young hipster, his hour come round at last, was slouching his way towards stardom. Country music would never be the same.*

California, or KDAV in Lubbock, Texas—the honor is yet undecided). Nashville stars had begun to tour in custom buses and bought lavish mansions. Country music, once entertainment's stepchild, had become Big Business.

Other signs were not so reassuring, and spoke of rumblings to come. Also in 1954, Bill Haley changed the name of his band from the Saddlemen to the Comets, and only a bit earlier in Memphis, Tennessee, a pimply-faced kid with sideburns had paid to record a song for his mother, an event duly noted by the perspicacious Sam Phillips at Sun Records. Country music in the early postwar years had seen tumult and change, but it was nothing compared to what was about to happen.

TOP TEN

GEORGE JONES FAVORITE RECORDS

''You Win Again'' is my all-time No. 1. The others are in alphabetical order. I hope you'll understand that ''He Stopped Loving Her Today'' has a very special place in my heart. I just couldn't help naming it, even if it was my record.
—George Jones

1 **"You Win Again"**
Hank Williams (MGM, 1952)

2 **"Always Late (With Your Kisses)'"**
Lefty Frizzell (Columbia, 1951)

3 **"Blue Eyes Crying in the Rain"**
Roy Acuff (Columbia, 1947)

4 **"Blue Moon of Kentucky"**
Bill Monroe (Decca, 1954)

5 **"Heartaches by the Number"**
Ray Price (Columbia, 1959)

6 **"He Stopped Loving Her Today"**
George Jones (Epic, 1980)

7 **"I Love You a Thousand Ways"**
Lefty Frizzell (Columbia, 1950)

8 **"I Love You Because"**
Leon Payne (Capitol, 1949)

9 **"Today I Started Loving You Again"**
Merle Haggard (Capitol, 1968)

10 **"Wreck on the Highway"**
Roy Acuff (OKeh, 1942)

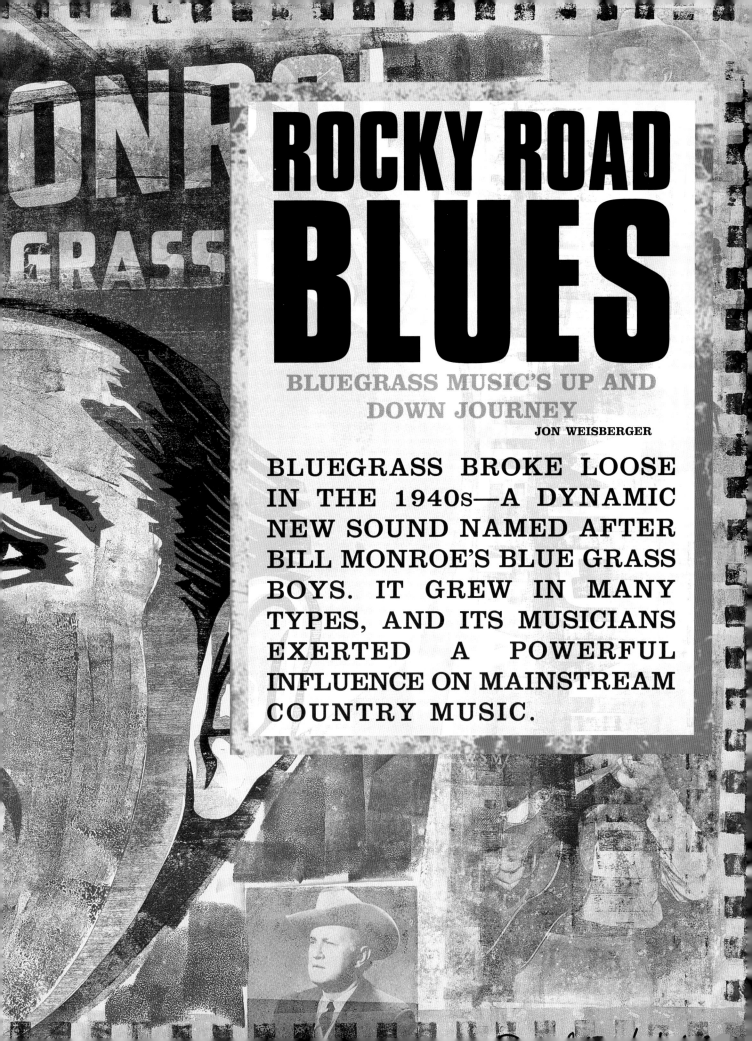

ROCKY ROAD BLUES

BLUEGRASS MUSIC'S UP AND DOWN JOURNEY

JON WEISBERGER

BLUEGRASS BROKE LOOSE IN THE 1940s—A DYNAMIC NEW SOUND NAMED AFTER BILL MONROE'S BLUE GRASS BOYS. IT GREW IN MANY TYPES, AND ITS MUSICIANS EXERTED A POWERFUL INFLUENCE ON MAINSTREAM COUNTRY MUSIC.

continues opposite

Although the term is sometimes used to indicate music "as old as the hills," and at other times to cover almost any kind of acoustic country music, bluegrass is actually a relatively specific and modern form of country music. Born on the stage of the Grand Ole Opry just a few years before Elvis Presley revolutionized the popular-music world, it was created by the 1946–1947 edition of Bill Monroe's Blue Grass Boys and is fittingly named after them.

Dynamic and brimming with virtuosity, yet also sentimental and fiercely loyal to tradition, bluegrass has survived long periods of estrangement from the country mainstream by creating a set of institutions—record labels, venues, publications, and traditions—to sustain itself.

MONROE'S GIBSON
Bill Monroe's 1923 Gibson F-5 mandolin symbolized his musical craft and his artistic drive. Today it resides in the Country Music Hall of Fame and Museum.

At the same time, it has acted as a kind of subterranean influence on that mainstream, furnishing a seemingly endless supply of supporting musicians, songs, and—from time to time—stars who freely acknowledge their debt to bluegrass. As much as the loyalty of the fans themselves, it is the often contentious, but symbiotic, relationship between bluegrass and the larger worlds of country and popular music that has enabled it to enter the 21st century as a vital and growing force.

By the time World War II came to an end, Monroe was already an established star of the Grand Ole Opry. Touring extensively during the war years, he had built a reputation as the leader of one of the Opry's most exciting string bands, which performed a mixture of traditional tunes and original songs at faster tempos and higher keys than those of his colleagues. Although accordionist Sally Ann Forrester and banjo player David "Stringbean" Akeman contributed occasional solos, Monroe's mandolin and the fiddle of Robert "Chubby" Wise were most often highlighted, with guitarist Tex

Willis and bass player Bill "Cousin Wilbur" Wesbrooks comprising the rhythmn section of the group.

That lineup was with Monroe when he went into a Chicago recording studio in February 1945 to make the first recordings for his new label, Columbia Records. (He had last recorded in 1941 for Bluebird.) But within seven months, all of its members except Wise were gone. Taking their places were guitar player Lester Flatt, who came from the band headed by Charlie Monroe (Bill's brother and former duet partner), bassist Howard "Cedric Rainwater" Watts, and, recruited in the closing days of the year, banjo player Earl Scruggs.

A revolutionary sound

A North Carolina youngster who had previously played with Lost John Miller & His Allied Kentuckians, Scruggs brought a revolutionary sound to the Blue Grass Boys. Stringbean and other Opry banjo players had played the instrument in the clawhammer style, employing a curled right hand to stroke downward on the strings, or rudimentary two-finger picking to sound out individual notes. But Scruggs had refined the three-finger picking style of his native Cleveland County into a technique he called a "roll," which allowed him both to pick out melodies with unprecedented precision and surround them with regular patterns of other notes

BIG MON *A towering figure in bluegrass, Bill Monroe guided and shaped this distinct strain of music for more than 50 years as a bandleader, singer, songwriter, and virtuoso mandolinist.*

1966 Carter Stanley of the Stanley Brothers dies. Ralph Stanley carries on without him.

1967 "Foggy Mountain Breakdown" appears in the soundtrack of the film *Bonnie and Clyde*.

1969 Flatt & Scruggs split.

1971 Two highly influential progressive bluegrass bands—New Grass Revival and the Seldom Scene—are formed.

1972 "Dueling Banjos" is featured in *Deliverance*.

1985 Ricky Skaggs is named CMA Entertainer of the Year. The International Bluegrass Music Association is formed.

1987 At age 16, Alison Krauss releases her first album, *Too Late to Cry*.

1988 A "Best Bluegrass Recording" category is added to the Grammy Awards.

1990 The first International Bluegrass Music Awards show staged in Owensboro, Kentucky.

1995 Alison Krauss wins three CMA Awards.

1996 Bill Monroe dies at age 84 in Nashville.

1997 Ricky Skaggs returns to bluegrass with the *Bluegrass Rules!* album.

2000 The film *O Brother, Where Art Thou?* is released, along with its bluegrass-flavored soundtrack. Ralph Stanley becomes a member of the Grand Ole Opry cast.

2002 *Billboard* magazine publishes its first bluegrass album sales chart. The soundtrack for *O Brother* wins a Grammy Award as Best Soundtrack.

2003 The Del McCoury Band joins the Grand Ole Opry cast.

"LESTER FLATT'S SINGING AND EARL SCRUGGS'S UNIQUE BANJO-PICKING WERE THE CORNERSTONES OF AN ACT THAT TOOK BLUEGRASS AROUND THE WORLD."

MARTY STUART

that created a smooth, yet rhythmically powerful texture. And though it was most exciting when used to drive up-tempo numbers, such as "It's Mighty Dark to Travel" and "Blue Grass Breakdown," it served equally well to accompany bluesy, syncopated songs, such as "Heavy Traffic Ahead," and even ballads like "Summertime Is Past and Gone."

Despite Scruggs's startling mastery of this innovative sound, he eagerly accepted Monroe's job offer because Lost John Miller's engagements were few and far between. Furthermore, it was only when the bold, new banjo sound was placed in the context provided by Monroe's band—with its hot, jazzy fiddle, quicksilver mandolin, and robust rhythm section—that it achieved its full potential. Rounding out the appeal of the Blue Grass Boys was the contrast between Flatt's mellow voice and Monroe's sharper, higher-pitched tenor, as well as the precision of the group's harmonies in trios and gospel quartets, and new songs written by Monroe and Flatt to take advantage of the quintet's strengths.

The impact of the new sound, heard on the Opry's far-flung broadcasts, at personal appearances throughout the South, and on 28 sides recorded for Columbia in September 1946 and October 1947, was both immediate and profound. Guitarist Norman Blake remembers that "it was a string band with a different sound," while North Carolina musician Curly Seckler recalled for a Lester Flatt biography that "everyone was saying, 'What has happened to Bill Monroe's music? It don't sound like it used to.'"

Audiences responded enthusiastically. They greeted George D. Hay's regular introduction on the Opry of "Bill, and Earl with that fancy banjo" with tumultuous applause, roaring as Monroe, Scruggs, and Wise launched into energetic solos. Most importantly, a growing number of young musicians were inspired to emulate the Blue Grass Boys' music.

BLUE GRASS BOYS (AND GIRL) *Although Bill Monroe (center) formed his Blue Grass Boys in 1939, bluegrass did not develop overnight. This 1945 incarnation of the group includes Lester Flatt (2nd left), Dave "Stringbean" Akeman, and Sally Ann Forrester.*

Showers of Notes—
Scruggs-style Banjo

For many listeners, the defining characteristic of bluegrass music is the five-string banjo, played with the fluid, three-fingered picking style popularized by Earl Scruggs.

Three-finger banjo styles can be traced back to nineteenth-century minstrelsy and ragtime players from the early days of sound recording. The Carolinas particularly nurtured banjo stylists who could pick out a melody while maintaining a steady beat. Charlie Poole did this in person (if rarely on record) during the late 1920s, while DeWitt "Snuffy" Jenkins and Johnny "Half-Pint" Whisnant were featured sidemen on Carolina radio prior to World War II. Three brothers from Flint Hill, North Carolina—Junie, Horace, and Earl Scruggs—all learned three-finger banjo, but Earl's abilities quickly surpassed those of his older siblings. While earlier stylists often used irregular patterns or an unbroken roll of nine notes to the bar, Earl played eight notes to the bar, often dropping his thumb for his first roll, giving him greater speed and flexibility. After joining Bill Monroe & the Blue Grass Boys in December 1945, Scruggs and his "fancy banjo" became a sensation over WSM's Grand Ole Opry. During his two years with Monroe, he began syncopating his roll to better match his bossman's backbeat.

Scruggs's impact upon other banjo players was enormous. Suddenly realizing their established two-finger styles were now archaic, Ralph Stanley and Don Reno scrambled to unlock Scruggs's

secrets. Other significant banjo stylists emerged during the 1950s. J. D. Crowe, Don Stover, Allen Shelton, and Bill Emerson became known for their explosive, right-handed drive. The more idiosyncratic Don Reno, Sonny Osborne, and Eddie Adcock often incorporated jazz phrasings or flashy single-string riffs. Scruggs continued to innovate as well. His detuning tricks on "Earl's Breakdown" and "Flint Hill Special" led to the development of "Scruggs tuners," headstock pegs that could rapidly and accurately detune a banjo from open G to open D and back again.

A new melodic bluegrass style emerged by the decade's end. More intricate and demanding than the three-fingered roll, it allowed banjo players to play fiddle tunes and other melodies note for note. Bobby Thompson and Eric Weissberg were the first to record in this style, but few noticed this innovation until Boston-bred musician Bill Keith joined Bill Monroe's Blue Grass Boys in 1963. Doug Dillard and John Hartford were influential melodic players who helped seed the rock-influenced "newgrass" movement of the 1970s.

DAVE SAMUELSON

FLATT & SCRUGGS *By the time of their appearance in the 1964 movie* Country Music on Broadway, *Lester Flatt (on guitar) and Earl Scruggs were easily the most visible act in bluegrass. Earl Scruggs's rapid-fire banjo outbursts not only drove the band, but in many ways defined bluegrass.*

Bill Monroe's Blue Grass Boys

When the Monroe Brothers—Bill and Charlie—went their separate ways in 1938, Bill, intent on building a new band and style to realize his own long-held vision, selected musicians who could play his music, yet were capable of adding something of their own. Starting in 1939, and continuing over the next 57 years, his Blue Grass Boys became a powerful incubator for talent, their living alumni still prominent, though Monroe himself died in 1996.

His earliest Blue Grass Boys lineups included singer-guitarist Clyde Moody, fiddler Tommy Magness, and bassist Bill Wesbrooks. During World War II, Monroe hired his first five-string banjoist. David "Stringbean" Akeman was no virtuoso, but he, too, became a beloved Opry comedian and later an early *Hee Haw* regular.

As World War II ended, the Blue Grass Boys attracted a blend of talent whose impact has yet to diminish. Singer-guitarist Lester Flatt, fiddler Chubby Wise, revolutionary five-string banjoist Earl Scruggs, and bassist Cedric Rainwater—led by Monroe—defined the sound and rhythms of classic bluegrass. When Flatt & Scruggs launched their own band in 1948, Monroe didn't miss a beat, continuing to hire talented musicians who added their flavor to his musical oeuvre. Some, like Flatt & Scruggs, formed bands that put their own spins on the music; others became respected instrumentalists.

The names of prominent 1940s and 1950s Blue Grass Boys are well known in the bluegrass pantheon—banjo innovator Don Reno; singers Jimmy Martin, Carter Stanley, and Mac Wiseman; fiddlers Benny Martin, Bobby Hicks, and a very young Sonny Osborne. During the 1960s, fiddlers Vassar Clements, Richard Greene, and Buddy Spicher; banjoists Bill Keith, Curtis McPeake, and Eddie Adcock; singer-guitarists Peter Rowan, Del McCoury, and Roland White passed through the band. Rowan and Richard Greene worked together in the 1970s rock band Seatrain before moving into respected solo careers as roots artists. Kenny Baker, an ex-honky-tonk fiddler, became a constant in Monroe's lineup.

In allowing band members to develop their talents as Blue Grass Boys, Monroe did more than simply launch careers. Realizing that each player in his own distinctive way would continue spreading the word, the Father of Bluegrass guaranteed the music's future.

RICH KIENZLE

"Bill Monroe is one of the ultimate 'feel' players. If he played it, it's because he felt it."
MANDOLIN PLAYER SAM BUSH

GUIDING LIGHT *Bill Monroe (on mandolin in this 1980s photo) provided a training ground for many of bluegrass's biggest stars, including Earl Scruggs, Lester Flatt, Jimmy Martin, Del McCoury, Mac Wiseman, Carter Stanley, Vassar Clements, and Kenny Baker (on fiddle in this photo).*

PROFILES IN COUNTRY

THE STANLEY BROTHERS

RALPH STANLEY
BORN STRATTON, VIRGINIA, FEBRUARY 25, 1927
PLAYED BANJO

CARTER STANLEY
BORN STRATTON, VIRGINIA, AUGUST 27, 1925
DIED DECEMBER 1, 1966
PLAYED GUITAR

FIRST RECORDED 1947
INFLUENCES THEIR PARENTS, WADE MAINER, SNUFFY JENKINS
HITS ''RANK STRANGER,'' ''MAN OF CONSTANT SORROW''

Carter and Ralph Stanley were born in the remote Clinch Mountain territory, and they sang in a primitive Baptist church where instruments weren't allowed. Yet by the end of high school they were regulars on local radio. Early fans of Bill Monroe's, the Stanleys became the first of many devotees to enlarge on the new sound of bluegrass. Their signature in their early Columbia recordings was a mournful mountain vocal style, stacked up in unique, three-part vocal harmonies.

The brothers recorded their best-remembered sides for Mercury between 1953 and 1958, even as the bluegrass market turned cold in the shadow of rock & roll. The folk revival brought the Stanleys back to prosperity, but the partnership ended when Carter died in 1966 at just 41 years old.

Ralph soldiered on, rebuilding his band on a vocal partnership with new-comer Larry Sparks. Over subsequent years, Stanley's band would prove a launch pad for major talents, such as Sparks, Keith Whitley, and Ricky Skaggs. In 2001 Stanley became the patriar-chal figure in the musical cast of the film *O Brother, Where Art Thou?* and on subsequent cast tours.

CRAIG HAVIGHURST

"The Original Bluegrass Band," as the Flatt-Scruggs-Wise-Rainwater lineup was dubbed in retrospect, lasted barely two years, but it established a distinctive template for what would become bluegrass in almost every respect. The instruments would be predominantly acoustic, with guitar, bass, banjo, mandolin, and fiddle the most widely used. The singing was stylized yet emotive, with prominent, tight harmonies. The repertoire would be composed of simply constructed songs that, whether old or new, dealt predominantly with romantic loss, nostalgia for the rural home and loved ones left behind, and the essentials of the Christian gospel. Instrumental prowess and jazz-like improvisation would always be given ample display, not only in instrumental numbers and in solos interspersed between vocal passages in songs, but in the musical embroidery of "backup," where players would take turns accompanying the vocals. And though there would be bandleaders and stars, it would be an ensemble music, in which musicians would be featured and recognized as

THE STANLEY BROTHERS *Carter and Ralph Stanley were among the first to adopt the new bluegrass sound of Bill Monroe in the late 1940s. Initially, Monroe accused them of being mere copycats, but as they refined their unique bluegrass sound he became a supporter.*

RALPH STANLEY *Following the 1966 death of older brother and partner Carter, Ralph Stanley soldiered on, refined his distinct old-time/bluegrass blend, and became by the 1990s virtually equal in stature to Bill Monroe as a bluegrass patriarch.*

individual contributors, pooling their unique talents and approaches to create a characteristic group sound.

The pattern for bluegrass was created by a single source, but it was not until it had been adopted—and adapted—by a variety of artists that it became identifiable as the hallmark of a genre. Even as Lester Flatt and Earl Scruggs were carrying the sound they had helped to create into their new joint venture—

the Foggy Mountain Boys, formed in early 1948—the process was getting under way.

The Stanley Brothers, from southwest Virginia, had led their own band—the Clinch Mountain Boys—since 1946 and had already made distinctive string-band recordings in early 1947. But they heard the Blue Grass Boys' new sound and absorbed it—apparently too well for

1954 POSTER *The most popular act in blue-grass in the 1950s and 1960s, Flatt & Scruggs had their pick of show dates.*

Opry shows, featuring new lead singer Mac Wiseman, and aspiring to sing on the Ryman stage himself.

Martin, Wiseman, the Osbornes, Jim & Jesse, the Stanley Brothers, Don Reno, and other pioneers would go on to build decades-long careers in bluegrass, and behind them came hundreds of other musicians. By the mid-1950s, virtually all the significant country-music labels had signed at least one bluegrass act. Flatt & Scruggs recorded for Mercury, then signed with Columbia in 1953, while the Stanleys headed from Columbia to Mercury the same year. Jim & Jesse signed with Capitol in 1952. In 1954, Martin and the Osborne Brothers teamed up briefly for RCA (which also recorded the Lonesome Pine Fiddlers between 1952 and 1954), before starting with Decca and MGM, respectively, in 1956. Monroe and Eanes recorded for Decca and Wiseman for Dot, while Don Reno

Monroe's taste. In mid-1948 they had cut a version of Monroe's "Molly and Tenbrooks," and their recording actually preceded Monroe's into the marketplace by several months. So closely did the Stanleys emulate the Blue Grass Boys' Opry performances of the song that when Columbia Records signed the Stanleys in 1949, an angry Monroe left Columbia for Decca in protest.

Like wildfire

But it was too late to put the genie back in the bottle. The new sound was catching like wildfire. Jim & Jesse McReynolds teamed up with Hoke Jenkins on banjo to perform around Augusta, Georgia, while in Bluefield, West Virginia, the Lonesome Pine Fiddlers—formed in the late 1930s by Ezra Cline and his brothers—recruited Scruggs-style banjo player Larry Richardson and mandolinist-singer Bob Osborne. In the meantime, Osborne's younger brother, Sonny, still at home in Dayton, Ohio, was teaching himself banjo. And in Sneedville, Tennessee, Jimmy Martin was listening to Monroe's

> ## "He's the one who brought the fire of rockabilly to bluegrass."
>
> **JEFF HANNA OF THE NITTY GRITTY DIRT BAND, ON JIMMY MARTIN**

KING AND HIS COURT *Known for much of his career as "The King of Bluegrass," Jimmy Martin (center) rarely disappointed with his sky-high vocals and aggressive attack. Joining him for this late 1950s performance in Ligonier, Pennsylvania, are Paul Williams (mandolin) and a young J. D. Crowe (banjo).*

began a long association with guitarist-lead singer Red Smiley on Cincinnati's independent label, King Records, in 1951.

Recognizing that commercial success depended on developing a distinctive sound of their own, each of these acts sought to differentiate itself from the others, even as they retained many of the characteristics of the original bluegrass model. Flatt & Scruggs downplayed the role of the mandolin, while adding Josh Graves's dobro to the bluegrass instrumental arsenal in 1955. The Stanley Brothers emphasized a mournful mountain vocal style. Jim & Jesse featured the unique cross-picking mandolin style of Jesse McReynolds (derived from Scruggs's banjo rolls) and soaring duet harmonies. Martin laid claim to a "good 'n' country" sound built around his booming rhythm guitar and uninhibited singing. The Osborne Brothers perfected a smooth vocal sound that emulated pedal steel guitar voicings by placing Bobby's high, emotive lead singing on top of a trio; they then surrounded it not only with Sonny's banjo but also with the trappings of a country band, complete with drums.

If the major record labels hoped to recreate the commercial success of Monroe's original bluegrass band—five of their records made the *Billboard* country charts in 1948 and 1949—they were largely disappointed. Although bluegrass artists were winning devoted fans, record sales and airplay lagged behind those of the country mainstream. Nashville acts were now shifting away from the rural sounds of bluegrass to the electrified honky-tonk of artists such as Webb Pierce and the more uptown stylings of Eddy Arnold and Red Foley. And though Elvis Presley's first record contained a rocked-up version of Monroe's "Blue Moon of Kentucky," the rock & roll boom of the 1950s and the sophisticated Nashville Sound served mostly to push bluegrass artists away from country and youthful southern audiences.

MARTHA WHITE EXPRESS *(Overleaf) Flatt & Scruggs were one of the first country acts to tour by bus. This is their first, nicknamed "The Martha White Express," after their sponsor. (From left) Flatt, Scruggs, Charles Elza, Josh Graves, Curly Seckler, Paul Warren, Onie Wheeler.*

JIMMY MARTIN

BORN SNEEDVILLE, TENNESSEE, AUGUST 10, 1927
DIED MAY 14, 2005
PLAYED GUITAR
INFLUENCES ROY ACUFF, HANK WILLIAMS, BILL MONROE
HITS "OCEAN OF DIAMONDS," "WIDOW MAKER," "20/20 VISION"

Jimmy Martin combined soaring vocals, an aggressive stage presence, and an accessibility that allowed his bluegrass to exist alongside mainstream country records on jukeboxes across America.

In 1949, he began singing lead and playing guitar with Bill Monroe & the Blue Grass Boys. Martin's soaring and insistent lead vocals forced Monroe's tenor harmonies into the stratosphere and helped Monroe refine the heart-tugging, edgy vocal confluence that came to be known as the "high lonesome sound."

After leaving Monroe, Martin became a bandleader in his own right. Beginning in late 1954, he made recordings that signify him as one of the genre's all-time greats. The raw emotion of "20/20 Vision," "Ocean of Diamonds," and "Hit Parade of Love" is unmatched in bluegrass.

His tempestuous personality cost him opportunities, including the Grand Ole Opry membership he prized. Yet his legacy is secure, thanks to his marvelous recordings with his Sunny Mountain Boys band, and with the Nitty Gritty Dirt Band on three *Will the Circle Be Unbroken* volumes.

PETER COOPER

Yet the music survived, in part precisely because its down-home aspects now represented a clear alternative to trends that some rural audiences found objectionable. (Urbanites—who moved to border areas, such as Cincinnati, Dayton, Detroit, and the Washington-Baltimore corridor—agreed.) Furthermore, by the second half of the decade, the word "bluegrass" and phrases such as "featuring five-string banjo" were being used to identify records and artists whose music contained enough common elements to be grouped together. This enabled fans to focus not only on their favorite artists, but to consider buying records or attending shows by new or unfamiliar ones, secure in the knowledge that they were likely to find them enjoyable.

However, for some artists, such as the Stanley Brothers, who were forced to move from Mercury to the more marginal King

label, the late 1950s were, nevertheless, a lean period. Even Monroe, who continued to make regular Opry appearances, often found himself, like the Stanleys, unable to maintain a full complement of band members, and so he traveled with one or two key players, hiring local pickers on a show-by-show basis. While the practice allowed bluegrass bandleaders to keep an eye on promising up-and-comers, who were honing their skills by learning the stars' repertoires, the quality of the music at personal appearances often suffered. Fortunately, their recordings usually featured outstanding session players or former band members recruited for the day.

In marked contrast to most bluegrass acts, Flatt & Scruggs suffered few reversals. Not only were the duo and their group Opry stars, but by the end of the decade they were traveling a weekly circuit of close to 2,500 miles, appearing on live TV shows in half a dozen cities, and interspersing those performances with concerts at music parks, auditoriums, and theaters. In early 1959, they hit the *Billboard* charts for the first time in seven years with the nostalgic "Cabin on the Hill." From then on, they were a regular presence on the country hit parade. Then at the end of 1962, they broke into the pop chart with their recording of "The Ballad of Jed Clampett," the theme to the popular *Beverly Hillbillies* TV show.

Flatt & Scruggs were also among the first to take advantage of the growing urban folk revival as a means to reach new audiences. Spurred by characterizations like folk music guru Alan Lomax's description of Flatt & Scruggs's sound as "folk music with overdrive," folk revivalist audiences largely discounted bluegrass's

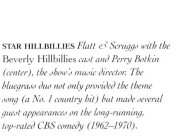

STAR HILLBILLIES *Flatt & Scruggs with the Beverly Hillbillies cast and Perry Botkin (center), the show's music director. The bluegrass duo not only provided the theme song (a No. 1 country hit) but made several guest appearances on the long-running, top-rated CBS comedy (1962–1970).*

HIP TO BE SQUARE
By the time of this 1967 performance at San Francisco hippie enclave the Avalon Ballroom, Flatt & Scruggs had won over legions of fans, young and old.

commercial origins and the country-music aspirations of artists like Flatt & Scruggs, the Stanley Brothers, Jim & Jesse, and the Osborne Brothers.

Folk darlings

Instead, they saw bluegrass as a music of the people, born on the front porches of Appalachia and practiced by talented amateurs. (And when an artist like Doc Watson emerged from Appalachia, steeped in folk balladry and fully formed as a rural artist, the convenient stereotype seemed startlingly true; never mind that Watson played electric guitar in dance bands before Ralph Rinzler showed him that acoustic folk concerts were far more lucrative.) Record companies responded to the interest by emblazoning LP records

THE GOOD DOCTOR *A virtuoso guitar flatpicker and singer, Doc Watson has been a grandfatherly figure for the acoustic music revival. Southbound (1966) was his first album with son Merle, a talented picker in his own right.*

with titles like the Stanley Brothers' *At the Folk Festival*. Folkways Records called on Pete Seeger and his brother, Mike, to compile and annotate a seminal 1958 collection of music by DC-Baltimore bluegrass musicians.

In the first half of the 1960s, a virtual Who's Who of top bluegrass acts appeared at the Newport Folk Festival, where they were generally welcomed with open arms. (One New York critic sniffed about Hylo Brown's Newport show, carping that the more countrified aspects of the performances appeared "phony and cheap.") Still, as performers learned to adjust their presentation and repertoire to suit folk audience's tastes, highlighting their versions of old-time songs and tunes, while skipping recent releases aimed at country music fans, the folk circuit became an important part of their business.

DOC WATSON *Doc with son Merle.*

DOC WATSON

BORN DEEP GAP, NORTH CAROLINA, MARCH, 2, 1923
PLAYED GUITAR
FIRST RECORDED 1961
INFLUENCES JIMMIE RODGERS, CARTER FAMILY, MERLE TRAVIS
KEY RECORDINGS "BLACK MOUNTAIN RAG," "WINDY AND WARM," "SHADY GROVE"

A landmark acoustic guitarist and premiere interpreter of American song, Arthel "Doc" Watson is not easily pegged. His work is steeped in traditional country, bluegrass, gospel, blues, British Isles folk, and even rockabilly.

An illness in infancy left him blind, but he mastered harmonica, banjo, and guitar, while shuttling between home and a state school for the blind in Raleigh. He started playing in dance bands to support a new family, initially on electric guitar, and developed the speedy playing that made him famous.

Watson was almost 40 when folklorist Ralph Rinzler ushered him into the New York folk revival. Not only did he set a new standard for so-called "flatpicking" (a bluegrass style played with a pick), he proved to be one of the great finger-pickers as well, with a technique that enlarged upon the innovations of Mississippi John Hurt and Merle Travis.

From 1967 on, Doc and son Merle, a dazzling picker and slide player, toured as one of folk's best-loved duos. That era came to a tragic end in 1985, when Merle was killed in a tractor accident.

CRAIG HAVIGHURST

In many ways, however, the most important bluegrass development of the 1960s was in the establishment and proliferation of multiday, multiartist bluegrass festivals. Although musician Bill Clifton had presented a one-day festival in northern Virginia in 1961 that featured, among others, the broad-ranging Country Gentlemen, Jim & Jesse, the Stanley Brothers, and Bill Monroe, it wasn't until 1965 that the model for a subsequent explosion of multiday festivals was presented—the Roanoke Bluegrass Festival, held in Fincastle, Virginia. Produced by colorful country-music manager and promoter Carlton Haney, the festival combined a fully fledged stage show featuring a host of well-known acts with elements drawn from a variety of other events. These included the instrumental workshops found at many folk festivals, as well as instrumental contests that had long been a feature of regional fiddlers' conventions.

Bluegrass festivals

Soon bluegrass festivals were being presented at music parks and in pastures from Georgia to Indiana and beyond.

To marquee artists, who were struggling to keep their major label affiliations (and to local and regional groups trying to get out of the frequently rowdy hillbilly clubs), the festivals offered an opportunity to connect with larger audiences. To long-time enthusiasts, they offered an economical way to hear old favorites and promising newcomers; to new fans, drawn by exposure to "Foggy Mountain Breakdown" (an integral part of the soundtrack to the 1967 film *Bonnie and Clyde*) or "Dueling Banjos" (featured in *Deliverance*, 1972), they presented an attractive introduction to the increasingly wide range of bluegrass styles. Festivals also created a marketplace where vendors of records, instruments, and souvenirs could easily deal with customers. Also, they offered an opportunity for amateur musicians to buy instruments, gain instruction—sometimes one-on-one—from the masters, and gather in jam sessions to swap songs and trade licks. Drawing a cohesive community from country people and citybillies alike, festivals quickly became essential to the music's continued vitality and viability.

HOLLYWOOD OUTLAWS *In 1967, Flatt & Scruggs's blistering 1950 instrumental "Foggy Mountain Breakdown" figured prominently in the soundtrack to the movie* Bonnie and Clyde *and even hit the pop charts. Flatt & Scruggs capitalized with this 1967 LP.*

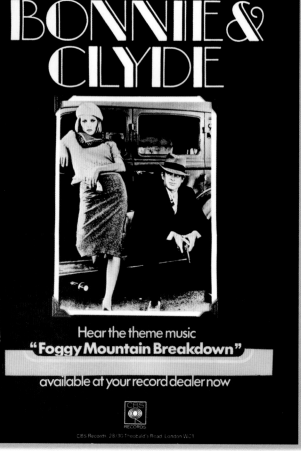

EARL SCRUGGS REVUE *After splitting with Lester Flatt in 1969, Earl Scruggs pursued folk, rock, and bluegrass in the Revue, a band he formed with his sons. (Clockwise from lower left) Steve Scruggs, Vassar Clements, Bob Wilson, Gary Scruggs, Randy Scruggs, Jody Maphis, Earl Scruggs.*

By the mid-1970s, when the festival movement reached its first peak in popularity, the face of bluegrass had changed considerably. Although festivals, record labels, publications, and radio shows helped to maintain a degree of cohesiveness, the music itself was increasingly diversified. Heated arguments developed among fans and performers over whether new developments crossed a boundary separating bluegrass from other forms of music. And though the conflicts were sometimes depicted in generational terms, the truth of the matter was more complicated.

While some of the first- and second-generation greats continued to perform in largely the same fashion that they had for two decades or more, others, such as the Osborne Brothers (who were using electric pickups to amplify their instruments and regularly appeared with a full drum kit) had changed their music considerably. Still others, including Carter Stanley and Red Smiley, had passed away. That left their respective partners, Ralph Stanley and Don Reno, to carry on with other musicians. Lester Flatt and Earl Scruggs had parted ways in 1969, with Flatt continuing on in the classic Foggy Mountain Boys style, and Scruggs joining his sons and other youngsters in the fused bluegrass-country-rock of the Earl Scruggs Revue.

PROFILES IN COUNTRY

DEL MCCOURY

BORN BAKERSVILLE, NORTH CAROLINA, FEBRUARY 1, 1939
FIRST RECORDED
1964 AS SIDEMAN
INFLUENCES BILL MONROE, FLATT & SCRUGGS
HITS "I FEEL THE BLUES MOVIN' IN," "COLD HARD FACTS," "1952 VINCENT BLACK LIGHTNING"

Del McCoury started out as a banjo player. In 1962, he was hired by Bill Monroe and, moving over to guitar, spent a year as one of Monroe's more memorable lead singers. Afterward, he became leader of the hard-driving Dixie Pals. With the addition of sons Ron on mandolin (1981) and Rob on banjo (1987), the current Del McCoury Band began taking shape.

McCoury signed with Rounder and moved to Nashville at the beginning of the 1990s, releasing a series of CDs that drew attention for their elegant mix of blue-grass classics, country songs, and material gleaned from non-bluegrass writers, such as Steve Earle.

They collaborated with Earle on *The Mountain* (1999), and by the year 2000, Del and the boys were playing as many rock clubs and concert halls as bluegrass festivals, always reaching out to fans with a blend of old and new that epitomizes 21st-century hard-core bluegrass.

JON WEISBERGER

Instant Community—Carlton Haney and the Emergence of Bluegrass Festivals

Like the music itself, bluegrass festivals are often assumed to be as old as the Southern hills, but both are modern reinventions of earlier forms. And both are dominated by larger-than-life figures— Bill Monroe in the music and, for the festivals, Carlton Haney.

Born September 19, 1928, in Rockingham County, North Carolina, Haney was a former battery-factory worker, who became a country-music impresario. First handling regional bookings for Monroe in 1953, he later helped the early careers of Don Reno & Red Smiley, Loretta Lynn, the Osborne Brothers, Merle Haggard, and Conway Twitty.

In November 1957, Haney was in a Grand Ole Opry dressing room while Monroe jammed with ace banjoist Reno and other former sidemen. Monroe kicked off a number, and his distinctive timing so electrified the session that other Opry performers crowded in to listen. Instantly, Haney realized that an event built around reunions of classic Blue Grass Boys lineups could be a huge musical and commercial success.

There had been fiddlers' convention contests in the South since the 1800s, and a circuit of mom-and-pop country-music parks had grown up after World War II. And in the late 1950s and early 1960s, as bluegrass developed an identity and audience separate from country music, there had been many all-bluegrass shows.

But in 1965, folklorist and Monroe manager Ralph Rinzler showed Haney around the popular Newport Folk Festival, with its format of main stage and smaller educational workshop areas. Newport directly influenced Haney's production of the first outdoor, weekend-long, all-bluegrass festival, held that Labor Day Weekend on a horse farm near Fincastle, Virginia.

The climax on Sunday was an artistic and historical triumph for Haney. Cadre after cadre of former Blue Grass Boys (most appearing with their own bands on the festival's under card) reunited with Monroe. Rinzler rapidly wrote introductions and handed them up to emcee Carlton, who devotedly narrated "the bluegrass STOW-ree!"

Even without Monroe reunions, the festival concept proved to have powerful appeal, and for crew-cut southerners and long-haired northerners alike: a back-to-basics experience; feelings of group identity; parking lot and campground jamming that thrilled both pickers and listeners; a chance to meet the stars one-on-one; relatively little overhead for promoters; and welcome record table sales for performers.

Haney's first festival attracted only about 500 people. Now there are more than 300 bluegrass festivals held annually in the USA alone—and more internationally. Their godfather is the zealous Carlton Haney, who (in his own words) "did somethin' GREAT!"

RICHARD D. SMITH

HOME COOKING *Most bluegrass festivals are several-day affairs that draw hundreds of fans. But some are smaller. Here, a garage in Asheville, North Carolina, serves as the site for an intimate annual bluegrass jam.*

EXPERIENCED HANDS *One of the beautiful things about bluegrass festivals is the way they welcome players and fans of all ages —from the youngest whippersnappers to the most senior pickers.*

BLUE HIGHWAY *A favorite on the festival circuit since forming in 1996, Blue Highway have proven to be power-houses instrumentally and vocally. (From left) Shawn Lane, Jason Burleson (obscured), Wayne Taylor, Rob Ickes, Tim Stafford, 1996.*

DEL MCCOURY BAND *Since the 1990s, the Del McCoury Band has consistently been one of the most popular attractions in bluegrass. In this 2005 shot from MerleFest, singer Del is at right, son Ronnie McCoury is at left, on mandolin. His brother Rob is the group's banjo player.*

Other established acts were spinning off new groups—the Country Gentlemen's original mandolin player, John Duffey, for example, formed the popular progressive Washington, DC, area band, the Seldom Scene.

Tradition and innovation

Yet tradition-oriented bluegrass was still in good hands. Musicians such as Del McCoury and the Bluegrass Cardinals' Don Parmley led bands that concentrated on fresh material, rather than new stylistic twists. And young musicians Ricky Skaggs and Keith Whitley served years-long apprenticeships with the likes of Ralph Stanley. Others, influenced by

the wide variety of music around them, explored ways of incorporating rock, jazz, country, and even more far-ranging influences into nominally bluegrass settings. And while youthful groups, such as the New Grass Revival, served as lightning rods for the discontent of the traditionally minded, they weren't the only ones experimenting.

As festivals began to lose ground in attendance in the late 1970s—due to marginal fans moving on to other kinds of music, and rare, but well-publicized, incidents of violence—the music and the community that it spawned entered a period of retrenchment. During this time, it gained clarity and focus as it shed some of its more exotic offshoots.

Then, in the latter part of the 1970s, a new blend of modern influences and traditional sounds emerged. Banjo player J. D. Crowe, whose roots stretched back to a long stint with Jimmy Martin in the 1950s, had already turned heads with his band, the New South, in 1975. The group, which included Skaggs and sensational young California-bred guitarist Tony Rice, had released a self-titled album that included songs from writers Gordon Lightfoot and Rodney Crowell, as well as Flatt & Scruggs. Rather than stretch their bluegrass in the direction of the songs' sources, the group, featuring guest dobro virtuoso Jerry Douglas, recontextualized the songs in bluegrass settings underpinned with rhythms that reflected Martin's legacy.

That edition of the New South would soon disband. Skaggs and Douglas would move on to form the more progressive, yet still tradition-based, Boone Creek. Rice would explore jazz-influenced "new acoustic music" with mandolinist David Grisman; and Crowe would take the New South in a more countrified direction with the addition of Keith Whitley. But the impact of their 1975 album is hard to overstate.

Taking an even more aggressively traditional approach, the Johnson Mountain Boys came together in the late 1970s to recreate not just the sounds of first-generation bluegrass, but its typical stage presence, too. Wearing suits, string ties, and spotless, white western hats, the quintet tackled long-neglected gems from the 1950s, while adding well-conceived versions of classic country songs and stylistically faithful originals to their repertoire.

Further west, Colorado's Hot Rize incorporated progressive touches, including banjo player Pete Wernick's use of a phase shifter to add swirling tones to his melodic playing. Yet they, too, based their set lists on a mixture of idiomatic originals, old country songs, and evergreens from the likes of the Stanley Brothers. They also restored a long under-utilized comedic element to bluegrass with the creation of an alter ego—Red Knuckles & the Trailblazers—a dim-witted ensemble that, nonetheless, performed convincing honky-tonk, western swing, and occasional rockabilly numbers.

Enduring trends

Still, the most durable trends to emerge at the end of the 1970s were associated with long-time veteran Doyle Lawson. The bandleader had served as one of Jimmy Martin's Sunny Mountain Boys, then with J. D. Crowe's Kentucky Mountain Boys in the 1960s, and finally with the Country Gentlemen before striking out on his own in 1978. It was then that Lawson formed Quicksilver, a quartet embodying a kind of contemporary bluegrass that split the difference between traditional and progressive with a new vitality.

> **"What I like about the Del McCoury Band is the soul, the passion, and the conviction that they have for what they're doing. And the energy."**
>
> **EDDIE STUBBS, WSM ANNOUNCER AND DJ**

THE NEW SOUTH *Former Jimmy Martin banjoist J. D. Crowe (right) formed the New South in 1975, and in various incarnations his band proved to be a leading progressive bluegrass outfit. This lineup is (from left) Jimmy Gaudreau, Steve Bryant, Bobby Slone, future star Keith Whitley, Crowe.*

RICKY SKAGGS

BORN CORDELL, KENTUCKY,
JULY 18, 1954
PLAYS MANDOLIN, GUITAR
FIRST RECORDED 1971
HITS "CRYING MY HEART OUT OVER
YOU," "UNCLE PEN,"
"SOLDIER OF THE CROSS"

Between 1981 and 1989, no one
was hotter on the country charts
than Ricky Skaggs. His innovative
integration of bluegrass and
country led to 11 chart-toppers,
and, in 1985, a CMA Entertainer
of the Year Award and a second
Grammy. By the early 1990s,
though, his sales tapered off.

In 1994, Skaggs signed with
Atlantic Records and recorded
two country albums—1995's
Solid Ground and 1997's *Life Is
a Journey*. But when he asked
the label to release the 1997
acoustic album *Bluegrass Rules!*
they declined, and the singer
formed his own Skaggs Family
Records. The bluegrass
community welcomed him
back, and nearly annual awards
followed from the International
Bluegrass Music Association.

Skaggs's 1999 album *Ancient
Tones* was the best bluegrass
album of his career, while his
2000 tribute, *Big Mon: The Songs
of Bill Monroe*, found Skaggs
paying respects to his biggest
hero. Ricky Skaggs & Kentucky
Thunder grew to nine members
by 2003, creating the
unprecedented sound of
all-star, big-band bluegrass.

GEOFFREY HIMES

Making frequent use of the high lead-vocal trio pioneered by the Osborne Brothers, and bolstering the hard-driving banjo of Boone Creek alumnus Terry Baucom with a punchy electric bass, Doyle Lawson & Quicksilver offered tightly arranged, crisply executed versions of songs by Monroe, Flatt & Scruggs, and the Stanley Brothers. But the band also incorporated recent pop, rock, and country numbers, and their 1979 debut was hailed for its promising new sound. But it was with the all-gospel *Rock My Soul* (1981), a set that mixed songs from the bluegrass

MASTER AND PUPIL *Ricky Skaggs (right) never made any secret of his admiration for the music of Bill Monroe (left). By the time of this 1980s photo, it was as if a torch were being passed.*

gospel, southern gospel, and African-American gospel traditions, that the group scored its biggest breakthrough, reaching beyond bluegrass audiences to find favor with the growing audience for country-flavored sacred music.

At nearly the same time, Lawson joined with Crowe, Rice, bassist Todd Phillips, and former Monroe fiddler Bobby Hicks, to record *The Bluegrass Album*, a tribute to Monroe, Flatt & Scruggs, Jimmy Martin, and other pioneers. Eventually spawning nearly half a dozen follow-up albums and occasional tours, *The Bluegrass Album* introduced to new audiences first-generation songs that had long been difficult to obtain. Well-recorded and spectacularly performed with a blend of admiration, affection, reverence, and energy, *The Bluegrass Album* offered little more in the way of modern touches than Rice's lithe, groundbreaking lead guitar work. But the fact that these popular contemporary masters chose to play blue-grass classics in a manner close to the originals was enough to convince many young players of the value in paying closer attention to the music's roots.

A difficult decade

Despite these and other promising developments, the 1980s were largely a difficult period for bluegrass. The shrunken festival scene was a harder arena for artists trying to make a living, and it was widely believed that not only artists, but audiences, too, were growing older. And so, though there were those who muttered about betrayal and abandonment, many in the bluegrass community welcomed the rapid and unexpected country-music success won by Ricky Skaggs in the first half of the decade—especially when it brought the sound of the banjo to the top of the country charts for the first time in nearly 20 years.

Having left Boone Creek to work in the band of Emmylou Harris, whose compelling neotraditional slant on country music had earned her a steady stream of hits from 1975 on, Skaggs released his own solo album, *Sweet Temptation*, in 1979, while still in Harris's employ. To the surprise of many, the Kentucky native—still well shy of 30—cracked the country charts with a crystalline version of the

Stanley Brothers' "I'll Take the Blame," backing precise bluegrass lead and harmony singing with a spare mixture of classic and modern country sounds.

Signed to Epic Records as a solo artist and given free rein to produce his records himself, Skaggs quickly perfected the formula. Between 1982 and 1986, he scored an impressive string of mainstream hits, including ten No. 1s that alternated songs drawn from bedrock bluegrass, classic country, and a canon of edgier new songs by fresh writers, such as Guy Clark and Larry Cordle. New Grass Revival member Bela Fleck's banjo helped drive Skaggs's recording of "Highway 40 Blues" to the top of the charts in early 1983; the following year, Skaggs savored another victory when he earned Bill Monroe his first No. 1 hit as a songwriter with a scorching version of the latter's signature memoir, "Uncle Pen." Invited to join the Grand Ole Opry in 1982, Skaggs then took the CMA's top Entertainer of the Year honor in 1985—and never tired of praising mentors such as Ralph Stanley and extolling the virtues of bluegrass.

The IBMA is created

In another significant development, 1985 also saw the creation of the International Bluegrass Music Association, a trade organization that brought together artists, record labels, show promoters, instrument makers, and others who made a living from bluegrass. Charged with promoting the music to a wider audience, the association lobbied successfully for a bluegrass Grammy award (1988), organized an annual trade show to facilitate networking among its members, and created a Hall of Honor and an annual awards show to recognize achievements old and new. It also strove to bring a higher degree of professionalism to the industry, especially in its dealings with the larger music framework.

Skaggs's presence on the country charts began to slip soon thereafter, as he was overtaken by waves of neo-traditionalists and pop-country artists. But bluegrass maintained the friendly territory he had helped to carve out in the country-music world, thanks to the sudden and spectacular appearance of Alison Krauss.

CLASSIC COUNTRY RECORDING

BILL MONROE
"Uncle Pen"

Late in the evening about sundown, high on the hill above the town.
Uncle Pen played the fiddle, Lord, how it would ring…
WRITTEN BY BILL MONROE AND RECORDED OCTOBER 15, 1950

At the end of an arduous day, the teenage Bill Monroe would put a horse team away in a barn in Rosine, Kentucky. Often, from nearby and above, came fiddling that sounded like a conversation. He never forgot it.

By then an orphan, he worked for his uncle John Monroe, cutting corn and hauling timber, and living in a cabin on Tuttle Hill with his mother's brother, Pendleton Vandiver—a fiddler and Bill's nurturing mentor, "Uncle Pen."

Many of Monroe's formative musical experiences came while backing up Pen at square dances, and in 1950 Monroe set about honoring his uncle. Monroe built upon an elegant, sashaying melody by Merle "Red" Taylor (his fiddler in the Blue Grass Boys band), singing the verses with courtly declaration, then leaping to a proud, high tenor harmony during the chorus trio. At the end of the recording, Taylor segued into one of Pen's favorite tunes, "Jenny Lind."

Pendleton Vandiver died in 1932, after Bill had moved away. Being unable to attend the funeral, Monroe later said, was one of the worst things in his life. In 1973, he had a headstone created for Pen's hitherto unmarked grave in the Rosine cemetery.

RICHARD D. SMITH

TWO GENERATIONS *One of the female pioneers of bluegrass, Gloria Belle (left) was a featured vocalist and backing musician in the bands of Jimmy Martin and Charlie Monroe. More recently, Rhonda Vincent has emerged as one of the genre's favorite bandleaders, winning the IBMA's Female Vocalist award a record six times (2000–05).*

Steel-String Magnolias—
Women of Bluegrass

The prominence of Alison Krauss, Dolly Parton, Rhonda Vincent, and the Dixie Chicks in today's bluegrass scene belies the bumper sticker that once sputtered, "Bluegrass is man's music."

Women have been a part of bluegrass since Sally Ann Forrester stepped on stage with Bill Monroe in 1942. Bessie Lee Mauldin, Wilma Lee Cooper, the Stoneman sisters, and Gloria Belle were all in the trenches early on. Family gospel groups offered a way off the farm and out of the factory for the women in the Sullivan Family and the Lewis Family. Later, the Marshall and Isaacs Families would follow in their footsteps.

Rose Maddox met the material of Bill Monroe with panache on *Rose Maddox Sings Bluegrass* (1962), and Donna Stoneman filled in ably for Monroe on mandolin when he left those sessions after the first day of recording.

But it was the birth of bluegrass festivals—and their intersection with the women's movement and the fading folk boom—that set the stage for large numbers of women to enter the music. Rising from this fertile conjunction were all-female bands, such as New York's feisty Buffalo Gals, California's eccentric Good Ol' Persons, and Vicki Simmons's tenacious New Coon Creek Girls. Male-female partnerships flourished in the IInd Generation; Red, White, and Bluegrass; and the Front Porch String Band; while family groups, such as the Whites, the McLains, and the Cox Family, provided safe musical havens for young girls. Yet few women, with the exception of Katie Laur and Betty Fisher, were bold enough to lead their own bands.

However, an explosion of women-led groups was on its way. Often excluded from all-male bluegrass bands and finding themselves both capable and self-assured, women began to assume the role of bandleader in the 1980s. Lynn Morris, Laurie Lewis, Kathy Kallick, and Alison Krauss led the pack. Standing on their shoulders is the newest crop of female bandleaders—Valerie Smith, Jeanette Williams, Alecia Nugent, Honi Deaton, and, the most successful of this second wave, Rhonda Vincent.

Just over the horizon is recognition for women as instrumentalists. Blazing the trail are Alison Brown (banjo), Missy Raines (bass), Sally Van Meter (dobro), young Sierra Hull (mandolin), and Nickel Creek's Sara Watkins (fiddle). Can a jaw-dropping female Doc Watson be far behind?

MURPHY HENRY

Signed to Rounder Records in 1985, when she was just 14, Krauss released her debut album in 1987, drawing instant acclaim for her soulful fiddling and diaphanous vocals. She quickly became one of bluegrass's most prominent figures. Krauss solidified her broad appeal by alternately issuing largely traditional albums with her group, Union Station, that satisfied bluegrass audiences, and more wide-ranging solo albums that reached out to country and folk audiences. The Illinois native won her first Grammy in 1990, and was made a member of the Grand Ole Opry in 1993. Two years later, she scored a sizable crossover hit with a new version of "When You Say Nothing at All" that paid tribute to the late Keith Whitley's original. The cut earned the CMA's Single of the Year award and pushed sales of her *Now That I've Found You* compilation to more than two million copies.

A new generation

Still, Krauss was not the only success story among bluegrass artists. Although the country-music industry was chasing the crossover success of Garth Brooks and other megastars, the new artists it promoted were, thanks to Skaggs, Whitley, and Krauss, familiar with and receptive to bluegrass influences. (Mainstream country acts Vince Gill, Joe Diffie, and Patty Loveless also acknowledged their bluegrass backgrounds.) At the same time, a growing number of young bluegrass musicians were moving to Nashville, spurred by the difficulty of making a living in bluegrass, and drawn by the prospects of finding work in country recording studios and artists' touring bands. Although they weren't playing bluegrass as such, they brought its musical vocabulary to country records and performances, and more than occasionally introduced their employers to both classic and contemporary examples of the genre.

Meanwhile, other young bluegrass musicians, who had absorbed the lessons offered by Doyle Lawson & Quicksilver and others, were creating bands that combined traditional elements with a new energy, which captured the spirit and, at times, the rhythmic drive of rock music. Leading the way in the early part of the decade were groups such as IIIrd Tyme Out and the Lonesome River Band, who inspired still younger musicians to take up bluegrass instruments and form their own groups.

With the death of Bill Monroe in 1996, the bluegrass community found itself taking stock. The picture was far from uniformly bright, but there was plenty of hope and vitality. In 1997, at Vince Gill's insistence, the National Academy of Recording Arts and Sciences devoted the country-music portion of their Grammy

ALISON KRAUSS *A leading artist in bluegrass from the age of 16, Alison Krauss continues to expand its horizons. While dedicated to bluegrass, she has nevertheless collaborated impressively with country artists. And she has won big— 20 Grammys as of 2006. Her involvement in* O Brother, Where Art Thou? *helped ensure its musical quality.*

It was easy to predict that the prodigiously talented teenager Alison Krauss would have a big impact on the world of bluegrass. The surprise was that she would help bluegrass make such a big impact on the world. Her voice—a delicate, bell-toned wonder—has captivated millions, from the cultured to the common, largely without the support of mainstream radio.

Krauss confounded the standard formula for the traditional bluegrass star—a rural male raised in Kentucky, Virginia, or the Carolinas. Instead, she played violin in a family of music teachers in the college town of Champaign, Illinois. Fiddlers Randy Howard and Stuart Duncan shaped the way she attacked her instrument, while Suzanne Cox of the Cox Family deeply affected her vocal style. These influences were manifest in Krauss's debut album, *Too Late to Cry*, released when she was 16. With her 1990 album *I've Got That Old Feeling*, another side of Krauss emerged —that of the gifted interpreter, who infused contemporary songs with acoustic intimacy and the rhythms of bluegrass. She found further creative outlets producing albums for the Cox Family and Nickel Creek. A platinum live album with her band Union Station in 2002, and a 2004 studio CD, *Lonely Runs Both Ways*, further showcased her abilities.

CRAIG HAVIGHURST

awards broadcast to bluegrass and bluegrass-flavored music. The segment—featuring Gill, Alison Krauss and Union Station, and Patty Loveless—closed with a riveting take on a Monroe gospel favorite, "I'm Working on a Building," performed before a backdrop that featured portraits of the Father of Bluegrass. It was not only a gesture of the musicians' respect for Monroe, but also a symbol of the status that the music had gained in recent years.

Prominent again

Over the next few years, bluegrass's prominence—both on its own and as a valued part of country music—continued to rise. Ricky Skaggs made a triumphant return to bluegrass in 1997 with his

DIXIE CHICKS *Though they aren't a bluegrass band, the Dixie Chicks (banjoist Emily Robison, singer Natalie Maines, and fiddler Martie Maguire) proudly include bluegrass influences and styles in their eclectic, string-driven brand of country music.*

Bluegrass Rules! album. Then the banjo- and fiddle-playing Dixie Chicks burst on to the country scene with a sophisticated sound that blended their bluegrass roots and instruments with powerful, energetic country and pop influences. The Del McCoury Band, featuring McCoury's sons Rob and Ron in prominent instrumental roles in the award-winning band, earned national attention with a 1999 collaboration with alternative country hero Steve Earle. And 2000's *Big Mon*, produced by Skaggs, found a host of country and pop stars paying tribute to Monroe by performing his songs.

In that light, the epic success of the seven million-selling soundtrack to the Coen Brothers 2000 film, *O Brother, Where Art Thou?*, which featured a variety of roots artists and a driving bluegrass version of the Stanley Brothers' favorite "I Am a Man of Constant Sorrow" was more a ratification of an already evident trend than a wholly unexpected surprise. Indeed, Mercury Records, which originally released the CD, anticipated even before it hit the stores that it might sell at least 100,000 copies—twice what a typical successful bluegrass album sells.

Today, more than five years after the beginning of the *O Brother* boom, bluegrass continues to enjoy unprecedented popularity. First-generation heroes, ssuch as Earl Scruggs and Ralph Stanley, as well as newcomers including Mountain Heart, have enjoyed a degree of success that would have been unimaginable during the low points of earlier decades. With its simple, yet elegant appeal, and its combination of virtuoso musicianship and down-to-earth values, bluegrass seems at last to have found a permanent niche on the American musical landscape.

BLUEGRASS RULES! *Alison Krauss, Vince Gill, and Ricky Skaggs at Carnegie Hall, November 14, 2005. As these three artists demonstrate whenever they hit the stage, bluegrassers have become some of the brightest lights in country music.*

TOP TEN

PRE-1955 TOP TEN BY MARTY STUART

1 "The Wicked Path of Sin"
Bill Monroe & the Bluegrass Quartet (1946) *The architects of bluegrass offer a glimpse into the terrors of hell, with an altar call built into the last stanza.*

2 "Honky Tonkin'"
Hank Williams (1948) *Country's greatest songwriter designs a blueprint of Saturday-night escape for lonely hearts and troubled souls.*

3 "Waiting for a Train"
Jimmie Rodgers (1929) *Hard luck, hard traveling, hard times, wrapped in a romantic bow, sung and played by the original Mississippi rounder.*

4 "Foggy Mountain Breakdown"
Lester Flatt, Earl Scruggs & the Foggy Mountain Boys (1950) *This original Mercury recording is more powerful than lightning in a bottle. The music is as inspired as anything ever written by Bach or Beethoven.*

5 "The Winding Stream"
The Carter Family (1932) *A gift from heaven.*

6 "Wabash Cannon Ball"
Roy Acuff & the Smoky Mountain Boys (1947) *America, country music, and trains were made for one another. Here's further proof.*

7 "I Hear a Sweet Voice Calling"
Bill Monroe & the Bluegrass Quartet (1947) *This is what happens when angels sing a sad story.*

8 "The Titanic"
Ernest V. Stoneman (1925) *This could possibly be one of the finest story songs ever offered.*

9 "Rainbow at Midnight"
Ernest Tubb (1946) *Not for the faint of heart. Only true hillbillies are allowed here.*

10 "Step It Up and Go"
The Maddox Brothers & Rose (1951) *Listen to this, and then let's talk about rock and roll.*

ALL SHOOK UP

THE ROCK REVOLUTION AND THE NASHVILLE SOUND

COLIN ESCOTT

ELVIS CHANGED EVERYTHING IN 1956. AT FIRST, IT SEEMED AS THOUGH ROCK & ROLL WOULD BE THE DEATH OF COUNTRY MUSIC. BUT AS IT TURNED OUT, IT PAVED THE WAY FOR COUNTRY MUSIC TO GROW AND DEVELOP. THROUGH ELVIS AND HIS PEERS, COUNTRY MUSIC REACHED NEW LEVELS, AND STARTED TO CONSISTENTLY CROSS OVER TO THE POP MARKET.

I n November 1955, Steve Sholes signed Elvis Presley away from Sun Records for $40,000, a move so risky that it would have blotted—if not ended—his career had it backfired. "A great many people in and out of RCA figured that Steve had just aced himself out of the business," recalled Brad McCuen, one of the company's field reps. Instead, RCA's country-music chief had inadvertently ushered in perhaps the greatest change ever to overtake the way in which music was made and played in Nashville.

Sholes called Elvis to RCA's Nashville studio on January 10, 1956, for a session that became an epic cultural collision. Elvis arrived at RCA with his three-piece band shortly before 2:00 p.m. RCA, like all major labels operating in Nashville, expected its country artists to record four songs in three hours with local union musicians. Using his own guys— guitarist Scotty Moore, bassist Bill Black, and drummer D. J. Fontana— as the nucleus of the group,

NEW DAY DAWNING
Steve Sholes and Elvis Presley at his RCA signing, November 1955. (Below) Elvis in his element with Scotty Moore (guitar), Bill Black (bass), and D. J. Fontana (drums) at Ellis Auditorium, Memphis, 1956.

Elvis worked from 2:00 until 10:00 p.m., then clocked up another three hours the following day. He emerged with just five songs. That was the way he'd worked at Sun, and it says much about his strange solipsism that he never even thought of accommodating RCA or the Nashville way of doing things.

Elvis dressed like nothing the Nashville musicians had ever seen (the difference between Nashville's cowboy chic and Elvis's

ONE OF A KIND *In his second movie,* Loving You *(1957), Elvis played a Hollywood version of himself—a country boy on his way to singing stardom. He was costumed in Hollywood's dim conception of the sort of singer he was, too. But of course he was not your standard country star.*

Jerry Lee Lewis has his second No. 1, "Great Balls of Fire." Elvis Presley is inducted into the US Army for two years. Johnny Cash and Carl Perkins leave Sun Records for the Columbia label. Charlie Rich makes his first recordings for Sun Records.

1959 Fidel Castro seizes power in Cuba. Johnny Horton records the No. 1 hit "Battle of New Orleans." Buddy Holly dies in a plane crash near Clear Lake, Iowa. Marty Robbins records the No. 1 pop and country hit "El Paso."

1960 Elvis Presley returns from the US Army. John F. Kennedy is elected US president. Loretta Lynn scores her first hit with "I'm a Honky-Tonk Girl." Johnny Horton dies in a car crash near Milano, Texas. A. P. Carter of the Carter Family dies.

1961 The Berlin Wall is built in Germany. Jimmie Rodgers, Fred Rose, and Hank Williams are the first to be elected to the Country Music Hall of Fame. Patsy Cline gains a No. 1 country hit with "I Fall to Pieces." Loretta Lynn signs with Decca Records. Johnny Cash and June Carter make their first appearance on stage together. Bill Anderson joins the Grand Ole Opry cast.

1962 Columbia Records buys Owen Bradley's Music Row recording studio. Ray Charles records his pioneering *Modern Sounds in Country and Western Music.* Andy Warhol exhibits his Pop Art soup cans.

The Sun King—Sam Phillips

Although Sam Phillips was one of the first record "producers," in that his records bore his stamp, he was reactionary as much as revolutionary. He believed in the sanctity of the performance; consequently, he failed to embrace many technological innovations, including multitrack recording. "I don't go for overdubbing," he said. "I understand all the techniques and the bullshit, but I just don't see the spontaneity. You can have too many crutches."

Raised on a tenant farm near Florence, Alabama, Phillips worked for a mortician before becoming a radio announcer. In 1945, he moved to Memphis where he heard the music of the bluesmen, the edge-of-town hillbilly musicians, and the big-band orchestras. He loved it all. In January 1950, after several debilitating bouts of depression, the 26-year-old radio man opened the Memphis Recording Service. Over the next couple of years, he discovered and recorded B. B. King, Howlin' Wolf, and Jackie Brenston for Chess and RPM/Modern Records, and when Brenston's "Rocket 88" became one of the best-selling R&B records of 1951, he decided to go it alone.

If Phillips had a plan, the early Sun releases don't reveal what it was. But then, in July 1954, Elvis Presley suddenly revealed himself, and it's a measure of Phillips's insight that he immediately saw the way forward.

Nothing like Elvis's "That's All Right" was selling or had ever sold, but Phillips didn't care. By late 1955, Sun was skirting bankruptcy, and the major labels were enquiring about Elvis. As of November 16, 1955, Elvis Presley was on RCA, and Phillips was $40,000 richer. He already had Johnny Cash and Carl Perkins, and "Blue Suede Shoes" was in the can. Within weeks, he was spectacularly vindicated. Perhaps only Phillips could have seen the promise in Cash and his ragged two-piece band. Likewise, Jerry Lee Lewis had been turned away in Nashville, but Phillips saw only potential. He discovered Roy Orbison and Charlie Rich as well. Yet by 1963, all of them—Perkins, Cash, Lewis, Orbison, and finally Rich—had left Phillips. Sun limped on for another six years until Phillips sold the label and its catalogue for a still-undisclosed amount to Shelby Singleton. Phillips never produced another session.

COLIN ESCOTT

GUIDING HAND *Sam Phillips (left) not only discovered Elvis and produced the young singer's incendiary first recordings, but went on to build a whole stable of revolutionary singers.*

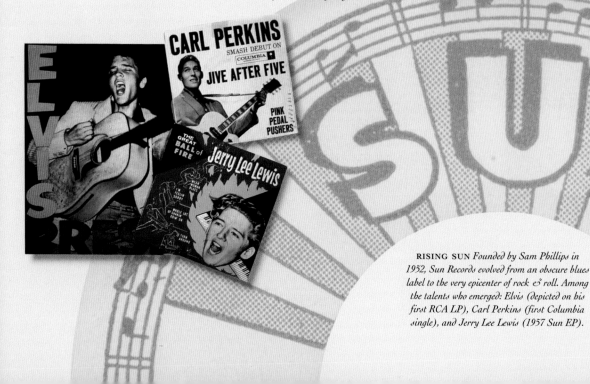

RISING SUN *Founded by Sam Phillips in 1952, Sun Records evolved from an obscure blues label to the very epicenter of rock & roll. Among the talents who emerged: Elvis (depicted on his first RCA LP), Carl Perkins (first Columbia single), and Jerry Lee Lewis (1957 Sun EP).*

Johnny Cash

TALENT TO BURN *Artists who began their careers at Sun Records include Johnny Cash (above), Jerry Lee Lewis (right), Carl Perkins, Roy Orbison, and Charlie Rich. Though Sam Phillips recognized their talent and harnessed it, he couldn't hold onto them. In time they all left for greener pastures at other record labels. (Below) Elvis, the first to leave, returned to the Sun recording studio for an impromptu reunion on December 4, 1956. As luck would have it, Sun's hottest new artists were on hand and in the mood to sing with Elvis, and Sam Phillips shrewdly turned on the recorder, capturing the spontaneous recording known today as "The Million Dollar Quartet." (From left) Lewis, Perkins, Elvis, Cash.*

CLASSIC COUNTRY
RECORDING

ELVIS PRESLEY
"That's All Right"

That's awright now, mama, any way you do.

WRITTEN BY ARTHUR "BIG BOY" CRUDUP AND RECORDED JULY 5, 1954 DID NOT CHART ON RELEASE, BUT REACHED NO. 2 IN ENGLAND UPON 50TH ANNIVERSARY RERELEASE, JULY 2004

When Elvis took a break from recording a country ballad on July 5, 1954, and began fooling around with **"That's All Right,"** he was unselfconsciously distilling all he knew into something completely original. "All of a sudden, Elvis just started singing this song, jumping around and acting the fool," recalled guitarist Scotty Moore. "And then Bill Black picked up his bass and started acting the fool, too. And I started playing with them. Sam Phillips stuck his head out and said, 'What are you doing?' And we said, 'We don't know.' 'Well, back up,' he said. 'Try to find a place to start, and do it again.'"

Arthur Crudup had recorded "That's All Right" in 1946, so Elvis might have been reconfiguring the song in his mind for perhaps seven or eight years. Crudup's faster numbers had a countrified—almost hillbilly—swing, and were quite dissimilar from standard A-A-B blues. "Down in Tupelo," Elvis famously remarked in 1956, "I used to hear old Arthur Crudup bang his box the way I do now, and I said if I ever got to the place where I could feel all old Arthur felt, I'd be a music man like nobody ever saw." And now he was.

COLIN ESCOTT

pimp chic was real), and he sounded like nothing the Nashville pickers had ever heard. Sholes's assistant, Chet Atkins, called his wife to come witness what he regarded as a freak show and later told one of the Jordanaires that Elvis would be a flash-in-the-pan. Sholes, who had asked Sam Phillips for assurance that he had "bought the right boy," packed up the tapes with some misgivings but shouldn't have worried. "Heartbreak Hotel" was among the songs he took back to New York.

Sholes had signed Elvis as a country act, but from the beginning he recognized Presley's crossover potential. He also knew the economic imperative behind such an acquisition. An inveterate workaholic, who would bring a portable disc player to the beach to audition new songs, Sholes had been employed at RCA since 1929. In his role of Director of Specialty Singles (which included R&B, kiddies' music, and country), he had thought long and hard about the future of country music and came to the conclusion that he needed Elvis or someone like him. "Your older listeners who want old country-music sounds are wonderful people," he said in an address to country DJs. "They're the backbone of this country, loyal radio listeners (when the kids aren't around), but they don't buy records. Not enough

> **"I'd always thought that Sun Records and Sam Phillips himself had created the most crucial, uplifting and powerful records ever made. Next to Sam's records, all the rest sounded fruity."**
> **BOB DYLAN**

ROCK & ROLL DREAMS *In 1954, Elvis was a pimply teenager, still dreaming of a recording career. Two years later, he was the biggest-selling artist in music and had turned the music world upside down. Here he surveys the competition at a Memphis record store, 1957.*

GOOD ROCKIN' *Elvis Presley onstage in Memphis in 1956, with bassist Bill Black in the background. Although he appeared first on the country record charts, ultimately Elvis proved too big for a single genre.*

to keep us in business. Not enough to keep the old-fashioned country artist in guitar strings. It's the kids who . . . want and buy the newer sounds."

Taking a chance

And so Sholes pressured his sales manager, John Burgess who, in turn, pressured his staff. "It's imperative that you follow up this all-market approach to every station receiving Pop or Country service," Burgess wrote to his reps. "Use the trade articles to sell your dealers and one-stops across the board." "Heartbreak Hotel" was released on January 27, 1956, and there was an

agonizing five weeks when Sholes's long career at RCA was on the line. But then the single began showing up on several local charts. Then it showed up on both the national pop and country charts, and neither country nor pop music would ever be quite the same again.

KING'S AXE *This Martin D18 acoustic was one of the first guitars Elvis used professionally. He customized it using stick-on lettering to spell his name.*

WANDA JACKSON

BORN MAUD, OKLAHOMA,
OCTOBER 20, 1937
PLAYED GUITAR
FIRST RECORDED 1954
INFLUENCES WESTERN-SWING
VOCALISTS, ELVIS PRESLEY

Wanda Jackson discovered early
that she was meant to sing. Born
in small-town Oklahoma,
Jackson lived in California until
she was 12. Returning to her
home state, she became a
protégé of Hank Thompson,
who placed her with Decca
Records, and then with Capitol.

In 1955, she toured with
Elvis Presley. They rode around
and flirted between shows.
Jackson's recordings edged
ever closer to rock & roll, but
her first success came in Japan
with "Fujiyama Mama." In 1960,
her recording of "Let's Have a
Party," recorded with the racially
mixed band, Bobby Poe & the
Poe Kats, became a Top 40 hit.

Jackson returned to country
music in 1961 and racked up a
number of hits beginning with
"Right or Wrong" and "In the
Middle of a Heartache." In 1973,
beset by personal problems, and
with her career on the decline,
she forsook secular music
altogether, but gradually
returned. In 2004, an alternative
country label produced a tribute
CD, *Hard Headed Woman: A
Celebration of Wanda Jackson*.
She might not approve of the riot-
grrrl cult she inspired, but there's
no doubt that while other girl
singers were simpering about
"where the boys are," Jackson
sang as if she knew all too well.

COLIN ESCOTT

Within months of signing to RCA, Elvis
triggered a three-alarm anxiety attack in
Nashville. Country DJs, a relatively new
species, began chasing the youth dollar.
They spun Elvis's records and other
rockabilly records, and quickly squeezed
out the older artists. Booking agent Hal
Smith handled veteran Ernest Tubb at the
time. "We came to the conclusion that the
best thing to do would be to get out of the
business," Smith told Tubb's biographer
Ronnie Pugh. "Ernest's brother was in the
insurance business in Texas, so Ernest
said, 'I could go into business with Bud,
but this is all I've ever done.' It was so sad."

Tubb, in fact, hung in there long enough
to see his career revive, but things looked
bleak in 1956. Television was tempting
country music's traditional audience to stay
at home, and, as Steve Sholes had seen, the
teenagers didn't want older country music.
The Grand Ole Opry was three-quarters
empty some nights, and NBC dropped it
from the network schedule in 1957. Other
radio barn dances folded one by one. It
was one of those moments, like the end
of World War II or the onset of the
Great Depression, when all bets
were off, and no one knew what
would happen next.

Because Elvis had been signed
by RCA's country division, the
head offices of the other major
labels—Decca, Columbia, and
Capitol—brought pressure on
their country A&R chiefs (Paul
Cohen, Don Law, and Ken Nelson,
respectively) to find the "next
Elvis." Hundreds of young hopefuls
were sucked in and spat out. A
few, such as Buddy Holly, Johnny
Burnette, and Conway Twitty,
would resurface another place,
another time, but they, along with
most others, were cut loose after
one or two sessions in 1956.

Rockabilly and pop

Since at least the 1970s, there
has been a strong cult following,
mostly in Europe, for some of
the rockabilly recordings from
Nashville, circa 1956. But they
certainly didn't sell at the time,
and neither did the attempts by
older artists to cut rock & roll.

Ernest Tubb recorded Chuck Berry's
"Maybellene." Webb Pierce recorded a
benighted vocal version of Bill Justis's
hit instrumental, "Raunchy," and tried
covering the Everly Brothers' "Bye, Bye
Love." Buck Owens cut rockabilly under
the pseudonym of Corky Jones. George
Jones tried it too as Thumper Jones.
The desperation was almost palpable.
Looking back on that era, Faron Young
concluded, "Hell, we all started trying to
put a bit of that jiggery in there. You're
making a quarter million a year, and
suddenly you're down to seventy-five,
eighty thousand. You'll do anything."

Slowly, it became clear that Elvis
represented an opportunity more than
a threat, because he'd opened up pop radio.
Country musicians had adapted pop songs
long before the first phonograph records,
and pop singers had been making hits out
of country songs for almost as long.

SONNY JAMES *Though he had had minor hits previously,
"Young Love" in 1957 was a breakthrough for Sonny James.
The record went No. 1 on both the pop and country charts.
He followed it with 21 more country No. 1s through the '70s.*

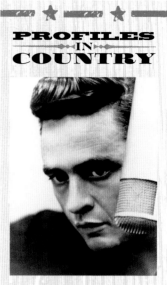

JOHNNY CASH

BORN KINGSLAND, ARKANSAS,
FEBRUARY 26, 1932
DIED SEPTEMBER 12, 2003
PLAYED GUITAR
FIRST RECORDED 1955
INFLUENCES JIMMIE RODGERS,
ROY ACUFF, THE LOUVIN BROTHERS
HITS "FOLSOM PRISON BLUES,"
"I WALK THE LINE," "RING OF FIRE"

At the dawn of his career in the 1950s, while his peers reached for pop stardom or stuck to the Hank Williams formula, Johnny Cash and his Tennessee Two punched out an unusually stark and distinctively rhythmic sound in the Sun Records studios. He wrote lyrics pulled from the joys and desperation of his own rural experience, then later, inspired by epochs and peoples not his own, recorded concept albums that diverged from commercial pressures.

His real gamble came in 1968 with a concert album, *Johnny Cash at Folsom Prison*, which fueled the myth that he had once served hard time. *Folsom* hoisted Cash to another level—his own ABC-TV series—and even when his sales declined in the mid-1970s, he remained country's quintessential personality. With help from producer Rick Rubin, Cash recaptured his artistry in the '90s and was a symbol of artistic adventurousness up until his death.

MICHAEL STREISSGUTH

Country songs first entered pop music *en masse* in the early 1940s, when the National Association of Broadcasters (NAB)—i.e., the radio station owners— boycotted pop songs protected by the ASCAP, because ASCAP had exorbitantly raised its licensing rates. In response, the NAB formed its own song-licensing agency, BMI. Trying to generate repertoire in a hurry, BMI cultivated the areas that ASCAP had ignored, notably country music. As a result, country songs such as "You Are My Sunshine" and "Pistol Packin' Mama" became gigantic pop hits. By the late 1940s, it seemed as though virtually every major country hit was

YOUNG LIONS
Johnny Cash and Elvis Presley meet backstage at the Grand Ole Opry, December 21, 1957. Unlike older country stars, Cash wasn't threatened by Presley's success. He had a fresh new sound of his own. (Right) Cash's first LP on Sun Records.

"He was everything I thought an artist ought to be."
KRIS KRISTOFFERSON ON CASH

"covered" for the pop market. "Jealous Heart," "Tennessee Waltz," "Slippin' Around," and most of Hank Williams's biggest songs became pop hits for top artists such as Patti Page, Tony Bennett, Frankie Laine, and Guy Mitchell. The same thing happened later with R&B songs, such as "Wheel of Fortune," "Hearts of Stone," and "Sincerely." It was nothing new for the pop charts to have a good sampling of country and R&B songs then, but after Elvis there was an opportunity for the original artists to cross over alongside their songs.

RCA's Steve Sholes had seen far enough ahead to know that he needed Elvis, but soon became so engrossed in Elvis's career that he let the country division slide. Capitol's Ken Nelson was the first to take advantage of the change that Elvis had wrought. Nelson had two struggling artists on his roster—Ferlin Husky and Sonny James. Husky had spent most of his career in the Bakersfield beer joints, while James worked southern

barn dances. They had both recorded for Capitol since 1952. Husky had seen a few hits, but none recently, while James had made minor hits but little impact.

At the end of October 1956, Nelson flew from his base in Los Angeles to Nashville. An Atlanta music publisher, Bill Lowery, had given him a record by a kid called Ric Cartey, and Lowery wanted to license the record to a major label. The top side was a rockabilly tune, "Ooh-Eee," and the flip side was a song that Cartey and his girlfriend had composed, entitled "Young Love." Nelson told Lowery that he would like Sonny James to do the song on the B-side, and Lowery agreed. It wasn't a song about drinking, cheating, dying mothers, or train wrecks; it was about the first blush of romance. Nelson sensed that it needed a new backdrop. Out went the fiddle, the banjo, and the steel guitar; in came the electric guitar and a chorus. James was from rural Alabama, but on "Young Love" he sounded curiously placeless. The regionality and nasality had gone, along with the hard-country instruments, such as fiddle and steel guitar. The result was easily digestible by pop radio.

A new sound

A week later, Nelson was still in Nashville when Ferlin Husky arrived. Four years earlier, Husky had recorded a ballad called "Gone" under the pseudonym Terry Preston. Now he rerecorded it; again the country instruments were replaced, and the chorus moved way up in the mix. By February 1957, "Young Love" was at No. 1 on the pop charts, and "Gone" followed right behind it at No. 4. Nelson was so self-effacing that it's hard to tell if this was a visionary act on his part or dumb luck. "Golly, were others trying to copy the sound that I created?" he once remarked incredulously to a journalist. "I didn't create the sound. The musicians and the singers created the sound. I guess it's possible that it did have some influence on the recording industry."

But Sonny James remembers Nelson telling Bill Lowery that "Young Love" would be a hit and remembers that he was as skeptical as Lowery. "Are you sure, Ken?" James asked, and Nelson was sure.

FERLIN HUSKY *Recording in the studio, ca. 1952, the year he signed with Capitol Records. Husky labored five years before scoring his first country No. 1, "Gone," which proved to be an early template for the Nashville Sound.*

It was also Nelson's idea to bring the chorus into the mix, quite possibly because Dean Martin had scored a big pop hit on Capitol with "Memories Are Made of This." Martin's record shaded toward country and had a very upfront chorus.

"Young Love" clarified the situation for the Nashville A&R men and music publishers—there was no point in goading older country singers into performing rock & roll; the challenge was to find someone who could sing convincingly about adolescent ardor.

Nashville Sound—in NY

Marty Robbins told Don Law that he could. Back in 1954, he had covered Elvis's first record, "That's All Right," and he, not Elvis, had scored the hit. In doing so, however, Robbins hadn't made the first major label rockabilly record. In his version, "That's All Right" was an up-tempo country song; there was none of Elvis's twitchy energy. One year or so later, Robbins issued an album, *Rockin' Rollin' Robbins*, that he hated with all his heart. (Toward the end of his life he said that he wanted to buy up every copy.) When the flirtation with rock & roll didn't work, Robbins reverted to straight country with "Singing the Blues" and surprised everyone by scoring one of the biggest country hits of 1956. Guy Mitchell covered it for the pop market, and Robbins was outraged because Mitchell was on his label, Columbia Records. Robbins knew that his record had sold around 750,000 copies, while Mitchell's had sold three million. He felt that Mitchell's chance should have been his and insisted on recording in New York with Mitchell's producer, Mitch Miller, and arranger, Ray Conniff.

> **I THINK IF YOU WENT AROUND TOWN ASKING PEOPLE WHO WAS THE BEST SINGER WE EVER HAD AROUND HERE, EVERYBODY WOULD PRETTY MUCH SAY, 'THE REST OF US ARE JUST TRYIN'. IT'S MARTY ROBBINS.'**
>
> **MARTY STUART**

MARTY ROBBINS

BORN GLENDALE, ARIZONA,
SEPTEMBER 26, 1925
DIED DECEMBER 8, 1982
PLAYED GUITAR, PIANO,
INFLUENCES GENE AUTRY,
EDDY ARNOLD
HITS "SINGING THE BLUES,"
"A WHITE SPORT COAT (AND A
PINK CARNATION)," "EL PASO"

From 1953 through 1983
Marty Robbins was never
off the country charts, and
he hit with every kind of
song—hard country, rocka-
billy, teen pop, cowboy, and
Nashville Sound crossover.

Although he tried his
hand at a variety of odd
jobs, no vocation interested
him until he found work
singing in Phoenix night-
clubs and on broadcasts.
Gene Autry had been his
childhood hero, but his
early singing was styled
after a newer idol, Eddy
Arnold. A No.1 hit on "I'll
Go On Alone" brought him
to Nashville and the Grand
Ole Opry in 1953.

When rock & roll
came, Robbins competed
on the pop charts with
prom hits, such as "A
White Sport Coat (And a
Pink Carnation)." Later, he
turned to cowboy music
and had a huge hit with
"El Paso." He was elected
to the Country Music Hall
of Fame in 1982. Two
months later, he died of
heart disease at 57.

RONNIE PUGH

In January 1957, Robbins went to New
York with four songs very much like
"Young Love," and one of them, "A White
Sport Coat (And a Pink Carnation),"
became a No. 2 pop hit. For the next 18
months, Robbins made early Nashville
Sound records in New York. In that time,
he notched up three more pop and country
hits with Miller's confections—"The
Story of My Life" (the first hit for the
partnership of Burt Bacharach and Hal
David), "Just Married," and "She Was
Only Seventeen." Robbins's restlessness
and versatility led him back to Nashville
and then on to western music, but the
success of the New York productions
didn't go unnoticed in Nashville.

Sonny James, Ferlin Husky, and Marty
Robbins had shown the way, but the
record that really sent country music in a
new direction was Jim Reeves's "Four
Walls." Unlike "Young Love" and "White
Sport Coat," it was identifiably a country
song. Reeves's career had taken off at the
Louisiana Hayride radio barn dance in
Shreveport, and his first hit came in 1953
with a novelty song, "Mexican Joe." Elvis
joined the *Hayride* a year later, so Reeves
had a front-row seat for the birth of rockabilly but wanted absolutely no part of it.
Others could make fools of themselves
with this new music; Reeves would not.
Steve Sholes bought his contract from the
tiny Abbott label in 1955 (a deal that

BEST OF THE WEST *In 1959, when most singers had
abandoned cowboy songs, Marty Robbins devoted this LP
to them, scoring a pop and country No. 1 with the single
"El Paso."*

became a template for his acquisition of
Presley later that year), and Reeves moved
to Nashville. Chet Atkins took over
Reeves's sessions after Sholes became con-
sumed with all things Presley, and Atkins
took his cue from "Young Love" and
"White Sport Coat." Ironically, Reeves
found "Four Walls" by chance. The demo
and lead sheet were sitting in a pile on
Atkins's desk that toppled over into the
trash. Reeves retrieved them, read through
the lyrics, and told Atkins he'd like to cut
the song. Out went the fiddle and steel
guitar, and in came the piano, electric guitar, vibraphone, strings, and vocal chorus.

An intimate vocal sound

"It was a lot of stress," Atkins told
journalist Dave Bussey, "because I had to
run back and forth to the control room, but
Jim liked my guitar sound and wanted me
to play the introduction and the bridge. He
also wanted the Jordanaires, and I called
and couldn't get them. Jim said he wanted
that sound, so we moved the session back
to when we could get them. He also wanted
to rehearse the song, and we were both
working on WSM, and we arranged to
rehearse 'Four Walls' one evening after the
radio program. The Jordanaires were
there, too. All great things are an accident.
You don't just sit down and say, 'I'm going
to develop this or that.' I wasn't trying to
change the business, just sell records. I
realized at that time [that] you had to
surprise the public and give them something
a little different. At that time, we had an
engineer from New York who was from
the old school, and he didn't believe in
artists getting too close to the microphone,
in case they popped a 'p' into it. Jim
wanted an intimate sound, and wanted to
get real close and whisper the lyrics, and he
had many arguments with this engineer.
Then it so happened that we recorded
'Four Walls' with [engineer] Selby Coffeen.
Steve Sholes was amazed. He said, 'How
did you get that beautiful vocal sound?'"

"Four Walls," sung in a warm, enveloping
baritone with no trace of Reeves's dirt-
poor east Texas background, was almost
embarrassingly intimate and changed the
way things were done in Nashville. Its quiet,
claustrophobic desperation ("Four walls to
hear me, four walls to see. Four walls too
near me, closing in on me.") ushered in the

new era. The record reached No. 11 on the pop charts, topped the country lists, and predicated much of what happened in country music through the next ten years.

Reeves's enormous achievement wasn't rock & roll; it was a response to the opening up of the airwaves that had been triggered by rock & roll. At the time "Four Walls" was recorded, Nashville

BOARD DIRECTORS *Chet Atkins (left) and recording engineer Bill Porter monitor a session in RCA's Nashville studio, now known as Studio B, ca. 1960. Atkins had ascended to the role of producer by 1957; Porter was his right-hand man from 1959–1964.*

A&R men had yet to develop a consistently successful rock & roll act. But one month after "Four Walls" entered the pop charts, the Everly Brothers' first hit, "Bye, Bye Love," also cracked the charts.

PROFILES IN COUNTRY

JIM REEVES

BORN PANOLA COUNTY, TEXAS, AUGUST 20, 1923
DIED JULY 31, 1964
PLAYED GUITAR
FIRST RECORDED 1949
INFLUENCES JIMMIE RODGERS, EDDY ARNOLD, GENE AUTRY
HITS "MEXICAN JOE," "FOUR WALLS," "HE'LL HAVE TO GO"

In the late 1950s, as Nashville producers wove popular sounds into country music, singer Jim Reeves best epitomized their work. Virtually nothing about his lush recordings reflected traditional country flavor. Few pop fans who bought "Four Walls" and "He'll Have to Go" guessed that the former baseball player began as a hillbilly singer, delivering novelty tunes for tiny Abbott Records. Although Reeves disliked the unsophisticated ditties, their success landed him a spot at RCA Victor.

In 1956 and 1957, RCA released two songs that signaled a new direction for Reeves—"My Lips Are Sealed" and "Am I Losing You." Both featured Reeves's romantic style and foreshadowed his pop breakthroughs.

The emergence of "Four Walls" literally opened a new world to the polished crooner. RCA dispatched Reeves on overseas tours, where he became Nashville's premier emissary. But he had little time to enjoy it. In 1964, Reeves and pianist Dean Manuel perished when the plane Reeves piloted crashed in the woods south of Nashville. Reeves remained on the charts 20 years after his death.

MICHAEL STREISSGUTH

VELVET TONES *Working with producer Chet Atkins, mellow-voiced Jim Reeves found a smooth, intimate sound that crossed over to the pop charts regularly through such hits as "Am I Losing You" (1957), "Four Walls" (1957), and "He'll Have to Go" (1959).*

"The Everly Brothers were my favorite rock & roll duo in the 1950s. Their harmonies were impeccable, and the songs and musicianship on the records excellent."

PAUL MCCARTNEY

EVERLY BROTHERS *Don (left) and Phil Everly brought the timeless brother-duet harmony style of the Delmore Brothers and the Louvin Brothers right up to date, becoming rock & roll stars and teenage idols, launched by their first big hit, "Bye, Bye Love" (1957).*

In the years ahead, the Everlys would become the first successful rock & roll act to be based, recorded, and managed out of Nashville. Although Don Everly was 20 years old and his brother, Phil, only 18, they had been performing for a decade. Their hits brought the sound of the country brother duet into the rock & roll age.

Where once the brother duets had sung of God, tragedy, and the home place, the Everlys had more pressing concerns— "How Can I Meet Her?" "Should We Tell Him?" "When Will I Be Loved" They experimented with R&B riffs and unusual open tunings. There were relatively few guitar solos on the Everly Brothers' records; instead, acoustic guitar riffs punctuated the verses. Two country songwriters, Felice and Boudleaux Bryant, had written the Everlys' breakthrough hit, "Bye, Bye Love," and were given the job of cranking out teen dramas for the duo. The Nashville session men proved adept at

providing the accompaniment. But for all their success, the Everlys were out on a limb in Nashville. They recorded for a New York label, Cadence Records, that didn't have a full-time or even part-time staff member in Tennessee, and their records didn't seem to change the way music was made in Nashville.

The Nashville way of doing things had changed, though. A year or so after Jim Reeves broke through with "Four Walls," Nashville music journalist Charlie Lamb coined the phrase "Nashville Sound" in his trade magazine, *Music Reporter.* Two years later, *Time* magazine published a piece about country music, using Reeves as its focus. With that article, "The Nashville Sound" became a phrase on everyone's lips. No one quite knew what it was (Chet Atkins famously jingled the change in his pockets when anyone asked him), but it became a music-industry catchphrase, nonetheless.

POP PRINCES *The Everlys' blend of country urgency and pop polish was so modern-sounding that most teenage fans never knew that all of the Everlys' early hits were recorded in Nashville. (Left) The Everlys' first LP from 1958.*

"they're off and rolling," says Archie

THE EVERLY BROTHERS

The minute *Bye-Bye Love* hit, the Everlys were in. Frails sent mail by the bale. The same thing happened with *Wake Up Little Susie* —only more so. Their pickin' and singin' won everybody with an ear to hear. The whole country woke up and spoke up for the Everlys. That's why Archie brings you more of the kind of music that made them famous on this Cadence LP.

a high-fidelity recording by
CADENCE CLP-3003

The Pickers

Capitol's Ken Nelson said that the Nashville Sound was all down to the musicians, and there was no doubt that the city's fabled "A-Team" had much to do with it. From the mid-1950s onward, the city's burgeoning music business had attracted a cadre of musicians who could make

their living solely from sessions. In the 1950s, the core group comprised guitarists Grady Martin, Hank Garland, Harold Bradley, and Ray Edenton; pianists Floyd Cramer and Marvin Hughes; bassist Bob Moore; and drummer Buddy Harman. Most of the vocal harmonies were by the Anita Kerr Singers and the Jordanaires. Harman reckoned that he worked 15,000 sessions during his stint as Nashville's preeminent session drummer. Most of the work was done in two studios — RCA's custom-built studio on Hawkins Street that had opened in 1957 (later known as Studio B), and Owen Bradley's studio. In 1955, Bradley had opened the first studio (in fact, the first music-related

Who You Gonna Call?
The A-Team!

For most of the 1950s and 1960s, the same select group of local musicians played on most Nashville recording sessions. These first-call studio pros earned the nickname "The A-Team."

The core group coalesced in the late 1940s and early 1950s, as country recording sessions became more frequent in Nashville. WSM music director and local orchestra leader Owen Bradley played a pivotal role. As he became involved in recording sessions, he enlisted other local sidemen to work those sessions, including guitarists Jack Shook and Harold Bradley (Owen's younger brother), bassist Bob Moore, drummer Farris Coursey, and vocal arranger Anita Kerr.

Chet Atkins, who arrived in Nashville in 1950, gradually went from A-Team studio guitarist to producer. Also pivotal was Grady Martin, whose arranging skills often placed him in the position of studio bandleader. Joining that cadre were guitarists Hank Garland, pianist Floyd Cramer, drummer Buddy Harman, and rhythm-guitar specialist Ray Edenton.

Around the mid-1950s, after Atkins and Bradley became producers for RCA and Decca, respectively, they worked to revitalize country record sales, hurt by rock & roll's ascendancy, by producing records appealing to country fans but catchy enough to reach pop audiences as well. Under their direction, fiddles and steel guitars gave way to smooth, pop-sounding background, often aided by one of Nashville's two premier vocal quartets—the Anita Kerr Singers or the Jordanaires.

This new production technique, christened the Nashville Sound, required versatile, creative instrumentalists. Martin, Garland, Harold Bradley, Bob Moore, Buddy Harman, Ray Edenton, and Floyd Cramer, later joined by saxophonist Boots Randolph, were the nucleus of the original "A Team." Flexibility ruled—to achieve the pickaxe clang on Jimmy Dean's "Big Bad John," Cramer banged a hammer on a piece of metal.

The A-Team's work accelerated Nashville's expansion into a world-class recording center, though the lineup changed with musical trends and generational shifts. Several A-Teamers became stars, among them Floyd Cramer, Jerry Reed, Ray Stevens, and Boots Randolph. Today, a select crew of first-call musicians still handle most Nashville recording, carrying on and building upon the traditions of the original A-Team.

RICH KIENZLE

NASHVILLE SESSION *In this scene from a 1960 Roy Orbison session, you can see the casual interplay that characterized the Nashville studio system. (from left) Guitarist Hank Garland, Anita Kerr, Dottie Dillard, Louis Nunley, guitarist Harold Bradley, Roy Orbison (without glasses), James Wilkerson, and producer Fred Foster.*

REACHING FOR A NOTE *Slim Whitman records in Owen Bradley's Nashville studio with a gang of session musicians that includes bassist Bob Moore (left), Owen Bradley (background, on piano), and violinist Lillian Vann Hunt, 1950s.*

MAKING ARRANGEMENTS *Anita Kerr was a key contributor to the sophisticated musical arrangements of the Nashville Sound. Not only did she lead a background chorus group used on many sessions, but she also helped Chet Atkins (pictured) arrange and produce many recordings.*

enterprise of any kind) on 16th Avenue, or what is now Music Row, and in 1962 he sold the studio to Columbia Records.

The "A-Team" even drew Elvis back to Nashville. He'd hardly recorded there after the "Heartbreak Hotel" session in 1956, but from the time he left the Army in March 1960 he recorded the majority of his nonsoundtrack sessions in Nashville. Elvis no longer carried a band because he'd stopped performing, but he found the Nashville cats very much to his liking. They were stereotyped as country musicians, but in addition to Elvis, they worked for Roy Orbison, the Everly Brothers, Brenda Lee, Perry Como, Ann-Margret, Al Hirt, and many other pop acts.

It wasn't widely known that Elvis, Orbison, and other acts of that ilk recorded in Nashville, so it was assumed that Nashville's session musicians could play only country music. In fact, they were supremely adaptable and inventive, and were more likely to play jazz than country or pop on their rare days off. The key element of their style was that they worked up spontaneous arrangements in the studio—"head arrangements"—drawing on a deep knowledge of country, R&B, gospel, and classic pop.

"I worked weekends with Owen Bradley's society dance band," said bassist

Bob Moore. "I knew more than three-chord country music, and so did most of the others. I led a rehearsal band on Sundays because some of the younger musicians wanted to practice. Bill Porter, who was a high school friend, engineered the sessions at RCA's Studio B. Forty or fifty musicians would come by, and the younger arrangers would bring arrangements. That's where the big sound came from. We were like a young prizefighter—hungry, lean, and wanting the recognition so bad you could taste it."

The classic sound

Moore hinted at a little-known fact about the classic Nashville Sound era—most of the key players had grown up with pop music. In fact, Nashville had a more

extensive pop-music scene than just about any other city in the South. Nashville's pop orchestras are barely remembered today, but to a generation of Americans "The Nashville Sound" meant the pop sounds of orchestra leaders, such as Beasley Smith and Francis Craig. Arranger-composer-conductor Smith cowrote Roy Acuff's "Night Train to Memphis," and led an orchestra at the Andrew Jackson Hotel in Nashville before taking over the WSM radio ensemble in 1933. Smith had a major role in the career of another local singer, Dinah Shore, and cowrote a pop standard, "That Lucky Old Sun." Craig led a band at Nashville's downtown Hermitage Hotel, and like Smith had a show on WSM (the Opry's parent station) that was picked up by the NBC network for

Hitmakers' Workshops—Nashville's Bradley Studios and RCA Studio B

From 1955 to 1970, two recording studios were the primary workhorses of Nashville's budding music industry. In late 1954, Owen Bradley bought an old house at 804 16th Avenue South and remodeled the basement, tearing out the first floor to create a two-story studio space. The studio, which opened in 1955, was the first on what became Nashville's Music Row. Later Bradley acquired a surplus military Quonset Hut and built a second, adjoining studio for both sound recordings and films. Bradley himself produced many sessions there, especially after he became Nashville's chief of Decca Records in 1958. His friendly rivals Don Law at Columbia Records and Ken Nelson at Capitol Records also frequently used the studios. Columbia bought the Bradley studios in 1962 and built new offices around the Quonset Hut. Through the years, the studios yielded hits such as Sonny James's "Young Love," Gene Vincent's "Be-Bop-a-Lula," and Marty Robbins's "El Paso."

Bradley's success inspired RCA to strengthen its Nashville presence. In 1957, RCA country producer Steve Sholes convinced his superiors to build a Nashville studio in a building leased long-term from businessman Dan Maddox. Located at 17th Avenue South and Hawkins, this small facility was commonly known as Little Victor until 1964, when the label built a bigger studio next door. The larger facility then became Studio A; the smaller one was dubbed Studio B. Like the Bradley operation, Studio B quickly became a hit factory, turning out country and pop hits alike for RCA and other labels, including Presley's "Are You Lonesome Tonight," Jim Reeves's "He'll Have to Go," and Roy Orbison's "Crying."

By the 1970s, the two studios no longer dominated the local scene as before. RCA closed Studio B in 1977, and the Country Music Hall of Fame and Museum began to operate it as a historic site. Columbia finally shuttered the former Bradley facilities two years later.

JOHN W. RUMBLE

HOME OF A THOUSAND HITS *Built in 1957, RCA Studio B in Nashville was home to numerous hits, including Elvis Presley's "Are You Lonesome Tonight," the Everly Brothers' "Bye, Bye Love," and Roy Orbison's "Only the Lonely."*

Music TV from the Heartland—
The Ozark Jubilee

Between 1955 and 1960, ABC's *Ozark Jubilee* dominated the country-music TV landscape. While broadening the fame of host Red Foley, it also served as a launching pad for talented newcomers, such as Porter Wagoner and Brenda Lee.

The *Jubilee* began as a local radio production of Springfield, Missouri's station KWTO in 1953. The following year, ABC picked up a portion of the show for live radio network broadcast from the Jewell Theater on South Jefferson Street. Next, Crossroads TV Productions' ramrod E. E. "Si" Siman—backed by his partners John Mahaffey, Lester E. Cox, and KWTO founder Ralph Foster— convinced the ABC network that this country show from the heartland had the potential to engage a national audience.

Siman's ace in the hole was Red Foley, who had hosted his own network radio shows and headlined the Grand Ole Opry's NBC network segment from 1946 to 1953. When Foley's personal problems caused a falling-out with WSM officials, Siman recruited Foley for the *Ozark Jubilee* radio show. Blessed with a warm, rich baritone, the sincere, easygoing star was equally ingratiating on the small screen. After the *Jubilee* made its first telecast on January 22, 1955, viewers began watching in droves.

Over its brief life, the show's cast included top names, such as Webb Pierce, Jean Shepard, Sonny James, Wanda Jackson, Billy Walker, and Brenda Lee, who was 11 years old at the time of her 1956 debut. Pete Stamper provided stand-up comedy, as did the team of Uncle Cyp and Aunt Sap. The Foggy River Boys gospel quartet (soon renamed the Marksmen) and square dancers added variety. The production was relatively involved for a country show of the day, including special sets and overhead camera shots achieved with mirrors.

Although never a Top 25 prime-time show, the *Jubilee* nevertheless managed strong ratings. Eager to reach rural customers, national advertisers such as Massey-Ferguson (farm equipment) and Williamson- Dickie (work clothing) became faithful sponsors.

During the show's five-year run, the *Jubilee*'s track record as an advertising tool and talent vehicle did much to ensure the future of country music television.

JOHN W. RUMBLE

BRENDA LEE *Discovered by* Ozark Jubilee *host Red Foley in 1956, 11-year-old Brenda Lee was a cast member of the TV show into 1957.*

coast-to-coast transmission. In 1947, Craig recorded what is statistically the best-charting pop record of all time, "Near You." It spent 17 weeks atop the *Billboard* chart; no record ever stayed longer. Craig recorded his song in Nashville for a small, local independent label—Bullet Records.

The vibrant music scene attracted a core of musicians, including Owen Bradley and Anita Kerr, who began their careers with an older generation of bandleaders but would go on to have a profound influence on the development of the Nashville Sound. Nashville's pop- music scene of the 1930s also attracted Fred Rose, who would leave, but eventually return, to start the first major music publishing house in Nashville—Acuff- Rose Publications. Rose became Hank Williams's producer, publisher, and mentor. Acuff-Rose's earliest rival—Tree Music— was launched by Jack Stapp, who had

been hired by WSM in 1938 to originate essentially easy-listening music shows that could be networked nationwide.

Many of the musicians and music business people, who had come to Nashville to work in pop music, looked down their noses at the country-music scene. When Owen Bradley made a countrified boogie record for Bullet in 1946, he insisted that it be issued under a pseudonym, Brad Brady. It was only after it had sold several thousand copies that he told Bullet's proprietor, Jim Bulleit, "I think you might have something with this hillbilly thing," and requested that later pressings be under his real name. Anita Kerr, who led the chorus that became such a feature of many Nashville Sound records, came to Nashville from Memphis and assembled her first choral group in the late 1940s to work with Beasley Smith on WSM's *Sunday Down South* network radio

"I wasn't that familiar with country music, but I learned fast."

ANITA KERR

DON GIBSON
"Oh Lonesome Me"

There must be some way I can lose these lonesome blues...

WRITTEN BY DON GIBSON
AND RECORDED
DECEMBER 3, 1957
NO. 7 POP; NO.1 COUNTRY
AUGUST 14, 1958

Don Gibson was living in a trailer park outside Nashville, his home appliances repossessed, his past littered with failed record deals. Then, on the same day in 1957, the songwriter conjured two classics—"I Can't Stop Loving You" and **"Oh Lonesome Me."**

"Oh Lonesome Me" proved especially strong. RCA producer-guitarist Chet Atkins, seeking an antidote to country's waning sales, infused the song with up-tempo elements borrowed from the newer sounds of rock & roll. In a savvy production move, he miked Troy Hatcher's bass drum to accentuate the beat and heaped on liberal helpings of the Jordanaires' background vocals to enhance a pop feel. A peppy electric guitar solo from Atkins himself sealed the deal. "Oh Lonesome Me" spent 21 weeks on the pop charts, rising to No. 7, while nesting for eight weeks at No.1 on the country side.

For the next two decades, Gibson's vocals—masculine, dramatic, and vulnerable—would seldom fail to air on country radio.

MICHAEL STREISSGUTH

ANITA KERR SINGERS *Anita Kerr's quartet — (from left) Gil Wright, Anita Kerr, Dottie Dillard, and Louis Nunley — provided background chorus vocals on numerous Nashville hits of the 1950s and early '60s, such as Bobby Helms's "My Special Angel" and Jim Reeves's "He'll Have to Go."*

show. In 1950, Paul Cohen at Decca Records wanted a chorus on a Red Foley record, "Our Lady of Fatima," initiating Kerr's career in the recording studios. "I wasn't that familiar with country music," she said tactfully, "but I learned fast."

The men in charge

All the pieces were in place by the mid-to-late 1950s. Top 40 radio had embraced the zone where pop and country met; the Nashville musicians and studios were world class; the producers were attuned to crossover; and country songwriters were learning how to write about young love rather than tears in beers. The three men in the producer's chair, for most of what is now regarded as the classic Nashville Sound era, were Chet Atkins, Owen Bradley, and Don Law. All three took criticism from country purists for betraying country music, but they were contending with the economic reality that Steve Sholes had spelled out a few years earlier. Their jobs didn't depend on records that cultists would reissue half a century later but on crossover hits. "The way you keep your job," Atkins told Alanna Nash and anyone else who tried to criticize him, "is to sell records."

Atkins had been a journeyman country guitarist, but his taste, as revealed in a series of LPs made throughout the 1950s and 1960s, ran to light classics, jazz, pop, and Spanish music. He had effectively taken over RCA's country division from Steve Sholes in 1957, when he was made manager of the Nashville studio, but didn't assume total creative control until 1958. His initial signings included Don Gibson, who had been recording since 1949 with very little success. Gibson immediately scored with his original versions of "Oh Lonesome Me" and "I Can't Stop Loving You," issued on the A and B sides of the same single. "Oh Lonesome Me" was a breakthrough record in Nashville in that it was the first time anyone could remember miking the drums. Usually, drums were in the background and were picked up by the microphones on other instruments, but Atkins loved the double-timed bass drum lick and placed a microphone on the drum kit. The revolution came in small

increments, and it came from a willingness to experiment. Atkins was overjoyed with the success of "Oh Lonesome Me" because he no longer worked in Sholes's shadow. "I was my own man then," he said often.

Owen Bradley, who had taken over Decca's country division from Paul Cohen in 1958, brought his experience with the big bands and WSM's studio orchestra to country music. Like Atkins, his personal taste can be judged by his own records, which were a fair distance from country. He not only produced Patsy Cline's Decca sessions, reckoned by many to be the apogee of the Nashville Sound, but also made pop records with Brenda Lee, Bobby Helms, and Burl Ives. Bradley also continued to record the old-timers he had inherited from Cohen, including Ernest

IN THE TRENCHES *Before he was a producer, Chet Atkins (left) was a top session guitarist. Here he works a 1954 Davis Sisters session with guitarist George Barnes. (Above) One of Chet's many albums, this one from 1958.*

CLASSIC COUNTRY RECORDING

PATSY CLINE
"Crazy"

*Crazy, I'm crazy for
feelin' so lonely.
I'm crazy, crazy for
feelin' so blue.*

WRITTEN BY WILLIE NELSON AND
RECORDED AUGUST 21, 1961

In 1961, ten weeks after a near-fatal car collision, Patsy Cline still needed crutches to get around. That summer, she hobbled into Owen and Harold Bradley's Quonset Hut studio and recorded **"Crazy."**

At the time of her session, the big-voiced singer had taken over the No. 1 slot with "I Fall to Pieces." But songwriter Willie Nelson's partially spoken performance on the four-minute "Crazy" demo made for a confusing template, and Cline struggled to find her phrasing.

Although the A-Team laid an elegant foundation and the Jordanaires provided velveteen vocal support, Cline had difficulty transforming Nelson's steel-shaded honky-tonk ballad into a torch song. She spent the entire four-hour session on the song, but left unhappy with her performance. Producer Owen Bradley offered to let Cline come back at a later date and overdub a new vocal over the instrumental tracks they had created. The next session, she delivered magic in a single take.

"Crazy" became not only a country classic, but a Top Ten pop hit. In 2000, VH-1 ranked it among the 100 greatest rock & roll songs of all time; in 2004, the Library of Congress added it to the National Recording Registry.
TOM ROLAND

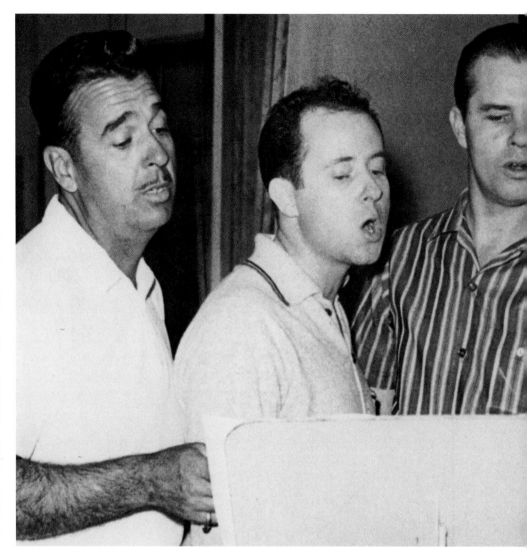

FULL VOICE *The Jordanaires provided background vocals for hundreds of hits, including those of Elvis Presley and Patsy Cline. Here they join Tennessee Ernie Ford in the studio. (l-r) Ford, Gordon Stoker, Neal Matthews Jr., Hoyt Hawkins, Ray Walker.*

Tubb, Kitty Wells, Bill Monroe, and Webb Pierce. He steered them all skillfully into the new era, finding a zone where they could feel comfortable, yet still make records true to themselves.

Columbia's Don Law was a British émigré, who had sung with the London Choral Society in his youth, but that was a distant memory by the late 1950s. Despite his age and background, Law had an excellent ear for country songs with crossover potential, and when he found one, he spared no expense in going all out for pop airplay. Stonewall Jackson's "Waterloo," Jimmy Dean's "Big Bad John," Johnny Horton's "Battle of New Orleans," and Claude King's "Wolverton Mountain" were classic Don Law productions—full,

ballsy, and crammed with hooks. In 1962, Law saw some blues recordings he had made in 1936 and 1937 with Robert Johnson reissued to great acclaim, and it seemed as though his long experience in the business told him that you never knew what would sell. As a result, like Atkins, he was willing to experiment, whether by placing the fuzz-toned guitar way up front on Marty Robbins's "Don't Worry," or letting Floyd Cramer bang a piece of metal for the hammer strike on Jimmy Dean's "Big Bad John."

Capitol's Ken Nelson, who'd set the pace when he recorded "Gone" and "Young Love," still recorded in Los Angeles as a matter of preference, and, as the infrastructure of the Nashville

IT'S A HIT *Though she's all smiles in this 1950s photo with producer Owen Bradley (left) and Decca executive Paul Cohen, Patsy Cline labored for years before gaining her first No. 1, "I Fall to Pieces" (1961).*

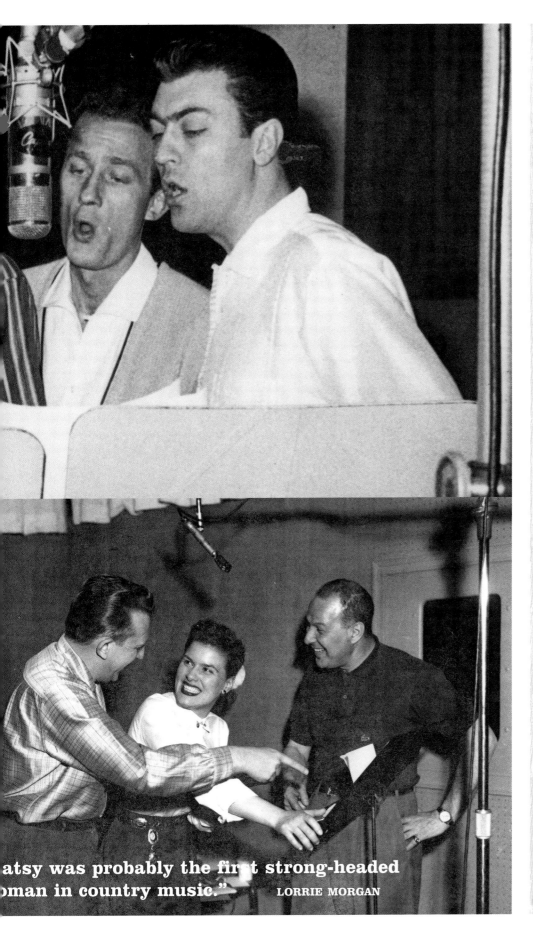

"atsy was probably the first strong-headed oman in country music." LORRIE MORGAN

PATSY CLINE

BORN GORE, VIRGINIA,
SEPTEMBER 8, 1932
DIED MARCH 5, 1963
FIRST RECORDED 1955
INFLUENCES KAY STARR,
KATE SMITH, HELEN MORGAN
HITS "CRAZY," "I FALL TO PIECES,"
"SWEET DREAMS"

Patsy Cline endured years of
struggle until she became one
of country music's leading
ladies with the 1961 release of
"I Fall to Pieces." Born Virginia
Hensley, she grew up in
Winchester, Virginia, where she
began singing in church. She
listened regularly to the Grand
Ole Opry, but also had an affini-
ty for pop vocalists, including
torch singer Helen Morgan and
the big-voiced Kate Smith.

In 1957, following an appearance on *Arthur Godfrey's Talent
Scouts*, she scored her first hit
with the bluesy "Walkin' After
Midnight." But she hit her stride
with "I Fall to Pieces," a crossover
hit that deftly balanced her country heritage with a big melody.
Despite both a serious car accident and nervous breakdown
that year, Cline began recording
with more regularity, mixing
torchy ballads with traditional
pop covers, country standards,
and western-swing classics.

Her life ended tragically in
March 1963 during a plane trip
from Kansas City. Piloted
through a storm by manager
Randy Hughes, the craft
crashed in Camden, Tennessee.
Cline remains one of country's
most significant figures.

TOM ROLAND

TOP TEN

MY TOP TEN FAVORITE SONGS OF ALL TIME
BRENDA LEE

This was a very difficult exercise for me. I have made so many friends in the music business over the years, and I have thousands of favorite songs in every genre. I was asked to pick only ten, but keep in mind . . . this is just the tip of the iceberg!
—Brenda Lee

1 **"Mansion over the Hilltop"**
the first gospel song my mother taught me; Elvis Presley, Tennessee Ernie Ford, George Jones, and many others have recorded it.

2 **"If You Love Me"**
Lavern Baker (Atlantic, 1959)

3 **"Stand by Me"**
Ben E. King (Atco, 1961)

4 **"At Last"**
Etta James (Argo, 1961)

5 **"I'm So Lonesome I Could Cry"**
Hank Williams (MGM, 1949)

6 **"Yesterday"**
The Beatles (Parlophone/Capitol, 1965)

7 **"Are You Lonesome Tonight?"**
Elvis Presley (RCA, 1960)

8 **"I Can't Stop Loving You"**
Ray Charles (ABC-Paramount, 1962)

9 **"Wind Beneath My Wings"**
Bette Midler (Atlantic, 1989)

10 **"(I Can't Get No) Satisfaction"**
Rolling Stones (London, 1965)

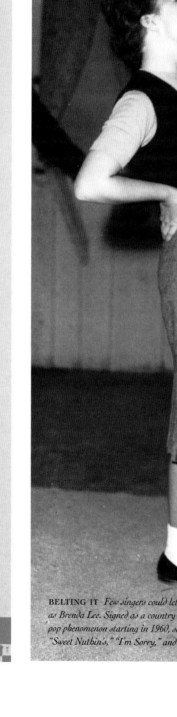

BELTING IT *Few singers could let it rip as powerfully as Brenda Lee. Signed as a country act, she became a pop phenomenon starting in 1960, scoring big hits with "Sweet Nuthin's," "I'm Sorry," and numerous others.*

business grew, his absences meant that he wasn't on hand to grab the best new songs. Unlike Atkins, Bradley, and Law, he wasn't buying into the notion of Nashville as Music City USA. Instead, Nelson cultivated the original alternative country scene in Bakersfield, California. Many of the recordings he made in California with Buck Owens, Merle Haggard, and others amounted to the music that Nashville forgot. Warped and hardened in the isolation of the California honky-tonks, it started with the sound of steel guitars and Fender Telecasters playing off each other. Drums made it danceable. This was music that had migrated from Oklahoma, Texas,

and Arkansas, kept alive as a statement about roots in the vast melting pot of Southern California.

In *Time* magazine's Nashville profile of 1960, it was revealed that Nashville had edged out Los Angeles as the second-largest recording center in the US. On October 26, 1963, *Cash Box* magazine reported that Nashville accounted for 20 percent of the nation's Top 50 singles. Few, of course, knew that Elvis, Orbison, Brenda Lee, and the Everlys figured into Nashville's total. But even without them, the statistic showed the degree to which the Nashville Sound had penetrated all levels of popular music.

TEENAGE IDLING *American teenagers became influential music consumers for the first time in the 1950s, and the prosperous kids of the Baby Boom let their tastes be known, elevating Elvis Presley, the Everly Brothers, and Brenda Lee to stardom.*

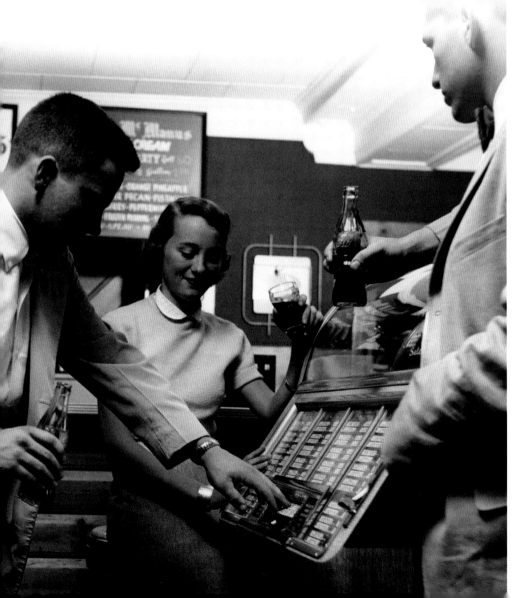

TOP TEN

TOP TEN FAVORITE PERFORMANCES BY NASHVILLE SESSION MUSICIANS— HAROLD BRADLEY, THE MOST RECORDED GUITARIST IN HISTORY

1 Grady Martin's electric guitar solo on Red Foley's **"Chattanoogie Shoe Shine Boy"** (1950)

2 Hank Garland's cascading electric guitar intro on Patsy Cline's **"I Fall to Pieces" (1961)**, using an Ecofonic tape slapback echo machine

3 Chet Atkins's electric guitar solo on Don Gibson's **"Oh Lonesome Me"** (1958)

4 Hank Garland (and me) playing the electric guitar intro on Bobby Helms's **"Jingle Bell Rock"** (1957)

5 Grady Martin's bass guitar fuzz solo on Marty Robbins's **"Don't Worry"** (1961)

6 Grady Martin's acoustic guitar fills on Marty Robbins's **"El Paso"** (1959)

7 Jerry Kennedy's dobro on Jeanie C. Riley's **"Harper Valley P.T.A."** (1968)

8 Scotty Moore's lead electric guitar on Elvis Presley's **"Heartbreak Hotel"** (1956)

9 Floyd Cramer's piano intro and fills on Patsy Cline's **"Crazy"** (1961)

10 Don Helms's steel guitar intro on Patsy Cline's **"Walkin' after Midnight"** (1957)

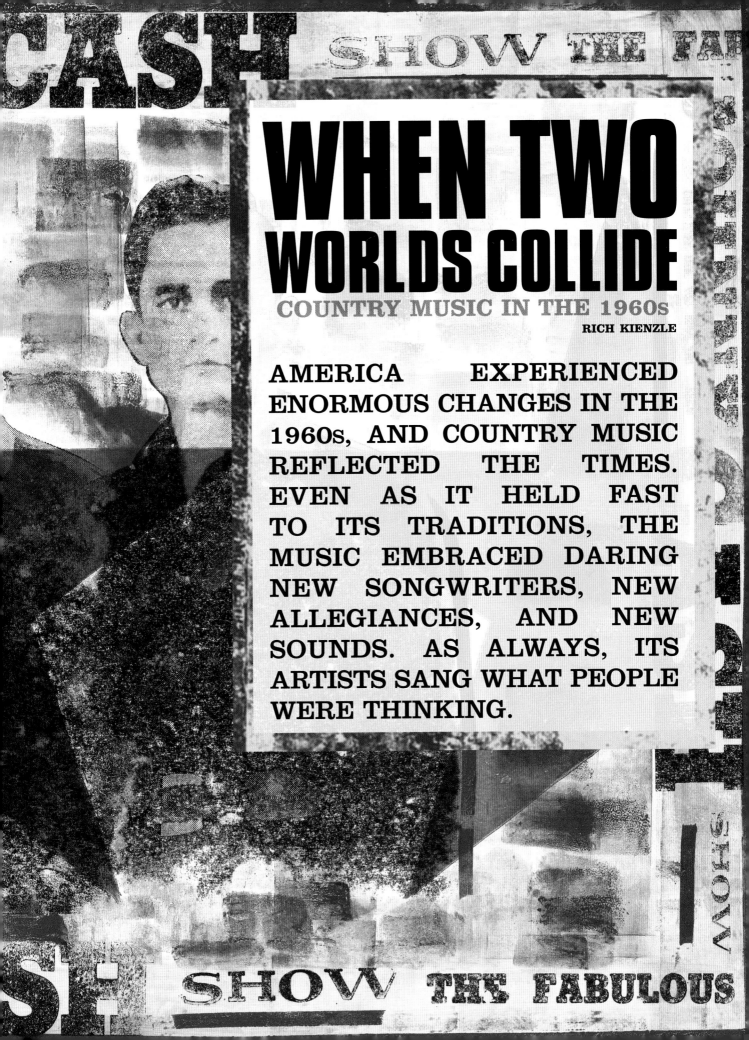

WHEN TWO WORLDS COLLIDE

COUNTRY MUSIC IN THE 1960s

RICH KIENZLE

AMERICA EXPERIENCED ENORMOUS CHANGES IN THE 1960s, AND COUNTRY MUSIC REFLECTED THE TIMES. EVEN AS IT HELD FAST TO ITS TRADITIONS, THE MUSIC EMBRACED DARING NEW SONGWRITERS, NEW ALLEGIANCES, AND NEW SOUNDS. AS ALWAYS, ITS ARTISTS SANG WHAT PEOPLE WERE THINKING.

1963 *The Jimmy Dean Show* debuts on ABC-TV. Patsy Cline dies in a plane crash in Tennessee. "Act Naturally" becomes the first of 21 No. 1 country singles for Buck Owens. Ray Charles wins a Grammy for "I Can't Stop Loving You." President John F. Kennedy is assassinated in Dallas.

1964 The Beatles perform on *The Ed Sullivan Show* during their first US visit. Jim Reeves dies in a plane crash near Nashville. Roger Miller wins five Grammy Awards. Tom T. Hall moves to Nashville with $46 and a guitar. Johnny Cash's *Bitter Tears*, an album about the struggles of Native Americans, is released. Cash and Bob Dylan meet at the 1964 Newport Folk Festival.

1965 Charley Pride makes his first records. Roger Miller wins six more Grammy Awards for a total of 11 in two years. Merle Haggard leaves the tiny Tally label for Capitol Records.

1966 Tammy Wynette makes her chart debut with "Apartment No. 9."

1967 Israel defeats Egypt, Syria, and Jordan in the Six Day War. The Country Music Hall of Fame and Museum opens on Music Row. "Gentle on My Mind" becomes Glen Campbell's breakthrough hit. Porter Wagoner hires Dolly Parton as duet partner for his TV show and road appearances.

continues opposite

o country singer but Johnny Cash would have recorded *Bitter Tears*, a 1964 concept album that confronted the mistreatment and neglect of Native Americans head-on. His angry, passionate performance of folksinger Peter LaFarge's "The Ballad of Ira Hayes" told the tale of Hayes, the Arizona Pima Indian and World War II combat hero whose tragic death in 1955 followed a decade of readjustment problems and alcoholism. When country stations proved skittish about playing the single, Cash unleashed his frustration in a full-page ad in *Billboard*'s August 22, 1964 issue. Here's what he said in part.

"DJs – station managers – owners, etc.: Where are your guts?"Ballad of Ira Hayes" is strong medicine. So is Rochester—Harlem—Birmingham and Vietnam. I've blown my own horn now, just this once, then no more. Since I've said these things now, I find myself not caring if the record is played or not. I won't ask you to cram it down their throats. Just one question: WHY?"

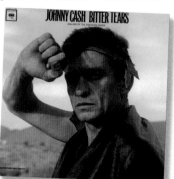

MORAL STATEMENT *Johnny Cash's Bitter Tears (1964) reflected his hunger for justice. Four years later, so would At Folsom Prison.*

respect but yielded clear economic benefits. That growth manifested itself in the annual *Country Music Who's Who* directories, published by Thurston Moore. The first, in 1960, was 182 pages; 1972's edition was over 400. Urban journalists began making regular pilgrimages to Nashville to visit the Opry, hang out with local label chiefs like Chet Atkins and Owen Bradley, and file stories—often filled with wide-eyed amazement—about the huge revenues these seemingly down-home, unassuming types generated.

The single eventually reached No. 3 on the country charts. The 1960s were an era of amazing progress and bitter conflict in America, and country music reflected the nation's struggles, particularly in the music of its greatest artists, such as Cash and Merle Haggard. The years 1960–72 constituted an immensely creative period for country music that cemented its place in America's mainstream. Record buyers who wouldn't be caught dead near the Grand Ole Opry began routinely snapping up singles by country singers. They marked the ultimate triumph of the Nashville Sound and gave solid credibility to the city's country-music enclave, once an embarrassment to Nashville's genteel, old-money establishment. As a multimillion-dollar industry, it didn't just earn official

Nonetheless, this era of expansion didn't come easy. Broadening the music's appeal was only one aspect. Some performers made an impact by holding to tradition or swimming against the tides. Artists renowned for one style unexpectedly reinvented themselves. Nor did all country's growth originate in Nashville. As time passed, once-fresh ideas grew tired. New, unexpected concepts arose and prospered. Controversies broke out like brushfires. Most importantly, during that era country, try as it might, could not ignore America's socio-cultural and political upheavals. In short, it was the start of a wild ride.

Modern sounds

Ray Charles, already an established star for his string of arresting gospel-flavored R&B hits, explored his lifelong love for country music on his two lavishly arranged, groundbreaking *Modern Sounds in Country and Western Music* albums, both released in 1962. His soulful pop take on Don Gibson's "I Can't Stop Loving You" gave it stature that transcended its beginnings as a country favorite. Charles wisely selected country songs that, despite their lineage (some were written in the 1940s), possessed elements of melody and lyric that, like "I Can't Stop Loving You," also reflected pop sensibilities.

TRAILBLAZER *Ray Charles won new fans and respect for the genre with* Modern Sounds in Country and Western Music *(1962).*

In a 1994 interview, Owen Bradley explained the fundamental requirements for a crossover hit: "The song has to be pop and country. You can't just make a crossover with a real hillbilly song or vice versa." This required a different type of songwriter. In previous decades, most country singers wrote their own material. Professional tunesmiths, such as Carson Robison, Bob Miller, Fred Rose (who began in pop), Cy Coben, or Cindy Walker, were a distinct minority in country. Except for a few instances where

1968 Conway Twitty records the first of his 50 No. 1 hits. The first televised CMA Awards Show airs on NBC-TV. The Byrds (with Gram Parsons) record the landmark country-rock album *Sweetheart of the Rodeo.* *Johnny Cash at Folsom Prison* album is recorded. Johnny Cash and June Carter marry. Tammy Wynette's "Stand By Your Man" is a No. 1 country hit. Martin Luther King Jr. and Robert F. Kennedy are assassinated. Communists in North Vietnam launch the Tet offensive on the south.

1969 US astronauts Neil Armstrong and Buzz Aldrin walk on the moon. *Hee Haw, The Glen Campbell Goodtime Hour*, and *The Johnny Cash Show* are all launched on network television. George Jones and Tammy Wynette marry. Merle Haggard's "Okie from Muskogee" becomes a No. 1 hit.

1970 Merle Haggard dominates the CMA Awards, winning for Single, Album, Male Vocalist, and Entertainer of the Year. Conway Twitty and Loretta Lynn record their first duets. Johnny Cash performs for President Richard Nixon at the White House.

1971 The Nitty Gritty Dirt Band records *Will the Circle Be Unbroken* — uniting the rock band with Nashville's old guard. Charley Pride wins the CMA's Male Vocalist and Entertainer of the Year awards.

CLASSIC COUNTRY RECORDING

RAY CHARLES
"I Can't Stop Loving You"

I can't stop loving you,
so I've made up my mind,
To live in memory of old
lonesome times.
WRITTEN BY DON GIBSON AND
RECORDED FEBRUARY 15, 1962
NO. 1 POP, JUNE 2, 1962

For a while, no one had a greater impact on how country music was made, nor brought more new fans to the music, than Ray Charles. At a time when his contemporaries were cutting "twist" albums, Charles—who had played country music early in his career, but had rarely recorded it—vented his country soul. The vehicle was his trailblazing 1962 album *Modern Sounds in Country and Western Music.*

His label, ABC-Paramount, counseled against it, but Charles had written artistic control into his contract. A&R man Sid Feller put out the call for songs, and every country publisher sent a stack. Charles whittled 250 songs down to 12 that he could refashion in his likeness. The stash included Don Gibson's **"I Can't Stop Loving You,"** written in 1958.

Charles heard just two lines before deciding it was for him. Feller considered "I Can't Stop Loving You" one of the album's weakest tracks and placed it near the end of side two. The label had no thought of issuing it as a single until Feller heard that Tab Hunter had copied Ray's arrangement. An edited version was rushed to the streets and was atop the pop charts within weeks.

COLIN ESCOTT

producers had backdoor ties to certain publishers and pushed their material on singers, most producers recorded whatever songs a singer wanted to do.

A new breed of writers, most inspired by Hank Williams, appeared on the horizon in the late 1950s. A few later became stars themselves. Their subjects were the time-honored ones—drinking, adultery, love lost and found—yet their lyrics delved far deeper, probing the essence of emotions instead of just singing of events. Some songs were philosophical or contemplative. Others tried a stream-of-consciousness narrative or incorporated dreams or metaphor.

Ray Price—still a hard-line honky-tonker, renowned for his Nudie suits, the fiddle and steel sound of his Cherokee

CHEROKEE COWBOYS *Ray Price (right) and Darrell McCall harmonizing onstage, 1963. Price led the Cherokee Cowboys band in the '50s and '60s, costumed in Nudie finery emblazoned with Indian motifs. (One of his classic jackets is displayed here.) Price kept the flame burning for hard-country music in the 1960s with propulsive fiddle-and-steel shuffles like "Heartaches by the Number" (1960) that regularly topped the charts.*

Cowboys, and trademark shuffle beat—became a catalyst for this fresh approach to country songwriting. In 1958, he hit with "City Lights," written by Bill Anderson, a college-educated ex-sports-writer who wrote the song one night on a hotel rooftop in tiny Commerce, Georgia. That year, Price hired another promising newcomer, Roger Miller, as a Cherokee Cowboy band member. The Oklahoma native wrote both complex, emotional ballads and zany, eccentric novelties. Miller's ballad, "Invitation to the Blues," became another 1958 success for Price. The same year, Ernest Tubb hit with Miller's ballad "Half a Mind." In 1959, Jim Reeves scored with two more Miller compositions—the amiable "Billy Bayou" and "Home." Price unveiled another new songwriting talent a year later, when he took Harlan Howard's now-classic "Heartaches by the Number" (also a pop hit for singer Guy Mitchell) to the top of the country charts.

In 1959, Price, manager Hal Smith, and Californian Claude Caviness founded the Pamper Music publishing company.

Pamper quickly signed Nashville newcomers Harlan Howard and Hank Cochran to staff songwriting contracts. The following year, Cochran brought Pamper another newcomer—Willie Nelson, newly arrived from Texas after "Family Bible," an original he'd sold for $150, became a Top Ten hit for Claude Gray.

Both Cochran and Nelson found success fast. In 1961, Cochran's "I Fall to Pieces" became Patsy Cline's first No. 1 country hit. Then Faron Young topped the country charts with Nelson's "Hello Walls," a lonely man's conversational monologue with his suddenly empty house. Both numbers packed an emotional wallop beyond the usual garden-variety weeper, as did Nelson's reflective "Crazy," Cline's follow-up hit to "I Fall to Pieces."

These Young Turks also found fresh emotional perspectives on the working man's life. Florida native Mel Tillis got his first break as a writer when Webb Pierce started recording his songs in the 1950s.

BANGING OUT HITS *Harlan Howard was a warehouse forklift driver when he learned his "Heartaches by the Number" was a smash. The proceeds financed his switch to full-time songwriting.*

Ray Price's Cherokee Cowboys & Ernest Tubb's Texas Troubadours

In 1953, a fan remarked that Ray Price, touring with the Drifting Cowboys, the backup band of Price's late mentor Hank Williams, sounded "just like Hank." Realizing he needed his own musical identity, Price amicably parted with the Cowboys. A year later, he hired the Western Cherokees, a Texas honky-tonk band, which he renamed the Cherokee Cowboys. Price's insistence on hiring musicians who blended outstanding musicianship with personality made the Cowboys an incubator for future superstars. The role of front man, the bandmember who sang to warm up audiences at shows, proved valuable training for Roger Miller, Willie Nelson, Johnny Paycheck, Darrell McCall, and Johnny Bush. Among the band's instrumental stars were future Nashville studio guitarist Pete Wade, pedal steel stars Jimmy Day and Buddy Emmons, and swing fiddle masters Wade Ray, Keith Coleman, and Curly Lewis. Price was not one to put on airs. He traveled on the bus with the band, encouraged their offstage jam sessions, and arranged for them to record an LP for Columbia.

Ernest Tubb's band was also a hotbed of talent. Following the style of his first hit, "Walking the Floor over You," Tubb required simple, uncluttered accompaniment from his Texas Troubadours. So long as they gave him what he needed, Tubb

showcased band members' talents in solo spots onstage. As the band evolved in the early 1960s, that concept reached a different level. New lead guitarist Leon Rhodes and pedal-steel guitarist Buddy Charleton kept it simple behind the boss. But during their showcases they became a scintillating country-jazz ensemble. Two other newcomers, drummer Jack Greene and guitarist Cal Smith, were talented vocalists. The band became self-contained, and at Tubb shows they presented their own act before Tubb appeared. Proud of his "boys," Tubb arranged a Decca recording contract that yielded four Troubadours LPs. Greene was still a Troubadour in 1965 when he recorded his first No. 1 single, "There Goes My Everything," followed by "All the Time," "Until My Dreams Come True," and "Statue of a Fool." Smith began recording two years later and reached stardom in the early 1970s with "The Lord Knows I'm Drinking" and "Country Bumpkin."

RICH KIENZLE

TEXAS TROUBADOURS *Ernest Tubb's band was an exceptional training ground for musicians. In this 1960 photo, Tubb (second left) is joined by Johnny Johnson (guitar), Jan Kurtis (drums), Leon Rhodes (electric guitar), Buddy Emmons (pedal steel guitar), and Jack Drake (bass).*

COUNTRY'S FIRST COUPLE *Tammy Wynette and George Jones were country's storybook couple of the late '60s. Following their 1969 marriage, their duets charted the progress of their marriage—from its first romantic stirrings ("Take Me," 1971) to its denouement ("Golden Ring," 1975).*

Tillis and Danny Dill's evocative "Detroit City," a 1963 hit for Bobby Bare, captured the plight of rural southerners who fled poverty to work in northern auto plants, only to find themselves lonely, alienated, and desperately homesick. The "I wanna go home" chorus became an almost primal cry for deliverance.

Howard, Cochran, Nelson, Anderson, Miller, Tillis, and others triumphed as songwriters throughout the 1960s. All of them also made records of their own, but at first only Anderson's career sustained itself, beginning with the Owen Bradley-produced "The Tip of My Fingers" and "Still." Miller and Nelson also had early hits—Miller with the brilliant "When Two Worlds Collide" (cowritten with his

pal Anderson), and Nelson with "Touch Me." Unfortunately, neither found strong follow-ups. Tillis wouldn't catch fire for years. Though Chet Atkins ruled RCA Records in Nashville, he ultimately reported to New York corporate executives. Displeased by Miller's faltering sales, they pressed Atkins, despite his deep admiration for Miller, to drop him from the label.

Not everyone embraced the new crossover paradigm. Hard-core traditionalists like Ray Price, Kitty Wells, Hank Thompson, Little Jimmy Dickens, and Lefty Frizzell all stuck to no-frills country through the 1960s, as did George Jones, who was fast being recognized as a master vocalist during that decade. And in the case of Conway Twitty, a former rock & roller became one of the champions of basic honky-tonk music, once he was given the opportunity to record country music, beginning in 1965.

PROFILES IN COUNTRY

CONWAY TWITTY

BORN FRIAR'S POINT, MISSISSIPPI, SEPTEMBER 1, 1933
DIED JUNE 5, 1993
PLAYED GUITAR
INFLUENCES ELVIS PRESLEY, EDDY ARNOLD
HITS "IT'S ONLY MAKE BELIEVE," "HELLO DARLIN'"

Conway Twitty became one of the most consistent and focused giants of country music. With canny concentration on women and why they buy records, reclusive Harold Lloyd Jenkins gave his stage persona an air of laconic, luxurious mystery.

Twitty signed with Mercury, then MGM, before recording "It's Only Make Believe" in Nashville in 1958. The song was a million-seller, and Twitty continued in rock & roll well into the 1960s. Then in 1965, producer Owen Bradley signed Twitty to Decca Records as a country artist.

Twitty adamantly professed allegiance to country and, eventually aided by the all-out duet support of Loretta Lynn, became a leading exponent of Nashville traditionalism—with a twist. A master of explosive lyrics, he penned and sang romantically visceral hits such as "You've Never Been This Far Before."

Twitty never won the industry's most prestigious awards and described that as a boon, attributing his unusual longevity to lack of overexposure. He died suddenly, while on tour, of a ruptured stomach aneurysm.

JACK HURST

LORETTA LYNN

BORN BUTCHER HOLLOW, KENTUCKY, APRIL 14, 1935
INFLUENCES KITTY WELLS
HITS "DON'T COME HOME A'DRINKIN' (WITH LOVIN' ON YOUR MIND)," "COAL MINER'S DAUGHTER," "THE PILL"

Loretta Lynn has created much more than great hit recordings. The combination of the songs she has written, the records she has made, the books she has cowritten, and the film of her life story that was based on all this work ultimately yields one of the most fascinating life stories of the 20th century.

Married at 13, Lynn had four children by her 18th birthday. Her husband convinced her to sing in public in local honky-tonks in Washington state and in Canada, where she was heard by the owner of Zero Records. The tiny label released her first song, "I'm a Honky Tonk Girl," in 1960.

Emboldened by the record's success, Loretta and her husband headed to Nashville, where her husband convinced the Grand Ole Opry to allow her to perform. She was made a member of that show two years later, and her career has thrived ever since, earning her every conceivable award, including election to the Country Music Hall of Fame. Her most recent award was a Grammy for best country album—2004's *Van Lear Rose*.

MARTHA HUME

Twitty's longtime duet partner, Loretta Lynn, was the antithesis of crossover. In the 1960s, the newcomer emerged unheralded from the Kentucky Appalachians by way of Washington State with her hit original "I'm a Honky-Tonk Girl" on tiny Zero Records, produced in Los Angeles by steel guitarist Speedy West. Her vocal style made her an important transitional figure, since it sat between Kitty Wells's demure persona and Cline's passion-packed delivery. Lynn's songwriting—personal, feisty, and often edgy—drew inspiration from her keen observation ("You Ain't Woman Enough") and firsthand experience ("Fist City"). Her writing and vocal styles were so distinctive and so much of a piece that few singers dared cover her originals. When Owen Bradley signed Lynn in 1961, he recognized her uniqueness, kept her sound country, and supplemented her solo success by teaming her for duets with Ernest Tubb and later, more spectacularly, with Twitty. In the early 1970s, her renown transcended her core

MADE FOR EACH OTHER *Conway Twitty and Loretta Lynn proved a natural duet partnership, scoring multiple hits and awards for their impassioned recordings. Indeed, their chemistry was so palpable that many fans assumed they were married.*

audience as she projected blunt-talking, blue-collar feminism on songs like "One's on the Way" and "The Pill," elevating her to the status of an American icon.

Another female country superstar emerged later in the 1960s from Appalachia—this time, Tennessee's Smoky Mountains. Unlike Lynn, who was already a mother when her career began, Dolly Rebecca Parton had set her sights on a musical career from the very beginning, making her first records as a young teen. She found early success on Monument Records after moving to Nashville to pursue a singing career at age 18. When Porter Wagoner hired her in 1967 to replace longtime vocalist Norma Jean on his syndicated television show, he recognized that Parton's talents (a soulful Appalachian voice and a painterly song-writing gift) transcended her flamboyant appearance. Some of her songs were light and humorous, others dark, foreboding, and even Gothic, reflecting deep veins of morality and an eye for nuance and detail. Her first hits came as duets with Wagoner before she emerged on her own in the early 1970s, a prelude to a later crossover stardom few ever expected.

Music City—East and West

Dozens of song publishers popped up in Nashville during the 1960s, along with large and small record companies, booking agents, managers, publicists, and small studios, most congregating near the Bradley Studio on 16th Avenue South, in a neighborhood soon known as Music Row. Country radio's growth exploded. In 1961, 81 stations had all-country formats. There were 150 by 1963, and double that in 1966. Radio barn dance broadcasts, however, were vanishing. The Opry remained dominant, and Wheeling, West Virginia's *WWVA Jamboree* maintained its

A STAR IS BORN *Prior to joining forces in 1967, Porter Wagoner was the star, and Dolly Parton was the ingénue. In time she would outgrow his TV show and their duets.*

CLASSIC COUNTRY RECORDING

LORETTA LYNN
"Coal Miner's Daughter"

Well, I was borned a coal miner's daughter In a cabin on a hill in Butcher Holler.

WRITTEN BY LORETTA LYNN AND RECORDED OCTOBER 1, 1969
NO. 1 COUNTRY, DECEMBER 19, 1970

"Coal Miner's Daughter" tells the story of Loretta Lynn's family and origins in Butcher Hollow, Kentucky. Released October 31, 1970, the song rapidly rose to No. 1 on the country charts. More important, it served as the impetus for Lynn's best-selling biography (1976) and the Oscar-winning biopic starring Sissy Spacek (1980), both of which share the song's title.

"Coal Miner's Daughter" was a departure for Lynn, who was known mainly for sassy, back-talking tunes of domestic strife such as "Fist City," "You Ain't Woman Enough (To Take My Man)," and "Don't Come Home a'Drinkin' (With Lovin' on Your Mind)." Songs such as these had led some to describe her as an advocate for women's rights. But, in truth, these songs were part of an incredibly detailed tapestry of one woman's experience of triumphing in 20th-century America. "Coal Miner's Daughter" pulled all the threads of the story together.

MARTHA HUME

PROFILES IN COUNTRY

BUCK OWENS

BORN SHERMAN, TEXAS,
AUGUST 12, 1929
DIED MARCH 25, 2006
PLAYED GUITAR
INFLUENCES HANK WILLIAMS,
CHUCK BERRY
HITS "ACT NATURALLY," "CRYIN'
TIME," "TOGETHER AGAIN"

Alvis Edgar "Buck" Owens, son of a sharecropper, became not only an adept guitarist and celebrated singer but also a gifted businessman. He was a Capitol Records session sideman before signing with the label in 1957. His own first hit, "Under Your Spell Again," did not come until two years later. It was followed by "Act Naturally," a smash that startled the Nashville-centered industry.

Racking up 20 No. 1 country hits between 1963 and 1972, Owens aggressively capitalized by buying radio stations and opening a song-publishing company, a booking agency, and a recording studio, giving country artists more artistic freedom than they enjoyed in Nashville. He never lost sight of the core of Buck Owens Enterprises. "The . . . secret," he once said, "is to write a song, record it, and control it."

His decline began in 1969 with a lucrative gig cohosting the *Hee Haw* TV show, which reduced his image to that of a buffoon. His artistic demise was finalized with the 1974 motorcycle death of his friend and lead guitarist Don Rich. Yet after leaving *Hee Haw* in the late 1980s, his reputation recovered, and he became what he remains—an icon.

JACK HURST

popularity. But both the *Louisiana Hayride* and Southern California's *Town Hall Party* folded in 1960 as television took over.

Two thousand miles west in Bakersfield, the temperatures, terrain, and oilfields were nearly identical to Texas and Oklahoma. In the 1930s, thousands of southwestern refugees displaced by Depression-era dust storms relocated there and brought along their favorite country music—western

YOUNG BUCK *In 1954, an unknown Buck Owens made a pilgrimage to Nashville and sat on the steps of the Ryman Auditorium. Nashville would know him soon enough.*

swing and honky-tonk. That led to a robust local country scene in Bakersfield during the 1940s. The city became a regular stop for Bob Wills and other stars.

Texas-born Buck Owens arrived in Bakersfield from Phoenix in 1951 and joined a local bar band—Bill Woods's popular Orange Blossom Playboys. A masterful guitarist who loved rockabilly, honky-tonk, and western swing, Owens soon defined Bakersfield's musical style. His first hits for Capitol Records were textbook Ray Price shuffles. Eventually,

"Buck Owens, more than any other country artist of his time, brought the bandstand into the production of his records."

RODNEY CROWELL

Owens found his own voice with a stripped-down twang built around Fender Telecasters, trebly pedal steel, and a driving 2/4 rhythm he likened to a freight train, inspired by his love for rock and Bob Wills's dance beat.

That sound, as well as his fame, came into its own with Owens's 1963 hit version of Johnny Russell's "Act Naturally," which launched a nearly unbroken streak of No. 1 singles that stretched through the rest of the decade. Owens attracted country fans across America who, unmoved by the decorous Nashville Sound, loved his catchy songs and elemental style. While Owens didn't publicly condemn Nashville production techniques, he made it clear to his fans that he had no interest in crossing over to the pop market. That didn't hem him in. After publicly pledging that he would cut only country material, in 1965 he shocked many fans by recording

"Memphis," previously a huge rock & roll hit by Johnny Rivers, and written and first recorded by Owens's longtime hero Chuck Berry. Owens's totally plausible defense? The song's lyrics were pure country. When Owens formed his first band in 1963, his bass player, Merle Haggard, suggested he call the group the Buckaroos. That bright idea was just the first glimmer in a brilliant career.

Merle Haggard emerges

Soon afterward, Haggard joined the band of Bakersfield favorite Wynn Stewart and pursued his own singing career as he worked to overcome a troubled past that included a stint in

GUITAR MAN *Glen Campbell—formerly a top LA session guitarist who had backed Frank Sinatra, Merle Haggard, and the Beach Boys—got his own TV variety show, where he revealed the full range of his talent.*

BUCKAROOS TRIUMPHANT *Buck Owens and his crack Buckaroos band were at the top of their game when they made their classic live album at New York's Carnegie Hall in 1966.*

PROFILES IN COUNTRY

MERLE HAGGARD

BORN OILDALE, CALIFORNIA, APRIL 16, 1937
FIRST RECORDED 1963
INFLUENCES LEFTY FRIZZELL, BOB WILLS, JIMMIE RODGERS
HITS "OKIE FROM MUSKOGEE," "WORKIN' MAN BLUES"

From birth in a boxcar to enduring fame, Merle Haggard has written, played, and lived an American epic. In making many of country music's most timeless hits, he also gave a voice to Middle America.

After serving time, Haggard signed with Capitol Records in 1965. His success with "I Am a Lonesome Fugitive" prompted him to pen a series of eventual classics about imprisonment and wanderlust. "Workin' Man Blues" set off a series of songs that profiled the white laboring class.

In 1969, his "Okie from Muskogee" not only earned him the CMA's Entertainer of the Year title, but placed him in the vanguard of superpatriot flag-wavers. To escape the latter position, he recorded an album exploring his deepest musical interests, *A Tribute to the Best Damn Fiddle Player in the World*, Bob Wills. Although he no longer inhabits the charts, Haggard continues to surprise listeners in his golden years.

JACK HURST

San Quentin prison for a failed robbery attempt. Inspired by Bob Wills and Lefty Frizzell, Haggard's first hit single—a version of Stewart's ballad "Sing a Sad Song"—followed the austere guitar-steel sound Owens established. Haggard, though, proved a different and far more formidable writer. His originals were generally somber and reflective, ranging from rowdy honky-tonkers to eloquent, thoughtful vignettes reflecting his deep-seated populism. Loyal to his friends at Bakersfield's Tally Records, he spurned the entreaties of A&R man Ken Nelson to join Capitol Records until 1965, when Haggard scored a Top Ten hit with his remake of Liz Anderson's "(All My Friends Are Gonna Be) Strangers."

Glen Campbell, born in Arkansas, made country music that reflected the flash of Hollywood more than it did the dusty streets of Bakersfield. He started out as a versatile, in-demand Hollywood studio guitarist, playing on hits for a wide range of artists, such as Merle Haggard, the Byrds, the Righteous Brothers, Frank Sinatra, and Dean Martin, and even toured with the Beach Boys. Campbell's style—exemplified on late 1960s hits, such as Jimmy Webb's "By the Time I Get to Phoenix" and "Wichita Lineman"—was smooth, slick country-pop with full-blown orchestral backing. Fittingly, he also figured in country's expansion into prime-time network TV. In 1969, CBS slipped his *Glen Campbell Goodtime Hour* variety show into the time slot vacated by *The Smothers Brothers Comedy Hour*, canceled by CBS for its controversial political satires. CBS also premiered *Hee Haw* that year (starring Buck Owens and Roy Clark), while ABC unveiled The *Johnny Cash Show*.

The rise of Roger Miller

Cash's and Campbell's shows owed much to an early precursor—ABC's *Jimmy Dean Show*, a weekly variety hour that ran from 1963 to 1966. Famous for his 1961 crossover single, "Big Bad John," Dean was a supremely qualified host who had hosted Connie B. Gay's local *Town and Country Time* on WMAL-TV in Washington, D.C., in the early 1950s. He later stepped up to short-lived CBS programs. Taped in Manhattan, the ABC show included the usual network variety

show trappings and mainstream showbiz acts. To his credit, Dean insisted that the show's many country guests be presented with dignity and class. During the 1965 season, two landmark events occurred. One show presented the first televised country-music awards ceremony. On another, frequent guest Roger Miller premiered the song "King of the Road."

For Miller, the network TV appearance signaled a remarkable turnaround. Two years earlier, despite a successful writing career and network TV guest spots showcasing his zany personality, Miller prepared to leave Nashville to study acting in Hollywood, galled by his spotty success as a singer. To fund the move, he hastily recorded 16 numbers for producer Jerry Kennedy at Mercury-Smash Records in early 1964. Improbably, the tossed-off, spontaneous recording session yielded two hit country singles that made the pop Top Ten—the madcap, off-the-wall "Dang Me" and "Chug-A-Lug." "King of the Road" did likewise. With a hip, Bobby Darin-inspired, finger-snapping intro, "King of the Road" turned country music's tradition of hobo songs inside out by celebrating a modern-day, laid-back bum with style. Miller's success, which won him a record-setting 11 Grammys in 1964 and 1965, broadened country's audience and made less conventional singer-songwriters fashionable in country circles.

A wealth of talent

Chet Atkins had a soft spot for off-the-wall singer-songwriters. He already had the iconoclastic John D. Loudermilk at RCA and, in 1965, signed Willie Nelson, whom he'd long admired but whose singing career had faltered. Atkins then added three more unique singer-writers to RCA's roster—Waylon Jennings, Jerry Reed (also a virtuoso, in-demand studio guitarist), and John Harford (later Hartford), a singer-banjoist whose eccentric songs were influenced by Miller and Bob Dylan. Hartford's quirky albums may have gained only a cult following, but "Gentle on My Mind" established his songwriting credentials when Glen Campbell made it a hit.

Jerry Kennedy signed another unique voice in 1967—Tom T. Hall. A bluegrasser from Kentucky, Hall arrived in Nashville

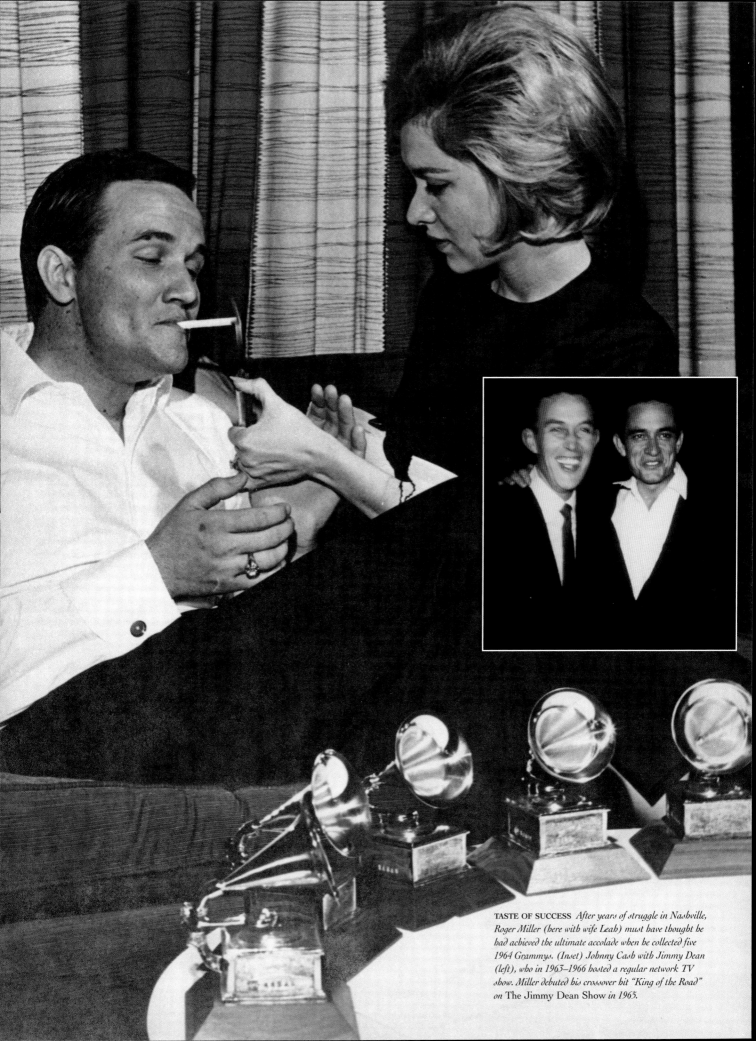

TASTE OF SUCCESS *After years of struggle in Nashville, Roger Miller (here with wife Leah) must have thought he had achieved the ultimate accolade when he collected five 1964 Grammys. (Inset) Johnny Cash with Jimmy Dean (left), who in 1963–1966 hosted a regular network TV show. Miller debuted his crossover hit "King of the Road" on The Jimmy Dean Show in 1965.*

Local Heroes— Syndicated Country Television in the 1960s

During the early 1960s, country music's presence on network television was slight, and progress slow. But country music made steady gains in syndicated television during the early years of the 1960s. In syndication, TV series were taped and sold to individual stations on a case-by-case basis, to be aired in a time slot at the station's choosing (rather than broadcast nationally at a time specified by the network). Syndicated country-music programming was particularly popular in the South and Southwest, and a staple of weekend afternoon programming in the 1960s and 1970s.

Porter Wagoner, Flatt & Scruggs, and the Wilburn Brothers were some of the first to create a television presence with shows produced and distributed by Nashville's Show Biz, Inc., which took the lead in making Nashville a significant TV production center. Quick to follow the trend were Ernest Tubb, Leroy Van Dyke, Kitty Wells & Johnny Wright, and the Stoneman Family—each of whom worked with Nashville companies. Jim & Jesse and Bill Anderson, also based in Nashville, teamed with firms based in Springfield, Missouri, and Charlotte, North Carolina. Charlotte-based Arthur Smith and Bakersfield, California's Buck Owens also launched popular syndicated series.

In addition to airing syndicated shows produced by others, some TV stations created their own syndicated series. Beginning in 1960, for example, Nashville's WSM-TV successively launched *Pet Milk Grand Ole Opry*, *National Life Grand Ole Opry*, and *That Good Ole Nashville Music*, all of which spotlighted four or five Opry acts and guests per week in productions taped mostly at the WSM studios.

Admittedly, commercials for Black Draught laxative and routines by rube comedian Speck Rhodes linked *The Porter Wagoner Show* to country's cornpone medicine-show heritage. But headline artists emphasized modern elements as well. For instance, Jim & Jesse added electric steel guitar to their band. And Wagoner himself featured Buck Trent's electrified banjo and contemporary guest stars.

Whatever a program's blend of tradition and innovation, these series were boons for all concerned. Above all, these programs celebrated the regionalism and artistic diversity that were still hallmarks of country music in the 1960s.

JOHN W. RUMBLE

BLUEGRASS TRANSMISSION *Bluegrass duo Jim & Jesse McReynolds hosted a TV show that ran from 1966 into the '70s. To broaden their appeal beyond the traditionalist bluegrass audience, they brought in drums and electric guitars for a more mainstream sound.*

in 1964 and began writing songs for Flatt & Scruggs. His breakout hit was Jeannie C. Riley's sassy 1968 rendition of his hypocrisy-busting "Harper Valley PTA," which topped both the country and pop charts, despite its raw, unvarnished arrangement. Around the same time, he began recording his songs. Although his voice was a limited and rather plain instrument, it was perfect for his keenly observed, cockeyed tales of real life, such as an arrest for speeding in a small town ("A Week in a Country Jail") and the loss of a beloved musical hero from his youth ("The Year Clayton Delaney Died").

When Don Law retired as Columbia's head of the country division in 1967, the company replaced him with Bob Johnston, a Texan who'd produced pop with Patti Page and Bob Dylan's classic *Highway 61 Revisited* album. Johnston found most of his success producing Dylan, Flatt & Scruggs, and Johnny Cash, but Billy Sherrill of Columbia's Epic subsidiary became the label's primary Nashville producer. Sherrill, rooted in gospel and rock, admired pop producer Phil Spector's elaborate "wall of sound" productions. He also disdained the Nashville Sound method as practiced by Atkins, Bradley, and Law, who relied on studio musicians' off-the-cuff creativity. By contrast, Sherrill controlled everything— songs, arrangements, even a singer's phrasing. He made his first splashes with David Houston's Grammy-winning 1966 ballad "Almost Persuaded," and later became one of Nashville's top producers turning out classic recordings by Tammy Wynette, George Jones, Charlie Rich, and Tanya Tucker.

Rock and folk

The 1950s rock boom had flattened Nashville, but the industry learned valuable lessons from the experience. Country music's growing strength allowed it to take 1964's British Invasion, which saw the Beatles and other English rock bands gaining a massive US foothold, in its stride. Buck Owens became an outspoken Beatles fan. The feeling proved mutual in 1965 when the foursome recorded a note-perfect "Act Naturally," sung by drummer and longtime country fan Ringo Starr. Another Brit band, the Nashville Teens, made a cacophonous rock hit of John D.

BRITISH INVADERS *In 1964, the Beatles stormed America, and ultimately country musicians were as affected by the Brits' heady blend of rock & roll, R&B, and country influences as rock and pop musicians were. Ironically, the Beatles themselves were big fans of country artists, including Carl Perkins, the Everly Brothers, and Buck Owens.*

PROFILES IN COUNTRY

TOM T. HALL

BORN OLIVE HILL, KENTUCKY,
MAY 25, 1936
HITS "HARPER VALLEY PTA,"
"THAT'S HOW I GOT TO MEMPHIS,"
"LITTLE BITTY"

When Tom Hall moved to
Nashville in 1964, he brought with
him only a guitar and $46. It was
apparently all he needed. The
next four decades would find him
contributing a slew of literate,
layered character studies that
helped transform the language
and scope of country music.

Hall drew on his love of literature and the skills he had honed
writing concise advertisements as
a radio DJ. He added melodies,
humor, and a shrewd perspective,
and arrived at a songwriting style
that was altogether distinct. In
1968, Jeannie C. Riley recorded
his droll hypocrisy study, "Harper
Valley PTA." Hall was suddenly an
in-demand solo act and a writer of
hits. He became a major country
star in the 1970s. "Old Dogs,
Children, and Watermelon
Wine," "The Year That Clayton
Delaney Died," "A Week in a
Country Jail," "Ravishing Ruby,"
and "I Love" helped him earn
the nickname given him by Tex
Ritter—"The Storyteller." While
Hall claims he "retired" in the
late 1990s, the songs he writes
with his wife, Dixie, routinely
reach the upper echelon of the
contemporary bluegrass charts.

PETER COOPER

Loudermilk's "Tobacco Road." Records by
Scottish folksinger Donovan—the British
Isles' Bob Dylan—appeared on Acuff-
Rose's Hickory Records label.

Other cultural changes proved more
problematic. America's Civil Rights movement, bent on ending racial segregation
and discrimination, had divided the US
amid the Cold War and the trauma of
President John F. Kennedy's assassination
in 1963. Southerners grew incensed when
Kennedy's successor, Lyndon Johnson,

advanced the Civil Rights legislation
that the late president had championed.
The folk-music community—urban and
liberal—maintained its longstanding,
active role in the Civil Rights movement,
and folk stars, such as Pete Seeger, Bob
Dylan, and Joan Baez, were prominent
in the Civil Rights movement in the
early 1960s.

Johnny Cash met Dylan when they
both appeared at 1964's Newport Folk
Festival. One of them began life poor and

WE SHALL OVERCOME
*During the '60s, the bravery
and determination of civil
rights leader Martin Luther
King Jr. symbolized the
struggles of black Americans
to achieve full equality in
America. After playing a
key role in the passage of the
Voting Rights Act of 1965,
King was tragically
assassinated in 1968.*

Protestant, the other middle-class and Jewish, but they shared many musical heroes. Dylan grew up in Minnesota absorbing mainstream country while Cash, who'd long identified with the poor and oppressed, admired many folk performers.

Cash gained stature in rock circles during the 1960s, but he paid a price for taking up the cause of Native Americans with *Bitter Tears* and "Ira Hayes." The Ku Klux Klan, offended by both records, slandered Cash's then-wife, Vivian—who was of Italian descent—and on at least one occasion burned a cross on his lawn. Klansmen also threatened to crash his shows and recording sessions. Cash armed himself, then filed (and later abandoned) a million-dollar defamation suit against the Klan.

For a time, civil rights violence and deaths increased, particularly (but not exclusively) in the South. The times were inflammatory. Crowley, Louisiana's "Reb

HITTING STRIDE *Charley Pride (right, with Jerry Reed) achieved his own breakthrough across the color barrier of country music. Yet Pride was against making his race an issue; he always sought to be embraced solely for music.*

Rebel" label, issued a series of vituperative racist country singles (sold under the counter in the Deep South) by singer "Johnny Rebel." Amid all that, RCA signed Charley Pride in the mid-1960s. It was a commercial risk, and Atkins knew that the African-American singer had to be carefully marketed. But he also realized Pride's solid, traditional style could score, ironic as it seems, with country's most arch-conservative fans, who disliked the pop slickness of the Nashville Sound. Despite some early problems (some major country promoters initially feared booking him), Pride gained endorsements from established singers and won over hard-core fans by giving them the kind of country that Ray Price and others seemingly abandoned by the end of the decade.

From "Desolation Row" to Music Row—
Bob Dylan Comes to Nashville

In 1965, Columbia Records producer Bob Johnston suggested to Bob Dylan that he come to Nashville to record an album. "I said, 'They've got the greatest musicians in the world, and there is no clock. It's just a great place to be,'" Johnston remembered more than 30 years later. Dylan seemed intrigued, but when he was out of earshot, Dylan's manager, Albert Grossman, and a Columbia record executive—both accustomed to recording close to home in New York—admonished the producer. "They came up to me," Johnston continued, "and said if I ever opened my mouth again about Nashville, they'd get rid of me."

But the seed had been planted, and Dylan called the shots. When Nashville session regular Charlie McCoy, visiting New York, contacted Johnston about tickets to a Broadway play, McCoy ended up in Columbia's New York Studio A, playing guitar on Dylan's "Desolation Row."

Presented with proof that Nashville cats could deliver the goods, Dylan came to Nashville in February 1966 to record tracks for what would become *Blonde on Blonde*. He brought three songs with him, cut them first, then sequestered himself for ten or twelve hours to come up with additional material for the double album. Released in May 1966, the album was a huge critical and commercial success.

Dylan returned to Nashville in October 1967, after recovering from a serious motorcycle accident and wood-shedded with The Band on the recordings now known as *The Basement Tapes*.

"I saw a marked difference," McCoy observed about Dylan as they worked on the second Nashville album *John Wesley Harding*. "It seemed like his whole vocal style changed. We did the whole album in nine and a half hours."

In 1969, Dylan came to Nashville again to make a more straightforward country album. The sessions for *Nashville Skyline*, Charlie Daniels said, "were loose, free, and, most of all, fun. Dylan was in a great mood and enjoyed the interaction with the players, and the players were really into what he was doing." On the last two days of recording, Johnny Cash joined Dylan in the studio. The album included the No. 4 pop single "Lay Lady Lay." Other rock artists took notice and followed Dylan to Nashville.

"All the guys who worked on the Dylan albums realized what an impact this was going to have on Nashville," McCoy remembered. "This opened the door to a whole different group of people."

JAY ORR

NASHVILLE SKYLINE *Bob Dylan (left) in the Columbia Records Quonset Hut studio on Music Row with bass player Charlie McCoy and guitarist Charlie Daniels (right) working on Dylan's third Nashville LP,* Nashville Skyline *(1969).*

NASHVILLE CAT *At the peak of his career in 1966, Bob Dylan made the surprising decision to record in Nashville with Nashville session musicians and created the groundbreaking* Blonde on Blonde *double LP. Pleased with his musical experiment, he returned to Nashville for two more albums that redefined his career—John Wesley Harding (1967) and Nashville Skyline (1969). After Dylan pronounced Nashville cool, other pop and rock singers followed in droves.*

CLASSIC COUNTRY RECORDING

TAMMY WYNETTE
"Stand by Your Man"

*Stand by your man
And show the world
you love him.*

WRITTEN BY BILLY SHERRILL
AND TAMMY WYNETTE AND
RECORDED JULY 28, 1968
NO. 1 COUNTRY,
NOVEMBER 23, 1968

Reportedly written in the studio in about 15 minutes from an idea that originated with Wynette's producer, Billy Sherrill, **"Stand by Your Man"** was released at a time when the women's movement was beginning to stir. Thus, the song's message—that a woman should stick with her man, even if he is weak and adulterous—immediately became a lightning rod for feminists. Then, in 1992, the song was again national news when Hillary Clinton, whose husband, Bill Clinton, was running for president amid rumors of behavior that perfectly fit the song's description, announced that she was not like Tammy Wynette, "standing by my man." A furious Wynette demanded, and got, an apology from Mrs. Clinton, who belied her words anyway by sticking with the president.

The song, which has been recorded hundreds of times by such disparate artists as Lyle Lovett, Tina Turner, and Henry Mancini, enjoyed a brief vogue as a camp anthem for the gay community when Elton John recorded it in the late 1990s.

MARTHA HUME

VIETNAM BLUES *(Above) A US Marine at Khe Sanh in Vietnam, 1968. The Vietnam War drove a huge wedge between Americans on the right and the left. At the time, most country songwriters and artists believed the war was a just cause—and said so in songs such as "Vietnam Blues" and "Hello Vietnam." Although Kris Kristofferson (right), a former Army helicopter pilot, wrote "Vietnam Blues," he soon turned from political commentary to songs that explored more intimate subjects.*

Race was just one issue that played into the music of the time. America's growing involvement in Vietnam generated vocal supporters and vehement critics.

Mel Tillis's "Ruby (Don't Take Your Love to Town)," a Top Ten hit for Johnny Darrell in 1967 (and a No. 6 pop hit for Kenny Rogers & the First Edition in 1969), centered on a Vietnam vet disabled in "that crazy Asian war," who bemoaned his wife's adultery. But most country singers and composers viewed Vietnam through the black-white absolute patriotism of World War II, as exemplified by Johnny Wright's 1965 "Hello Vietnam" (written by Tom T. Hall), which offered a soldier's reflections on the need to fight.

"That Crazy Asian War"

In 1966, as antiwar and antidraft protests spread across America's college campuses and elsewhere, Nashville struck back — hard. Dave Dudley's hit "Vietnam Blues," which defended the war and assailed protesters, encouraged its composer — West Point grad and Army chopper pilot

Kris Kristofferson — to consider a career change from soldier to songwriter. Meanwhile, Columbia Records refused to release outspoken conservative Marty Robbins's "Ain't I Right," which flatly branded antiwar protesters as communist sympathizers. Autry Inman's "The Ballad of Two Brothers," Johnny Sea's "Day for Decision," Stonewall Jackson's "The Minute Men (Are Turning in Their Graves)," and Ernest Tubb's "It's for God, Country, and You Mom (That's Why I'm Fighting in Viet Nam)," all took a similar hard line in questioning protesters' patriotism. Bill Anderson's 1970 "Where Have All Our Heroes Gone?" lamented fading traditional values; Loretta Lynn's "God Bless America Again" was less ideological.

Willie Nelson saw things differently, but his hard-hitting 1968 antiwar ballad, "Jimmy's Road," issued on a single, drew little notice. A few Nashville acts endorsed conservative Republican candidate Richard Nixon during the 1968 presidential campaign, but many others, Tammy Wynette

GEORGE WALLACE *Much as Martin Luther King Jr. stood for civil rights, Alabama governor George Wallace stood for segregation. In 1968, he ran for president as an independent candidate. He lost, and later renounced his racist politics.*

PROFILES IN COUNTRY

TAMMY WYNETTE

BORN ITAWAMBA COUNTY, MISSISSIPPI, MAY 5, 1942
DIED APRIL 6, 1998
INFLUENCES MOLLY O'DAY, SOUTHERN GOSPEL MUSIC
HITS "STAND BY YOUR MAN," "D-I-V-O-R-C-E," "TIL I CAN MAKE IT ON MY OWN"

She began her adult life as a dirt-poor single mother of three. She lived in government housing, waited tables, and fixed hair. One day in 1966, she walked into producer Billy Sherrill's office at Epic Records, and two weeks later Virginia Wynette Pugh Bird emerged as Tammy Wynette.

With a voice that could shake the rafters and a life story that could curl the hair of a battle-hardened Marine, Wynette was the embodiment of country music.

Her talent went much deeper than her great, sobbing voice. She adopted as her subject romantic discord and the difficulties this presented to women who were still trying to live the fairy-tale, including herself. Tellingly, Wynette always kept her beauty operator's license up-to-date.

She sang about romance in "Take Me" (a duet with George Jones, the best-known of her husbands). She sang about fidelity ("Stand by Your Man"), infidelity ("Your Good Girl's Gonna Go Bad"), divorce ("D-I-V-O-R-C-E"), and the insecurity of the newly single woman ("'Til I Can Make It on My Own"). Most important, she sang what she lived, letting her audience come along with her.

MARTHA HUME

COUNTRY-ROCK MILESTONE
The Byrds, led by Roger McGuinn, were a top rock group when they brought singer-songwriter Gram Parsons into the fold. Parsons led the band's pioneering foray into country-rock with the 1968 album Sweetheart of the Rodeo.

> **WE JUST HIRED A PIANO PLAYER, AND HE TURNED OUT TO BE [GRAM] PARSONS, A MONSTER IN SHEEP'S CLOTHING. AND HE EXPLODED OUT OF THIS SHEEP'S CLOTHING. GOD! IT'S GEORGE JONES! IN A SEQUIN SUIT!**

ROGER MCGUINN OF THE BYRDS

and Grandpa Jones among them, entertained at rallies for third-party candidate George Wallace—the segregationist Alabama governor and self-proclaimed alternative to Nixon or Democrat Hubert Humphrey.

The hippie movement—with its "Turn on, tune in, drop out" philosophy, its recreational drug use, loud rock music, antiwar protests, and long-haired males—polarized the generations and outraged adult America, including most country artists and fans. Yet many long-haired American rock musicians actually loved country music, including Roger McGuinn, leader of the pre-eminent folk-rock band, the Byrds, and the band's bassist, Chris Hillman, a veteran bluegrass mandolinist. To explore the genre, McGuinn and Hillman added Gram Parsons, whose obscure, Hollywood-based, International Submarine Band helped pioneer country-rock.

Parsons was the impetus behind the Byrds' landmark *Sweetheart of the Rodeo* album in 1968, featuring songs by Dylan, the Louvin Brothers, Parsons, Cindy Walker, Woody Guthrie, George Jones, and Merle Haggard. The band recorded nearly half the album in Nashville in March 1968, during which time Columbia Records got them an Opry guest spot. Even though they were neatly dressed and their long hair was trimmed, the audience reacted with stony silence and catcalls. Ralph Emery, who invited them to visit his late-night WSM *Opry Star Spotlight* radio show, treated the quartet with obvious hostility, an event which later inspired the acerbic McGuinn-Parsons composition, "Drug Store Truck Drivin' Man."

Similar conflicts divided bluegrassers Flatt & Scruggs. As Earl Scruggs

and producer Bob Johnston began adding folk-rock hits to Flatt & Scruggs albums, the musically conservative Lester Flatt vehemently objected to singing such tunes, including Donovan's antiwar ballad "Universal Soldier." The disagreement over the duo's musical direction led to their 1969 split.

Haggard vs. counterculture

The divisions continued. Buck Owens displayed his patriotism quietly and symbolically by playing a red, white, and blue acoustic guitar onstage. Merle Haggard, passing through Muskogee, Oklahoma, in his tour bus, heard his bass player remark, "I bet they don't smoke marijuana in Muskogee." That led to "Okie from Muskogee," Haggard's light-hearted celebration of small-town values versus the counterculture, which gave him a No. 1 single in 1969. Haggard's compelling working-class stance and hard-edged tunes earned him fans among rock musicians, including the Grateful Dead. *Rolling Stone* magazine, the counterculture Bible that admiringly profiled Haggard in 1967, ran a post-"Okie" profile entitled "We Don't Smoke Marijuana in Muskogee, We Steal" that detailed his ex-con past.

Haggard, however, never tied himself to a single ideology. While his song "Irma Jackson" dealt sympathetically with interracial romance, "Okie's" follow-up, "The Fightin' Side of Me," projected such a fist-shaking hostility to anyone questioning American policies that it smacked of political pandering.

He soon left political commentary behind, however, and subsequent masterpieces ("Daddy Frank") and album-length homages to Jimmie Rodgers and Bob Wills broadened his audience far beyond country's largely conservative core.

President Nixon's White House handlers felt exploiting country music's patriotic base—called the "Silent Majority" in those days—gave the president a political advantage. In 1970, Nixon invited Cash and his entire show to

SHOWING HIS COLORS *As Americans argued the morality of the Vietnam War, Buck Owens preferred to do his talking with his red, white, and blue guitar.*

SIGN OF THE TIMES
*Hippies, ca. 1971. In the
'60s and '70s, hippies
rejected bourgeois values
and the Vietnam War.
Most preferred rock to
country, but some hippie
bands—notably the
Grateful Dead—were
solid country fans.*

play the White House. Cash was advised
that the president had two specific
requests—"Okie from Muskogee" and
"Welfare Cadilac" [sic], Guy Drake's
1970 novelty hit mocking welfare abuse,
which some considered racist. Instead
Cash, while maintaining publicly that he
hadn't time to learn either song, sang his
own material, including "What Is Truth,"
a new song that bluntly defended the very
youth culture Nixon assailed.

Despite his longstanding battles with
drug addiction, Cash's popularity never
faded. When he initially beat his pill habit
in 1967, he and Bob Johnston decided to
record one of his prison concerts. *Johnny
Cash at Folsom Prison*, released in 1968, was
a raw, powerful document that connected
with country and noncountry fans alike.
Millions of new fans gravitated to Cash's
plain-spoken honesty. The 1969 follow-up,
Johnny Cash at San Quentin, yielded a classic single—a live performance of Shel
Silverstein's novelty, "A Boy Named Sue,"
complete with a bleeped "son of a bitch."
The record crossed over with a vengeance.

COUNTRY DÉTENTE *In 1970, President Richard Nixon (left,
with wife, Pat, beside him) invited Johnny Cash (right) and wife
June Carter Cash (2nd right) to perform at the White House in
an effort to reach Cash's fans. Cash sang "What Is Truth," a
song that defended the youth culture that Nixon feared.*

Cash's earthy, pulsating songs became a generation unifier. Conservative fans appreciated his values, while the young, whose own prejudices led them to write off most country fans and stars as "rednecks," revered his rebelliousness.

Cash, who recorded anything he liked, started cutting songs by a new group of Nashville composers, most notably Kris Kristofferson, who'd left the Army for Nashville in 1966, and wrote for Combine Music. He met Cash while working as a janitor at Columbia studios. However, his first songwriting success came in 1969 when Roger Miller hit with Kristofferson's "Me and Bobby McGee" (also a signature song for rock idol Janis Joplin). Kristofferson then expanded on the visions of Tillis, Miller, Howard, and Cochran with "For the Good Times";

REBELS IN ARMS *Johnny Cash went his own way from the very beginning. His uncompromising music and his principled stands influenced not only countless musicians but also his eldest daughter, Rosanne, who was one year old when this photo was taken at the Memphis Zoo in 1956. Like her dad, Rosanne Cash would be a musician to reckon with.*

JAILHOUSE ROCK *Johnny Cash famously recorded two best-selling live albums in prisons—* Johnny Cash at Folsom Prison *(1968) and* Johnny Cash at San Quentin *(1969). But those high-profile concerts were by no means his only prison performances. In fact, he gave numerous unheralded concerts behind bars, including this one for inmates at Arkansas's Cummins Prison in April 1969.*

The Hippest Show on Earth— The Johnny Cash Show

Country music was no stranger to network television when *The Johnny Cash Show* debuted on ABC-TV on June 7, 1969. Neither was Cash himself. He had appeared regularly before living-room audiences since 1957, when he sang "I Walk the Line" on the CBS network's *Jackie Gleason Show*.

Still, even after 12 years of intermittent exposure to the camera, Cash had hardly warmed to the medium. But when his *Folsom Prison* album of 1968 exploded onto the national scene, selling millions, Cash became an attractive personality to television executives and sponsors. Taped at Nashville's Ryman Auditorium (at Cash's insistence) and slotted as a summer replacement for *The Hollywood Palace, The Johnny Cash Show* encapsulated the major themes of Cash's recordings—rural dreams, common struggle, the West, and America's virtues and failings. In Cash's mind, America's soul lived in a heartland where dreams rode on trains, God saved men, and all races enjoyed a shot at justice and reward. The show reflected such beliefs and remains the clearest statement of Cash's inclusive artistic vision.

On Saturday nights (or later, Wednesday nights), viewers might see Cash singing gospel, sidling up to Ray Charles on a piano bench, or reverently introducing protest singer Pete Seeger (who appeared only after Cash battled with skittish network executives). And always there were trains. In the middle of each show, Cash featured "Ride This Train," a taped segment in which his monologues and songs narrated a video journey through hobo camps, prisons, Indian reservations, interstate highways, and other places where he saw the often forgotten lifeblood of America.

Of course, the show featured the inevitable concessions to ratings-obsessed executives. From time to time, he appeared incongruous with such guests as Broadway star Liza Minnelli, pop poet Rod McKuen, bubblegum rocker Neil Diamond, and, yes, a circus monkey. He was most comfortable with artists who worked closer to his tradition, such as Bob Dylan, Joni Mitchell, Glen Campbell, and Eddy Arnold. Yet Cash seemed always willing to stretch his comfort zone, inviting such disparate performers as Eric Clapton's Derek & the Dominos, Neil Young, the Who, Stevie Wonder, and Louis Armstrong. The show stoked the fire of Cash's popularity in the late 1960s, but as his flames cooled cancellation came in the spring of 1971. Yet for its time it was easily the hippest music show on television.

MICHAEL STREISSGUTH

CASH AND DYLAN *(Left) Johnny Cash and Bob Dylan had been friends for years when Dylan made this rare TV appearance on the opening episode of Cash's ABC-TV show, June 7, 1969. (Above) Early in his career, Cash would wear the occasional flashy red suit when he performed. But after country costumer Manuel Cuevas counseled Cash to garb himself only in black for dramatic effect, Cash saw the wisdom, even going so far in 1971 as to write a song called "Man in Black."*

ACROSS THE GREAT DIVIDE
The Nitty Gritty Dirt Band's John McEuen (left) works on a number with Roy Acuff (center) and Jimmy Martin (right).

recorded by Ray Price in a lushly arranged rendition it became a 1970 crossover favorite. That year, Cash's rendition of Kristofferson's "Sunday Morning Comin' Down," a tune that celebrated dissolution, won the CMA Song of the Year award. As Kristofferson, denim-clad, with shoulder-length hair, came onstage to accept his award, an uneasy Roy Clark and Tennessee Ernie Ford (who despised long-haired men) greeted him with obvious wariness.

Yet the hippie-redneck rift slowly began to mend. The Nitty Gritty Dirt Band's 1972 *Will the Circle Be Unbroken* album, which united the rock band with Maybelle Carter, Doc Watson, Jimmy Martin, Merle Travis, Earl Scruggs, and Roy Acuff, became a landmark generational bridge, and bands began integrating players from all strata. The California country-rock band Seatrain included two of Bill Monroe's 1960s Blue Grass Boys—fiddler Richard Greene and

guitarist Peter Rowan. Commander Cody & His Lost Planet Airmen played rockabilly, Bakersfield numbers, and swing. Ray Benson's band Asleep at the Wheel, inspired by Haggard's Wills tribute album, focused on recreating Bob Wills's classic western swing.

Outlaws on the horizon

With this came a turning point. The Nashville Sound had indeed expanded country's audience beyond anyone's expectations. But in 1972, though few dared admit it, the once-daring crossover concept, now pat and formulaic, had begun to ossify. Sherrill's revisionist approach aside, many producers used the Nashville Sound as a one-size-fits-all formula, naively assuming it would succeed with any singer. Granted, Eddy Arnold's and Ray Price's crossover triumphs with orchestrated pop vindicated their desires to change direction, but Cash's success proved that easy-listening arrangements weren't necessary to attract noncountry fans.

bands obtain unprecedented creative control, lavish recording budgets, and ample publicity. It infuriated him so much that when his contract came up for renewal that year, he went for broke. During lengthy, contentious negotiations, his temerity in demanding creative freedom that no other country singer had ever requested flummoxed Atkins and other RCA Nashville executives. At one point, Waylon pointed to a framed photo of Willie on the wall and commented, "You already made a mistake with that man, Hoss. Don't make the same mistake again."

In the end, Waylon's new RCA contract guaranteed him the creative control he'd long desired. Some of Music Row's establishment waited for him to fail. Willie, too, would find a more welcoming spirit when he signed with Atlantic Records around the same time. All this would guarantee him one thing. The next phase would be wilder yet.

Willie Nelson and Waylon Jennings realized Atkins had tried his best. But as RCA's artist roster grew, Atkins, elevated to an RCA vice-presidency, found that his corporate duties put him under increasing stress. Adding to that stress was a 1973 bout with colon cancer, from which he recovered after surgery. He cut back his production work and placed many of his artists in the hands of newly hired RCA staff producers. Both Waylon and Willie grew frustrated by promises that never seemed to assuage their continuing lack of recording success. After a fire destroyed his home in late 1970, a discouraged Nelson returned to Texas. In 1972, he and RCA called it quits. Jennings, still in Nashville and under contract, was outraged as he watched rock

TOP TEN PLUS

MERLE HAGGARD'S 14 FAVORITES FROM BAKERSFIELD

1 **"A Dear John Letter"**
Jean Shepard with Ferlin Husky (Capitol, 1953)

2 **"Kathleen"**
Wally Lewis (Tally, 1957)

3 **"Gone"**
Ferlin Husky (Capitol, 1957)

4 **"Whatcha Gonna Do Now"**
Tommy Collins (Capitol, 1954)

5 **"You Better Not Do That"**
Tommy Collins (Capitol, 1954)

6 **"All of the Monkeys Ain't in the Zoo"**
Tommy Collins (Capitol, 1964)

7. **"You Gotta Have a License"**
Tommy Collins (Capitol, 1953)

8. **"High on a Hilltop"**
Tommy Collins (Capitol, 1955)

9. **"Meanest Man in Town"**
Fred Maddox (4 Star, 1952)

10 **"Never Before Been in Love"**
Owen Charles (Guyden, 1959)

11 **"Foolin' Around"**
Buck Owens (Capitol, 1961)

12 **"Act Naturally"**
Buck Owens (Capitol, 1963)

13 **"Love's Gonna Live Here"**
Buck Owens (Capitol, 1963)

14 **"I've Got a Tiger by the Tail"**
Buck Owens (Capitol, 1965)

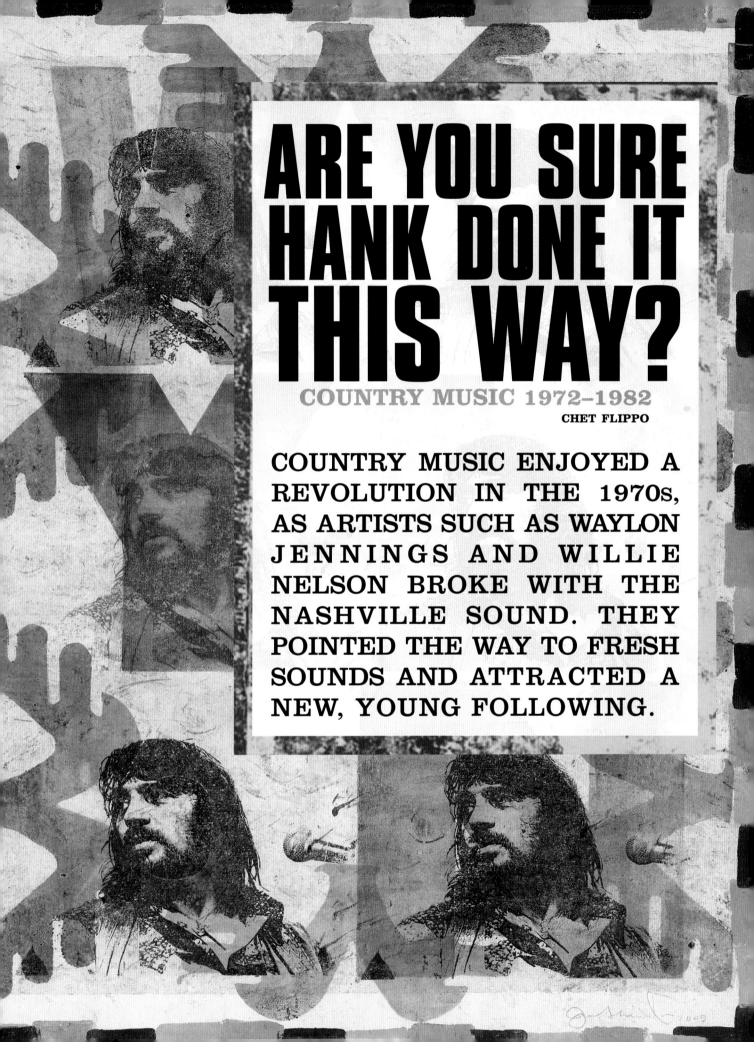

ARE YOU SURE HANK DONE IT THIS WAY?

COUNTRY MUSIC 1972–1982

CHET FLIPPO

COUNTRY MUSIC ENJOYED A REVOLUTION IN THE 1970s, AS ARTISTS SUCH AS WAYLON JENNINGS AND WILLIE NELSON BROKE WITH THE NASHVILLE SOUND. THEY POINTED THE WAY TO FRESH SOUNDS AND ATTRACTED A NEW, YOUNG FOLLOWING.

1972–1980 TIMELINE

1972 The first Dripping Springs Reunion festival takes place just outside Austin, Texas. Emmylou Harris begins recording with Gram Parsons. In her first session, 13-year-old Tanya Tucker records "Delta Dawn," destined to be a Top Ten hit. The first Fan Fair music convention takes place at Nashville's downtown Municipal Auditorium. The Eagles debut on the pop charts with "Take It Easy." The Opryland USA theme park opens in Nashville.

1973 The United States and North Vietnam sign a ceasefire agreement, and American troops leave Vietnam. Willie Nelson stages his first Fourth of July Picnic. Charlie Rich earns his first two No. 1 country hits, "Behind Closed Doors" and "The Most Beautiful Girl." Gram Parsons dies of a drug overdose at age 26 in Joshua Tree, California. Elvis and Priscilla Presley divorce.

1974 The Grand Ole Opry's new home—the Opry House at Opryland—opens. For the opening night's festivities President Richard Nixon joins the cast onstage. Porter Wagoner and Dolly Parton announce the breakup of their act. Olivia Newton-John is named the CMA Female Vocalist of the Year. President Richard Nixon resigns from office.

1975 George Jones and Tammy Wynette divorce after six years of marriage. Emmylou Harris makes her solo debut on the country charts with "Too Far Gone." Linda Ronstadt's "When

continues opposite

The 1970s were a strange voyage through the looking-glass for America and country music. As the decade began, the nation was still in the throes of the idealistic youthquake that had occurred in the middle of the 1960s. Revolutionary fervor was still in the air, along with scents of patchouli and marijuana. And yet by 1973 the youthquake was already morphing into a new generation of consumerism. Somehow rock & roll lost its way and its political force.

As rock music got tired, the rebels got tired and they grew up—just as big business and advertisers figured out what was going on.

Yet even as rock and the nation's youth were losing their revolutionary edge in the 1970s, country music was becoming a battleground for artistic integrity and truth-telling. In fact, in many ways the history of country music in the 1970s can be described as "Blows Against the Empire," a series of spontaneous uprisings, developments, and musical movements that amounted to a massive shift in what country music would become.

In that sense, the modern era of country music began on March 17, 1972. That was the day when the first ragged troops of hippie country fans joined traditional mainstream country lovers on a cow pasture near Dripping Springs, Texas. Some 60,000 music lovers congregated for a sort of country-music Woodstock to hear top traditional acts—Loretta Lynn, Roy Acuff, and Tex Ritter—as well as the best of the new breed—Kris Kristofferson, Tom T. Hall, Waylon Jennings, and Willie Nelson. Although the young, long-haired fans didn't create this festival (that was the work of some tuned-in music promoters), they energized and legitimized it. The outdoor festival would point to a new generation of country stars, a new direction in music, a new era of country

AGE OF AQUARIUS *In the early '70s, long hair and wild clothes were still badges that said "Hippie!" to most country fans. But during this decade, artists like Waylon and Willie would help bring young and old together.*

songwriting, a revolution in country music recording, and ultimately—ironically—to a revolution in country-music packaging and marketing. There were other developments in the 1970s that echoed the message of change that came from Dripping Springs, but that event was a watershed for the era.

Over the course of the three-day Dripping Springs Reunion, tens of thousands of long-haired marijuana smokers encountered tens of thousands of burr-headed, cowboy-hatted, beer-drinking rednecks. Surprisingly, they bonded—over a shared love of music. Both sides realized that the traditional music that was falling out of favor was merging with a new, progressive, beat-heavy, rock-tinged country sound. Country was changing, but in a good way.

Winds of change

This was the culmination of a movement that had been building in Nashville since the late 1960s. After much commercial and artistic success in the late 1950s and throughout much of the 1960s, the pop-flavored experiments that Chet Atkins, Owen Bradley, and others had pioneered in the heyday of the Nashville Sound had devolved into tired formula. The same overworked cadre of studio musicians (the A-Team) were playing the same

SLICK WILLIE *In the 1960s, Willie Nelson was having trouble getting noticed, no matter where his face appeared. But with a new look—and a fresh outlook on music—he became the '70s' most unlikely superstar.*

Will I Be Loved" becomes a No. 1 country hit. Willie Nelson releases the album *Red Headed Stranger* and scores his first No. 1 hit with "Blue Eyes Crying in the Rain." John Denver wins the CMA's Entertainer of the Year Award; his "Back Home Again" is named Song of the Year. Dolly Parton and Waylon Jennings win the CMA's Female and Male Vocalist of the Year Awards.

1976 *Wanted! The Outlaws*, featuring Waylon Jennings, Willie Nelson, Jessi Colter, and Tompall Glaser, becomes country's first platinum album.

1977 Elvis Presley dies at age 42 at Graceland.

1978 Willie Nelson's *Stardust* album goes to No. 1 on the *Billboard* country charts and remains on the country charts for a record 551 weeks. *Esquire* magazine publishes "The Ballad of the Urban Cowboy," the article that inspires the movie *Urban Cowboy*. Dolly Parton wins the CMA's Entertainer of the Year Award. Kenny Rogers's single "The Gambler" becomes a No. 1 country hit.

1979 Willie Nelson wins the CMA's Entertainer of the Year Award. *The Electric Horseman*, starring Robert Redford and Willie Nelson, premieres in December.

1980 A spate of country music movies: *Urban Cowboy*, *Coal Miner's Daughter* (the biopic of Loretta Lynn's life), *Honeysuckle Rose* (starring Willie Nelson), and *9 to 5* (starring Dolly Parton). Alabama scores a first No. 1 single, "Tennessee River." George Jones's "He Stopped Loving Her Today" hits No. 1. Rosanne Cash records "Seven Year Ache," destined to become her first No. 1 hit.

It Takes Two—
The Great Duet Teams

Country music's greatest duet teams flowered in the late 1960s and 1970s. What made them special was chemistry: Dolly & Porter, Conway & Loretta, and George & Tammy had it in spades, as if they'd been born to sing together.

The most chemically compatible male-female duo in country-music history has to be George Jones and Tammy Wynette. Their duet career began in 1971, not long after their storybook marriage in 1969, and ended in 1980, five years after their soap-opera divorce. In addition to having two of the greatest voices in country music, Jones and Wynette kept fans glued to the story of their marriage, with hits that traced the arc of their relationship from 1971's "Take Me," through "We're Gonna Hold On," (1973) and "Two Story House" (1980). Put it all together, and the songs tell the story of a love gone wrong as compelling as any grand opera.

Loretta Lynn and Conway Twitty, whose duet career spanned roughly the same period, didn't have a real-life romance, but they did have a real-life business partnership in the form of the United Talent booking agency. Still, they were the closest of friends, and the chemistry between them was undeniable. Their duets were sassy, competitive, and tender at times, leading some fans to decide that there just had to be a romance somewhere in the background. Their hits, which include 1971's "After the Fire Is Gone" and 1973's "Louisiana Woman, Mississippi Man," never did anything to dispel that notion.

Similar rumors of romance stalked Dolly Parton and Porter Wagoner in their duet years (1967–1974), but again, the impetus for their 13-album collaboration was commercial—their work was an outgrowth of Parton's featured role on Wagoner's widely syndicated television show. The quality of their sugar-and-vinegar duet work is often underestimated because their rhinestone-encrusted appearance was so spectacular, but their success made "Porter 'n' Dolly" a household phrase. The end came in 1974 (though duet recordings in the can were released for another two years), after Parton's solo career had soared, and she made a much-publicized and anxiety-ridden professional break with Wagoner, leaving fans to wonder if her song "I Will Always Love You" was the ultimate Dear John letter.

MARTHA HUME

STAND BY YOUR MEN
The 1970s were the heyday of male-female duets in country. Two of the best were Loretta Lynn and Conway Twitty (featured on their 1973 album), and George Jones and Tammy Wynette (right).

things on too many records, while rewritten versions of the same old song were being trotted out for the singers to sing. The Nashville Sound was becoming an assembly-line version of creativity in the studio. And there seemed to be no way of breaking out of the successful formula. In Nashville, artists had to record in the label's studio, with whatever producer the label assigned to them. They also had to record the songs that the producer picked for them, with the musicians that the producer selected.

As a result, many fledging artists were giving up on Nashville and its sweetened Nashville Sound as being musically bankrupt. The No. 1 country radio hit on the *Billboard* charts the week of the Dripping Springs Reunion was Freddie Hart's cloying "My Hang-Up Is You," which would go on to be the biggest country hit of the year. In retrospect, the song reflected a last gasp of country's sedate past. The same could be said of another of the biggest country songs of

GATHERING STORM *The Ryman Auditorium in Nashville had been home to the Grand Ole Opry since 1943. But in 1972, the Opry's owners opened the Opryland theme park, moved the Opry to new quarters there two years later, and threatened to tear down the Mother Church of Country Music. Loud civic outcry saved the landmark building.*

the year, which was debuting on country radio stations the week of March 17, 1972. Donna Fargo's "Happiest Girl in the Whole U.S.A" echoed a simpler era of country music that would soon be eclipsed by a more up-to-date reality.

Strangely, even as Nashville music executives tended to hold fast to tired old ways, they seemed perfectly willing to dispense with genuinely valuable traditions. For example, during this period there was talk in Nashville that the only visible symbol of country music's heritage, the Ryman Auditorium, the "Mother Church of Country Music," would be torn down once the Grand Ole Opry's owners finished building Opryland outside of town, where the Opry would soon be moved. It didn't happen, thanks to wide public outcry. But it was a close call. Opryland, a vast musical theme park filled with roller coasters and dancing girls in gingham pinafores, opened in 1972; the Opry moved out to the new Opry House there two years later. Much was made at the time of the circle of

THE FAITHFUL AT THE MOTHER CHURCH *Fans wait in line outside the Ryman for another weekend show of the Grand Ole Opry, 1972.*

Ryman flooring that was installed in the new Opry House stage—tradition preserved—but the fact remained that the Ryman itself was left to languish as a virtually derelict building for 20 years until it was finally renovated and reopened in 1994.

In marked contrast to Nashville's ambivalence for the past, at the Dripping Springs Reunion, past and present seemed to be able to coexist just fine. Tex Ritter—a walking, living, breathing link to country music's rich past—could be seen puffing on a pipe backstage and looking very grandfatherly. He strode around backstage, talking to and encouraging the younger artists, as well as saying hello to such old friends and legends as Ernest Tubb, while rubbing shoulders with the long-haired avant garde of country. The Reunion could not have happened in

PARTNERS IN RHYME *Pictured offstage at the first Dripping Springs Reunion festival in 1972 are the three amigos — (from left) Kris Kristofferson, Willie Nelson, and Waylon Jennings.*

MAN WITH THE BLUES *Willie Nelson in the '60s, at RCA Studio B. Despite eight years at RCA, his career seemed stymied until he moved back to his native Texas to find his rightful audience.*

Nashville, with its musical class lines, as it clearly created a demilitarized zone in the culture wars, where hippies and rednecks could get along and be united in a common love of country music. The Reunion gave hope to the performers that there was a future beyond Nashville record labels and mainstream country radio stations. It united them.

Common grievances

At this point, some of the musical ringleaders felt an urgent need for banding together. Like America's revolutionary forefathers, scruffy outsider artists like Willie Nelson, Waylon Jennings, Tompall Glaser, and Bobby Bare had common grievances. For example, Nelson, Jennings, and Bare were all on RCA, and all three were dissatisfied with the label, chafing at the limitations it placed on them as Chet Atkins increasingly delegated A&R and producing responsibilities to junior

producers with less vision and less willingness to experiment. Bare and Jennings, especially, were on a parallel road to Outlawdom and independence with their recording careers. (The term "outlaw" had not yet been coined to describe this exciting new outsider movement. But when Glaser's publicist Hazel Smith came up with the name in 1973, it stuck.) At this point, Jennings's reputation was building not just in country music but in rock circles. As a result, he had been out in the world at large and was astonished to learn just how much artistic freedom rock & rollers had compared to Nashville's artists.

A recording artist for RCA since 1965, Jennings had felt ill-served by the system for years, and rightly so. He mainly wanted a little freedom: to record with his road band and to record what songs he wanted to, when he wanted to—without a producer who had been assigned by Atkins—and especially where he wanted to.

It was this last wish that led to his alignment with Glaser and the formation of Outlaw Headquarters at Hillbilly Central, Glaser's studio on 19th Avenue South, just off Music Row. Jennings and Glaser, and their friends and musicians, hung out there, and played pinball and drank in nearby joints like the Bump-Bump Room. And in 1972, after discovering that RCA had not

automatically picked up Waylon's option to re-sign with the company, his manager Neil Reshen soon had Columbia, Atlantic, Capitol, and Mercury Records wooing Waylon. After tense negotiations, RCA eventually re-signed Jennings, but only after giving him the greatest artistic freedom of any of its country artists. This move proved to be precedent-setting, and would have major implications for country music ever after. A form of indentured servitude was passing, and the music would open up as a result.

OUTLAW'S BEST FRIEND *(Left) Bobby Bare blazed a trail for the Outlaws in getting creative control of his records in the early '70s. He also recorded songs by poetic new songwriters, including Kris Kristofferson, Shel Silverstein, Billy Joe Shaver, and Townes Van Zandt.*

TOMPALL GLASER *(Above) Although he never enjoyed a lot of hits, Tompall Glaser played a key role behind the scenes in persuading his friend Waylon Jennings to throw off the shackles of his Nashville producers and pursue his own artistic vision.*

"Kris is, of course, one of the best songwriters of all time. He shows more soul when he blows his nose than the ordinary person does at his honeymoon dance."

WILLIE NELSON ON KRIS KRISTOFFERSON

HANDS OF TIME *One of Willie Nelson's longtime trademarks is his worn nylon-string, Martin N-20 classical guitar, autographed by his many heroes and friends.*

But at Dripping Springs in March 1972, things were still in transition. Willie Nelson, another disgruntled RCA artist at the Texas festival, was just plain miserable about his career. His ten-year major-label recording career seemed over. His records weren't selling. Beyond all that, he was trying to find his identity. At this point, with his casual street clothes, he still looked remarkably like a short-haired insurance salesman, especially in comparison to Kris Kristofferson who, along with his Band of Thieves, sported long hair, tight-fitting black leather suits, and silver-and-turquoise jewelry that practically dripped off them. Kristofferson had broken through a few years earlier, in 1969, with his own bag of heretical tricks. He had already begun to change the musical landscape with songs that were frank, literate, sensual and sometimes openly sexual—songs that carried rock's revolutionary

message in a country idiom. Though Willie Nelson didn't know it at the time, he and Kristofferson were comrades in arms.

BLOOD BROTHERS *Willie Nelson (left) and Kris Kristofferson discovered in the '70s that they were kindred spirits. Each wanted to stretch the boundaries of country songwriting; each ended up writing hits that have become standards.*

WATERING HOLE *A legendary Nashville bar, Tootsie's Orchid Lounge is situated behind the Ryman Auditorium. In the '60s and '70s, that proximity gave hungry songwriters like Willie Nelson a prime spot for pitching songs to thirsty Opry singers.*

Nelson, a native Texan, had only recently given up on making it as a recording artist in Nashville and moved with his family to Austin. After a fire in Nashville destroyed his house (and after an episode in which he lay down on lower Broadway outside Tootsie's Orchid Lounge and waited for a car to run over him), he decided that Nashville was not for him. As a songwriter, he had had numerous hits ranging from "Crazy," with Patsy Cline, to "Hello, Walls," with Faron Young, and "Funny How Time Slips Away," with soul singer Joe Hinton. But his own solo records proved fruitless, so he figured that he could do worse than move to Texas, where he could always earn a living playing clubs. One of the clubs he accidentally landed in was a curious hippie emporium in a converted National Guard Armory in Austin, known as the Armadillo World Headquarters. It opened in 1970, around the time Nelson hit town from Nashville, and it quickly became a center of the city's

countercultural activity. Nelson called his friend Waylon and told him, "I think I've found something here."

"It was like going to church," one Armadillo fan said of Nelson's earliest concerts there, and it was a sentiment that was echoed by many a Willie fan. Nelson loved all American music—pop standards, blues, old hillbilly songs, western swing, rock, soul. As so many great American artists do (Jimmie Rodgers, Elvis Presley), Willie mixed them all up, wrote honest new songs like "Me and Paul" and "Bloody Mary Morning," and reached a young Texas audience that was ready and waiting. As Nelson recalled in an interview years later, "All the ingredients were there. The audience was there. I just happened to stumble on to an audience, really. I just saw that there was a lot of young people who liked country music, and I may have been one of the first ones to see that." It seemed only a matter of time before the wider world would catch on to Willie Nelson.

Red Headed Stranger
In 1973, Nelson left RCA for the more progressive Atlantic Records—the label that launched Ray Charles and Led

Zeppelin—after A&R chief Jerry Wexler decided that Atlantic should have a country division.

"It was 1973," Wexler recalled in his autobiography, "when Willie was looked down on by Nashville's assembly-line producers as eccentric. But his eccentricity was exactly what attracted me. I suggested he use his own band, something he'd always been denied, since I wanted him to be comfortable....

"Other than Willie, we never broke any [country] artists. Given time, I'm sure we would have pulled it off, but as Atlantic's chief financial officer, Ahmet [Ertegun] made the call: it's in the red, so close it down."

Running a country division was an interesting idea that could have further changed country if Atlantic had not too easily abandoned the idea, as Wexler, one of the most accomplished producers in pop and R&B (after successes with the likes of Aretha Franklin) could have wrought unimaginable wonders in country. As it was, Nelson's two Atlantic albums, *Shotgun Willie* (1973) and *Phases and Stages* (1974), were well-thought-out aural sagas that have stood up remarkably well over the years. *Phases and Stages* actually was something of a hit for Willie, selling nearly half a million copies. More significantly, though, at Atlantic Nelson learned who he was as a recording artist.

His next record, *Red Headed Stranger*, was a natural outgrowth of where Nelson was headed after his brief but fruitful stint at Atlantic. When Columbia Records signed Nelson he was suddenly a hot property, and after a small bidding war with Warner Bros. Records, Nelson got what he had wanted all along: total artistic control. So he headed down to tiny Garland, Texas (near Dallas), to a studio that had been used mostly for recording advertising jingles. There, in three days and for only $20,000 of studio costs, he cut *Red Headed Stranger*. When he brought the album to Columbia Records in Nashville, head A&R man Billy Sherrill argued against releasing the album. It was unfinished, he said. It sounded like a demo. Other execs agreed with him.

IN HIS ELEMENT *Nelson loved all American music—pop standards, blues, old hillbilly songs, western swing, rock, and soul. He mixed them all up in fresh combinations, wrote new songs, and reached a young Texas audience that was ready and waiting.*

TURNING POINT *Recording first with his own band, and then with Muscle Shoals pickers, Willie Nelson achieved artistic breakthroughs with these two albums for Atlantic Records:* Shotgun Willie *(1973) and* Phases and Stages *(1974).*

But Nelson stuck to his guns and noted that his contract gave him final say. "They thought it was underproduced, too sparse, all those things," Nelson wrote in his autobiography. "Even though they didn't like it, they had already paid me a bunch of money for it, so they had to release it under my contract. And since they had money in it, they had to promote it."

It is impossible now to overstate the impact of this seminal 1975 album. It legitimized and intellectualized country, and immediately made country a mainstream popular phenomenon. A concept album about a mysterious hombre who rides into town from nowhere, kills a saloon girl who tries to steal one of his horses, and then rides off, *Red Headed Stranger* had mythic resonance. It is a brilliant saga-song western epic album, a very minimalist work, but one that plucks every heartstring, wrings every emotion, subtly explores eerie aspects of the human condition. And it just plain sounded good. Buoyed by the album's first single, "Blue Eyes Crying in the Rain"—Nelson's first No. 1—*Red Headed Stranger* built into a massive seller and proved the worth of country-music concept albums. Above all, though, it turned Willie Nelson into a star.

PROFILES IN COUNTRY

BILLY SHERRILL

BORN PHIL CAMPBELL, ALABAMA, NOVEMBER 5, 1936
BUSINESS AFFILIATIONS COLUMBIA RECORDS/ EPIC RECORDS

By expanding upon the pop-inflected Nashville Sound, Sherrill became the dominant record producer of the late 1960s and 1970s. He signed on with Epic Records in 1962, but he didn't have much luck until 1966 when he co-wrote and produced the No. 1 single "Almost Persuaded" for David Houston. Later that year he launched the career of Tammy Wynette; under Sherrill's direction she racked up 20 No. 1 hits in ten years. The producer found his next big success with George Jones, whom he signed in 1971. Sherrill revamped the singer's sound by surrounding him with lusher arrangements. He also encouraged Jones to rely more on the bottom end of his enormous range. The result was a revitalization of Jones's career and many hits.

In 1972, Sherrill took 13-year-old Tanya Tucker and seized on her precocious voice to fashion seven Top 10 hits in two years. Sherrill also transformed jazz-soul singer Charlie Rich into a country-pop crooner, with "Behind Closed Doors" and "The Most Beautiful Girl." Sherrill also produced hits for Johnny Cash, Johnny Paycheck, and Lacy J. Dalton, and developed the young Shelby Lynne. He retired from the music business in the early 1990s.

GEOFFREY HIMES

> **TO US, OUTLAW MEANT STANDING UP FOR YOUR RIGHTS, YOUR OWN WAY OF DOING THINGS.**
>
> WAYLON JENNINGS

Ol' Waylon

A couple of years before, Jennings had recorded his own career-changing album. This one had its genesis at the 1972 Dripping Springs Reunion. The story goes that Jennings stepped into a backstage trailer at the festival and met songwriter Billy Joe Shaver for the first time. Shaver was a Jennings fan, and he immediately grabbed a guitar and played a new song that caught Waylon's ear. It was a song inspired by Willie Nelson called "Willy the Wandering Gypsy and Me." Jennings asked if Shaver had more songs like that. Shaver said he had more than Jennings could count. At that point, the two agreed that Waylon would cut an album of Shaver songs and "Willy the Wandering Gypsy" would definitely be among them.

As it happened, Tom T. Hall also appeared at Dripping Springs, and got so involved and spirited that he took his shirt off during his fevered—for him—performance, and flung his guitar into the very appreciative crowd at the end of his set. Hall also paid close attention to Shaver's songs and promptly recorded "Willy the Wandering Gypsy and Me" on his next album, *The Story Teller*, released in September 1972. Jennings was not pleased by this development.

Months later, back in Nashville, Shaver repeatedly tried to reach Jennings on the phone but could not get through. When was Jennings going to record his songs? Eventually, Shaver tracked him down at a recording session. Shaver threatened to "kick his ass" if he didn't listen to the songwriter's compositions. Jennings gave in, and Shaver spun out song after song, including "Old Five and Dimers Like Me," "Black Rose," and "Honky Tonk Heroes." Waylon allowed that there was nothing to do but record those songs.

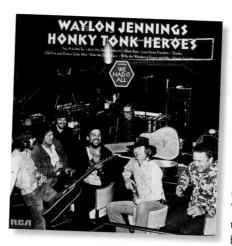

HONKY TONK HEROES *Waylon Jennings scored a breakthrough of his own when he recorded nine songs by newcomer Billy Joe Shaver for this 1975 album. Waylon holds the guitar; Shaver is immediately left of him.*

Even so, there were still some rocky moments between the two, especially after Shaver heard Jennings changing the tempo of more than one song, especially the title cut, "Honky Tonk Heroes," which enraged the writer. "Trust me," Jennings told him, and Shaver finally did. True to Jennings's word, all but one of the tracks on the *Honky Tonk Heroes* album were written or co-written by Shaver. It was the artistic validation Shaver needed to forge his way in Nashville as both hit songwriter and recording artist. For Jennings, it was an early creative high point, and proof positive that his artistic freedom was producing art of undeniable merit.

Yet it was *Wanted! The Outlaws* (1976) that became country music's breakthrough album of the 1970s—country's first album to be certified platinum for sales of more than one million copies. In a town and music community with low expectations, sales of 300,000 for an album had been considered exceptional.

The Outlaws also marked a shift in packaging and marketing. Jerry Bradley at RCA Nashville noticed Jennings's success, and, seeing the flurry of stories about the emerging Outlaw movement in rock as well as country magazines, decided to take advantage of that momentum with a commercial package. After Jennings suggested me as a candidate for liner notes for the package, Bradley next put together old tracks by Jennings, Nelson, Jennings's wife, Jessi Colter, and Waylon's compadre from Hillbilly Central, Tompall Glaser. The record-company executive slapped a faux Old West cover on the package and touted it as the latest and hottest new thing out of Nashville. Lo and behold, that's what it became. Nashville's million-selling ceiling was suddenly shattered.

WANTED *It was an idea made in marketing heaven: an album of previously released tracks and outtakes, pulled together with a new brand name (Outlaws!). Nevertheless, it sounded fresh and daring, and in 1976 it became country music's first album to be certified platinum.*

WAYLON JENNINGS *The former DJ and one-time bass player for Buddy Holly was nearly 40 years old when, suddenly, after a decade of unfulfilled potential, he became a country-music superstar.*

PROFILES IN COUNTRY

ROSANNE CASH

BORN MEMPHIS, TENNESSEE,
MAY 24, 1955
PLAYS GUITAR
FIRST RECORDED 1978
INFLUENCES THE CARTER FAMILY,
THE BEATLES, BUFFALO SPRINGFIELD,
EMMYLOU HARRIS, RODNEY CROWELL
HITS "SEVEN YEAR ACHE," "I DON'T
KNOW WHY YOU DON'T WANT ME,"
"TENNESSEE FLAT TOP BOX"

With her 1979 debut, *Right or Wrong*, which spawned three Top 25 hits, Rosanne Cash arrived as an important new female voice. But it was her second album, *Seven Year Ache* (1981), that established her as a uniquely qualified hybrid artist, Tennessee bred, and California cured. With the title song, her first No. 1, she paired an intensely personal lyric about her marriage to Rodney Crowell with the tough street vibe of pop's Rickie Lee Jones. Everything about it spoke of her fierce independence, and of the tug-of-war between her steely eyed realism and lush romanticism. *Newsweek* termed her "the most intensely modern of Nashville's new women."

Cash continued to blend genres before settling on an introspective style with 1990s *Interiors*, which foreshadowed her divorce from Crowell. In 1995, she married John Leventhal, who helped her reach a new maturity of songwriting. It found its zenith in her 2003 duet with her dying father, "September When It Comes," set to the tempo of tears, and in *Black Cadillac* (2006).

ALANNA NASH

DOLLY PARTON

BORN LOCUST RIDGE, TENNESSEE, JANUARY 19, 1946
PLAYS GUITAR, BANJO
INFLUENCES AVIE LEE PARTON (HER MOTHER); REV. JAKE OWENS (GRAND-FATHER); BILL OWENS (UNCLE)
HITS "JOLENE," "COAT OF MANY COLORS," "I WILL ALWAYS LOVE YOU"

"I started writing serious songs when I was about seven," Dolly Parton says, "but I was fiddling with it before that." It shows. Now into her fifth decade of recording, Parton is country's greatest living star. Others may have been more consistent hitmakers, but no one has so successfully spanned "old" and "new" country, or reinvented herself with such frequency and vision. Her personal story of growing up in the mountains of East Tennessee and moving to Nashville and joining *The Porter Wagoner Show* is well known. So is her pop-country phase and movie-star stint of the '70s and '80s. Parton's entrepreneurial talents—the Dollywood theme park, a film production company, music-publishing concerns, and a forthcoming Broadway musical—have earned her a fortune estimated at $400 million and taken her far beyond the Smoky Mountains. Yet she returns there in her art. Her spate of acoustic mountain/bluegrass albums capture quintessential backwoods themes. Beneath her flash and "trash," beats the heart of a hillbilly savant.

ALANNA NASH

Jennings later had the first triple-platinum album in country history with his *Greatest Hits* offering, again proving that rock fans brought their album-buying habits over to country.

The rock bible

A contributing factor to the shift in Nashville's national persona in the 1970s was undoubtedly the coverage of country music in rock magazines, particularly in *Rolling Stone*. The latter began in San Francisco in 1967 as a journal of rock music and its attendant counterculture, with its issues of drugs, radical politics, the Vietnam War, and ecology. Called the "rock bible" by *Time* magazine, *Rolling Stone* began to assume respectability and commercial success in the early 1970s. I was a contributing editor to *Rolling Stone* while in graduate school at the University of Texas at Austin during that time and had been filing articles on rock musicians. I began suggesting articles to Jann Wenner, the magazine's editor, on country artists who might also be of interest to their readers. It seemed apparent that many country artists also appealed to the rock audience, and that proved to be the case in subsequent coverage.

Dolly Parton, for example, quickly became a favorite with *Rolling Stone* readers, especially after she left Porter Wagoner's television show in 1974 for a solo career. In early 1977, it became clear that the time was right for *Rolling Stone* to do a major take on Dolly. She had been country music's best-kept secret for years: one of the most original and most sensitive songwriters since Hank Williams, blessed with an achingly sweet voice to boot. She was bound and determined to break out of the country-music ghetto, find a national audience, and carry her music and her message to the world at large. Traveling across Connecticut for a week or so as Dolly played small venues around the state, I interviewed

her in-depth. After that, I knew, as I seldom knew with an artist, that she could accomplish whatever she wanted to accomplish. It was only a matter of will—and time. In December of that year, Dolly scored her first big pop crossover hit, "Here You Come Again," and soon there was hardly a person in America who didn't know the woman with the hourglass figure and the shimmering, childlike trill of a voice.

AMERICA'S SWEETHEART *Although she was well known to country fans from her 1967–1974 stint on* The Porter Wagoner *TV show, Dolly Parton achieved a whole new level of stardom once she left Wagoner and spread her wings for the pop market.*

The South's Gonna Do it Again: The Influence of Southern Rock

In the late 1960s, Macon, Georgia record maven Phil Walden helped bring to light the music of the Allman Brothers—a spirited, virtuoso group of players who blended rhythm and blues, country, and rock & roll into a swirling, jam-oriented concoction now known as "southern rock."

Defined by twin guitar leads, storytelling lyrics, and southern imagery, what began in Macon as a regional rock movement is now a core element in modern country music. Travis Tritt, Tim McGraw, Montgomery Gentry, and other acts cop the sound and sing the praises of southern-rock heavyweights like the Allman Brothers, the Marshall Tucker Band, Charlie Daniels, and Lynyrd Skynyrd.

The Allman Brothers—a group that featured an inventive rhythm section, a soul singer in Greg Allman, and two masterful guitarists in Duane Allman and Dickey Betts—laid the groundwork with songs like "Ramblin' Man" and "Melissa," released through Walden's Capricorn Records. Capricorn also became the record-company home of Spartanburg, South Carolina's Marshall Tucker Band, a group that scored genre-crossing hits "Heard It in a Love Song" and "Fire on the Mountain." The Tuckers' Toy Caldwell was a prime influence on the music of his friend, Hank Williams Jr.

Charlie Daniels has been the most successful in crossing over from southern rock to country, scoring numerous country hits. He has also undergone the biggest change in image and outlook: where Daniels once boasted in song of getting "drunk" and "stoned," he eventually became a hard-line political and social conservative who opined that drug dealers should be hung from trees. Throughout all the transitions, he remained an instantly identifiable force on fiddle, a fine guitarist, and an idiosyncratically appealing singer.

Unlike the Tucker Band or Daniels, Florida group Lynyrd Skynyrd's songs didn't cross over on to country charts. Yet "Sweet Home Alabama" became the anthem for the country-reared, rock-ready New South, and the group's multi-guitar sound has been approximated time and again in Nashville studios. In 2005, Skynyrd member Johnny Van Zant and his brother Donnie released a country album together, and they were delighted to hear Tim McGraw assert that if Skynyrd came out now the band would be on country radio.

PETER COOPER

REBEL ROCK (left) Gregg Allman of the Allman Brothers Band, in concert here in 1979, was a key leader in the southern-rock movement of the '70s. Together, he and his older brother Duane brewed up a heady mixture of blues, rock, jazz, and country that continues to influence rock and country musicians alike. (right) In his long career, Charlie Daniels has played sessions for Bob Dylan (see p. 260), scored rock hits with songs like "The South's Gonna Do It Again," and ultimately became accepted as a mainstream country-music star.

Duet Till You're Satisfied—
Willie Nelson's Singing Partners

Since making his earliest recordings in the mid-1950s, Willie Nelson has deliberately crossed stylistic boundaries, not only through his solo recordings but also by singing with artists spanning the musical spectrum. By the end of 2004, his famous vocal collaborators amounted to more than 80 people, who sang with Nelson in duets and in various other combinations. This list includes two duets created by overdubbing Willie's voice onto recordings that had been made previously: The 1975 hit "Good Hearted Woman," by Nelson and longtime buddy Waylon Jennings, and 1985's "I Told a Lie to My Heart," on which Nelson sings harmony to a demo vocal recorded by Hank Williams nearly 40 years earlier. Years listed are those of earliest identified release, and those listed are named only once—the year they first recorded with Nelson.

JOHN W. RUMBLE

1962
Shirley Collie

1974
Tracy Nelson

1975
Waylon Jennings
(overdub)

1977
Darrell McCall
Mary Kay Place

1978
Hank Cochran
Johnny Paycheck

1979
Leon Russell

1980
Dyan Cannon
Emmylou Harris
Amy Irving
Ray Price

1981
Jody Payne

1982
Johnny Bush
Merle Haggard
Roger Miller
Dolly Parton
Webb Pierce

1983
Brenda Lee
Steve Fromholz

1984
Ray Charles
Julio Iglesias
Kris Kristofferson
Hank Wilson
   (Leon Russell)

1985
Johnny Cash
Lacy J. Dalton
As member of
   The Highwaymen
George Jones
Hank Snow
Mel Tillis
Hank Williams
   (overdub)
Faron Young
Neil Young

1986
David Allan Coe

1992
Boxcar Willie
Ray Wylie Hubbard

1993
Shawn Colvin
Bob Dylan
Lyle Lovett
Sinead O'Connor
Bonnie Raitt

1994
Willie Nelson Jr.
Curtis Potter
Buckwheat Zydeco

1995
Grandpa Jones
Kimmie Rhodes

1997
B. B. King

1999
Beck
Manhattan Transfer

2000
Dr. John
Johnny Lang
Keb Mo
Francine Reed
Kenny Wayne
   Shepherd
Susan Tedeschi

2002
Ryan Adams
Jon Bon Jovi
Sheryl Crow
Vince Gill
Patty Griffin
Norah Jones
Toby Keith
Brian McKnight
Aaron Neville
Keith Richards
Rob Thomas/
   Matchbox Twenty
Lee Ann Womack

2003
Kenny Chesney
Eric Clapton
Elvis Costello
Crystal Gayle
Wyclef Jean
Diana Krall
Shelby Lynne
The Mavericks
John Mellencamp
Paul Simon
Shania Twain
Steven Tyler
ZZ Top

2004
Al Green
Ben Harper
Toots Hibbert
Holmes Brothers
Ricky Lee Jones
Kid Rock
Carole King
Jerry Lee Lewis
Joni Mitchell
Paula Nelson
Joe Walsh
Lucinda Williams

Admittedly, though, Dolly was something of an anomaly for *Rolling Stone*. Originally, the magazine's country coverage was heavily devoted to the 1970s Austin scene, which was a rich mixture of folkie artists and other musical misfits who adopted a quasi-country persona. Michael Martin Murphey, Doug Sahm, Jerry Jeff Walker, B. W. Stevenson, Ray Wylie Hubbard, and many others led a dynamic Austin club culture. This progressive-country scene and its music went through many nicknames, including "Redneck Rock" (after Hubbard's "Up Against the Wall, Redneck Mother"), and "Cosmic Cowboys" (after Murphey's 1973 Cosmic Cowboy Souvenir album, and his anthemic song "Cosmic Cowboy"), and coalesced around free-form radio station KOKE-FM. The significance of the call letters was more than a local in-joke, as

Austin's more mellow marijuana atmosphere began to give way to an influx of cocaine from the California music pipeline.

Drugs were only one reason why Austin never developed a formal music industry; it has never gone beyond being one of the liveliest club and live music centers in the world. There were sporadic attempts throughout the 1970s to develop a large recording, managerial, and publishing presence in Austin, but forces working against that involved an increasingly hostile attitude toward Nashville, and a large amount of what can only be described as hippie laziness.

As a final legacy from Dripping Springs, in 1973, Nelson—sensing the potential of what he had glimpsed with this new dynamic audience—launched the first of his Fourth of July picnics, which were also, in those early years, staged near Dripping Springs. He invited a similar line-up of traditional artists and up-and-coming kindred spirits, and the event quickly became a fan favorite and media darling.

Outlaws ascendant

The game was over. The Outlaws won. Their creative period ended, and the commercial period began. Jennings would be named the CMA's Male Vocalist of the Year in 1975 (displaying a career-long obliviousness to awards—he didn't attend the ceremony). In 1976, Waylon and Willie won the CMA Award for Duo of the Year. In 1979, Willie was named the CMA's Entertainer of the Year, the top award. In addition, Jennings and Nelson were all over radio in the late 1970s with the most-played singles in country for three years straight—in 1976 with their duet of "Good Hearted Woman," in 1977 with Jennings's "Luckenbach, Texas" and in 1978 with their duet "Mammas Don't Let Your Babies Grow Up to be Cowboys." The record labels bowed before them, and threw a big party for Willie and Waylon at New York's Rainbow Room, and another big party for Dolly Parton at Windows on the World.

Commercially, the Outlaw movement reached its apogee in 1978, the year Nelson appeared on the cover of *Rolling Stone*. (He would be the last country artist on the magazine's cover until Dolly Parton appeared there in 1980, followed

HELLO, DOLLY *It was a sure sign that Dolly Parton had arrived as a major music star when* Rolling Stone *featured her on the magazine's December 11, 1980 cover. Her media blitz had begun even earlier— she appeared on the cover of* Playboy *in December 1979, also in a Santa suit.*

many years later by Garth Brooks in 1993.) Also in 1978, the Willie-Waylon connection delivered four No. 1 albums: Nelson's *Stardust* and *Willie and Family Live*, Jennings's *I've Always Been Crazy*, and their collaboration, *Waylon & Willie*. Furthermore, 1978 saw Jennings write and record "Don't You Think This Outlaw Bit's Done Got Out of Hand." Jennings did not write many songs, and he obviously meant the sentiment of this one. It is in part a vocal retelling of the drug raid that year on his Nashville studio. Unfortunately for Jennings, one of the other lessons he learned from his rock & roll friends was a fondness for cocaine, which led to a $1,500-a-day habit. It began eroding his career and his health, leading, in 1981, to drug treatment and recovery.

In retrospect, it's clear that Nelson and Jennings supplied the main thread of continuity for country's bedrock musical values—values that continue to this day. Jennings's staunch preservation of the role of the traveling troubadour (and his improvement upon honky-tonk) can be heard in many young artists throughout the past decades, as well as in contemporary performers. Nelson's fearless experimentation has grown stronger as an influence through the years, as has his insistence on respecting his elders in country music: Bob Wills, Lefty Frizzell, Ray Price, Cindy Walker.

And what of mainstream country in the face of the tenacious Nashville Sound and the Outlaw Barbarians at the Gate? It survived, but only the very best of the traditional country artists would endure: Jones, Haggard, Cash, and the women who stepped out of the shadow of the men—Dolly Parton, Loretta Lynn, and Tammy Wynette.

One result of the Outlaw breakthrough for mainstream country was that the lines between country and rock became increasingly harder to define. The Outlaw movement opened the doors of artistic freedom wide—perhaps a shade too wide for some. Country music (and its new pop

WAYLON & WILLIE *After scoring a No. 1 hit with their duet on "Good Hearted Woman" in 1976, Waylon Jennings and Willie Nelson became country music's favorite team of the late '70s. They made two best-selling albums together and scored another No. 1 with "Mammas Don't Let Your Babies Grow Up to Be Cowboys."*

"The Berlin Wall fell for the same reason. A lot of people wanted to see that happen. They wanted to see the artist have a little more control."

WILLIE NELSON ON THE CHANGES IN ARTISTIC CONTROL IN THE 1970s

CLASSIC COUNTRY
RECORDING

KENNY ROGERS
"The Gambler"

*You got to know when
to hold. Know when to
fold 'em...*

WRITTEN BY DON SCHLITZ
AND RECORDED 1978
NO. 1 COUNTRY, DECEMBER 16,
1978, NO. 16 POP

"The Gambler" is a story song
with an ending that, on first listen,
comes as a mild surprise. It's a
conversation in which a mentor
passes on a bit of common-
sense wisdom, and the trappings
of the tale include such standard
country imagery as a train,
alcohol, and ultimately death.
What makes "The Gambler"
particularly unique is its digression
from the standard emotional
content of most songs. It concerns
neither love nor anger, and the
words from the gambler to his
fellow train rider are a rather
matter-of-fact lesson in life.

"The Gambler" represented
the first success for Don Schlitz,
a songwriter who would go on
to compose such hits as "On the
Other Hand," "Forever and Ever,
Amen," and "When You Say
Nothing at All." Schlitz, who
composed the song around an
open D tuning on his guitar,
recorded the first charted
version. But Rogers delivered
the definitive rendition, with
producer Larry Butler adding a
key change and small percussive
elements to create a little more
aural activity.

In addition to a slew of
awards, the song also provided
the basis for five television
movies between 1980 and 1994.
And it gave Rogers a permanent
image on which to hang his hat.

TOM ROLAND

audience and attendant prosperity) had not
only made room for an Emmylou Harris
or a Rosanne Cash or a Rodney Crowell;
it had also made room (too much, some
said) for crossover crooners like Kenny
Rogers, Ronnie Milsap, Crystal Gayle,
and Barbara Mandrell.

That was the yin and the yang of 1970s
country. For even as country was becoming
more rough-edged, progressive, and relevant,
thanks to artists like Waylon and Willie and
Gram Parsons and Kris Kristofferson, it
was also filled with plenty of performers

KENNY ROGERS *Known as a pop singer early in his
career, Kenny Rogers made a shrewd move to country music
in the '70s. His gritty voice was perfectly suited to country
story-songs like "Lucille" (1977) and "The Gambler" (1978).*

who seemed more pop than country. Not
everyone in Nashville was happy about
the turn of events.

On the surface, the conflict appeared to
be an "outsider" versus "insider," "pop"
versus "traditional" issue, but in effect it
amounted to the final evolution of the
Nashville Sound: if you want pop-sounding
country, who better to sing it than pop

singers? In 1974, when mainstream country was still leaning heavily toward pop records, the sugary Olivia Newton-John was named the CMA Female Vocalist of the Year. The only basis for the vote seemed to be the young Australian's three country-charting singles from 1973 and 1974: "Let Me Be There" (which peaked at No. 7), "If You Love Me (Let Me Know)" (No. 2), and "I Honestly Love You" (No. 6). These singles were also massive pop hits, as well they should have been. They were pop.

Following the 1974 CMA Awards show, tempers flared up and down Music Row. The great traditional singers George Jones and Tammy Wynette were still married at the time, and their house was the scene of a meeting of angry traditionalists and pop-leaning country artists. Getting together to talk about the situation were two dozen country stars, including Bill

OLIVIA NEWTON-JOHN
Nashville's country-music establishment fully embraced pop crossover in 1974, the year the CMA voted breathy Australian singer Olivia Newton-John its Female Vocalist of the Year.

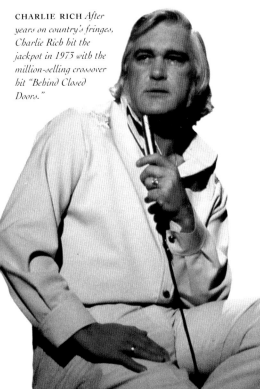

CHARLIE RICH *After years on country's fringes, Charlie Rich hit the jackpot in 1973 with the million-selling crossover hit "Behind Closed Doors."*

Anderson, Porter Wagoner, Jim Ed Brown, Dottie West, Brenda Lee, Faron Young, Conway Twitty, Cal Smith, Hank Snow, Mel Tillis, Barbara Mandrell, and Dolly Parton. The upshot of this gathering at George and Tammy's house was the formation of a country solidarity movement called the Association of Country Entertainers (ACE). Their major stated concerns—which would be no less relevant today— were valid representation of traditional artists on the CMA board of directors and a musical balance on country radio's playlists.

As a result of that 1974 flap, a memorable CMA Awards event came the next year, when an obviously well-lubricated Charlie Rich ended his reign as 1974's Entertainer of the Year by announcing the new recipient of the CMA's top prize. "The award goes to my good friend, John Denver," said Rich, who had been drinking gin-and-tonics backstage. At which point he pulled out his Zippo lighter and set fire to the card holding the name of his successor. Rich held the burning card up for the cameras on the nationally televised live show and smiled a big smile of triumph. The message to anyone watching seemed clear: in Rich's eyes, a West Coast neo-folkie like John Denver, who had built his career on pop radio, was not welcome in country music.

West Coast country-rockers

The West Coast equivalent of the Outlaw movement was country-rock. Its prime mover had been Gram Parsons, the Georgia boy who hijacked the folk-rock Byrds to forge the definitive country-rock statement *Sweetheart of the Rodeo* in 1968. But Parsons burned out early, the victim of a drug overdose in 1973, before he could find his commercial stride. Although Parsons had exquisite taste in songs and musicians (he

PROFILES IN COUNTRY

GEORGE JONES

BORN SARATOGA, TEXAS,
SEPTEMBER 12, 1931
INFLUENCES ROY ACUFF,
HANK WILLIAMS, LEFTY FRIZZELL
HITS "SHE THINKS I STILL CARE,"
"THE GRAND TOUR," "HE STOPPED
LOVING HER TODAY"

At Jones's first recording session,
producer Pappy Daily complained:
"George, for the last few hours
you've sung like Roy Acuff, Lefty
Frizzell, Hank Williams, and Bill
Monroe. Can you sing like George
Jones?" It took him a few years,
but by the 1960s Jones had developed into the most emotionally
powerful voice in country music.
By nearly unanimous agreement,
it is a rank he still holds.

Like his hero Hank Williams,
Jones struggled with alcoholism
and drug abuse. Unlike Hank,
Jones survived his demons. His
wild years (1955–1982), however,
produced his greatest musical
performances and 127 chart hits.
Gifted with a prodigious vocal
range, Jones is capable of rum-
bling and hiccupping his way
through a rollicking novelty like
"White Lightning" (1959) or mim-
icking the gliding moan of steel
guitar on "He Stopped Loving Her
Today" (1980). Most importantly,
he has a deep understanding of
sorrow and an uncanny ability to
convey its infinite shades in song.
Married four times (the third was
Tammy Wynette), Jones had settled into the role of revered elder
statesman by the 1980s. His election
to the Country Music Hall of Fame
in 1992 was long expected.

PAUL KINGSBURY

DESPERADOS *The Eagles capitalized on country-rock more
successfully than any act in the '70s, and the rockers' influence
on today's country remains strong. They're shown here in an
outtake from sessions for their 1973* Desperado *album.*

discovered Emmylou Harris and brought
her to the spotlight as his duet partner),
he couldn't connect with a mass audience.

That achievement fell to his Southern
California rivals, the Eagles. Country-rock
reached its commercial peak in the 1970s
with their string of soft-rock hits on the pop
charts. They began as Linda Ronstadt's
backing band. A true pioneer of the genre,
Ronstadt formed the folk-rockish Stone
Poneys in Los Angeles in the mid-1960s,
and after going solo, recorded the acclaimed
country-rock album *Hand Sown … Home
Grown*. She then recorded the album *Silk
Purse* in Nashville in 1970, and appeared
on both the Grand Ole Opry and on
Johnny Cash's television show. In 1974,
she hit No. 2 on the country singles chart
with a remake of Hank Williams's "I Can't
Help It (If I'm Still in Love with You)."
The following year, she had a No. 1 country
hit with "When Will I Be Loved" (a remake
of the Everly Brothers' 1960 pop hit, also
recorded in Nashville), and—more significantly for her—a No. 2 pop hit. Though
she would continue to occasionally dabble
in country, from this point forward
Ronstadt became for all intents and
purposes a mainstream pop star.

Emmylou Harris, in many ways, turned
out to be Ronstadt's counterpart in country.
But whereas Ronstadt moved from a
countryish sound to rock and pop, Harris
moved in the opposite direction, from folk,
rock, and pop into country. Beginning as
a folkie in the Washington, D.C. area and
in New York City, she had met Parsons
in 1971. By then he had already made
country-rock history with his International
Submarine Band in 1967, and with his
groundbreaking work with the Byrds and
the Flying Burrito Brothers. Harris sang
harmony on his 1973 album, *GP*, toured
with him, and then recorded with him on
his 1974 album, *Grievous Angel*.

Understandably, Harris was devastated
by Parsons's death that year from a drug
overdose, and eventually landed in Los
Angeles, where her 1975 album *Pieces of the
Sky* became a country-rock benchmark.
The willowy singer put together a series of
stellar backing groups, beginning with the
Hot Band, which included former Elvis
Presley sidemen James Burton and Glen
D. Hardin, as well as future country star
Rodney Crowell. Harris moved to
Nashville where she became a pillar of
the music community. Some of her later

MAVERICK *Gram Parsons pioneered country-rock with the
Byrds and the Flying Burrito Brothers, then discovered Emmylou
Harris. Here he flaunts his country-rock clothes, custom-made to
his specifications by Nudie (with Parsons in inset photo).*

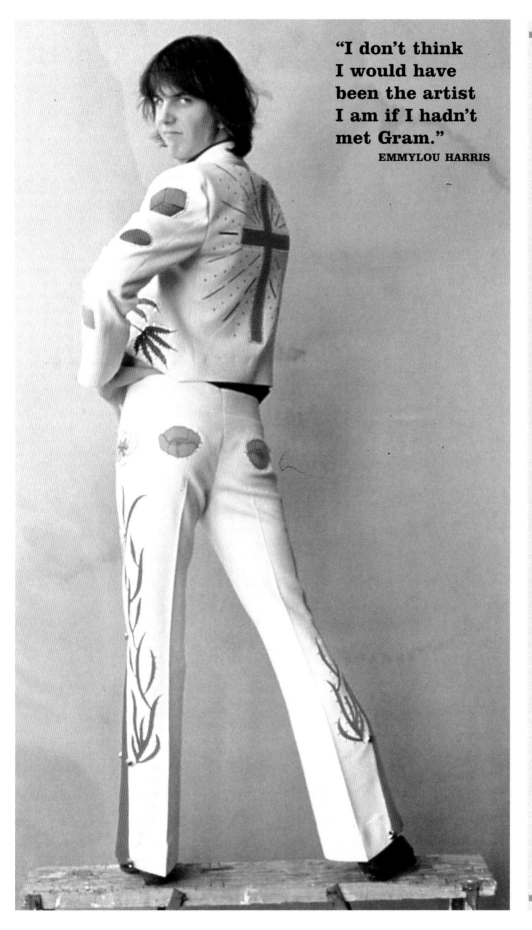

"I don't think
I would have
been the artist
I am if I hadn't
met Gram."
EMMYLOU HARRIS

PROFILES IN COUNTRY

GRAM PARSONS

BORN WINTER HAVEN, FLORIDA,
NOVEMBER 5, 1946
DIED SEPTEMBER 19, 1973
PLAYED GUITAR
FIRST RECORDED 1963
INFLUENCES ELVIS PRESLEY,
GEORGE JONES, LOUVIN BROTHERS
HITS "HICKORY WIND," "SIN CITY,"
"OOH LAS VEGAS"

Gram Parsons never sold many
records while he was alive, but
the few that he did sell inspired
careers that changed the face of
country music. While at Harvard,
he founded the International
Submarine Band, his first country-
rock outfit. He dropped out of
school, moved the band to LA,
and recorded an album (*Safe at
Home*). But just as the record was
coming out, Parsons accepted an
invitation to join the Byrds, a band
that had pioneered folk-rock and
psychedelic rock. On the only
album he recorded with them,
Sweetheart of the Rodeo (1968),
Parsons helped them pioneer
country-rock as well.

In 1968, Parsons and Chris
Hillman quit the Byrds and
cofounded a new country-rock
band called the Flying Burrito
Brothers. But after two albums,
Parsons quit this band as well.
Then he found his perfect vocal
partner, Emmylou Harris. He
featured her prominently on his
two solo albums: *GP* (1973) and
Grievous Angel (1974). Before
the second disc could be
released, Parsons died of a
heroin overdose. He was 26.
GEOFFREY HIMES

sidemen—including Crowell, Ricky Skaggs,
and producer Emory Gordy—would be
leaders in country's rebound in the 1980s.

Urban cowboys

As the 1970s began winding down, a
curious phenomenon spread. Willie Nelson
wannabes blossomed wherever country-
music fans gathered, particularly throughout Texas, and Nelson lookalikes elbowed
each other for standing room in front of
Willie's stage. Feathered cowboy hats,
red scarves, and flowery cowboy shirts
eventually morphed into the fashion excesses
of what became the Urban Cowboy era,
named for the John Travolta film of 1980.

The film itself stemmed from an *Esquire*
magazine article about a young oil-patch
roughneck (Travolta) who pursues a pretty
young hellion (Debra Winger) in the
wilds of Gilley's, the cavernous Texas
honky-tonk named for singer Mickey
Gilley, who had enjoyed a low-key music
career, but remained in the shadow of his
more famous cousins, piano-pounder
Jerry Lee Lewis and televangelist Jimmy
Swaggart. Pasadena, where Gilley's was
located (the club has since burned and
been demolished, although a modern
namesake exists in Dallas), was and
remains, a blue-collar petrochemical-
industry town outside Houston, on the
polluted Houston Ship Channel. Gilley's
was a hell-raising behemoth of a club
where nightly fights were plentiful. Those
who visited the club (the regulars were
called "Gilley Rats") quickly discovered it
was a low-budget operation with cheap,
stained mattresses scattered on the floor
as padding around a mechanical bull—set
up so patrons could show off their rodeo
skills after a beer or six.

Urban Cowboy made a country star out
of smooth-singing Johnny Lee, an easygoing regular at Gilley's who appeared on
the movie's platinum-selling soundtrack,
a mishmash of mostly easy-listening pop
songs from (in addition to Lee) the
Eagles, Jimmy Buffett, Joe Walsh,
Bonnie Raitt, Dan Fogelberg, Bob Seger,
Charlie Daniels, Kenny Rogers, Boz
Scaggs, Linda Ronstadt, and J. D.
Souther. Lee had never before charted
higher than No. 15, and the soundtrack's
"Lookin' for Love" became his first No. 1
single. He married *Dallas* star Charlene
Tilton at the height of his newfound
fame, and suddenly found himself in the
uncomfortable role of tabloid, as well as
country, star. He would have four more

VOCAL SUPPORT *Country-rockers Emmylou Harris (left)
and Linda Ronstadt became friends and occasional collaborators
in the '70s. By the time of this 1977 concert photo, Emmylou had
a string of country hits, and Linda Ronstadt ruled the pop charts.*

The Roots of Progressive Country

With the albums *Pieces of the Sky* and *Elite Hotel*, both released in 1975, Emmylou Harris and her producer Brian Ahern invented a new kind of country music. Here was music that talked about the perennial country themes of marriage, home, and work, but with the modernist irony of Bob Dylan and his singer-songwriter heirs. Here was music that blended Appalachian string-band instruments with the rhythmic thump of Bakersfield country and rockabilly. Here was music that took the freedom and energy of Gram Parsons's country-rock, and subtracted the clutter and sloppiness so it could be heard on country radio.

Harris had ten Top Ten hits of her own in the 1970s. But what started out as an individual sound became a full-fledged movement by the end of the decade, as her past and current musicians became evangelists for this new approach. Her rhythm guitarist, Rodney Crowell, became a producer who applied the Harris-Ahern sound to his own recordings, as well as to those of Rosanne Cash and Guy Clark. Crowell's replacement in Harris's band, Ricky Skaggs, produced similar recordings by himself and the Whites. Harris's bassist, Emory Gordy Jr., became a producer who interwove the sound on records by Steve Earle and Patty Loveless. Harris's pianist, Tony Brown, became an MCA executive who signed and produced albums by Earle, Loveless, Marty Stuart, Joe Ely, Lyle Lovett, and Nanci Griffith. Vince Gill, who played guitar and sang on many of these albums, became a solo star in his own right.

This tight-knit group of friends created such enduring albums as Cash's *Seven Year Ache*, Skaggs's *Highways & Heartaches*, Clark's *The South Coast of Texas*, Earle's *Guitar Town*, and Loveless's *Honky Tonk Angel*. They also found commercial success along the way. Between them, Harris, Skaggs, Cash, and Crowell scored 31 No. 1 country hits, and 57 Top Ten hits in the 1980s. In addition, Gill, Loveless, Earle, and Lyle Lovett would all have Top Ten country hits in the 1980s.

This progressive bunch pursued innovation in the face of the business-as-usual forces on Music Row. Not only did they lend a new sound and a new sensibility to country music, but they enjoyed hits while doing it.
GEOFFREY HIMES

THE HOUSTON KID *After apprenticing in Emmylou Harris's Hot Band, Rodney Crowell emerged as one of country's most gifted progressive singer-songwriters.*

Hard hat days and honky-tonk nights.

JOHN TRAVOLTA URBAN COWBOY

No. 1 hits through the early 1980s, before the Urban Cowboy bubble burst. Gilley, who also could be heard on the soundtrack, went on to have ten No. 1 singles from 1980 to 1983, including remakes of pop songs like Buddy Holly's "True Love Ways" and Ben E. King's "Stand by Me." The movie's success also spurred a rash of nationwide dance clubs, most with their own mechanical bulls.

Urban Cowboy has been described as a backlash against disco, which would explain its widespread acceptance by pop audiences. By 1981, country was America's best-selling music. As the genre became more oriented to crossing over to pop, the music became slicker, and veered toward self-parody. It would be years before the pendulum would again begin to swing.

BULL MARKET *Starring young heartthrob John Travolta, the movie* Urban Cowboy *was a surprise hit in 1980, playing to a rising national infatuation with all things country.*

TELL ME 'BOUT THE GOOD OLD DAYS

TRADITION AND CHANGE IN THE 1980s

MICHAEL MCCALL

EVEN AS THE "NEW YORK TIMES" WAS SOUNDING THE DEATH KNELL FOR COUNTRY MUSIC, A FRESH GENERATION OF ARTISTS WAS COMING TO PROMINENCE ON RADIO AND RECORDS. ALTHOUGH THE BRASHEST OF THIS NEW BREED GENERATED THE MOST PRESS, IT WAS THE STEADIEST THAT SOLD THE MOST RECORDS AND HAD THE GREATEST INFLUENCE.

A screenwriter would boil down country music's revival in the early 1980s to two personable leaders. There's the Texas rancher, whose gentlemanly conduct and classic Marlboro Man style made him a sex symbol to women, and whose solid, Gary Cooper-like sense of self appealed to men. As with all great cowboys, he bolstered his mild-mannered appearance with an uncompromising set of values. He resisted Nashville's attempts to smooth and sweeten his sound, insisting on recording the western swing and honky-tonk he had performed in Lone Star clubs.

As with all great heroes, his timing proved him right, too, as he matured into the most enduring and respected star of his generation.

Then there's the other lead character—the ebullient son of Appalachia, an immensely talented instrumentalist and capable vocalist who brought the mountains down to the city. He was steeped in the fierce, yet unashamedly sentimental sounds of bluegrass, though he had continued his education as a member of a highly regarded road band based in Southern California. By the time the fair-haired, moralistic country boy arrived in Nashville, he was determined to prove that blending down-home picking and uptown rhythms would appeal to traditionalists and modernists alike. He succeeded beyond anyone's expectations, reviving both country music and bluegrass along the way.

Indeed, any discussion of the early 1980s, when Nashville entered a new era of renewed vitality and commercial success, usually begins with Texas cowboy George Strait and Kentucky prodigy Ricky Skaggs. Starting in 1981 and 1980 respectively, they slowly built steam until, by 1983, they dominated the country charts and pushed many slick 1970s artists off the charts.

SADDLE PAL *George Strait, who donated this saddle to the Country Music Hall of Fame and Museum, is a genuine rancher and horseman.*

Strait had his first No. 1 in 1982, with the loping mid-tempo tune "Fool Hearted Memory," then released a string of consecutive No. 1 hits that would carry him through 1984. He never looked back, eventually scoring more chart-toppers than anyone in country-music history. Skaggs also achieved his first No. 1 hit in 1982, and the next 10 singles he released also went to No. 1 or No. 2. Anyone who turned on the radio between 1982 and 1985 would surely have heard a Skaggs or Strait song within an hour. For that, traditionalists rejoiced, and Nashville moved toward a new future.

Music Row opens up

It would be a mistake, though, to put the whole turnaround on their strong backs. A confluence of events led to widespread changes in Nashville in the early '80s, transformations that opened up Music Row to the possibility of giving long shots like Strait and Skaggs an opportunity.

The revolution really began in front offices and in recording studios, where a wholesale shift in leadership created new gatekeepers—and a new modern country sound. Most of the primary executives came from outside the Music Row

HOT PICKIN' *Ricky Skaggs wedded elements of country and bluegrass to become one of the most influential mainstream stars of the '80s. In 1982, he was inducted into the Grand Ole Opry, at the time its youngest member.*

1986 Warner Bros. Records debuts two very different new artists, Randy Travis and Dwight Yoakam. "Touch Me When We're Dancing," a remake of the Carpenters' pop hit, becomes Alabama's 20th straight No. 1 country hit.

1987 Randy Travis's debut album, *Storms of Life*, is certified platinum.

1988 George Bush (the elder) is elected the 41st US President. Keith Whitley gains his first No. 1 singles, "Don't Close Your Eyes" and "When You Say Nothing at All." Buck Owens and Dwight Yoakam's duet on "Streets of Bakersfield" becomes a No. 1 hit. Hank Williams Jr. wins the CMA's Album and Entertainer of the Year Awards.

1989 The Berlin Wall is brought down. Garth Brooks, Alan Jackson, and Clint Black release their debut singles. Mary Chapin Carpenter debuts on the country charts with "How Do." Keith Whitley dies at age 33 of an alcohol overdose. Tim McGraw moves to Nashville determined to further his music career. Garth Brooks scores his first No.1 single, "If Tomorrow Never Comes."

1990 British scientist Tim Berners-Lee conceives and develops the World Wide Web, built upon the US government's Internet system. Garth Brooks's first two albums are certified platinum. George Strait wins his second consecutive CMA Entertainer of the Year Award.

PROFILES IN COUNTRY

HARLAN HOWARD

BORN DETROIT, MICHIGAN,
SEPTEMBER 8, 1929
DIED MARCH 3, 2002
HITS "I FALL TO PIECES,"
"WHY NOT ME,"
"BLAME IT ON YOUR HEART"

Harlan Howard ranks as the
most successful and prolific
commercial songwriter in
country-music history, racking
up more than 100 country hits
across six decades.

He was driving a forklift in
Los Angeles when Ray Price
released "Heartaches by the
Number," Howard's second hit
as a writer. With the royalties,
he left his job and moved to
Nashville in June 1960. He then
hit upon the hottest streak any
writer has experienced in
Nashville. During one week in
1961, he had 15 songs in the
Top 40.

His early successes include
Ray Charles's "Busted," Patsy
Cline's "I Fall to Pieces," and
Buck Owens's "I've Got a Tiger
by the Tail" and "Above and
Beyond." In the 1980s, Howard
enjoyed a popular resurgence,
with his stripped-down, earthy
poetry fitting the back-to-
basics movement of the neo-
traditionalists. His songs, nearly
always about relationships, often
showed a wry humor and
reflective wisdom, as in such
1980s hits as John Conlee's
"I Don't Remember Loving You,"
the Judds' "Why Not Me,"
Conway Twitty's "I Don't Know
a Thing About Love," and Ricky
Van Shelton's remake of "Life
Turned Her That Way."

MICHAEL MCCALL

STRAIT TO THE TOP *George Strait has racked up more
No. 1 hits than any living country performer. He's also one of
a handful of '80s luminaries to survive the generational shift
of the '90s and beyond.*

system. They included veteran musicians
and producers such as Jimmy Bowen,
Tony Brown, Jim Ed Norman, Tim
DuBois, Jim Foglesong, Harold Shedd,
Allen Reynolds, Kyle Lehning, Emory
Gordy, and Garth Fundis. Just as
important were the accountants and
marketers who graduated into the
president's chair, such as career
executives Joe Galante, Rick Blackburn,
Bruce Hinton, and Roy Wunsch.

These men brought with them
wide-ranging backgrounds and
unconventional attitudes, most of them
having left New York and Los Angeles
businesses offices to put down stakes in
Nashville. Greeted as carpetbaggers at
first, they were persistent or perhaps
egotistical enough to believe they could
lead country music in a new, viable
direction. Their fresh perspectives

resulted in a sound based on live-wire
talents, many of whom wrote their own
material and sounded like no one else.

Young artists who'd been around for
a few years—Reba McEntire, Rosanne
Cash, Hank Williams Jr., Emmylou
Harris, Rodney Crowell, Michael Martin
Murphey, the Nitty Gritty Dirt Band,
and Gail Davies—got more promotional
juice and were able to wield more artistic
control over their recordings.

Just as important, Nashville signed
scores of new artists who changed the
look and direction of country music,
making it more contemporary while
holding on to what was important about
its origins. The 1980s are sometimes cast
as the neo-traditionalist era that brought

FAMILY TRADITION *Rosanne Cash and Rodney Crowell (then
Mr. and Mrs.) and Hank Williams Jr. represented the opposite
ends of country's wide-open and individualistic styles of the '80s.
Cash and Crowell were a total team during their 12-year marriage.
After a youth of replicating his dad's hits on stage, Hank Jr.
finally became a successful artist in his own right. Father and
son collaborated electronically on "There's a Tear in My Beer."*

How I Became a Girl Singer

I grew up listening to all kinds of music. My sisters and I had little Sears record players, the kind with a squeaky little speaker under the turntable. We each had our record collections that either grew or decreased depending on who was stealing from whom. I particularly went for my older sister's Beatles and Mamas & the Papas records. My other older sister had Judy Collins records, which I enjoyed filching as well. I especially loved my Bob Dylan albums and records by the Band.

In the den, my parents had their Herb Alpert, Brazil '66, and Tom Lehrer albums, as well as Dad's great collection of jazz 78s and Mom's folk albums. Country music was represented in our house by Johnny Cash, Merle Haggard, and Dolly Parton.

Every Saturday afternoon, the *Texaco Opera Theatre* from the New York Met blasted through the house. That was Mom's passion. I remember hearing the voice of the announcer—with his very precise and upper crust inflection—telling us the synopsis of the opera about to be performed. My mother grew up loving classical music and opera. She has a picture of herself and all her girlfriends as young college coeds, backstage in New York with the great tenor Laurence Melchior. But her daughters didn't exactly get it: we liked the Rolling Stones, the Band, Motown, and Johnny Cash.

My mother and older sister were teaching themselves to play guitar during the "great folk scare" in the early '60s. I wanted to join in, and picked up a bass ukulele. Eventually, I got my mother's gut-string guitar. I would get out the generic songbook—something along the lines of "America's Best Loved Songs"—and match my finger positions to the chord charts above the lyrics of each song. That was how I learned the chords. After that it was just a matter of cherry picking the records around

the house to teach myself the songs I loved. I relied heavily on my ear to get where I wanted to go. I wore that Sears record player out.

When I got a record deal out of Nashville, the question I was asked most often was, "How did a girl who grew up in New Jersey end up playing country music?" This question quickly became the bane of my existence, mostly because I didn't have a good short answer. The way I saw things, there was something of a sea change taking place in Nashville; labels were signing artists who didn't fit the longtime ideal of a country artist. People like Lyle Lovett, Rodney Crowell, and Steve Earle were getting a lot of attention, and artists like Lucinda Williams, Nanci Griffith, and Rosanne Cash were celebrated for their intelligent and literate songs. There was nothing out of place to me that these women were writing and producing their own records.

I put out my first album in 1987. It barely created a ripple in the big commercial ocean. But it got some decent reviews, and it was a start. I found myself sitting on the panel one night at the now-defunct TV show *Nashville Now*. During a commercial break, Ralph Emery, the host, or maybe it was one of the other guests, asked me how I enjoyed being a "girl singer" in Nashville. I was flabbergasted. I had never heard that term before. It sounded so marginalizing. Sexist. Unenlightened. Someone had to explain to me that, for example, Dolly Parton was probably the most popular "girl singer" in country music when she was a regular on *The Porter Wagoner Show*. But I had never seen *The Porter Wagoner Show*. I knew Dolly from her own records, and from her television show that often featured guests like Emmylou Harris and Linda Ronstadt. She was an incredible artist, songwriter, performer, entertainer. She was the ultimate country-music icon.

It took me a minute to think it through, but then it was like, "Oh yeah!"

I realized it's a pretty good thing to find oneself in the same orbit, if only for a transcendent moment, as Dolly Parton. We should all dream of being such grand "girl singers."

MARY CHAPIN CARPENTER

IVY LEAGUE AND LUCKY
Mary Chapin Carpenter, educated at Brown University, was one of the few folkie singer-songwriters to translate her gifts into country gold. She did it by mixing country-rock dance tunes and confessional ballads.

CLASSIC COUNTRY RECORDING

LEE GREENWOOD
"God Bless the USA"

*'Cause there ain't no doubt
I love this land, God bless
the USA.*

WRITTEN BY LEE GREENWOOD,
AND RECORDED 1983

NO. 7 COUNTRY, JULY 28, 1984

GLAD-HANDING *At the 1990 CMA Awards, George Jones reaches out to Roy Rogers, who joined Randy Travis (far right) on his* Heroes and Friends *album along with Jones, Vern Gosdin (second from left), and Tammy Wynette.*

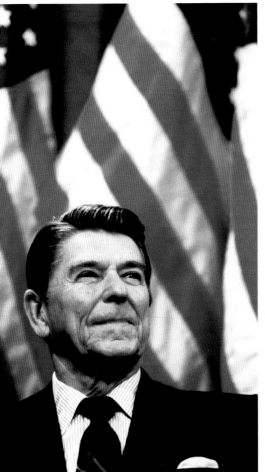

HAIL TO THE CHIEF *President Ronald Reagan (who as California governor pardoned country music star and former prisoner Merle Haggard) rallied patriotic fervor in the '80s for his conservative economic and foreign policies.*

country back to its earthy roots. That was part of it, but it discounts the variety and progressiveness of the era, too.

Not only did the '80s bring forth traditionalists such as Strait, Skaggs, Randy Travis, Keith Whitley, the Judds, Dwight Yoakam, Patty Loveless, Ricky Van Shelton, and the O'Kanes, it also gave country music progressive singer-songwriters including Kathy Mattea, Mary Chapin Carpenter, Lyle Lovett, Nanci Griffith, and K. T. Oslin; roots-rockers in the form of John Anderson, Steve Earle, k. d. lang, Highway 101, Pam Tillis, Sawyer Brown, the Desert Rose Band, and Foster & Lloyd; and out-and-out modern crossover acts such as Gary Morris, Lee Greenwood, Restless Heart, Exile, Mark Gray, and Neal McCoy.

While veterans including George Jones, Ronnie Milsap, Anne Murray, the Oak Ridge Boys, and Don Williams continued to score top hits, what made the 1980s vital was the greatest invasion of swaggering young artists to burst on to the scene since Nashville's burgeoning days of the 1950s. Country artist development in the '60s and '70s moved carefully and conservatively; the '80s changed all that.

Just before Labor Day in 1983, a Korean Airlines flight headed from New York to Seoul was shot down when it entered Soviet air space, killing 269 passengers, including 63 US citizens. President Ronald Reagan called the act "barbaric," and many Americans were angered at what appeared a senseless attack against defenseless civilians.

Within days, Greenwood wrote a personal statement of devotion to his homeland, **"God Bless the USA."** Producer Jerry Crutchfield encouraged him to cover the national map in the second verse by inserting the names of cities from every geographical region, and Greenwood recorded it with a grainy reverence and polished vibrato, enlisting Larry Gatlin and the Gatlin Brothers for backing vocal assistance. He also lobbied MCA Records' pop chief, Irving Azoff, to release it.

"God Bless the USA" became an overwhelming signature song and an unofficial national anthem, casting much of Greenwood's other work into the shadows. In the ultimate full-circle conclusion, Reagan—who found himself at the center of the crisis that inspired it—and his Vice President, George Bush, developed personal friendships with Greenwood, citing "God Bless the USA" among their favorite songs.

TOM ROLAND

GUITAR TOWN, TEXAS STYLE *Steve Earle brought his fierce, uncompromising talent to Nashville from the Lone Star state, putting a gritty, sharp-edged stamp on the back-to-basics movement in '80s country. This photo graced his breakout album,* Guitar Town *(1986).*

As Steve Earle later described in a famous epithet, the '80s marked country music's "integrity scare." For a brief, but fruitful and exciting period, renegade songwriters and iconoclastic talents dominated record-label rosters and, in some cases, made strong inroads at radio. Nashville seemed to strike a good balance between those who broke through to massive stardom—Strait, McEntire, the Judds, Travis—and intriguing artists who built solid careers, some of them with radio's support and some without it.

A key turning point

One of the era's most infamous and controversial moments begat, in retrospect, a turning point of sorts. In September 1985, on what must have been a slow news day, the *New York Times* published a page-one report by respected staff music critic Robert Palmer. Headlined "Nashville Sound: Blues for Country Music," it insisted, as many interpreted it, that country music was dying. Palmer, citing the struggling careers of older stars such as Tammy Wynette, suggested that country had failed to attract younger listeners and that its aging audience no longer bought records or attended concerts in sizable numbers.

Palmer cited the short-lived Urban Cowboy fad, but said that sales had fallen hard in recent years. "These good times are gone and for most of the established country stars they won't be coming back," Palmer wrote. "It's not just the Nashville Sound that seems to be dying, it's the Nashville dream."

Boy, was he wrong.

The article became a rallying cry for Music Row, which disputed the charges, and accused Palmer of ignoring recent positive developments. Had he stuck to the fading fortunes of Wynette and older country stars, he'd have been right. But the article failed to acknowledge that sales at that moment were on an upswing, that several exciting new artists had been introduced, and that a new sound had replaced the old one.

By talking only to veterans and failing to interview Music Row's new leadership, Palmer missed the real story

of the moment. The rest of the tale involved changes in label management, the influx of new producers, and the sudden signing of youthful artists, both traditional and progressive, who were altering the music, bringing in new fans, and bringing back older ones.

Palmer failed to mention the emergence of Alabama as country's first million-selling country-rock band, and the first of a rush of new harmony-based, self-contained bands such as Restless Heart and Sawyer Brown, who were already enjoying hits when the *Times* article was published. The journalist didn't notice the sales racked up by John Anderson's single "Swingin'" or the emergence of Skaggs and Strait as powerhouse roots performers. Nor did he acknowledge the signing of the Judds and their quick emergence as stars, or Reba McEntire's breakthrough with her first platinum album, *My Kind of Country*.

Indeed, on the last week of August 1985, just days before Palmer's article, Randy Travis had released his first single, "On the Other Hand." Six months later, Steve Earle and Dwight Yoakam—two artists Palmer would praise—released their first hit singles. As producer and label executive Tony Brown stated in one of many rebuttal articles, "It was true some of the older artists had begun to fade away, but a new group of young performers had emerged [who] were energetic, attractive, intelligent."

The Nashville Network, or TNN, also emerged as a new form of promotion. With a cable channel devoted to country music, and with a new outlet for videos (it soon branched out to include a sister station, Country Music Television, or CMT), country's youth appeal took on greater significance. Yoakam, for example, who had a hard time at radio, gained great support from television because of his lean good looks.

For the first time in many years, the press began to take notice, too. By 1986, mainstream rock publications including *Rolling Stone* and *Spin* ran lengthy articles on country's new renegades. Brash talkers such as Earle and Yoakam drew more ink than bigger sellers Travis and

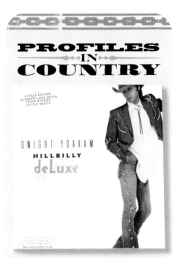

PROFILES IN COUNTRY

DWIGHT YOAKAM

BORN PIKEVILLE, KENTUCKY, OCTOBER 23, 1956
PLAYS GUITAR
FIRST RECORDED 1984
INFLUENCES BUCK OWENS, JOHNNY CASH, GRAM PARSONS, ELVIS PRESLEY
HITS "GUITARS, CADILLACS," "STREETS OF BAKERSFIELD," "AIN'T THAT LONELY YET"

In a whirl of traditionalism and rock-inspired grit, Dwight Yoakam became one of modern country music's most intriguing and intelligent voices. Here was a singer who used the word "hillbilly" as a signifier of what was cool and real rather than as an insult, who played throwback music while moving around the stage like a stripper, and whose uniform included a cowboy hat, spangled jackets, and ripped, tight jeans. In interviews, he talked more like a historian of southern culture than an "aw shucks" country singer, and he often derided Nashville's soundalike song factories.

He also refused to remain creatively static: even after 1987's *Hillbilly Deluxe* garnered four Top 10 country singles, he and producer Pete Anderson tweaked and experimented to arrive at 1988's *Buenos Noches from a Lonely Room*, an album that featured his duet on "Streets of Bakersfield" with Buck Owens. Strings, rock & roll organs, and other non-traditional elements were a significant part of every subsequent album of new material, and by the turn of the century Yoakam was seen as much as an innovator as a throwback.

PETER COOPER

Tony Brown's Texas Experiment

Early in Tony Brown's career, Nashville street talk tagged the producer and record executive as "too hip" for Music Row. A former pianist for Elvis Presley and Emmylou Harris, Brown became a record executive in 1978, and signed Alabama and Vince Gill, among others. But the young A&R man struck Music Row's old guard as too willing to gamble and too eager to bank on progressive talent.

Jimmy Bowen, in his autobiography *Rough Mix*, cited Brown's cutting-edge reputation as the reason he hired him. When Bowen took over the Nashville division of MCA Records in 1984, he chose Brown as his vice president of A&R.

As Bowen focused on recording MCA's hottest new stars, George Strait and Reba McEntire, Brown looked to the future. In fast succession, he signed three Texas iconoclasts—Steve Earle, Lyle Lovett, and Nanci Griffith—who would test country radio's willingness to stretch and accept young, singular singer-songwriters. Earle ran the working-class rock of Bruce Springsteen and John Fogerty through a concisely focused, roots-rebel sieve. Lovett drawled offbeat acoustic tunes that balanced a droll wit with devastatingly sensitive dramas. Griffith, a self-described "folkabilly," merged

WIZARD OF ODDS *Tony Brown always downplayed his abilities as a musician, but he had a visionary verve for cutting hit records and expanding the boundaries of mainstream country.*

the literate Lone Star folk of Carolyn Hester and Townes Van Zandt with stripped-down roots rock. All three artists became instant critical darlings, but despite some initial acceptance—Earle and Lovett had early singles go Top 10—none was embraced by country radio.

In the long run, all three artists confirmed Brown's instinct for discovering significant talent. Even without radio play, Earle, Lovett, and Griffith carved out long careers and became major influences on the next generation of songwriters. But to country music's detriment, they had to cut ties with Music Row to find their audiences.

Brown would make a career of giving distinctive talent a chance, with a list of signings that includes Patty Loveless, Marty Stuart, Trisha Yearwood, and, as recently as 2005, Shooter Jennings. He also produced Rodney Crowell's most commercially successful album, *Diamonds and Dirt*, and brought Vince Gill to MCA, where his talent finally flourished into superstardom. Like producers John Hammond and Jerry Wexler before him, Brown's impact can't be measured just in chart numbers, but in artistry and creative impact.

MICHAEL MCCALL

RENAISSANCE ROAD WARRIOR *Mississippi-born Marty Stuart logged years as a youthful sideman to such greats as Lester Flatt and Johnny Cash before emerging as one of country music's most progressive yet tradition-minded mavericks after being signed to MCA Records by Tony Brown.*

Skaggs, which irked some industry insiders, but the attention helped everyone. Still, a publicist working for Travis once asked the PR rep of Earle why she couldn't get stories on the soft-spoken traditionalist in national magazines. "Get him to cuss more often," Earle's publicist replied. "The rock press loves that."

By 1986–1987, the dam broke. Many of the young label heads had drawn harsh criticism for dropping veteran artists such as Dolly Parton, Johnny Cash, Ernest Tubb, Charley Pride, Bill Anderson, and others. But the barbs were soon replaced by critical acclaim for newcomers Lyle Lovett, the O'Kanes, k.d. lang, Foster & Lloyd, Highway 101, Holly Dunn, and Ricky Van Shelton—all of whom had at least some success at radio and on the sales charts. Country music suddenly had a hipper, more photogenic face.

By 1987, even the *New York Times* couldn't help but notice. *Times* correspondent Stephen Holden spent a few days in town, joining Jimmy Bowen in the studio and interviewing young artists and the current power structure. The resulting article commented that country music "had turned itself around," and once again had "captured the ears of a new audience."

The boys from Alabama

For all the attention drawn by the most progressive new artists, like Yoakam, Earle, Lovett, and lang, it was the polite, hard-working, consistent hit-makers who created the most lasting impact on the radio and sales charts.

Alabama, made up of three cousins and a Yankee drummer, were never critical favorites, but their long-haired, rock-band look and melodic, harmony-based sound proved immensely successful and influential. Until then, country groups largely consisted of vocal quartets such as the Statler Brothers and the Oak Ridge Boys, or string bands based on the Flatt & Scruggs model.

In the 1970s, when self-contained bands ruled rock & roll, country failed to introduce one band that had any significant radio success. The Nitty Gritty Dirt Band—a California roots-rock group—attempted to crack Nashville's conservative code, and while they found support from young fans, apart from the critical acclaim for their 1972 triple album, *Will the Circle Be Unbroken*, they didn't make much headway into the country establishment—at least not until after Alabama broke down the barriers. Randy Owen, Jeff Cook, Teddy Gentry, and Mark Herndon looked like southern rockers, but they were social conservatives from the small town of Fort Payne, Alabama, who offered up sweet love songs and nostalgic odes to rural life. The simple ear-candy drew the wrath of the rock

press, who preferred the rowdy edge of the Outlaw movement or the down-home, soul-baring style of George Jones and Loretta Lynn.

But Alabama ushered in a new, smoother country style, influenced more by the Eagles than Waylon and Willie or

HILLBILLY PRINCE *Dwight Yoakam resurrected the Bakersfield Sound via Appalachia and Los Angeles. His twangy tenor, smart songwriting, and neo-honky-tonk esprit (replete with strategically torn jeans) made him both a critical and commercial darling.*

> ## "My favorite male country singer? Dwight Yoakam."
> JOHNNY CASH

PROFILES IN COUNTRY

JIMMY BOWEN

BORN SANTA RITA, NEW
MEXICO, NOVEMBER 30, 1937
BUSINESS AFFILIATIONS
WARNER/REPRISE RECORDS,
MCA RECORDS,
CAPITOL RECORDS

No Nashville music chief in the '80s instigated more change—or more controversy—than Jimmy Bowen. He initially established himself as a pop A&R chief for Reprise Records, producing Frank Sinatra's "Strangers in the Night." Arriving in Nashville in 1977, he proved to be a restless label head; in 12 years, he moved from MCA to Warner Bros. to MCA (again) to Capitol. He was as ruthless as he was restless. At each company, he'd employ a slash-and-burn philosophy, firing other executives and drastically cutting artist rosters.

Believing Nashville had fallen behind in recording standards, he argued for larger investments in production and pushed studios to update to state-of-the-art technology. He also encouraged artists to co-produce their own records, usually with him as their partner. He also embarked in a legendary power struggle with Garth Brooks that he eventually lost.

However, there was no denying his success. Each label improved under his stewardship, and country music gained a larger slice of the pop-music pie.

MICHAEL MCCALL

George and Merle. Despite the critical disdain—*Entertainment Weekly* once crowned Alabama "the most overrated band in the history of country music," while a Los Angeles newspaper described their music as "flaccid" and "insipid"— they stand as one of the most important acts of their time. Recognizing their importance, the country-music industry inducted Alabama into the Country Music Hall of Fame in 2005.

The band thought their lack of cynicism worked against them, that in the days of anti-heroes and so-called musical outlaws, critics didn't respond well to artists who showed a zest for life and an appreciation of heritage and home. In an era when the press championed those who worked outside the music industry or openly battled with Music Row, Alabama embraced the business and happily cooperated with its leaders.

"We don't make a big hoopla about nothin', really," Randy Owen told journalist Bob Allen in the mid-1980s. "We're not out to teach big lessons or

SELF-CONTAINED *Alabama represented an innovation. Onstage, the members supplied all their instrumentation as well as vocals, in contrast to the traditional harmony-group structure of the Oak Ridge Boys and the Statler Brothers.*

speak philosophically about anything. We don't put hidden messages in our music."

By mid-decade, Alabama's influence showed in the number of other bands making inroads into the country charts. Suddenly, bands were everywhere. Restless Heart, a harmony-driven group, and the more outrageously attired Sawyer Brown were followed by Highway 101, Shenandoah, Atlanta, and other bands. Also, many bands from pop and rock entered the country sweepstakes, the most successful being Exile (which had previously had a '70s pop hit), the Desert Rose Band (led by Chris Hillman of the Byrds and Flying Burrito Brothers), the Nitty Gritty Dirt Band (finally embraced by Music Row), and Southern Pacific (featuring members of the Doobie Brothers and Creedence Clearwater Revival).

"I think one of the things we can take some pride in is that we knocked down some doors for other groups, and we continue to stay together as a band," Teddy Gentry told *Country Music* after the band announced its retirement from the road in 2003.

Vocal groups and small family ensembles remained active, too. The success of the Judds, a mother-daughter duo featuring the ambitious Naomi Judd and her gifted offspring Wynonna, foretold a rash of new signings, including Sweethearts of the Rodeo, The O'Kanes, Baillie & the Boys, and the Forester Sisters—all of whom took a sweet, spare approach to country music similar to the Judds' back-porch sound.

Strait country

George Strait's influence created just as large a seismic shift on Music Row as that of Alabama, even if his tradition-based approach couldn't have been more different. After the hat-act era of the '90s, when it seemed nearly every male country singer had to wear a Stetson, it's hard to remember that when Strait arrived in Nashville, western wear was considered an archaic mode of fashion that went out of date with Roy Rogers. Indeed, Asleep at the Wheel's Ray Benson, who has always worn a cowboy hat onstage, remembers attending a CMA Awards show in the late '70s when the only other guys wearing cowboy hats were fellow

COWPUNK'D *k.d. lang, who named her band the re-clines in homage to Patsy, originally commanded as much attention for her campy cowgirl couture as for her emotive vocals.*

CLASSIC COUNTRY RECORDING

ALABAMA

RANDY OWEN FORT PAYNE, ALABAMA, DECEMBER 13, 1949
TEDDY GENTRY FORT PAYNE, ALABAMA, JANUARY 22, 1952
JEFF COOK FORT PAYNE, ALABAMA, AUGUST 27, 1949
MARK HERNDON SPRINGFIELD, MASSACHUSETTS, MAY 11, 1955
INFLUENCES ALLMAN BROTHERS, BOB SEGER, THE EAGLES

HITS "TENNESSEE RIVER," "LOVE IN THE FIRST DEGREE," "THE CLOSER YOU GET"

Cousins Randy Owen, Teddy Gentry, and Jeff Cook formed their first professional band, Young Country, in 1969. In 1977, the band dubbed itself Alabama and charted its first single, "I Wanna Be with You Tonight." After running through a series of drummers, the band hired Mark Herndon in 1979, completing the group that would become the hottest country band for the remainder of the twentieth century.

Being authentic country boys themselves, Owen and Gentry, Alabama's best songwriters, had no trouble in coming up with the right formula. But there was an image involved as well: these long-haired, T-shirt and blue jeans wearing guys looked like southern rockers and acted that way onstage. In today's term, they "branded" themselves, right down to the distinctive band logo that decorated their albums, merchandise, and tour buses.

In 1980—by then signed to RCA Records—Alabama went No. 1 with the nostalgic "Tennessee River." It was the first of 20 consecutive No. 1s, a record that has yet to be equaled.

EDWARD MORRIS

"I am doing what I am doing today because of the good Lord, my family, and George Strait."

**GARTH BROOKS,
SPEAKING IN THE 1990s**

long-haired country boys Charlie Daniels and John Anderson. Then, as Benson said, "They asked us if we'd take them off for the show."

When MCA began talking to Strait about a record deal, they wanted him to ditch the Wranglers, the big belt buckle, and definitely the big hat. The label wanted to sell that boyishly handsome face, and the marketing director didn't want anything obscuring it. "They asked him to take his cowboy hat off," said Erv Woolsey, who has managed Strait since the days when he toured Texas clubs as the uncredited singer of the Ace in the Hole Band. "They wanted to put him in bell bottoms with studs up the sides. He told them, 'No, I'm not going to do that.' He dresses the same way he dressed when he was growing up. It's who he is."

Strait's success impacted the modern image of the male country singer more than anyone of his generation. "George Strait is definitely one of the main reasons I started wearing a cowboy hat," said Alan Jackson. "When I was singing

in the clubs, I was doing songs by George and John Anderson and Hank Williams Jr. They were my favorites, and they were wearing hats. I thought I should get me one, too."

Of course, Strait also changed how country music sounded. His smooth, seamless way of presenting swing rhythms, barroom two-steppers, and gently intoned ballads became one of the dominant sounds of the 1980s and beyond. "I can still remember the first time I saw George perform," said Bruce Hinton, the former chairman of MCA Records' Nashville division. "It was in a nightclub in Gardena, California, and what struck me is how many young men and women there were. That wasn't usually the case for traditional country music acts then. All the guys dressed like him. And as soon as the band kicked in, all the women went and sat right in front of him. I'd seen that in pop music, but never in country."

Lee Ann Womack, then still a teen back in Jacksonville, Texas, saw the enthusiasm Strait created from the ground up. "Every guy in my high-school class dressed like him, they all acted like him, they all wanted to be him," she said, laughing. "His influence in that part of Texas was so, so big."

Strait went against the grain of his generation of country singers in another way, too. As big as he became, he never looked for a way to expand his sound in search of a non-country audience. "Once an artist becomes successful, there can be a bewildering amount of options," Hinton said. "Sometimes artists make a decision in their heart that they believe is the right thing, though in hindsight, it turned out that they turned left when they should have turned right. But George has an instinct for doing what's right for him, and it's served him incredibly well."

SWANGIN' *John Anderson combined the plaintive honky-tonk style of Lefty Frizzell with an instantly recognizable vocal signature, attained through a technique of pulled-back phrasing and the habit of singing across, not into, the microphone.*

TORCHBEARERS *During the 1980s, George Strait (right) helped lead a resurgence of traditional country. In the '90s, admirer Alan Jackson followed his lead. In 2000, the two joined forces to record "Murder on Music Row."*

In a media-driven age, Strait also managed to live almost reclusively— at least for a superstar. Most modern entertainers are encouraged to be as visible as possible; Strait contradicted that theory, refusing nearly all media requests, whether from television, magazines, or newspapers. He rarely did interviews, and he refused to appear on celebrity-driven shows such as *Entertainment Tonight*. He even turned down repeated requests from *The Tonight Show with Jay Leno* and *Late Night with David Letterman*, two high-profile programs sought out by nearly all singers and actors.

Alan Jackson, for one, marveled at Strait's ability to keep to himself, yet still do so well. "I think it's a really smart plan, because it gives him a mystique or something," Jackson said, then paused

and changed his words. "You know, it's probably not a plan at all. He's probably just like me; he probably just doesn't like doing that stuff. He's a pretty down-to-earth guy who likes being at home."

Still, no one else in the 1980s had as enormous an impact. Garth Brooks, after he skyrocketed to fame, said he decided to pursue a country-music career after hearing George's debut album, *Strait Country*. When Brooks won his first CMA Entertainer of the Year award, he dedicated it to "two George's," as he put it—Jones and Strait. Tim McGraw even went as far as recording a tribute song called "Give It to Me Strait."

Of course, part of Strait's genius was smoothing honky-tonk's rough edges so

CLASSIC COUNTRY RECORDING

GEORGE STRAIT "Does Fort Worth Ever Cross Your Mind"

You're in someone else's arms in Dallas, Does Fort Worth ever cross your mind?
WRITTEN BY WHITEY AND DARLENE SHAFER, AND RECORDED JUNE 25, 1984
NO. 1 COUNTRY, JANUARY 5, 1985

"Does Fort Worth Ever Cross Your Mind," with its fiddle-and-steel high notes arcing over swinging, locked-in rhythms, is the perfect definition of 1980s neo-traditionalism, Nashville-style.

George Strait already had established a string of No. 1 hits when the Whitey and Darlene Shafer tune began its chart ascent in the closing months of 1984. His fifth consecutive chart-topper and sixth in two years, "Does Fort Worth Ever Cross Your Mind" also represents a milestone for the Texas rancher. It marked his first single produced by MCA Records' Jimmy Bowen. Over the next eight years, the two would collaborate on a remarkable 25 Top 10 hits, 17 of them No. 1s.

Former LA session player John Hobbs captures Nashville's classic slip-note piano style, and the precise rhythms come from former Toto bassist David Hungate and emerging Nashville drummer Eddie Bayers. At Strait's suggestion, Bowen brought in Texas fiddler Johnny Gimble and veteran steel player Weldon Myrick, giving the track its timeless swing accents.

Strait responded with one of the most slyly expressive vocals of his career, slurring and stretching words with a casual ease that doesn't bring attention to itself, yet gives the story of lost love a jaunty, rakish glint.

MICHAEL MCCALL

PROFILES IN COUNTRY

GEORGE STRAIT

BORN POTEET, TEXAS, MAY 18, 1952
PLAYS GUITAR
FIRST RECORDED 1976
INFLUENCES HANK WILLIAMS, BOB
WILLS, MERLE HAGGARD, GEORGE
JONES, FRANK SINATRA
HITS "DOES FORT WORTH EVER
CROSS YOUR MIND," "ALL MY EX'S
LIVE IN TEXAS," "THE CHAIR"

When George Strait first hit the
scene in 1981, he was considered a throwback and an anomaly. Arriving at the height of the
Urban Cowboy era's fixation
with middle-of-the-road pop
crossover, Strait deliberately
blended the western swing
and honky-tonk sounds of his
native Texas with modern
country music. His success—
artistically and commercially—
helped inspire a renaissance
of traditional country.

Strait figured out who he was
early on. Shortly after his first
major-label single (and Top Ten
hit) "Unwound" was released, he
told *Billboard*: "I want to reach
the point where people hear my
name and immediately think
of real country music."

Strait accomplished his
mission and more. Since his 1981
debut, he's racked up 25 million-
selling albums (far ahead of
anyone else in country music)
and 40 No. 1 hits on the *Billboard*
chart. Though he has starred in
a successful Hollywood movie
(*Pure Country*, 1992), the low-key
superstar seems content to focus
on what he does best: touring
with his crack band and
recording fresh twists on
classic country.

PAUL KINGSBURY

HEAVENLY HARMONY *By replacing Rodney Crowell in
Emmylou Harris's Hot Band, Ricky Skaggs brought a high-
lonesome sound which served Harris well. Skaggs helped craft
her landmark 1980 bluegrass album,* Roses in the Snow.

that it fit the clean, crisp ideals of modern
country music. Strait's oft-named
heroes—Bob Wills, Merle Haggard,
Hank Williams, George Jones, Ray
Price—tended to be raucous, hard-living
fellows. None of them possessed Strait's
calm, even-tempered, clean-living
character. Where hard-country singers
had tended to be hell-raisers, Strait was
inherently respectable and responsible. He
kept his wits and his appointments, and he
maintained his looks and his health, all in
a business that tends to fry the off-
balanced, wear out the insecure, and
re-mold the desperate. He wasn't eaten up
with the inner fire that burned holes in his
idols, but he recognized what flickers in
the best of country music's past and
delivered it with refinement and respect.

Therein rested his magic. Strait is a
casual, convincing country singer who
drew on authentic traditions while

presenting a marketing-director's dream
image. He's as respectable as Roy Rogers
and as convincing a balladeer as Eddy
Arnold, yet he also could re-fashion a
honky-tonk tune made famous by Faron
Young and glide with ease through a
western-swing standard.

Kentucky thunder

Skaggs's impact was even more
immediate than Strait's, with 16 Top
Ten hits between 1980 and 1986. Even
though his run at the top of the radio
charts wasn't as long as the Texan's,
Skaggs has continued to be a creative
pioneer in leading both country and
bluegrass toward its future.

The Kentucky native grew up playing
old mountain songs on mandolin, and
by age seven he had performed on a
television program hosted by bluegrass
stars Flatt & Scruggs. At 15, he joined
the band of one of his idols, Ralph
Stanley, and at 17 recorded an album
with his childhood friend, Keith Whitley,
who also was a member of Stanley's band.

Skaggs was a sought-after picker and singer in several progressive bluegrass bands through the 1970s, including the Country Gentlemen, New South, and his own Boone Creek. Emmylou Harris recruited him to join her Hot Band in the late '70s, and Skaggs began his solo career at Sugar Hill Records with the 1979 album *Sweet Temptation*, a big seller for a bluegrass release, and it led to a contract with Columbia Records. His single "Crying My Heart Out Over You" went to No. 1 in 1982, the first of 11 No. 1 hits in the 1980s.

Skaggs's bluegrass-flavored major label debut, *Waitin' for the Sun to Shine*, sold more than 500,000 copies in its first year, in an era when new country artists rarely had gold albums. He won the CMA's Male Vocalist of the Year award in 1982, the same year he won the Horizon Award; then in 1985, he took home the CMA's Entertainer of the Year award — the first time an artist had won country's biggest honor so early in a career.

As he gained fame, Skaggs also became more outspoken about his religious beliefs. A *Country Music* magazine profile from the 1980s tagged Skaggs as "High Energy with Moderation," nicely summing up both his music and his fundamentalist Christian outlook. He told the magazine his goal was "to put out good messages and songs—family values and Christian values of marriage and love and hope for the future of families and children."

Although Skaggs lost momentum by the late 1980s, his quick success helped push Music Row to take more chances on talented young artists. The bluegrass ranks proved fertile ground, with two hot bluegrass youngsters, Keith Whitley and Vince Gill, both signing with RCA and putting out debut albums in 1984, though Gill wouldn't have significant success until he switched to MCA in 1989 and worked with producer Tony Brown. The deeply talented Whitley, with his ability to cross honky-tonk and bluegrass worlds, was just beginning to achieve major hits when he succumbed to alcohol poisoning in 1989. Nonetheless, in 1988 and 1989 he had five consecutive No. 1 hits, marking what surely was just the

> ## I LEARNED AN INCREDIBLE AMOUNT FROM HAVING RICKY SKAGGS IN THE BAND. WE DID A DIFFERENT KIND OF HARMONY SINGING, AND THERE WERE A LOT MORE SPECIFIC PARTS.
>
> **EMMYLOU HARRIS**

POMPADOURED VIRTUOSO *Vince Gill looked as if he might always just run in Nashville's most elite musical circles (Rodney Crowell, Rosanne Cash, Emmylou Harris) until he found his own sound in the '90s and became a superstar.*

PROFILES IN COUNTRY

KEITH WHITLEY

BORN SANDY HOOK, KENTUCKY,
JULY 1, 1955
DIED MAY 9, 1989
PLAYED GUITAR
FIRST RECORDED 1971
INFLUENCES LEFTY FRIZZELL,
STANLEY BROTHERS
HITS "DON'T CLOSE YOUR EYES,"
"WHEN YOU SAY NOTHING AT ALL,"
"I'M NO STRANGER TO THE RAIN"

A hard-country singer whose bruised baritone was a wonder of nuanced phrasing, Keith Whitley was viewed by many as the heir apparent to the great George Jones. Tragically, the man who would be king was just realizing his potential when he died of an alcohol overdose in 1989.

A bluegrass prodigy who apprenticed with Ralph Stanley as a teenager, Whitley later logged a stint in J. D. Crowe's New South. But his deepest calling as a honky-tonk singer was evidenced early—as a child he appeared on a regional television show singing a hauntingly adult version of Hank Williams's "You Win Again."

Though Whitley began mainstream country recordings in 1984, he fully hit his artistic stride only after teaming with Garth Fundis, a sensitive producer who couched Whitley's hard-country vocals in sympathetic arrangements. Their alliance produced the two releases that have made Whitley's reputation: 1988's *Don't Close Your Eyes* and 1989's *I Wonder Do You Think of Me*. The latter was released posthumously, and to this day it remains as unforgettable as it is sadly finite.
CHRISSIE DICKINSON

start of one of country's most striking artistic and commercially successful careers. His influence would remain strong on many of the singers who came to fame in the 1990s.

Emerging women

So would the influence of certain of the female stars. Patty Loveless, like

BACKWOODS ANGEL *Patty Loveless came out of eastern Kentucky and even as a teen captured the attention of Porter and Dolly and the Wilburn Brothers. Her wild-and-wounded vocal style signaled an emotional and regional authenticity.*

Whitley, drew on Appalachian mountain harmonies, but also on rockabilly and honky-tonk, forging a fresh sound that gained power from Loveless's raw, rising voice and feisty song choices. Though she had difficulty overcoming a reticent nature, her career grew slowly but steadily. Loveless won over the rock press early on, and then gradually gained the respect of peers and the ears of radio programmers. She would continue to shine as a beacon of country-music integrity.

SITTING PRETTY *The West Virginia-bred Kathy Mattea scored with core country fans and CMA voters, but her real passion lay in folk, bluegrass, and Celtic music. She incorporated all three styles as her career matured.*

PROFILES IN COUNTRY
THE JUDDS

NAOMI JUDD
BORN ASHLAND, KENTUCKY,
JANUARY 11, 1946
WYNONNA JUDD
BORN ASHLAND, KENTUCKY,
MAY 30, 1964
INFLUENCES HAZEL & ALICE,
EMMYLOU HARRIS, BONNIE
RAITT
HITS "MAMA HE'S CRAZY,"
"WHY NOT ME," "GRANDPA
(TELL ME 'BOUT THE GOOD
OLD DAYS)"

The Judds helped welcome back traditional country in the 1980s with folksy, acoustic, yet blues-influenced songs revolving around nostalgic themes reminiscent of simpler times.

The daughter of a Kentucky gas-station owner, Naomi went from being a teenage mother to a divorced welfare mom, yet still dreamed of being a star. She became a nurse to support her two girls, and moved her family near Nashville. With unbridled determination, she wouldn't give up until she landed a recording contract for herself and her teenage daughter, Wynonna, who possessed a powerful and soulful voice.

Though the duo performed semi-regularly on Ralph Emery's early morning television show, it was Naomi's nursing job that led to her big break: she slipped a demo tape to a hospital patient, the daughter of producer Brent Maher. Their first single on RCA, "Had a Dream (For the Heart)," hit the charts in 1983.

During the Judds' eight-year career, they enjoyed 14 No. 1 hits and won four Grammies and eight CMA awards. They broke up in 1991, after Naomi contracted hepatitis C. The next year, Wynonna launched her solo career.

BEVERLY KEEL

Kathy Mattea, a West Virginia native, drew more on folk music and Southern California country-rock than on bluegrass, but there was an acoustic drive to her songs that incorporated the mountain sound, too. Down-to-earth and unafraid to show her intelligence, Mattea's graceful presence on radio eventually made her an award-winning artist with a solid, loyal fan base.

But the biggest acoustic act to follow in Skaggs's wake was the Judds. Mother Naomi's relentless drive and folksy homilies provided a public persona for the duo that was part storybook fairy-tale and part family drama, though it was daughter Wynonna's husky, growling alto that gave their sweet songs weight and power. The two became the most successful mother-daughter duo in music history. With gently rocking tunes and breezy acoustic numbers kissed with sweet harmonies, they sang of enduring family values, of banking on love, and on finding your own strength.

They shot to popularity quickly, scoring 14 No. 1 hits from 1984 to 1990, and they were going strong when Naomi announced her retirement due to a diagnosis of chronic hepatitis C. Naomi later wrote a book about how she overcame an untreatable illness, and Wynonna went on to an acclaimed solo career.

FAMILY FEUD *The Judds were as famous for their private spats as their public persona, but the tension between the mother-daughter duo translated into heavenly music.*

MY KIND OF COUNTRY

REBA McENTIRE

BORN CHOCKIE, OKLAHOMA,
MARCH 28, 1955
FIRST RECORDED 1971
INFLUENCES DOLLY PARTON,
BARBARA MANDRELL, PATSY CLINE
HITS "IS THERE LIFE OUT THERE,"
"WHOEVER'S IN NEW ENGLAND,"
"SOMEBODY SHOULD LEAVE"

Reba McEntire maintains one of the genre's most successful careers by continually incorporating contemporary sounds without changing her trademark traditional vocal style. The fiercely driven Oklahoman has sold nearly 50 million albums during her 30-year career. In 2004, she became the country female with the longest span of No. 1 hits when "Somebody" became her 22nd chart-topper.

McEntire began to seize more control of her career in the late 1980s, hiring her steel guitarist, Narvel Blackstock (whom she married in 1989) to manage her. The pair built a diversified entertainment company, Starstruck Entertainment, housed in a lavishly appointed office building on Music Row.

Raised on a 7,000-acre cattle ranch, McEntire and her siblings formed the Singing McEntires when she was in high school. Her first solo Top 20 hit came with a remake of "Sweet Dreams" in 1979, but big success began with 1984's *My Kind of Country*. She earned the CMA Entertainer of the Year Award in 1986.

Since then, she has acted in Hollywood movies, ventured out to Broadway (*Annie Get Your Gun*), and starred in a long-running television series (*Reba*).
BEVERLY KEEL

CINDERELLA STORY *Mother Naomi (left) envisioned the Judds' mega-success long before her daughter did. Wynonna went on to establish herself as an eclectic solo act, as admired by rock and blues fans as country.*

At the same time that the Judds accentuated country music's back-to-roots trend, a Nashville veteran finally found her groove with a retro-sounding album that showed off her strong Okie voice and down-home personality.

Reba

Reba McEntire had released 16 singles, only three of which even reached the Top Ten, before achieving her first No. 1 hit in early 1983, "Can't Even Get the Blues." But it wasn't until she left Mercury Records and moved to MCA in 1984 that she truly began to find her voice.

Her first MCA album, *My Kind of Country*, played up her love of twangy, traditional country music and her rodeo background, while shifting away from the sweet country-pop she'd previously recorded. Co-produced with Jimmy Bowen, McEntire's album jumpstarted her career with back-to-back No. 1 hits, "How Blue" and the stunning heartbreak ballad "Somebody Should Leave."

McEntire credited the turnaround to her record company giving her more say in her musical style. By the next album,

Whoever's in New England, McEntire aimed again at a more modern, pop-crossover style, but this time with gutsier, stronger material. Her forceful, yet admirable pluck came through, and McEntire would rank as the biggest country female star for the rest of the '80s and into the '90s. Future superstars such as Faith Hill, who worked for McEntire, and Shania Twain cited her ambitious drive and the way she took control of her business and image as role models for their own careers.

"I work hard, but I have a lot of fun, too," McEntire said, summing up her philosophy and strong business sense. "It's the greatest living I think I could have made. I'll tell you one thing for sure: it beats working cattle all to thunder."

By the late 1980s, McEntire had branched into acting and writing books while presiding over a string of start-up businesses that had been pulled together into an entertainment empire. Her Starstruck Entertainment branched into management, promotion, publicity, recording studios, and music publishing. She had a construction company, a jet-leasing company, and raised horses.

RODEO QUEEN *Reba McEntire vowed in the late '80s that she would always wear the silver belt buckle she got for singing the national anthem at the National Rodeo Finals as a reminder to stay traditional.*

CLASSIC COUNTRY
RECORDING

RANDY TRAVIS
"On the Other Hand"

But on the other hand,
there's a golden band,
to remind me of
someone who would
not understand.
WRITTEN BY PAUL
OVERSTREET AND DON
SCHLITZ, AND RECORDED
JANUARY 30, 1985
NO. 1 COUNTRY, JULY 26, 1986

Randy Travis became a
superstar in 1986 with the
release of his critically
acclaimed debut album,
Storms of Life. One of its
singles, "On the Other
Hand," a wrenching ballad
sung from the perspective
of an emotionally torn
husband teetering on the
verge of infidelity, remains
a classic of the era. With a
head-turning baritone and
subtle phrasing that
recalled the legendary
country singer Lefty
Frizzell, Travis imbued the
song with a masterful mix
of world-weary regret,
melancholy, and longing.

Yet "On the Other
Hand" had to be released
twice as a single to find its
audience. On September
14, 1985, the initial release
of the song stalled at No.
67 on the charts. Travis's
second single, "1982,"
cracked the Top 10 and
became his breakthrough
hit. Its success paved the
way for the re-release of
"On the Other Hand," and
on its second try, the ballad
went to No. 1, solidifying
Randy Travis as a new
traditionalist beacon.

CHRISSIE DICKINSON

Around that time, *Entertainment Weekly* deemed her "the Oprah Winfrey of country music." No one argued.

She later sold all her businesses, just as she moved into broader entertainment roles, starring on Broadway in *Annie Get Your Gun* and developing and starring in her own sitcom, *Reba*. "I don't believe in limitations," she said in a very Oprah-like statement. "I believe in possibilities. As a woman, I know I have to work twice as hard to get what I want. But I'm willing to do that."

New vehicle with old wheels

Randy Travis was another major '80s star who started out as a traditionalist, but eventually evolved into doing more crossover-oriented material while expanding into acting and other fields. If there's a crowning achievement of the neo-traditionalists movement, it's Travis's 1986 debut album, *Storms of Life*.

The late Grand Ole Opry humorist Minnie Pearl described Travis as "a new vehicle with old wheels," explaining that he sounded good, looked good, and moved country into the future by drawing on its past. She added, "A voice like his only comes along once in a generation."

Even after a series of fast-rising stars gave life to country music in the early '80s, Travis rose faster, sold more albums, and drew more praise than any of his predecessors. *Storms of Life* earned the distinction of becoming the first debut album by a country artist to sell a million copies within a year of its release. A decade later, such achievements were commonplace, but Travis's success set a benchmark that proved country music was gaining great momentum across the United States.

A troubled teen who was saved from jail time by his manager, Elizabeth Hatcher, who later became his wife, Travis entered country music as a solid, responsible young man whose voice bore great emotion, but whose presence had a rock-steady, reserved quality. Success didn't come easy; every record label turned down Travis at least twice before he signed with Warner Bros. Records while working as a short-order cook in an Opryland area nightclub.

> **"When the time is right, they're going to make a movie of Randy's life, and it will be a signature of hope for everyone who thinks their hardships cannot be overcome."**
>
> JON VOIGHT

Though credited for returning country music to its roots, Travis also joined Strait in setting the code for how future male country stars should carry themselves. Hard-drinking and wild living were passé; Travis was clean-cut and square-jawed, he dressed in a crisp, casual style with a slight western cut to his jackets—nothing too gaudy or flashy, and nary a rhinestone in sight. He was humble but not compliant, polite but not a pushover, and reverent to those who came before him. He closely monitored his diet and worked out daily with a personal trainer, maintaining a well-sculpted body that served him well in flexing his biceps or baring his chest in magazine layouts.

Strait and Travis, like McEntire and Mattea, mirrored the young professionals of their day. Country no longer belonged only to rural America, and even if some stars were raised on farms, they soon left the fields behind. They were ambitious, hard-working, and educated, and they built investment portfolios as their hit songs and concert income grew. They weren't much different from rising executives in other southern cities, or small-business owners in suburbs and small towns. And that's who bought the records and came to the shows. Contemporary country had changed, just as the South and America had changed.

And, like the rest of the nation, country music ended the '80s poised for a boom period.

COUNTRY CHARMER *Randy Travis, who altered the course of commercial country music with his neo-traditionalist debut,* Storms of Life *(1986), croons to Minnie Pearl at the 1987 CMA Awards.*

TOP TEN

TOP TEN FAVORITE COUNTRY RECORD PRODUCTIONS FROM TONY BROWN

1 **Don't It Make My Brown Eyes Blue**
(Capitol, 1977)
Artist: Crystal Gayle
Producer: Allen Reynolds

2 **Behind Closed Doors**
(Epic, 1973)
Artist: Charlie Rich
Producer: Billy Sherrill

3 **Too Far Gone**
(Reprise, 1975)
Artist: Emmylou Harris
Producer: Brian Ahern

4 **Seven Year Ache**
(Columbia, 1981)
Artist: Rosanne Cash
Producer: Rodney Crowell

5 **Somebody Like You**
(Capitol, 2002)
Artist: Keith Urban
Producer: Dan Huff

6 **Family Tradition**
(Elektra, 1979)
Artist: Hank Williams, Jr.
Producer: Jimmy Bowen

7 **Crazy**
(Decca, 1961)
Artist: Patsy Cline
Producer: Owen Bradley

8 **Stand by Your Man**
(Epic, 1968)
Artist: Tammy Wynette
Producer: Billy Sherrill

9 **Wide Open Spaces**
(Monument, 1998)
Artist: Dixie Chicks
Producers: Blake Chancey & Paul Worley

10 **Would You Lay With Me**
(Columbia, 1973)
Artist: Tanya Tucker
Producer: Billy Sherrill

POCKETFUL OF GOLD

COUNTRY MUSIC IN THE AGE OF PLENTY

PETER COOPER

COUNTRY MUSIC ENJOYED A POPULARITY BOOM EARLY IN THE 1990s. BUT AS MULTI-PLATINUM SALES BECAME THE NEW BENCHMARK, THE HUGE COMMERCIAL DEMANDS ON COUNTRY MUSIC BECAME APPARENT. WOULD COUNTRY GAIN THE WORLD ONLY TO LOSE ITS SOUL?

continues opposite

Along Music Row, all of 1989 felt like spring. It was a year when musical sophistication and commercial viability seemed of a piece. It was a year when country's arms spread to embrace singer-songwriters schooled in Bob Dylan and in Hank Williams, when "New Traditionalism" didn't mean aping Merle Haggard so much as it meant offering fresh perspectives on old models, and when "pop-country" was as likely to mean "edgy and intricate" as "syrupy and string-laden."

It was a year when country music could claim itself as the most critically acclaimed pop-culture genre: Emmylou Harris, Nanci Griffith, Foster & Lloyd, Merle Haggard, Rodney Crowell, Rosanne Cash, Kevin Welch, Kathy Mattea, Lyle Lovett, and the O'Kanes were all Music Row-based major label artists, while rock & roll was searching for an identity in the pre-grunge years.

The CMA Awards that November found industry voters making a case for well-rooted country music. Hat-wearing, stand-and-sing artist George Strait won the Best Entertainer prize, while Vern Gosdin's slow, lonesome, stone-country gem "Chiseled in Stone" was Song of the Year. Two well-constructed generational summits—the Nitty Gritty Dirt Band's *Will the Circle Be Unbroken, Vol. II*, and the Hank Williams Sr.–Hank Williams Jr. duet "There's a Tear in My Beer" (the son dubbed vocals over his long-gone daddy's decades-old track)—received awards as well. And Kathy Mattea, whose rich voice was in favor with radio programmers and music critics, was named Best Female Vocalist. The most intriguing aspect of the scene

SITTIN' IN *Democratic presidential nominee Bill Clinton plays the saxophone with the University of Arkansas band during a Fayetteville stop in the last days of the 1992 campaign.*

came from five newcomers who made their country chart debuts that year. Mary Chapin Carpenter was a folk-loving, erudite, Ivy League-schooled singer-songwriter whose music simultaneously recalled Joni Mitchell and the Carter Family. Travis Tritt's sound was informed by the Marshall Tucker Band, the Allman Brothers, and Lynyrd Skynyrd, and Tritt brought southern rock back to the country mainstream. Alan Jackson and Clint Black played meat-and-potatoes country music that was solid and smart. And then there was Garth Brooks—a curious, highly profitable amalgam of … everything.

Brooks loved rodeo songs, and his "Much Too Young (To Feel This Damn Old)" was a tribute to the solitary, bronc-busting life: "Sleep would be best/ But I just can't afford the rest/ I've gotta ride in Denver tomorrow night." But while his debut album was stripped-down enough for Brooks to be branded as a neo-traditionalist, he had a penchant for arena-rock theatrics and a degree in marketing. While the others in the Class of '89 would sell millions of albums, it would be Brooks who redefined country-music success.

FLYING HIGH *Garth Brooks brought dramatic rock-arena theatrics to country in the early '90s. Here, he makes a spectacular sweep over an enthralled throng in Dallas in 1993.*

2000 George Bush (the younger) becomes America's 43rd president. George Jones survives a near-fatal car crash. Garth Brooks announces his retirement at age 38. *O Brother, Where Art Thou?* premieres in American movie theaters at year's end.

2001 Islamic terrorists crash hijacked airliners into the World Trade Center and the Pentagon. The Country Music Hall of Fame and Museum opens in its new downtown location in Nashville. Keith Urban scores his first No. 1, "But for the Grace of God."

2003 US and allied forces launch the Iraq War. Apple starts its iTunes online music store. Johnny Cash dies, four months after the death of wife June Carter Cash. Alan Jackson repeats as CMA Entertainer of the Year.

2004 Gretchen Wilson scores her first No. 1 with "Redneck Woman." Big & Rich release their debut album. Kenny Chesney is the CMA's Entertainer of the Year.

2005 Loretta Lynn wins two Grammy Awards for her recordings with rocker Jack White. Kenny Chesney and Renée Zellweger marry, then annul their marriage. Garth Brooks and Trisha Yearwood marry. Keith Urban is named CMA Entertainer and Male Vocalist of the Year. Garth Brooks scores his first No. 1 hit since 1998 with "Good Ride Cowboy" on the *Radio & Records* chart.

2006 Buck Owens dies. Dixie Chicks release their first studio album since 2002.

ALAN JACKSON

BORN NEWNAN, GEORGIA,
OCTOBER 17, 1958
PLAYS GUITAR
INFLUENCES GEORGE JONES,
MERLE HAGGARD, RANDY TRAVIS
HITS "CHATTAHOOCHEE," "DRIVE,"
"WHERE WERE YOU"

From the start, it was clear Alan Jackson could write catchy traditional songs. What took a while to perceive was how often he drew on personal experience to create powerful lyrics that evoked universal truths. In that sense, Jackson stands as his generation's most successful heir to Hank Williams and Merle Haggard.

The evidence existed on his first album, from 1990: "Home" poignantly describes the life his parents built for their children. Over the years, Jackson continued to draw on his family and the things that had influenced him. The upbeat "Chattahoochee" name-checked the river he enjoyed as a child while recounting adventures he lived through as a teen and young adult. "Drive," another uptempo song, is a grand statement about what he learned from his father and how he's trying to pass the same lessons on to his daughters.

Not everything Jackson writes is personal (and he doesn't write everything he records). Occasionally he gets political but always from a grassroots way. That's what made his 9/11 song, "Where Were You (When the World Stopped Turning)," so striking: it took a singer of simple songs from Georgia to best describe the nation's visceral reaction to that day's terrorist acts.

MICHAEL MCCALL

HOWDY, FRIENDS *Alan Jackson's folksy persona serves him well with country's core audience. His down-to-earth songs about family, small-town life, and even southern cooking resonate with this 1995 concert crowd.*

HELP ME HOLD ON *Travis Tritt arrived in country's class of '89, riding a fast train of rowdy rock and honky-tonk. By 1992, when this concert photo was taken in Los Angeles, he had won a Grammy.*

With regular-guy looks and a voice that was earnest but not technically virtuosic, Brooks had struggled to even get a record deal in Nashville. Whatever he lacked, Brooks made up for with a conviction that burned across stages and seemed to reduce the space between singer and audiences. "The greatest compliment I ever got was from a woman who said, 'It's weird: You're like one of us that made it,'" Brooks said.

Though Brooks was well established by year's end with his smash ballad "If Tomorrow Never Comes," Clint Black was 1989's first breakout artist. Black's movie-star looks were compatible with the video era, and his cowboy image didn't ruffle any traditionalists' feathers. His debut single, "A Better Man," hit No. 1, his *Killin' Time* album topped the country charts for 28 weeks, and he was named the CMA's Horizon Award winner, given to country's top up-and-comer, in 1989. Though Black gave Brooks a run for the 1990s' country crown, he would eventually have to settle for being a certified hit-maker as opposed to Brooks's status as a pop icon.

GARTH BROOKS

BORN LUBA, OKLAHOMA,
FEBRUARY 7, 1962
PLAYS GUITAR
INFLUENCES GEORGE STRAIT,
THE EAGLES, KISS, JAMES TAYLOR
HITS "THE DANCE," "FRIENDS IN
LOW PLACES," "WHAT SHE'S
DOING NOW"

It's impossible to overstate Garth Brooks's impact on modern country music. In the 1990s, he ushered contemporary country into the arena age, filling 20,000-seat venues and eventually selling 100 million albums. It was a revolutionary concept for the time: a country singer who could compete on a par with superstar pop and rock acts.

The release of his third record, 1991's *Ropin' the Wind*, was a watershed event for both the artist and the genre, becoming the first country album to debut at No. 1 on both *Billboard*'s all-genre Top 200 chart and the country albums chart. His flashy stage concerts were filled with 1970s-style arena pyrotechnics: he swung from ropes, sang in staged rain and fire, and amped the energy and volume to ten. His savvy musical mix of traditional fiddle-and-steel country, sensitive folk balladry, and rock rave-ups appealed to both a new generation of country enthusiasts as well as fans of '70s arena rock.

After his last studio release, 2001's *Scarecrow*, Garth "retired" from the road and the recording studio but in 2005 returned to cut "Good Ride Cowboy," a tribute to the late Chris LeDoux, as well as a deal with Wal-Mart for distribution of his albums.

CHRISSIE DICKINSON

HAT TRICK *With 1989's "A Better Man," Clint Black became the first new male country performer to score a No. 1 hit with a debut single in 15 years. His freshman album,* Killin' Time, *went double platinum.*

CLASSIC COUNTRY
RECORDING

GARTH BROOKS
"The Dance"

Our lives are better left to chance. I could have missed the pain, but I'd have had to miss the dance.
WRITTEN BY TONY ARATA, AND RECORDED IN 1989
NO. 1 COUNTRY, JULY 14, 1990

Garth Brooks fought his first record-label battle when it came to "The Dance." It may have been the most important victory of his career. Brooks first heard the song at the Bluebird Cafe by its writer, Tony Arata, and played it for his producer Allen Reynolds. But Brooks questioned whether he should record it. Most of his debut featured guitar-driven, fiddle-spiked cowboy songs; "The Dance" was a sensitive ballad looking back at a relationship. Reynolds pushed for the song, and Brooks agreed to record it.

By April 1990, Brooks had released three singles, and his debut had sold decently, if not spectacularly. Jimmy Bowen, the veteran record executive, had recently taken over Capitol Records, and advised Brooks to move on to the second album. But Brooks and his managers balked—they'd seen the crowd reaction to "The Dance." Impressed by their passion for the song, Bowen green-lighted the single's release. "The Dance" leap-frogged up the charts and spent three weeks at No. 1.
MICHAEL MCCALL

NO FENCES *(Previous page) One of the most important country stars since Hank Williams, Garth Brooks, shown here in 1993, moved country to the forefront of American entertainment. In doing so, he sold more than 115 million albums.*

The year 1990 saw some of the edgier denizens of Music Row falling from commercial grace, while the "Class of '89" secured surer footing on radio stations. It also saw the continuing rise of a multi-talented Oklahoman named Vince Gill, who had kicked around the music business for years as a touring musician, session guitarist, and marginally successful solo act. Gill's ballad "When I Call Your Name" became his first Top 5 hit, won the CMA's Single of the Year Award, and established Gill as a major solo artist.

The same year Gill collected the CMA's Single of the Year prize, Brooks was named the winner of the Horizon Award, and the Academy of Country Music named him Entertainer of the Year, as well—the first of four straight ACM Entertainer crowns. Still, it wasn't until the next year that the magnitude of his contributions was fully understood.

The impact of SoundScan
In May 1991, *Billboard* magazine began using data acquired from SoundScan, a company that sought to report sales data via bar-code scans at cash registers. In the past, that data had been derived from sales clerks' estimates. Turns out, those estimates were wrong.

"The week the system came out, it became apparent that Nashville had been selling far more records than anyone realized," reported Bruce Feiler in his *Dreaming Out Loud* book. "[Garth Brooks's] *No Fences* album moved from sixteen to four on the pop chart, which

NASHVILLE ROYALTY *Emmylou Harris learned early that if she played with the best, she'd be the best. This 1993 performance reunited her with former band members Rodney Crowell (left) and Ricky Skaggs, and with Vince Gill (right).*

includes music from all genres." Later in 1991, Brooks's *Ropin' the Wind* album became the first country song set to debut at No. 1 on the *Billboard* pop charts.

The new data indicated that country sales comprised 17 percent of the overall total for American music, second only to rock. That information aided Nashville's cause in getting more radio stations to feature country, and a boom was on: by 1995, nearly 70 million people were listening to country songs on the radio. That figure put country ahead of the second-place finisher, adult contemporary music, by more than 18 million.

In Lisa Rebecca Gubernick's book, *Get Hot or Go Home*, Brooks was quoted talking about the marked change in the charts caused by the SoundScan reports: "It's like someone opened the closet door. Just because the light is on, does it mean it wasn't that way all along?" Even before

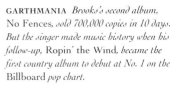

GARTHMANIA *Brooks's second album,* No Fences, *sold 700,000 copies in 10 days. But the singer made music history when his follow-up,* Ropin' the Wind, *became the first country album to debut at No. 1 on the* Billboard *pop chart.*

FOOT FETISH *In the early '90s, country nightspots transformed themselves into dance clubs as the new line dancing fever took hold. Dressed in contemporary western wear, dancers strutted, stomped, and swiveled to choreographed routines.*

SoundScan came into use, it had become apparent that country was booming. Between 1989 and 1991, sales more than doubled, from $460 million to nearly $1 billion. Then, between 1991 and 1994, those sales doubled again, to $1.97 billion.

Dance fads

Both a boost to and a beneficiary of the boom, the team of Kix Brooks and Ronnie Dunn—better known as Brooks & Dunn—first hit the charts in 1991, heading to No. 1 with a song called "Brand New Man." They would eventually become the most popular duo in country history, and in 1992 their "Boot Scootin' Boogie" was part of something that hadn't happened in country music since the days of Bob Wills: a dance craze.

HUNKY DORY *The well-chiseled Billy Ray Cyrus brought a brand-new kind of dance-hall fever to country with his smash debut "Achy Breaky Heart" (1992). His subsequent hits also packed a punch, but in recent years he has gained a higher profile through TV acting than music.*

Kentucky-bred Billy Ray Cyrus contributed to the new dance fad with "Achy Breaky Heart," a song that came complete with a video that depicted "Achy Breaky" fans doing a choreographed "line dance."

"The huge success of the song… brought line dancing to the awareness of the general public," wrote David Powell on his "Roots 'n' Boots" website in 2003. "Line dancing was suddenly 'in' all around North America."

In a celebrated dust-up, Travis Tritt charged that Cyrus was turning country music into an "ass-wigglin'" contest (they would later make nice). But "Achy Breaky Heart" ruled the country charts for five straight weeks, and it rose to No. 1 faster than any single in country history, topping the charts in its second week of release, while it peaked at No. 4 on the pop charts. Cyrus eclipsed even Garth Brooks as country's big story of 1992, but in the end it was Brooks who held the staying power: Cyrus would never again top the charts.

Another new star of the early 1990s was Trisha Yearwood, who first hit in 1991 with a mid-tempo story song called "She's in Love with the Boy." While that song's story of a young love that won't bow to parental wishes was Yearwood's initial hit, it in no way captured the breadth of her talent. A fan of the Eagles, Linda Ronstadt, and other West Coast pop acts, Yearwood combined a Georgia drawl, a strong and subtle voice, and an expansive vision of country music to become one of the modern era's finest vocalists.

Before she had a record deal with MCA, she worked as a demo singer and as a receptionist at MTM Records. She met a pre-fame Garth Brooks, who told her that he'd gladly help her if his own star were ever to rise. When Brooks became a headliner, he invited Yearwood to be his opening act. Over the years, the two would record several charting duets, the most successful of which was the No. 2 country hit "In Another's Eyes" (1997). The two later became romantically involved and married in December 2005.

In the 1990s, one of Yearwood's vocal heroes, Emmylou Harris, found herself shifting from a 15-year role as mainstream

"You're not going [to do this] in front of these people!"

TRISHA YEARWOOD TO GARTH BROOKS, REALIZING HE WAS ABOUT TO POP THE QUESTION ONSTAGE BEFORE A CROWD OF 7,000 AT BUCK OWENS'S CRYSTAL PALACE, MAY 2005

Americana the Beautiful

Americana music is best defined not by what it is than by what it isn't: It isn't on country radio, though many of its acts are more traditionally country-minded than many current country superstars. In fact, several performers who were once part of mainstream country— including Emmylou Harris, Steve Earle, Jim Lauderdale, Nanci Griffith, Kieran Kane, and Kelly Willis—are now known as Americana artists. This fluid subgenre encompasses dozens of acts whose roots may be found variously in the works of Hank Williams or Lightnin' Hopkins or Bob Dylan. Americana artists need not even be American, as Brit Nick Lowe and Australian Kasey Chambers are considered part of the fold.

The current Americana scene is an offshoot of what came to be known in the 1990s as "alternative country" or "No Depression" music. Acts like Uncle Tupelo, the Jayhawks, Jason & the Scorchers, and Robbie Fulks provided an edgy alternative to a commercial country scene dominated by mainstream performers like Garth Brooks and Reba McEntire.

In 1990, Illinois band Uncle Tupelo released an album called *No Depression* that drew its name from a Carter Family song. Subsequently, a "No Depression" Internet chat group sprang up, helping build the community of independent-minded listeners who would eventually patronize the music magazine *No Depression* when it began publishing in 1995. The magazine has become one of America's most respected niche periodicals, but the term "No Depression" proved too amorphous a term to describe a music scene.

In 1995, the Gavin music-trade publication began running an "Americana" chart, and in late 1999 the Americana Music Association was founded to further "American roots music based on the traditions of country." The Association hosts a yearly conference and an awards show that has enhanced the connections between traditional country music heroes and contemporary Americana artists: Loretta Lynn and Johnny Cash, for instance, received Americana awards at times when they weren't being recognized by the Country Music Association. The Americana genre is pleased to claim them—along with genre stalwarts Lucinda Williams, Gillian Welch, and John Prine—even as country radio shrugs its collective shoulders at the absence of such music makers.

PETER COOPER

ROOTS REVIVAL *Lucinda Williams (with rocker Willie Nile) is one of the most lauded performers of Americana music, made up of folk and alt-country artists. (Below, left to right) Polly Parsons, Rodney Crowell, John Prine, David Keith, Jim Lauderdale, Webb Wilder, Allison Moorer at the 2003 Americana Awards.*

country artist. Though Johnny Cash once remarked to journalist Patrick Carr that, "Every so often country has to get back to Emmylou Harris," the early 1990s found the genre moving from her well-rooted sound into something decidedly slicker. Yet Harris remained highly influential. Her three 1991 concerts at the severely decayed Ryman Auditorium brought attention to the beauty and importance of that long-closed relic and helped spur a successful renovation campaign. Captured on album in 1992's *At the Ryman*, and featuring an all-star acoustic band that included Sam Bush, Roy Husky Jr., and Jon Randall, Harris's bluegrass-inflected shows presaged the back-to-basics *O Brother, Where Art Thou?* movement by nine years.

By mid-decade, Harris was experimenting with moody, atmospheric, decidedly non-country elements on her *Wrecking Ball* album, and was championing the songwriting of Gillian Welch, David Olney, Lucinda Williams, and others who worked outside the

country mainstream. Her role as a matriarch of the so-called "alt.country" or "Americana" scene cannot be over-emphasized, as Harris's music has touched nearly every proponent of that hard-to-define sub-genre.

GRIT AND GRACE *Emmylou Harris, the godmother of the Americana movement, is revered worldwide, particularly in Europe, where the genre is more popular than main-stream country. Here she performs in Paris, France, 1995.*

TURBO TONKIN' *Ronnie Dunn (left) and Kix Brooks—better known as Brooks & Dunn—mix equal parts blue-collar honky-tonk and cranked-up country-rock to fuel their own brand of high-octane chart-toppers.*

High stakes

In the mid-1990s, Brooks, Yearwood, Gill, Tritt, Alan Jackson, Brooks & Dunn, Reba McEntire, Clint Black, Wynonna Judd, Mary Chapin Carpenter, and others enjoyed what proved to be a waning period of prosperity. The new rules of major label Music City commerce—"Sell a million, get on the radio or get out of mainstream country music"—meant that Harris, Nanci Griffith, Kevin Welch, and others who had previously been considered "country" were no longer members of the fold. Those artists stayed in Nashville, but by 1994 they seldom entered the big record-label buildings along Music Row. Those buildings housed labels and artists who made "New Country," the crossover-ready, multi-platinum music of the 1990s. Where gold sales of 500,000 were admirable in the

TABERNACLE TIME *Harris's* At the Ryman *(1992), an acoustic live album, is one of many benchmarks of her long, adventurous, and distinguished career.*

ANOTHER COAL MINER'S DAUGHTER
Patty Loveless, a distant cousin to Loretta Lynn and, like her, the child of a real-life miner, was one of few women who strove to keep country's traditional flame burning in the late '90s. This album dates from 1994.

AUSPICIOUS BEGINNING *Thirteen-year old LeAnn Rimes arrived out of nowhere in 1996 with "Blue," a haunting, yodel-laced song originally written for (but not recorded by) Patsy Cline. The album by the same name logged at No. 1 for more than three months.*

'80s, major labels in the '90s (and in the years since then) worked for platinum sales of more than one million. New listeners abounded, but all the attention came with a cost to many of country's veteran core artists, who were phased out of radio rotation.

That's not to say that interesting and acclaimed commercial country music wasn't produced in the mid-1990s. Yearwood provided numerous pleasures, as did Wynonna with her soulful, gospel-inflected song sets. Even as Garth Brooks's stage shows opted for over-the-top gestures and pyrotechnics, his albums favored warm sounds and smart songs. Alan Jackson released a string of hits buoyed by solid country sounds, subtle humor, and plaintive vocals. David Ball hit like a honky-tonk cannonball with "Thinkin' Problem" in 1994, the same year that Patty Loveless's *When Fallen Angels Fly* album revealed itself to be a modern classic.

But country radio formats were accepting of straightforward, down-the-middle country music only when it came from "hot" contemporary artists. Loveless's 1997 single "You Don't Seem to Miss Me" featured harmony vocals from Country Music Hall of Famer George Jones and garnered a 1998 Vocal Event of the Year trophy from the CMA. But by the late '90s several influential radio programmers refused to play anything with Jones on it, declaring Jones out of step with the format. At least one program director requested a re-mixed version of the song, sans Jones. Loveless refused to take Jones off the recording, and the song died on the wrong side of the Top 10.

"Jones needs to be on the radio," Garth Brooks said. "I don't care if he's 90 years old. If you don't think George Jones should be on the radio, then I understand you don't think Garth Brooks should be there, either. Because George Jones is country music."

With veteran performers exiting the mainstream, several important new performers emerged, tweaking their sounds until they reached commercial mass. Shania Twain, Tim McGraw, Faith Hill, Kenny Chesney, and Toby Keith did not arrive on the scene as fully-developed artists when their first records were released in the early '90s, but in time they would become major, multi-platinum stars. Young LeAnn Rimes, on the other hand,

experienced her greatest artistic and commercial triumph right off the bat, when she released "Blue" in 1996 at age 13.

Written in the 1960s, "Blue" came from the pen of Bill Mack, a Dallas radio personality and promoter. Like Brenda Lee and Tanya Tucker before her, Rimes was a child who sounded like a woman, and Mack thought Rimes's voice would be an ideal vehicle for "Blue," a ballad in the style of Patsy Cline. "Blue" helped Rimes land a deal with Curb Records, and it became an immediate smash on release. The album of the same name debuted at No. 3 on the pop charts, but though she followed with charting country singles, Rimes wasn't able to sustain the success of "Blue." As she grew into her twenties, what had seemed an idyllic youth gave way to a young adulthood marked by legal wranglings with her father/manager Wilbur Rimes, by a turn towards dance-pop music, and by a new image that involved revealing outfits and sexy poses.

Beauty and the beats

If Rimes peaked upon arrival, it took Shania Twain some time to perfect her genre-altering sound and style. Twain's

BRANCHING OUT *After Blue, Rimes, shown here in '96, moved on to inspirational ballads, which showed off her big-voiced talent. She turned her attention to pop music in the millennium, but returned to country with 2005's* This Woman.

SHANIA TWAIN

BORN WINDSOR, ONTARIO, CANADA, AUGUST 28, 1965
PLAYS GUITAR
FIRST RECORDED 1993
INFLUENCES DOLLY PARTON, PAT BENATAR, REBA MCENTIRE
HITS "WHOSE BED HAVE YOUR BOOTS BEEN UNDER," "ANY MAN OF MINE," "YOU'RE STILL THE ONE"

With the help of her husband-producer, Robert John "Mutt" Lange, Shania Twain has become the queen of contemporary crossover.

Despite her high-gloss image, her roots were undeniably hardscrabble. Tragedy struck in 1987 when Twain's mother and stepfather died in a car crash, leaving Twain, who began singing semi-professionally as a child, to support her younger brothers. She worked as a Canadian resort singer, and in 1991 headed to Nashville.

Her 1993 self-titled Mercury debut failed to excite listeners, but the reclusive Lange—who had guided hits for rock acts Def Leppard and Foreigner—spotted a Twain video. The two married in 1993, and working with Lange, Twain released *The Woman in Me* in 1995. It yielded seven hit singles, mixing Twain's warm, sassy vocals with infectious pop-country arrangements. In 1997, *Come On Over* solidified her superstar status: at 15 million sales and counting, it's the best-selling album of the SoundScan era.

CHRISSIE DICKINSON

1993 debut album was a bland pop-country effort that did little to distinguish the native Canadian from the New Country pack. After meeting Mutt Lange, who would become her husband and producer, she developed a sound that combined arena-rock drum sounds, pop hooks, and the occasional scampering

WONDER WOMAN *Shania Twain bombed with her 1993 debut album but rallied to set an enviable sales benchmark for country albums. Her 1997 effort,* Come on Over, *has sold 20 million copies in the US. Here she performs during half-time at Super Bowl XXVII in San Diego in 2005.*

SHANIA TWAIN

Come on Over

Why I Don't Love the Music Business—
And Why I'm Still in It

I don't particularly love the music business, in the same way that I don't particularly love gas-station restrooms, but I understand how they fill a societal need. Sometimes I am even compelled, against all better judgment, to take advantage of them. Or it.

This is not to say that the music business is utterly corrupt and bereft of a single person who actually cares about music beyond its profit potential. Or that there are not fine people with deep moral convictions and an intuitive understanding and appreciation of music in all its subtle forms currently working in the business. It is just to say that I have met only three of those people in my life—and one of them is dead.

I know what you're thinking: I am just old and bitter and wish things were like they were in the old days, before records and artists were completely image-driven and media became the soul-and flesh-eating disease it currently is. But you're wrong. I didn't like it any better in the old days.

Okay, I digress. Actually, I'm beating around the bush.

Here is the point of my cranky reflection: When my first record (*Right or Wrong*) was about to come out, in 1979, I had a marketing meeting at Columbia Records in Nashville. (This was not actually my very first record; I had made a record in Europe for Ariola the previous year, but it had never been released in the United States. Rick Blackburn, who was head of Columbia Nashville at the time, had heard it and had signed me to Columbia on the strength of that pathetic little album, God bless him.) In the marketing meeting, the talk turned to the subject of my "image." This alarmed me. I was 23 years old, a bit of a self-styled hipster, the key word being "self." I bristled at the idea that these corporate types were now going to tell me how to dress or style my eggplant-colored hair. But no, it was far more crass and vague than that. They wanted to make me—and I quote—"fuckable." To reiterate, this was the Year of Our Lord 1979. I know I had a powerful mix of emotions upon hearing this remarkable and innovative strategy to sell my record, but I don't recall my response, if any. I may have been too appalled to defend myself. That moment still stings in retrospect, for so many reasons: the implication that I was not already … well, you know … the implication that the music itself was not enough to carry me, the breathtaking insult of hearing this said directly to my face, the sexism, the reduction of my whole being to a commodity, etc.

Now, I look at what goes on in the music business, and I think how charming they were back in 1979. At least their marketing proposal seemed like a fresh idea. It's not like today, when the concept of fuckability is a hackneyed routine that has been laboriously broken down into all its repellent microscopic parts to be systematically slapped on to any person, no matter how natively unattractive, to achieve that very specific high-gloss packaging varnish of impeccable grooming and one-dimensional narrative. That narrative usually going something like this: an impeccably groomed, good ol' gal/prostitute wearing $300 jeans has just returned from a hayride in upper middle-class suburbia and wants to offer you her services for something upwards of a million bucks an hour—i.e., she's not available. Oh, and she sings. At least, that's the way I read most of these image-driven campaigns to sell records. But maybe that's just post-traumatic reasoning on my part, left over from that ill-fated marketing meeting.

I have a hidden agenda in telling you this story. As I write this in the spring of 2005, I have a new record coming out. My A&R man at Capitol, Julian Raymond—who is one of the three people mentioned above who really does have a passion and sensitivity for music, and who reminds me of a modern-day Dick Asher, the second in the tri-umvirate who commands my utmost respect—started talking to me about doing a video. A video, for God's sake. My first reaction was: Why? He knows I'm not going to show any skin, I'm not going to dance, and I'm not going to wear $300 jeans. It's just against my religion, and I dislike hayrides and suburbia. "But it can buy you more time at home and less on the road," he replied. Point taken. But why

do I put up with the shenanigans of major labels at all, you may ask. They have deep pockets and marketing machinery, and I don't. I also don't have the organizational skills or desire to go sovereign, as many of my musician friends have done. And despite my opening metaphor about gas-station restrooms, I do still have an attachment to the major-label model. I've had long relationships in the record business. Ten years from now, of course, it will be unrecognizable to itself. Maybe then I'll actually miss it.

So here I am, a few years shy of beginning a third decade in this business, looking a little less … well, you know … than I did in 1979, and enjoying the freedom of being less so in so many regards. There are certain aspects of the game from which I am happily exempt. No one would even dare to suggest the kind of marketing makeover proposed to me back in the old days, not only because the idea has been so seamlessly woven into the music business that it defies verbalization, but also because I'm old enough to be the label staff's mother, damn it.

But as I gear up for the release of my twelfth record album, I look back longingly to simpler times, when a girl just needed a little bare skin and a come-hither look to thrill the masses and push that product from gold to platinum. Today I'm a grown woman with children who loves being at home and who finds no thrill in dirty dressing rooms and buses filled with hairy musicians in sweat pants. Still, I want my record to do well—so that I can spend even more time at home. So I'm leveraging my options. The record is called *Black Cadillac*, and it's a somewhat dark but elegiac cycle of songs about loss, ancestry, and personal history. Not the kind of record that lends itself to high-gloss images of inane sexiness. But what the hell, look for a full-on media onslaught with super-modern, digitally enhanced images of a gorgeous relic from 1979 (me) and a vintage Cadillac. You'll have no problem recognizing me. I'll be the one in the $400 jeans, flicking pieces of hay from my belly button as I exit the mall.

ROSANNE CASH

HER OWN WAY *Throughout her career, Rosanne Cash has defied easy categorization. Since moving to New York in the '90s, her music has increasingly reflected an unfettered—and lyrically bold—mix of rock, pop, folk, and country influences. Her 2006 release,* Black Cadillac, *an aural memoir of grief, family, and continuing relationships with the deceased, brought Cash universal praise.*

fiddle or other country instrument. Twain also showcased a pinup-ready body in her videos and photo shoots, spurring country's glam-battles of the last part of the decade. Twain took mainstream country farther into the pop and rock arena than it had ever been, and her looks proved as influential as her sound. In the late 1990s, while male artists could carry a few extra pounds or have a "regular-guy" quality to their appearance, country females were expected to look and dress like runway models.

As it turned out, record labels found beautiful women to be in abundance. Singing talent was not as abundant, but technology was aiding producers' ability to stamp out bum notes from sub-par singers. The Antares company developed an "Auto-Tune" device that had nothing to do with helping cars run better: "Auto-Tune" was a studio and stage aid that nudged flat or sharp singing into perfect tune. Soon, roughly 90 percent of major-label country artists were using vocal tuning technology (including Pro Tools as well as Auto-Tune) in live performances. Brooks and his producer, Allen Reynolds, eschewed the new technology that most Music Row producers and engineers eagerly relied upon.

"Our flaws are one of the things that set us so far apart," Brooks said. "I've watched meetings where people said, 'Oh my God, she's gorgeous: Let's get her a record deal.' 'But she can't sing.' 'Well, we'll fix that.' I think the temptation is there."

In visual art, music, and architecture, idiosyncrasy often bows in the face of perfection. As producers delivered auto-tuned performances to record labels, which then delivered those well-scrubbed performances to radio stations, the country airwaves began to suffer from sound-alike syndrome. Country album sales declined about 20 percent in 1996, a dip that some in the industry correctly saw as evidence that the Garth-led boom was over. Faith Hill, though, was immune to country's downward commercial trend. She built a catalog of pop-leaning hits in the 1990s that helped her head into the

PRETTY IN PINK *Faith Hill grew up singing to her record collection, using a hairbrush for a microphone. The practice paid off: Her debut album, 1995's* Take Me As I Am, *produced two No. 1 singles.*

Sound Effects? The Debate over Pro Tools

For decades, snobs sneered at country music, denigrating it as hillbilly music where everyone sang through their noses and played off-key. By the 1990s, critics took the opposite tack: the recordings had become so air-tight and note perfect that they suffocated individuality and emotion.

Indeed, the music once seen as backward proved to be at the forefront of the Pro Tools engineering movement that revolutionized pop-music recording at the end of the twentieth century. Pro Tools, as the auto-tuning technique is widely known, is actually a brand name for a complex digital recording system; one feature of the system allows engineers to change the pitch or tone of a vocal or instrumental note.

For a music that once touted authenticity as a major aspect of its appeal, auto-tuning would seem to present some thorny ethical questions. It's one thing for a studio producer to fix notes on a teen dancing machine like Britney Spears or an image-driven artist like Ashlee Simpson. It's a different deal altogether for a country singer, where truth-in-advertising is part of the promotional package.

Nonetheless, auto-tuning became commonplace in Nashville in the 1990s. Several superstars never worked in the studio without it, and by the 2000s, use of the engineering technique began being used religiously during concert performances by several leading country acts. As the practice became the norm, a background debate ensued: Is it cheating, or is it simply using all the technology available to make the best, and most cost-effective, recording possible? Others argued over another question: does an obsession with studio perfection process out the peculiarities that, in the past, resulted in some of country music's best-loved recordings? Imagine Johnny Cash being auto-tuned. Or Hank Williams, Ernest Tubb, Kitty Wells, and Loretta Lynn. All of them sang off-key at times; a couple of them rarely, if ever, hit a "correct" note. Yet their performances are legendary, despite—or maybe partly because of—their imperfections.

In any case, pitch-correction technology created a counter-movement of performers who proudly refused to use the tools, among them Martina McBride, Trisha Yearwood, Vince Gill, and Allison Moorer. The latter noted on one of her album's liner notes, "Absolutely no vocal tuning or pitch correction used in the making of this record."
MICHAEL MCCALL

PROFILES IN COUNTRY

FAITH HILL

BORN JACKSON, MISSISSIPPI,
SEPTEMBER 21, 1967
FIRST RECORDED 1993
INFLUENCES REBA MCENTIRE,
ELVIS PRESLEY, TAMMY WYNETTE
HITS "IT MATTERS TO ME,"
"THIS KISS," "BREATHE"

Though she is half of country's highest-profile couple, Faith Hill already owned a pair of gold and platinum albums before her 1996 marriage to Tim McGraw. Her story also rivals his for triumph over difficult odds.

As an adopted child growing up in Star, Mississippi, she first sang publicly at age three at church. A 1975 performance by Elvis Presley was the first concert she attended. But it was a Reba McEntire concert 10 years later that convinced Hill she should pursue stardom, and within a few years Hill quit college and moved to Nashville, where she worked first for singer Gary Morris, and then for McEntire herself.

Hill's earliest recordings displayed a soulful hitch in her voice and an empathy for working-class women. But as her profile broadened, she moved toward an expanded sound. When 1998's "This Kiss" gave her entrée into the pop market, she embraced it wholeheartedly, and took a more cutting-edge approach with the nine-million-selling *Breathe* album, which made her a superstar.

She stepped even farther from her roots with 2002's heavily produced *Cry*, which was poorly received by music critics. In 2005, she released *Fireflies*, a record that returned her to a more traditional country stance.

TOM ROLAND

BLACK MAGIC *Mr. And Mrs. Tim McGraw perform at the 2000 Academy of Country Music Awards. Their "Soul2Soul Tour" that year, which drew nearly 400,000 fans, marked one of country's most successful outings.*

> ## "People fall in love with Faith every night at her shows."
>
> **TIM MCGRAW ON FAITH HILL**

BREATHLESS *With 1998's* Faith *establishing her crossover appeal, Hill recorded* Breathe, *an all-out bid for pop stardom. The album entered the charts at No. 1 in 1999 and made her a household name, with a film role to follow.*

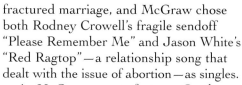

FAITH HILL
BREATHE

new millennium as one of country's most identifiable crossover stars. Though Tim McGraw, who became Hill's husband, began his rise as a singer of songs that risked being dismissed as mere novelties ("Indian Outlaw," "Refried Dreams"), he later became known for picking songs that were often more artistic and challenging than other material on the radio. He and Hill sang together on "Angry All the Time," Bruce Robison's story of a

fractured marriage, and McGraw chose both Rodney Crowell's fragile sendoff "Please Remember Me" and Jason White's "Red Ragtop"—a relationship song that dealt with the issue of abortion—as singles.

As McGraw rose to fortune, Garth Brooks's artistic and commercial influence took a tumble. In 1999, he issued *In the Life of Chris Gaines*, in which he tried on the role of a pop singer by masquerading as a fictitious rock idol, singing with

PROFILES IN COUNTRY

TIM MCGRAW

BORN DEHLI, LOUISIANA,
MAY 1, 1967
PLAYS GUITAR
FIRST RECORDED 1993
INFLUENCES KEITH WHITLEY,
MERLE HAGGARD
HITS "LIVE LIKE YOU WERE
DYING," "PLEASE REMEMBER
ME," "I LIKE IT, I LOVE IT"

When Tim McGraw emerged in 1994 with the novelty hit "Indian Outlaw," few guessed he would become country's reigning leading man. Yet his rough-around-the-edges delivery is instantly identifiable, and he blends traditional and contemporary country in a rock-style concert manner without alienating purists.

The illegitimate son of baseball pitcher Tug McGraw, he was raised as Tim Smith, a trucker's son who learned of his biological father at age 11. His musical breakthrough came with 1994's *Not a Moment Too Soon*. As husband to Faith Hill, he has evolved from a singer of radio-friendly songs to a mature father of three who tackles serious songs like "Drugs or Jesus" and "Angry All the Time." In addition to a career that garnered the CMA's Entertainer and Male Vocalist of the Year Awards, 21 No. 1 singles and sales of 33 million records, he delivered a powerful acting performance in the movie *Friday Night Lights*.

BEVERLY KEEL

"I like the unique, raspy timbre of Tim's voice. He has an innate country accent that shouts 'the real thing' to me. He phrases country, yet manages to cross all musical boundaries with the consistent delivery of good songs."

RONNIE DUNN ON TIM MCGRAW

> "The Dixie Chicks are free to speak their mind. They can say what they want to say.... [T]hey shouldn't have their feelings hurt just because some people don't want to buy their records when they speak out."
>
> **PRESIDENT GEORGE W. BUSH**

different inflections and with decidedly non-country backing. Brooks did so ostensibly to prime his audience for an upcoming Hollywood film in which he would play Chris Gaines. But the album was widely misunderstood and ridiculed. When it tanked, plans for the film were quickly scrubbed. That album's debacle marked the unofficial end of Brooks's eight-year term as country music's central player. Soon after, Brooks announced his pending retirement, celebrated with Capitol Records the milestone of 100 million albums sold, and released one more album, 2001's *Scarecrow*.

New Chicks in town

The new millennium gave us Hill and McGraw as country's first couple, Twain as the twang-pop princess rarely seen in Nashville, and the Dixie Chicks as country's top group. The Chicks' first two albums

featured sound mixes based in part on the mid-1990s recordings of Joy Lynn White, a splendid vocalist produced (to little commercial reward) by Paul Worley and Blake Chancey. Perhaps White's sound was ahead of its time, as the Chicks sold more than 12 million copies of their debut album, *Wide Open Spaces*. The group's next album, *Fly*, was also a tremendous success, and audiences flocked to see a female trio comprising a feisty vocalist, a virtuoso fiddle player, and a deft multi-instrumentalist.

Like McGraw, the Chicks used their success to exercise more creative control. By 2002, they were popular enough that

COWBOY PRESIDENT *Though he grew up a blueblood, President George W. Bush, who owns a ranch, says, "I'm a country music fan. I love it, always have."*

CHICKS RULE *The Dixie Chicks, the biggest-selling female band in history, proved themselves a power trio, vocally and instrumentally. (l-r) Emily Robison, Natalie Maines, Martie Maguire.*

they could release an acoustic album with a lead single ("Long Time Gone") that derided the failures of country radio ("They sound tired but they don't sound Haggard/They got money but they don't have Cash") and still raced up the radio charts. In March 2003, however, when Maines criticized President George W. Bush in a London concert, the group was pulled from many country radio playlists and effectively banished from the scene altogether. While Johnny Cash and Merle Haggard could have songs with differing perspectives on war and protest during Vietnam, there was no room in country music circa 2002 for an outspoken, alternative viewpoint. The reason for that had less to do with national culture than with the corporate culture of radio.

Business consolidation

With a single act of legislation, the Telecommunications Act of 1996 opened the doors for corporate conglomerates to own an unlimited number of radio stations. Beginning in the 1940s, the US Federal Communications Commission had strictly limited owners to a single station, but over the decades those restrictions eroded. Still, until 1996 station ownership remained

capped at 40 per owner. But the 1996 act allowed companies to acquire radio stations with no restriction. The result of this deregulation was swift consolidation. In seven years, Clear Channel Communications, the biggest radio owner of all, grew to own more than 1,200 stations. As of 2002, just 10 companies controlled a 65 percent share of the radio audience, and those companies were likely to program a station in Charlotte, North Carolina, in exactly the same manner as, for instance, a station in Buffalo, New York.

Through corporate edicts, the powerful Cumulus and Cox companies banned Dixie Chicks records from being played on their stations after Maines's statements, a situation that troubled even Bush allies such as

BUSHWHACKED *(Left) Not everyone held the Dixie Chicks' remarks against them. In 2003, when President Bush appeared at a political fundraiser in Lexington, Kentucky, one fan demonstrated her support.*

PROFILES IN COUNTRY

THE DIXIE CHICKS

MARTIE ERWIN MAGUIRE
BORN YORK, PENNSYLVANIA, OCTOBER 12, 1969
EMILY ERWIN ROBISON
BORN PITTSFIELD, MASSACHUSETTS, AUGUST 16, 1972
NATALIE MAINES
BORN LUBBOCK, TEXAS, OCTOBER 14, 1974

FIRST RECORDED IN CURRENT LINEUP 1997
INFLUENCES DALE EVANS, DOLLY PARTON, BLUEGRASS, AC/DC
HITS "WIDE OPEN SPACES," "GOODBYE EARL," "TRAVELIN' SOLDIER"

No act spiced up turn-of-the-millennium country like the Dixie Chicks, an iconoclastic trio from Texas whose talent was equaled by their penchant for drama. Born as a rootsy, retro cowgirl band in the 1990s, the Chicks put themselves through a mid-course, pop makeover—adding brassy lead singer Natalie Maines, yet refusing to pack up their old-school fiddle, banjo, and dobro.

Their first single together stirred interest, but "There's Your Trouble" and the title track of *Wide Open Spaces* exploded. The multiplatinum album earned numerous accolades. *Fly*, the follow-up, achieved similar success, and the Chicks became country's biggest superstars since Garth and Shania.

The band attracted controversy, but they ruffled feathers like never before, when Maines made a crack about President George W. Bush on the eve of the 2003 Iraq war. The London audience chuckled, but country radio bridled. The band more or less apologized, and then retreated to Texas to nurture new families.

Whether the lull portended the end is yet to be seen for a band that's proven as unpredictable as musically exciting.

CRAIG HAVIGHURST

CLASSIC COUNTRY RECORDING

ALAN JACKSON
"Where Were You (When the World Stopped Turning)"

Where were you when the world stopped turning on that September day?

WRITTEN BY ALAN JACKSON AND RECORDED OCTOBER 29, 2001

NO. 28 POP, NO. 1 COUNTRY, DECEMBER 29, 2001

In the wake of the terrorist attacks of September 11, 2001, the entire country was reeling from the devastation. So, too, was singer Alan Jackson. "For a couple weeks I couldn't do anything," he says. "Then I got kind of stabilized. I thought about writing something, but nothing would come naturally. I didn't want to write a patriotic song. So I didn't force it." In late October, Jackson woke up at three in the morning. "The song was just there," he says.

The song was **"Where Were You (When the World Stopped Turning),"** Jackson's moving ballad about 9/11. The quiet song was emotional and introspective, not political or preachy. It included a chorus of gentle, spiritual renewal: "But I know Jesus and I talk to God / And I remember this from when I was young / Faith, hope, and love are some good things He gave us / And the greatest is love."

In early November, Jackson performed the song for the first time on the nationally televised CMA Awards show. It hit a massive and immediate nerve. Inundated by listener requests, radio stations began playing the audio portion of Jackson's live CMA Awards performance. A studio version was soon released as well and headed straight for No. 1.

CHRISSIE DICKINSON

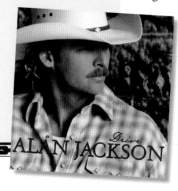

AGE-OLD SOUND *Alt-country star Gillian Welch, with partner David Rawlings, helped anchor the* O Brother, Where Art Thou? *soundtrack. Here they perform at Newport in 2005.*

Republican Senator John McCain, who called the ban "an incredible, incredible act." McCain cited the ban as an example of how deregulation could lead to "an erosion of the First Amendment," which guarantees free speech.

Whether or not deregulation curtailed free speech, it certainly affected the kinds of songs and sounds that reached radio. Though superstars such as Alan Jackson or the Dixie Chicks could record music that was quite individual, most songs were expected to fit neatly into a prescribed format, with one song's drums and bass not dissimilar from the next. The goal of radio programmers was not to sell albums for artists and labels—it was to keep people from turning the dial, as they might whenever they heard something out of the ordinary. Thus country blockbusters such as the *O Brother, Where Art Thou?* soundtrack could win Grammys and sell millions, but could not break through to FM country airwaves.

Radio was not the only facet of the music business to change through consolidation. In the boom years of the early 1990s, numerous record companies dotted Music Row. By mid-2005, only four major companies—Universal, Sony BMG, Warner Bros., and EMI—were left. Nashville's publishing houses have experienced a similar decline. Likewise, only four major publishers remain—EMI, Sony BMG, Universal, and Warner Bros.—all owned by the aforementioned companies, which control the record labels. Songwriters who work for these publishers have an accelerated chance of getting their songs recorded by major-label artists, but they are often encouraged to cowrite as many songs as possible instead of relying on the still, solitary, creative moments that produced many of country music's greatest songs. In 1961, there was an average of 1.12 writers per No. 1 *Billboard* country hit. By the mid-1990s, that figure was well above two writers per hit, and it continues to climb, meaning more hit songs are written by three writers than one. As with all things done by committee, the collaborations can sometimes lead to notions better than any one person would have conceived, but the final product can also end up more formulaic than the original idea.

When the writers at those companies turn in their work, the songs are sorted through, and the ones deemed most commercial are pitched to producers, A&R people and, on rare occasion, the artists themselves. There is safety in numbers, but safety is rarely an element of great art.

Timeless songs

Martina McBride, a masterful pop-country singer who won the CMA Female Vocalist of the Year prize in 1999, 2002, 2003, and 2004, is an artist who tends to value songs penned by one writer. Several of her hits have come from only one pen,

such as Leslie Satcher's "When God-Fearin' Women Get the Blues," and two songs by Gretchen Peters, "My Baby Loves Me" and "Independence Day." Like many of the country format's core artists, McBride arrived on the scene with inspirations that ranged from country icons (Patsy Cline and Loretta Lynn) to pop stars (Pat Benatar, the Eagles), and she regularly embraced pop keyboards, rock guitars, processed drums, and other elements that had through the years become central parts of the country-music soundscape.

Significantly, though, in 2005 McBride chose to record *Timeless*, an album of 18 country classics from the '50s, '60s, and '70s, including such gems as Hank Williams's hit "You Win Again," Loretta Lynn's "You Ain't Woman Enough," and

STAYING POWER *Martina McBride began as an opening act for Garth Brooks. Her expansive voice and wide-ranging themes won her a following beyond country, including a spot on two Lilith Fair tours.*

CLASSIC COUNTRY RECORDING

MARTINA MCBRIDE "Independence Day"

Roll the stone away, let the guilty pay, it's Independence Day.
WRITTEN BY GRETCHEN PETERS AND RECORDED ON JANUARY 20, 1993 NO. 12 COUNTRY, AUGUST 26, 1994.

When Martina McBride recorded her 1993 album, *The Way That I Am,* she had no idea that **"Independence Day"** would emerge as a career-defining song, or that it would become a validating anthem for women triumphing over domestic abuse. She just knew she loved it.

"I think people respond to the passion and power of this song," says McBride. "It's so well written; it's poetry, really, filled with imagery, compassion, strength, desperation—you just feel it on a gut level."

Still, the song didn't crack the *Billboard*'s country Top Ten list. Some radio programmers objected to the song's mother fighting back by burning down the family home. But the song received enough exposure that fans flocked to the stores, resulting in McBride's first million-selling CD.

"I've heard all kinds of stories about this song from fans," McBride says. "It has brought strength, relief, absolvement from guilt, and most notably, been the catalyst for women to leave abusive relationships."

BEVERLY KEEL

> ## COUNTRY MUSIC HAS ALWAYS BEEN A FORMAT OF MUSIC THAT WRITES TO AND FOR THE REAL PEOPLE OUT THERE, THE WORKIN' MAN.
>
> **ALAN JACKSON**

Kris Kristofferson's "Help Me Make It Through the Night." Martina and husband/sound engineer John McBride even went so far as to hire older Nashville session players and use outdated, analog recording equipment. The surprising result: the throwback album debuted at No. 1 on the *Billboard* country album chart; in its first two weeks on the market it sold more than 250,000 copies, the best sales start of McBride's career.

Yet despite such successes for traditional country, at times in the new century country radio has played music that featured no definably "country" elements: the answer to the "Why is this country?" question became, "Because the proceeds from sales end up lining Music Row pockets." And that was true enough.

Growing pains

"Country music has expanded so much in the last 15 years," said Troy Gentry of southern rock-tinged duo Montgomery Gentry. "Garth Brooks is probably the one to thank for that. In the next 20 years or so, I think pop and country are going to get very close to merging." If they haven't already.

Alan Jackson, a staunch advocate of traditional country, once sang, "Don't rock

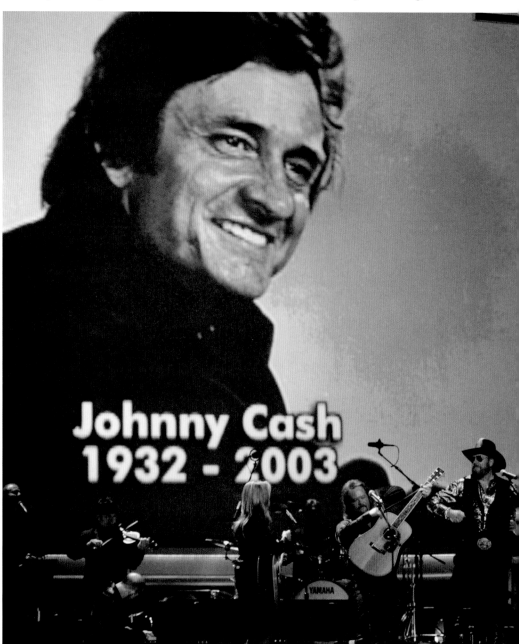

GOODBYE, OLD FRIEND *Two months after the death of Johnny Cash, Sheryl Crow, Travis Tritt, Hank Williams Jr., Kris Kristofferson, Willie Nelson, and the Nitty Gritty Dirt Band sang him home at the CMA Awards, November 2003.*

the jukebox/I want to hear some Jones." For his part, George Jones agreed in full with Jackson's statement, and he regretted what he saw as the dilution of country.

"I know things change, but you would not turn on a classical station to hear rock music, nor would you turn on a jazz station and expect to hear rap music," Jones explained. "I believe there is room for all genres of music, and we should hold on to our heritage and make true 'Country Music' that fans still love."

Increasingly, the kind of country music Jones talked about was seen by radio programmers as a dusty relic. In a song

called "Murder on Music Row" (2000) that garnered a deserving CMA Award, Jackson and George Strait asserted, "The almighty dollar and the lust for worldwide fame / Slowly killed tradition, and for that someone should hang." As if agreeing with the song's sentiment, 650 WSM-AM air personality Eddie Stubbs often quoted the Bailes Brothers in telling listeners, "We're living in the last days now." Meanwhile, Garth Brooks rested at home, Shania Twain recorded infrequently (releasing only one studio album between 1998 and 2005), and country album sales waned in the first years of the 2000s. And the period from 1989 to 2005 saw the deaths of legends including Johnny Cash, Roy Acuff, Tammy Wynette, Roger Miller, Bill Monroe, Conway Twitty, Chet Atkins, and Waylon Jennings.

Though each of those losses left holes that could not be filled, it was Cash's death, on September 12, 2003 at age 71, that most captured the world's attention. He had been in frail health and had been dealt a crushing blow when his wife, fellow performer June Carter Cash, passed away four months earlier. Yet he seemed such an indomitable force that news of his death (caused by respiratory failure brought on by complications from diabetes) was greeted more with shock than with understanding. "I guess I'll try to get numbly through the day as I start trying to adjust to the total alien concept of a world without Johnny Cash in it," said music industry executive Andy McLenon on the afternoon of the 12th.

After his passing, Cash was memorialized with concert tributes, musical reissues, and a major Hollywood biopic called *Walk the Line*. Again and again, his remarkable story was re-told: his dire and dusty youth in Arkansas; his presence at Sun Records in Memphis in the 1950s when he, Sam Phillips, Elvis Presley, Jerry Lee Lewis, Carl Perkins, Jack Clement, and a few others created the sounds we now call rockabilly and rock & roll; his 1960s embrace of folk-based artists such as Bob Dylan and Joan Baez at a time

REEL LIFE *Actress Reese Witherspoon won an Oscar for her portrayal of June Carter in* Walk the Line, *the 2005 film about her redemptive marriage to Johnny Cash. Joaquin Phoenix convincingly captured Cash's righteousness and rage.*

PROFILES IN COUNTRY

TOBY KEITH

BORN CLINTON, OKLAHOMA,
JULY 8, 1961
INFLUENCES HANK WILLIAMS JR.,
ALABAMA, WAYLON JENNINGS
PLAYS GUITAR
HITS "SHOULD'VE BEEN A
COWBOY," "COURTESY OF THE RED,
WHITE AND BLUE (THE ANGRY
AMERICAN)," "HOW DO YOU LIKE
ME NOW?!"

Toby Keith has a chip on his shoulder as big as the heartland. He cultivates, in hit after hit, a visceral sense of grievance, whether berating the woman in "How Do You Like Me Now?!" for passing him by before he was famous, or flipping off a Nashville establishment he thinks doesn't respect him. Keith's always on the lookout for anyone who might be looking down on him.

He grew up in Oklahoma, the son of an oil-company executive. After graduating high school, he worked as a roughneck and played semi-pro football, and spent most of the 1980s working the oil fields by day and the bars by night. His debut Mercury Records single, "Should've Been a Cowboy," topped the charts in 1993.

Keith bounced between record companies, but racked up 13 Top 10s in the 1990s. In the new century, the burly 6'4" singer kicked up the testosterone with a string of rollicking, egocentric hits, including the hawkish 9/11 anthem, "The Angry American (Courtesy of the Red, White, and Blue)," which some criticized as jingoistic. Keith reveled in the controversy, titling his 2003 album *Shock'n Y'all*. In 2005, he announced the formation of his own record label.

DAVID CANTWELL

when mainstream Nashville's politics ran counter to those antiwar voices; his support of disenfranchised people and of justice-seeking causes; his epic struggles with alcohol and drug addiction; his love affair with June Carter; his creative descent into contemporary irrelevancy in the 1980s, followed by his unprecedented return to Grammy-winning potency in the 1990s.

The day after the death of the Man In Black, Emmylou Harris said simply, "No body of work comes close to what his particular body of work is."

Toby, Kenny, and Keith

The early 2000s, however, were quite good to three artists who debuted in the '90s, but became stars in the new millennium: Toby Keith, Kenny Chesney, and Keith Urban. Keith's "Should've Been a Cowboy" (1993) was the most-played country radio song of the 1990s, but it wasn't until 2000 that he achieved blockbuster sales numbers, when he began recording songs that matched his brash image. A public war-of-words with Dixie Chick Natalie Maines didn't hurt his notoriety, nor did "attitude" songs such as "Courtesy of the Red, White and Blue (The Angry American)," "How Do You Like Me Now?!"

Chesney had been a perennial B-list country artist in the 1990s, but by 2004 he was selling more concert tickets than anybody in the music business except pop star Prince. Calling himself "the poster boy for hard work," Chesney transformed his body through intense workouts, and transformed his image and sound as well.

"I sit and listen to some of my early records and just cringe," he said in 2004. "I love George Strait with all my heart, but when I quit trying to be him and started just being myself, that's when my whole world changed."

Urban broke into Nashville in the 1990s as leader of a trio called the Ranch, and made his solo debut in

NASHVILLE MAKEOVER
Kenny Chesney, shown at the 2003 ACM Awards, transformed himself physically—and musically—from a cookie-cutter hat act to a rock-steady voice for kids caught in the uneasy coming-of-age transition from teen years to adulthood. In 2004, he was named CMA Entertainer of the Year.

PROFILES IN COUNTRY

KENNY CHESNEY

BORN LUTTRELL, TENNESSEE, MARCH 28, 1968
INFLUENCES GARTH BROOKS, GEORGE STRAIT, BRUCE SPRINGSTEEN, JIMMY BUFFETT
PLAYS GUITAR
FIRST RECORDED 1993
HITS "THE GOOD STUFF," "THERE GOES MY LIFE," "WHEN THE SUN GOES DOWN"

As with Garth Brooks, Kenny Chesney succeeded because he anticipated that audiences were primed to embrace country music embroidered with rock influences—in his case, the "classic rock" of the '70s and '80s.

A native of the Smoky Mountains, Chesney grew up in Chet Atkins's hometown. But when Chesney was learning to play guitar, he was more likely to crank Lynyrd Skynyrd's "Sweet Home Alabama" than anything in Atkins's repertoire. At East Tennessee State University, he played music while earning an advertising degree.

Most of Chesney's early successes were earnest piano-driven ballads. But the danceable rock & roll of "She Thinks My Tractor's Sexy" gave the newly buff-and-bronzed Chesney the image of an easy-rocking sex symbol for younger fans. On the title tracks to multiplatinum albums *No Shirt, No Shoes, No Problems* and *When the Sun Goes Down*, Chesney sings of lazing around on the beach and partying, an ideal soundtrack for spring-break getaways.

In 2005, he briefly wed actress Renée Zellweger.

DAVID CANTWELL

1999. The ensuing years found him becoming the first Australian-reared country star (discounting Olivia Newton-John) and the first major star to emerge from Capital Records' Nashville stable since Garth Brooks. His unabashed love of pop and rock melodies, and his affection for country, won fans including Loretta Lynn.

"I'm not a traditional country artist," said Urban, the singer of "Somebody Like You," and other hits. "At the same time, I'm not ashamed of the country side of what I do. It frustrates me that in this genre people think we have to push that country thing aside, like we're ashamed of it. What we're ashamed of is the ignorant perception of some people in society about country music. I don't put banjos on my record to make it 'country,' I put them on there because I think it sounds cool."

Redneck Woman

In 2004, her "Redneck Woman" single helped Gretchen Wilson become the first female country superstar to emerge since

GUITARZAN *Keith Urban, in concert in Greensboro, North Carolina, 2004, combined guitar wizardry with modern sex appeal and fetching country pop to become the 2005 CMA Entertainer of the Year.*

the mid-1990s, and the first rookie superstar the music had seen since the days of Clint Black, Garth Brooks, and Billy Ray Cyrus. A Jack Daniels-swigging antithesis of the fashion-plate female that had been in favor for years, Wilson was raised in the rural farming community of Pocahontas, Illinois. Like Garth Brooks, she was told she lacked the photo-spread looks and corporate-ready polish necessary to succeed in country music. And like Brooks, she was initially passed over by most of Music Row's major labels.

"My opinion is that a lot of people were just scared of me, because I had a vision," she said. That vision paid off to the tune of 3.2 million albums sold in 2004, and in 2005 Wilson won the Academy of Country Music and Country Music Association's top female vocalist trophies.

STILL COOL *Merle Haggard, one of the quintessential artists of the '60s, found it increasingly hard to get played on the radio after the millennium. But his music remained inventive, and new performers continued to show his influence.*

> ## THAT GRETCHEN WILSON, MAN, SHE REMINDS ME SO MUCH OF JANIS JOPLIN I CAN HARDLY STAND IT.

KRIS KRISTOFFERSON TO BIG & RICH'S JOHN RICH

"I hope I can help girls out there see that being yourself is the most rewarding thing you can do," Wilson said after collecting those awards. "You don't have to fit the right mold, weigh exactly a buck-twenty, and have the right hair."

Part of a tightly affiliated pack of artists called the Muzik Mafia—a group that includes the duo Big & Rich and an African-American rapper named Cowboy Troy—Wilson is the embodiment of the rags-to-riches story that draws music industry hopefuls to Nashville each year. Her success inspires hope, though not assurance, that country music could be moving into a spring season.

To be sure, the country-music industry is rife with difficulties. Corporate consolidation limits opportunities for artists and writers like never before, major record companies have not found ways to successfully market country outside mainstream radio or film exposure, and many of Nashville's finest singers, players, writers, and songs continue to go unnoticed by Music Row. In Nashville, music fans can go hear Kevin Gordon at the Family Wash, Todd Snider at the Belcourt Theatre, Pat McLaughlin at Douglas Corner, or David Olney at the Bluebird Café, and find songs and performances that are more

FAST-RISING STAR *Phoenix native Dierks Bentley came to Nashville at 19, but found the music business hard to crack. While working as a researcher at TNN television, he polished his demos and his performance chops.*

rooted, distinctive, and intelligent than much of what is played on country radio. And Johnny Cash's admonition that the music must occasionally get back to Emmylou Harris is, at present, being summarily ignored.

That said, Gretchen Wilson's rise offers an example of talent coming to the forefront in a way that was not predicted or prescribed by industry experts, and newcomers Dierks Bentley, Joe Nichols, and Shelly Fairchild are combining a solid sense of tradition with a contemporary flair. Mainstream country boasts two triple-threat stars who play lead guitar, sing, and write with considerable skill in Keith Urban and Brad Paisley. At the superstar level, Tim McGraw, Kenny Chesney, Toby Keith, and Alan Jackson have proven themselves willing to take creative chances with song selection and delivery. As sales figures wax once again after a significant turn-of-the-century dip, there is cause for optimism.

"There seems to be a freshness, the same way there was a freshness in the late 1980s and early 1990s," said Kix

Brooks of Brooks & Dunn in May 2005. "Things are coming back around."

If one of Jimmie Rodgers's fans from the 1920s could be transported into the front row for one of Brooks & Dunn's amped-up, high-energy, fire-spewing stage shows, that fan might have a tough time recognizing the connection between the acoustic hillbilly sounds of old and the rock-informed songs of today. What is now called "country" began as a simple but marrow-deep means of expression. Changes in technology, amenities, and consciousness are constant threats to render any static art form obsolete, and so country has never remained static. It electrified to adapt to honky-tonk jukeboxes, it took on a healthy backbeat to adapt to rock & roll, it shifted thematic perspective in the 1960s and '70s, and its latest incarnation would be dishonest if its purveyors did not acknowledge the impact of twenty-first century sounds and

ALL JACKED UP Gretchen Wilson, who galvanized young female fans, might have proved a one-hit wonder after the wildly popular "Redneck Woman." But her ongoing success suggests she'll be here for the party for years to come.

situations—from satellite television to terrorism to hip-hop.

But, at its best, country music's links to the past have to do with more than cowboy hats. The stories, in particular, continue to deal with toils and triumphs of common people. And the lyrical goal is still to deliver those stories simply but strongly, with quick impact and deep resonance. At the mid-point of the new century's first decade, Gretchen Wilson was singing those stories in a way that delighted both teenaged fans and heroes like Loretta Lynn. And Lee Ann Womack was winning the CMA's Album of the Year award for a piece of work many hailed as a return to tradition. It featured not only thrilling vocals with a distinctive twang and arrangements embracing both lush strings and prominent steel guitar—but also songs about drinking, cheating, and other old-fashioned subjects that can't be throwbacks because they remain as close as the local barroom. The title of that album may be taken as a threat, a boast, or a prayer. It rings true for country music no matter the interpretation: *There's More Where That Came From.*

TOP TEN COUNTRY GROOVES BY KEITH URBAN

1. "Tulsa Time"
Don Williams (ABC, 1978) *Recorded by Eric Clapton and Don Williams, but Don's is my favorite.*

2. "Swamp Witch"
Jim Stafford (MGM, 1973) *This is a killer song and a wicked groove.*

3. "I Think I'll Just Stay Here and Drink"
Merle Haggard (MCA, 1980) *A classic Haggard stomper. Great song, great voice, great groove.*

4. "Fly Away"
Don Williams (ABC, 1978) *Don Williams's records are some of the most original progressive and rhythmic grooves you'll ever hear.*

5. "Save a Horse, Ride a Cowboy"
Big & Rich (Warner Bros., 2004) *When I heard this song on the radio, I was floored.*

6. "Good Hearted Woman"
Waylon Jennings (RCA, 1972) *Ahhh—the all-time classic Waylon stomp. Peanut shells on the floor, cold beer in hand, and this song comin' out of a jukebox in the corner— who's with me??!*

7. "Rake and Ramblin' Man"
Don Williams (ABC, 1978) *Another great and original Don groove. Check out Don's spoken recitations. He's probably my favorite male country singer of all time.*

8. "Jolene"
Dolly Parton (RCA, 1973) *Congas and nylon-string acoustic guitar on one of the most infectious rhythms ever.*

9. "Do You Think Hank Done It This Way?"
Waylon Jennings (RCA, 1975) *More peanut shells, more beer, more jukebox in the corner. Wailin' with Waylon.*

10. "I Believe in You"
Don Williams (MCA, 1980) *Mature, sultry perfection. You da man, Don!*

Afterword

Dear Reader,

I hope you've enjoyed your journey through country music history. It's the same trip visitors take when they walk through the galleries of the Country Music Hall of Fame and Museum in Nashville. This book begins at the music's roots in folk song, blues, sacred music, and early popular music, and continues through changes brought about by technology, historical events, and popular taste, to arrive at country music present. We do the same in the museum, in our core exhibit, *Sing Me Back Home: A Journey Through Country Music.*

To help us tell the story in this book, we were fortunate to enlist two highly regarded country music authorities: former museum staff member Paul Kingsbury and noted journalist Alanna Nash. They, in turn, persuaded many of the top scholars in the field of country music to contribute to this important work. We owe a great debt of gratitude to Paul and Alanna.

Aided by photo researcher F. Lynne Bachleda, they drew upon the museum's rich collection of photos, artifacts, sheet music, songbooks, costumes, and other research materials. We are custodians of those materials because country artists, music business people, collectors, record companies, and photographers have entrusted their legacies to us. We are grateful for that trust. On this page you'll find the names of all the members of the Country Music Hall of Fame. This book honors them as recipients of country music's highest honor.

This book represents the most comprehensive sampling ever of our museum's treasures. Its cover and the chapter-opening artwork come from Jim Sherraden, manager of Hatch Show Print, a venerable show-poster shop located in downtown Nashville and owned by the museum. The Country Music Hall of Fame and Museum is a 501 (c)(3), not-for-profit organization, accredited by the American Association of Museums. The *Wall Street Journal* has called us a "Mecca with a mission." I hope this book will inspire you to visit the museum for the first time, or to come back again to see our ever-changing exhibit offerings. Just as much, I hope it will enrich your experience of country music, live and on record, leaving you—to borrow a phrase from the Skillet Lickers—"red hot and rarin' to go."

Kyle Young

Director
Country Music Hall of Fame and Museum (www.countrymusichalloffame.com)

The Members of the Country Music Hall of Fame®
(with years of induction)

1961 Jimmie Rodgers	1976 Paul Cohen	1988 Loretta Lynn	1999 Dolly Parton
1961 Fred Rose	1976 Kitty Wells	1988 Roy Rogers	1999 Conway Twitty
1961 Hank Williams	1977 Merle Travis	1989 Jack Stapp	2000 Charley Pride
1962 Roy Acuff	1978 Grandpa Jones	1989 Cliffie Stone	2000 Faron Young
1964 Tex Ritter	1979 Hubert Long	1989 Hank Thompson	2001 Bill Anderson
1965 Ernest Tubb	1979 Hank Snow	1990 Tennessee Ernie Ford	2001 The Delmore Brothers
1966 Eddy Arnold	1980 Johnny Cash	1991 Boudleaux and Felice	2001 The Everly Brothers
1966 James R. Denny	1980 Connie B. Gay	Bryant	2001 Don Gibson
1966 George D. Hay	1980 Original Sons of the	1992 George Jones	2001 Homer & Jethro
1966 Uncle Dave Macon	Pioneers	1992 Frances Williams Preston	2001 Waylon Jennings
1967 Red Foley	1981 Vernon Dalhart	1993 Willie Nelson	2001 The Jordanaires
1967 J. L. Frank	1981 Grant Turner	1994 Merle Haggard	2001 Don Law
1967 Jim Reeves	1982 Lefty Frizzell	1995 Roger Miller	2001 The Louvin Brothers
1967 Stephen H. Sholes	1982 Roy Horton	1995 Jo Walker-Meador	2001 Ken Nelson
1968 Bob Wills	1982 Marty Robbins	1996 Patsy Montana	2001 Webb Pierce
1969 Gene Autry	1983 Little Jimmy Dickens	1996 Buck Owens	2001 Sam Phillips
1970 Original Carter Family	1984 Ralph Sylvester Peer	1996 Ray Price	2002 Bill Carlisle
1970 Bill Monroe	1984 Floyd Tillman	1997 Harlan Howard	2002 Porter Wagoner
1971 Arthur Edward Satherley	1985 Lester Flatt & Earl	1997 Brenda Lee	2003 Floyd Cramer
1972 Jimmie H. Davis	Scruggs	1997 Cindy Walker	2003 Carl Smith
1973 Chet Atkins	1986 Benjamin F. "Whitey"	1998 George Morgan	2004 Jim Foglesong
1973 Patsy Cline	Ford (The Duke of	1998 Elvis Presley	2004 Kris Kristofferson
1974 Owen Bradley	Paducah)	1998 E. W. "Bud" Wendell	2005 Alabama
1974 Frank "Pee Wee" King	1986 Wesley H. Rose	1998 Tammy Wynette	2005 DeFord Bailey
1975 Minnie Pearl	1987 Rod Brasfield	1999 Johnny Bond	2005 Glen Campbell

Contributors

David Cantwell, coauthor of *Heartaches by the Number: Country Music's 500 Greatest Singles*, writes and teaches college English in Kansas City, Missouri.

Mary Chapin Carpenter has sold 12 million records, and won five Grammys and two CMA Awards.

Rosanne Cash is a Grammy-winning singer and songwriter, and the author of *Bodies of Water*, *Penelope Jane: A Fairy's Tale*, and numerous essays.

Kevin Coffey has written numerous articles and CD booklets about vintage country music. With Cary Ginell, he coauthored *A Discography of Western Swing and Hot String Bands, 1928–42*.

Peter Cooper writes about music for the *Tennessean*. He is the author of *Hub City Music Makers*, a book about the musical history of Spartanburg, South Carolina.

Wayne W. Daniel is an old-time music authority and the author of *Pickin' on Peachtree: A History of Country Music in Atlanta, Georgia*.

Chrissie Dickinson, a Chicago freelance writer, is a former editor of the *Journal of Country Music*.

Colin Escott was born in England but currently resides in Tennessee. His books include *Good Rockin' Tonight*, *Hank Williams: The Biography*, and several collections of journalism.

Chet Flippo is editorial director of CMT and CMT.com. He has worked as senior editor of *Rolling Stone* and as Nashville bureau chief of *Billboard*.

Holly George-Warren, an award-winning writer and editor, is the author of several books, including *Cowboy! How Hollywood Invented the Wild West*.

Michael Gray is associate editor of the *Journal of Country Music*. He is the co-producer of the Grammy-winning *Night Train to Nashville*.

Douglas B. Green, Ranger Doug of the Grammy Award-winning quartet Riders in the Sky, is the author of three books, including *Singing in the Saddle*.

Craig Havighurst was a writer for the *Tennessean* and is now an independent journalist and producer based in Nashville. He is the author of a forthcoming history of Nashville's WSM radio.

Murphy Henry is a bluegrass musician and a columnist for *Bluegrass Unlimited* and *Banjo Newsletter*; she is at work on a book about women in bluegrass.

Elek Horvath, a regular contributor to the *Journal of Country Music*, is coauthor of *Hatch Show Print: The Story of a Great American Print Shop*.

Geoffrey Himes has written about pop music for the *Washington Post* since 1977. His latest book, *Born in the U.S.A.*, spotlights Bruce Springsteen.

Martha Hume, former editor of the *Journal of Country Music*, is a freelance writer and editor who has contributed to many national publications.

Jack Hurst wrote a syndicated country column for the *Chicago Tribune* for 24 years. He was presented the Country Music Association's inaugural Media Achievement Award.

Beverly Keel is a professor at Middle Tennessee State University and an award-winning freelance journalist.

Rich Kienzle, author of *Southwest Shuffle*, has written about country since 1975. He's also co-produced numerous album reissues and annotated more than 300 such collections.

Paul Kingsbury has written and edited numerous books on country music, including *The Grand Ole Opry History of Country Music* and *The Encyclopedia of Country Music*.

Barbara Biszick-Lockwood, a trained musician and computer-software specialist, is at work on a biography of Jean Aberbach of Hill & Range Music.

Guy Logsdon is a western music expert, and author of *"The Whorehouse Bells Were Ringing" and Other Songs Cowboys Sing*.

Bill C. Malone is a retired history professor who has written several books, including *Country Music USA*, the first general survey of the subject ever written.

Michael McCall, a former editor of *Country Music* magazine, contributes regularly to national publications. He has authored biographies of Johnny Cash, Garth Brooks, and Shania Twain.

Edward Morris is a former *Billboard* country music editor, and reports for CMT.com. His books include *Garth Brooks: Platinum Cowboy* and *Edward Morris' Complete Guide to Country Music Videos*.

Michael Martin Murphey is a western recording artist and historian, and the founder of Michael Martin Murphey's Westfest, an annual celebration of the American West.

Alanna Nash won the Country Music Association's Media Achievement Award in 2004, as well as the Belmont Award for the Best Book in Country Music. She is the author of six books, including *Dolly: The Biography*.

Robert K. Oermann is a former *Tennessean* reporter, and has been author or coauthor of seven books, as well as writer for many TV and radio productions on country music.

Jay Orr, senior director for museum programs at the Country Music Hall of Fame and Museum, has been writing about country music for more than 20 years, including stints at the *Nashville Banner* and the *Tennessean*.

Nolan Porterfield is the author of five books, including acclaimed biographies on Jimmie Rodgers and folksong collector John Lomax.

Ronnie Pugh is a Nashville librarian and writer, and is the author of *Ernest Tubb: The Texas Troubadour*.

Tom Roland is a former *Tennessean* reporter and has written about country music for over 25 years. He is author of the *Billboard Book of #1 Country Hits*.

John W. Rumble is senior historian at the Country Music Hall of Fame and Museum, and has contributed liner notes to many historic reissue albums.

Dave Samuelson has been writing about music for nearly 40 years and has produced and annotated many LP and CD reissues.

Tamara Saviano is the president and founder of American Roots Publishing. She won a 2005 Grammy for coproducing *Beautiful Dreamer: The Songs of Stephen Foster*.

Mike Seeger has devoted his life to singing and playing southern traditional music and producing documentaries and concerts of traditional music.

Charlie Seemann is executive director of the Western Folklife Center in Elko, Nevada, and author of numerous articles about western and country music.

Richard D. Smith is a bluegrass musician and writer. He is the author of *Bluegrass: An Informal Guide* and *Can't You Hear Me Callin': The Life of Bill Monroe*.

Michael Streissguth is the author of *Johnny Cash at Folsom Prison: The Making of a Masterpiece*, and three other books, including a biography of Eddy Arnold.

Jon Weisberger is a freelance writer, songwriter, and musician, and is a contributing editor for *No Depression*.

David Wilds was born in Nashville, and grew up backstage at the Ryman watching his father, Honey Wilds of Jamup & Honey.

Charles K. Wolfe, a historian of early country music, is author of over twenty books, including *A Good Natured Riot: The Birth of the Grand Ole Opry*.

Illustrator: printmaker Jim Sherraden has been manager of Hatch Show Print since 1984. He is coauthor of *Hatch Show Print: The History of a Great American Poster Shop*.

Glossary

A&R
Abbreviation for "Artists and Repertoire," the department at a record company responsible for finding artists and songs for them to record, and for overseeing the production of recordings.

AFM
The American Federation of Musicians, the American musicians' union, founded in 1896. The Nashville chapter was founded in 1902.

ASCAP
The American Society of Composers, Authors, and Publishers, a performing rights organization created in 1914 to collect payments for songwriters and music publishers for public performance of their works in live venues and via radio, television, and other means. Its chief rival in the US is BMI.

Artist
A recording artist; usually a singer.

Alt-country
Alternative country music, i.e., music outside the mainstream of country music played on Top 40 country radio stations and appearing on the country-music record charts. Also known as Americana.

Ballet book
Colloquial for "ballad book"; a homemade collection of ballads and songs.

Barbershop quartet
A group of male singers specializing in improvised, unaccompanied, four-part harmony singing of sentimental songs; this style of singing was popular from the turn of the 19th century to the 20th.

Barn dance
A radio or television variety show featuring country music. The Grand Ole Opry is the longest-running radio barn dance.

Blackface minstrelsy
See **Minstrel show.**

Blue yodel
"Blue Yodel (T for Texas)," released in 1928, was the first big hit by Jimmie Rodgers, the Father of Country Music, but the term itself refers to his distinctly original vocal style, which incorporated folk, jazz, stage show yodeling, and blues.

Bluegrass
A distinct form of string-band music typically involving acoustic stringed instruments such as the fiddle, banjo, guitar, mandolin, dobro, and string bass, and incorporating freewheeling improvisational instrumental solos and high-pitched vocals. Bluegrass emerged in the 1940s and is named for the band that originated the style: Bill Monroe's Blue Grass Boys.

BMI
Broadcast Music Incorporated, a performing rights organization created in 1940 to collect payments for songwriters and music publishers for public performance of their works in live venues and via radio, television, and other means. Its chief rival in the US is ASCAP.

Boogie-woogie
An American, blues-derived musical style popular in the 1940s and 1950s, distinguished by a 4/4 beat and rhythmic, syncopated left-hand figures on the piano.

Border radio
Radio programming in English aimed at US listeners from stations located in northern Mexico. Border radio stations (whose call letters began with X) broadcasted from 1930 to 1986 at power levels much higher than allowed by the FCC in the United States.

Cajun
A Louisiana native descended from French Canadians exiled from Acadia, Canada, in the 18th century. Cajun music is usually performed in Cajun French, and the chief instruments are the fiddle and the accordion.

Camp meeting
A religious gathering held outdoors, especially one lasting several days with participants camping nearby.

Catalog
All the songs a songwriter has written or a music publisher controls.

Changes
Chord changes; the chord structure of a song.

Clawhammer
A traditional, rhythmic banjo-playing style in which the middle or index fingernail brushes a single string or strums on a downstroke, while the thumb plays between beats by plucking the fifth string (and occasionally other strings).

CMA
The Country Music Association, the Nashville-based marketing association that promotes country music and which was founded in 1958. The CMA has presented its annual CMA Awards Show since 1967.

Control room
The part of the recording studio where the producer and engineers monitor the recording.

Country-rock
A blend of country and rock music that emerged in the late 1960s. Chief early progenitors included Gram Parsons and Chris Hillman (who performed together in seminal country-rock bands the Byrds and the Flying Burrito Brothers), Linda Ronstadt, Dillard & Clark, Bob Dylan, the Grateful Dead, Neil Young, and the Eagles.

Cowpuncher
Cowboy.

Cover
A recording of a song that has been previously recorded by another performer.

Crossover
A hit country music recording that becomes a hit on the pop-music charts.

Demo
A demonstration recording: that is, a recording typically made by songwriters that is not meant to be released to the general public but instead shared with recording artists and producers to demonstrate how the song might sound as a finished commercial recording.

Dobro
A resonator guitar, played Hawaiian style (i.e., strings up, tuned to an open chord, and noted with a metal slide). Originally, Dobro was the brand name of resonator guitars made by the Dopyera brothers, but today the name has come to stand for all resonator guitars.

Engineer
The assistant to the record producer and the person who takes care of the technical aspects of recording.

Event song
A topical ballad dealing with actual news events, such as deaths, murders, train wrecks, ship sinkings, and natural disasters. Such ballads were common in country music of the 1920s and 1930s.

Field recording
Recording sessions held in remote locations, away from big-city recording studios, using portable recording gear. Many country recordings made prior to World War II were made in field recording sessions.

Flatpicking
Playing a steel-stringed acoustic guitar with a pick (also known as a plectrum), using a rapid, up-and-down picking motion, usually playing lead lines on individual strings. Doc Watson has long been recognized as a master of flatpicking.

Folk song
A traditional song of unknown origin passed down through oral tradition.

Frailing
Traditional banjo strumming on the downstroke; see "clawhammer."

Gig
Concert booking.

Hard country
Old-style country music, usually featuring fiddles and steel guitars; vocals with strong southern accents; and often lyrics dealing with life's harsher realities. See "honky-tonk."

Head arrangement
An arrangement developed by a performer or an ensemble spontaneously during rehearsals, and not written out or charted.

Hillbilly
A pejorative term in some circles, and a badge of pride in others, the word originally meant a dweller of the mountain hollers, particularly in the southeast United States. The sounds of that region—played on acoustic instruments such as the fiddle, guitar, and banjo and often delivered in a nasal twang—came to be known as hillbilly music, and this term was used to refer to the commercial genre as early as the mid-1920s. In the 1940s, led by Ernest Tubb, the Nashville music industry spurred the campaign to rename the genre "country."

Hobo song
A song celebrating the life of the hobo—a poor, homeless, nomadic person who traveled around the United States in the 1920s and 1930s, frequently by freight train.

Honky-tonk
A style of country music named after the bars where the music emerged in the Southwest in the late 1930s. Although there is great variety within the style, honky-tonk is usually characterized by a pronounced 4/4 beat, prominent fiddle or steel guitar, strong southern accents in the vocals, and lyrics dealing with life's harsher realities such as lost love, loneliness, drinking, adultery, and sorrow. The term "honky-tonk" is often used interchangeably with "hard country."

House band
Resident band at a venue.

IBMA
The International Bluegrass Music Association, a Nashville-based trade association founded in 1985 to market bluegrass and promote professionalism and growth in the genre. The IBMA has presented the annual International Bluegrass Music Awards since 1990.

Jaw harp (Jew's harp)
A small metal instrument held between the teeth and plucked with the fingers. Its vibration produces a twanging musical tone, which can be altered by moving the mouth.

Jukebox
A coin-operated music-playing machine.

Label
A record company.

Lead sheet
A simplified musical score, consisting of the basic melody line with chord names or symbols, and sometimes including lyrics.

Master
A disc, tape, or digital file that is the final recording version used to produce multiple copies for the general public.

Melisma
A decorative phrase or passage in which one sings several notes for a single syllable of text. Lefty Frizzell was a master of melisma.

Minstrel show
A popular form of musical stage show that emerged in America in the 1800s in which white performers "blacked up" with burnt cork, imitated black music, and caricatured black speech and behavior. Though held in disrepute today for its intolerable racial stereotypes, blackface minstrel music was widely popular into the early 20th century, and its songs and comedy routines exerted an influence on early country music and some of its early stars, such as Jimmie Rodgers, Roy Acuff, and Bob Wills.

Moonshine
Illegal homemade liquor.

Multitracking
A method of sound recording in which different instruments or vocal parts are recorded onto separate tracks on a recording tape or computer drive. These tracks are then mixed together to achieve the desired balance of sound.

Nashville Sound
A style of country music that emerged in the late 1950s as a commercial response to rock & roll. Producers such as RCA's Chet Atkins (who termed it only a "sales tag") and Decca's Owen Bradley removed or downplayed fiddles and steel guitars, substituting background choral singers and, sometimes, orchestral string sections to create a softer sound, meant to appeal to pop and country listeners alike. Jim Reeves and Patsy Cline were closely associated with the style.

Newgrass
Progressive bluegrass music, which often blends in elements from other genres of music.

Pickup band
A house band or local group that performs with a star singer from out of town during a nightclub date.

Old-time
A catch-all term used to describe country music styles prevalent during the 1920s and 1930s, such as string-band music, duet and group harmony singing, and yodeling.

Outlaws
A group of outside-the-mainstream performers who came to the forefront in country music in the mid-1970s. This group included Willie Nelson, Waylon Jennings, Tompall Glaser, Jessi Colter, Billy Joe Shaver, Kris Kristofferson, David Allan Coe, and others who blended elements of rock and modern, frank lyrics with traditional country music.

Pedal steel guitar
An electric steel guitar that uses knee levers and pedals to alter various string pitches. Pedal steels first came into widespread use in country music in the mid-1950s, following the success of Webb Pierce's No. 1 hit "Slowly," featuring the pedal steel work of Bud Isaacs.

Producer
The person who supervises all aspects of a recording session.

Rockabilly
A rhythmic musical style that fused elements of country boogie, blues, R&B, and bluegrass, and paved the way for rock & roll through its most commercial catalyst, Elvis Presley.

Rube
A country bumpkin; also, a stock character in country comedy.

Scruggs-style banjo
A bluegrass fingerpicking technique popularized by Earl Scruggs in which the thumb, index finger, and middle finger of the picking hand move in rapid, alternating, rolling fashion creating a driving rhythm and a rapid-fire series of notes.

Sheet music
Printed music, published in single sheets, not bound.

Sideman
A musician who plays in the road band for a country singer.

Sock rhythm
Playing closed (i.e., barre) chords on the backbeat to provide a snare-like rhythm, especially in the absence of drums.

Songster
A small songbook.

String band
A band comprising acoustic stringed instruments, such as the fiddle, guitar, mandolin, banjo, and string bass. Such bands were common in 1920s and 1930s America.

Tent show
A performance staged in a tent, which was usually carried and put up by a traveling ensemble of musicians. During the 1940s, several Grand Ole Opry artists, including Roy Acuff, Bill Monroe, and Jamup & Honey took traveling tent shows to rural areas and small towns.

Trail drive
A long (often four months) trek during which cowboys roped, handled, and moved herds of cattle between states, e.g. from Texas to northern markets. Cowhands often sang and played guitar at night to quiet the livestock and while away the time.

Travis picking
Fingerpicking technique popularized by guitarist Merle Travis, which involves playing a steady alternating bass pattern with the thumb while using the fingers to pick out a syncopated melody.

Twang
The sharp ringing sound made by a plucked string; also, the nasal sound of southern regional accents. The term has come to stand as a signifier for the sound of hard country music.

Vaudeville
Musical variety shows and theater circuit popular in America from the late 1800s to the early 1900s.

VFW Hall
A clubhouse for Veterans of Foreign Wars, an association of American military veterans. VFW halls have often been located in working-class communities and have frequently served as performance venues for country musicians.

Vibraphone
A percussion instrument (struck with mallets) with a double row of metal tuned bars, each above a tubular, electrically driven resonator, which produces a vibrato effect.

Western swing
A hybrid style of country music combining fiddle tunes with elements of big-band jazz, pop, and blues and usually intended for dancing. It emerged in the Southwest in the 1930s, and its key progenitors were Bob Wills and Milton Brown.

White lightning
Illicit homemade whiskey. It is usually colorless and made from corn.

Index

Acknowledgments and picture credits

Acknowledgments

Books like this don't happen without the talent, cooperation, and help of a lot of creative people. Among those we would like to single out for thanks: Country Music Hall of Fame and Museum staff members past and present Denny Adcock, LeAnn Bennett, Leia Buchanan, Mick Buck, Daniel Cooper, Kira Florita, Michael Gray, Elek Horvath, Bill Lloyd, Dawn Oberg, John Rumble, Jeremy Rush, Jim Sherraden, Jeff Stamper, Alan Stoker, Carolyn Tate, Liz Thiels, Tina Wright, and museum director Kyle Young; museum legal counsel Chris Horsnell of Bass, Berry & Sims; the talented Palazzo team including art director David Costa, photo researcher Emily Hedges, designer Terry Jeavons, managing editor Sonya Newland, and managing director Colin Webb; US photo researcher F. Lynne Bachleda; Willie Nelson and Mark Rothbaum; Top Ten list contributors Ray Benson, Harold Bradley, Tony Brown, Ranger Doug Green, Merle Haggard, Brenda Lee, George Jones, Marty Stuart, Eddie Stubbs, Travis Tritt, and Keith Urban; Don Edwards; Deborah Evans-Price; Holly George-Warren for sharing her two Prologue interviews; Tony Russell; Mary Chapin Carpenter, Rosanne Cash, Michael Martin Murphey, and Mike Seeger; and all the writers and photographers who gave so generously of their time and expertise for this book. You love country music, and it shows.

Lastly, we would be remiss if we did not single out one more very key person—Jay Orr of the Country Music Hall of Fame and Museum. It was Jay who brought us on board for this book after he, Kira Florita, Colin Webb, and David Costa had initially conceived it. By that point, Jay had already sketched out preliminary outlines for all the chapters—the man knows what he wants—and he had very definite ideas about the direction and content of the book. After that, Jay was always available for advice about author assignments; for intense transatlantic conferences about photos and layouts; for reviewing text and captions, suggesting a key factual point here or felicitous turn of phrase there; and for generally making sure the incredibly rich staff and archival resources of the Country Music Hall of Fame and Museum were always available and brought to bear for this book. The end product would not be what it is without you, Jay, and your colleagues at the Country Music Hall of Fame and Museum. Now, let's find a honky-tonk with a good country jukebox and some cold longnecks. The first round's on us!

Paul Kingsbury and Alanna Nash

Picture credits

Every effort has been made to trace the copyright holders. Dorling Kindersley apologises in advance for any unintentional omissions and would be pleased, if any such case should arise, to add an appropriate acknowledgement to any future edition of the book.

All images not otherwise credited are from the **Country Music Hall of Fame and Museum's Frist Library and Archive**

Alabama Department of Archives and History, Montgomery, Alabama: 165(cr and br)

Tony Baker: 314(r)

Collection of Russ Barnard: 276(t) Photo by Stanley W. Farrar

Brown University, Providence, RI: 29(bl) (Digital ID#rbaasm 1193), 29(br) (Digital ID#rbaasm 0475)

Camden County Historical Society: 46

Courtesy of Capitol Records: 348(l) Photo by Pamela Springsteen

Courtesy of Rosanne Cash: 266

Chansley Entertainment Archives: 76(l)

Corbis: 22, 68-69(b), 72, 90-91, 145(b), 265(b), / © Nubar Alexanian 326-327, 333(t), / © Mario Anzuoni/Reuters 213(b), / © AZZARA/SYGMA 208(t), / © William A. Bake 54, / © Bettmann 17 l, 34(r), 48(r), 72, 102(t and bl), 129, 130(tr), 138, 144 b, 146, 149 bgrd, 150 t, 257, 262 t, 263 tl, 266 r, 279 r, / Bureau L.A. Collection 345(r), / © Tami Chappell/Reuters 339(tr), 344-345, / © CinemaPhoto 91 (r), / © Richard A. Cooke 204 and 204-5(bgrd), / © Christopher Cormack 103(b), / © Henry Diltz 292(r), 294(r), 324(b), / © Owen Franken 205(t), /David J. & Janice L. Frent Collection 128(t), 258(c and bc), 263 (bl), / © Philip Gould 87 (m), 273, / © Rune Hellestad 341(t), / © Henry Horenstein 275(r), / © Hulton-Deutsch Collection 130(br), / © Brooks Kraft 340(t), / © Douglas Kirkland 291(t), / © Lake County Museum 32-33, / © Micheal Levin 231(t), / © Wally McNamee 303(b), / © M. J. Masotti Jr./Reuters 349, /The Mariner's Museum 140(r), / © Minnesota Historical Society 37, / © Jason Moore/ZUMA 210(r), 347(l), / © Keven Morris 205(b), / © Tim Mosenfelder 347(r), / © Genevieve Naylor 241, / © PEMCO - Webster & Stevens Collection; Museum of History and Industry, Seattle 25(l), / © Neal Preston 212-213, 285 l, 316(r), 337, / © Nell Redmond/ZUMA 206, / © Roger Ressmeyer 284(r), / © Reuters 211, 335 l, 338-339, 346(l and r), / © Flip Schulke 258(r), / © Mike Simons 340(b), / © Brian Snyder 342(t), / © Vince Streano 265(t), / © SYGMA 334(br), / © Peter Turnley 322, / ©Will van Overbeek 333(bl), / © Jeff Vanuga 124-125

Culver Pictures: 26(t)

Courtesy John de Grote with thanks to Dick Boak of Martin Guitars: 140(b)

Denver Public Library: 100-101(b) (LOC Repro and call # X-219360), 101(tr) (LOC Repro and call # X-21939); 102(br) (LOC Repro and call # NS-104)

Dorling Kindersley Picture Library: 180(ac), 181(tr)

Rare Book, Manuscript and Special Collections Library, Duke University, Durham, North Carolina: 24 (Music #B-277; 1-2), 28(tl) (Music #B-584), 28(cl) (Music #311), 28(cr) (Music #353), 28(bl) (#807), 28(br) (Music #A-8868), 29(tl) (Music #572 no.10), 29(tr) (Music #B-694)

Colin Escott: 160-61, 216(t), 218(t)

Foster Hall Collection, Center for American Music, University of Pittsburgh Library System: 17(m)

Getty Images: 272 /Image Bank 330(t)

Grand Ole Opry Archives: 152-53, 156-57 Photo by Gordon Gillingham, 172, 299, 312r, 317, 324(tl), 325(l) Photo by Chris Hollo

Courtesy of Paul Kingsbury: 264(l), 311(b), 329(br), 329(cr), 333(br), 338(bl), 339(b), 342(b)

The Kobal Collection: 108-109, 114, 115(r)

kued.org: 123(b)

Les Leverett: 169(b), 178, 183(r), 189, 208(b), 301(b), 303(tr)

Library of Congress, Washington DC: 15 (LC-USF34-054519-E DLC), 16 (Digital ID sb30333b), 23 (LC-USZC4-4438), 73 (LOCRepro #LC-USF34-016404-E DLC), 74-75 (LOC Repro #LC-USF33-006292-M2), 85 (LOC Repro #LC-USF33-011902-M2 DLC), 92-93 (LOC Repro #LC-USF33-006017-M2DLC), 94(b) (LC-USZC4-4840), 96-97 (LOC Repro #LC-USF331-006139-B-M1 DLC)

Janet Mayer: 283(r)

Alan Mayor: 302, 310, 313, 323, 331, 308-09, 303(tl), 308(l), 311(t), 314(l), 316(l), 319(l), 324(tr), 328-29, 329(t), 330(b), 341(b), 343(b)

Alan Messer: 6, 137(br), 278(t and b), 304

Brett Mielke: 342(t)

http://www.nashvilleportraits.com: 201(t), 201(b), 209, 274-75, 300(l), 301(t)

Pictorial Press: 155, 159(r), 162(b), 173(b), 217, 219(tl and bl), 220, 223(tl and tr), 227(r), 228-229, 230, 251(bl), 253(t), /Alamy 292(l)

Redferns: Richard E Aaron 294(l), / GAB Archives 295(r) / Beth Gwinn 300(r), / Mick Hutson 307, / Elliot Landy 261(br), / Michael Ochs Archives 245(m), 246(l), 249(l), 254, 260, 260-261(t), 262(br), / Jan Persson 260-261(b), / Mike Prior 285(r), / Andrew Putler 263(l), / Bill Rouda 4-5, 279(l)

Rex Features: 261(l)

Rolling Stone: 288

Raeanne Rubenstein: 293r, 332(b), 332(t), 348(r)

Courtesy of Earl and Louise Scruggs: 202(r)

Courtesy of Sears Archive: 27(b)

Courtesy of Mike Seeger: 35 Photo by Dane Penland

Cecil Sharp MSS Collection, reproduced courtesy of EFDSS, London: 30(r)

Terra Foundation for American Art, Chicago / Art Resource, NY: 20

westernjubilee.com: 123(t)

Charles K. Wolfe: 31, 84, 132-33

Interviews for prologue

Doc Watson by Paul Kingsbury, 1994
Buck Owens by Holly George-Warren, 1995
Loretta Lynn by Alanna Nash, 2004
Charley Pride by Paul Kingsbury, 1995
Tammy Wynette by Holly George-Warren, 1994
Vince Gill by Alanna Nash, 2003
Patty Loveless by Alanna Nash, 1993
Randy Travis by Daniel Cooper, 2001